50 yrs since
Beatles land in
NYC

02. 07. 14

Li Jane
with affection

Raphael

Storyteller

Other books from The Baltimore Sun:

Storybook Season: The 2000 Baltimore Ravens' Run to the Super Bowl
Pumpernickel Tickle and Mean Green Cheese
KAL Draws the Line
John Steadman: Days in The Sun
Off-Season: Living the Retirement Dream
Miss Prudence Pennypack's A Month of Manners
A Century in The Sun: Front Pages of the 20th Century
Miss Prudence Pennypack's Perfectly Proper
Marylanders of the Century
Are We There Yet? Recollections from life's many journeys
A Century in The Sun: Photographs of Maryland

Other books by Rafael Alvarez

The Fountain of Highlandtown (Woodholme, 1997)
Hometown Boy (Baltimore Sun, 1999)
Orlo and Leini (Woodholme, 2000)

Storyteller

LIGHT FOR ALL
THE SUN
www.sunspot.net

RAFAEL ALVAREZ

Published by
The Baltimore Sun
501 N. Calvert Street
Baltimore, MD 21278

Edited by Scott Shane
Layout and design by Jiho Kim
Cover photograph by Chiaki Kawajiri
Back cover photograph by Amy Davis

ISBN – 1-893116-22-0

Storyteller: a publication of The Baltimore Sun Company - 2001 - Baltimore, MD:
Baltimore Sun Co.: 2001

For my brothers:

Danny, who can fix anything

and

Victor, who can write anything

A writer ought to have no job, no boss, no teacher, no students . . . ought to follow no one else's routine . . . have no masters, no servants . . .

— V.S. Naipaul via Paul Theroux

Contents

RAFAEL ALVAREZ

Introduction

Those masterful images because complete
Grew in pure mind, but out of what began?
A mound of refuse or the sweepings of a street,
Old kettles, old bottles, and a broken can,
Old iron, old bones, old rags, that raving slut
Who keeps the till. Now that my ladder's gone,
I must lie down where all the ladders start,
In the foul rag-and-bone shop of the heart.
— William Butler Yeats

ALL LITERATURE, LIKE ALL POLITICS, IS LOCAL. GREAT STORIES REACH THE universal by way of the particular. They grow from stubble fields and back streets, whether of Joyce's Dublin or Dostoevsky's St. Petersburg or Faulkner's Yoknapatawpha County, Mississippi. And it is from a long immersion in the newspaper facts of Baltimore and environs that Rafael Alvarez has begun to create his own rich fictional locale, the Holy Land of East Baltimore.

What a ride he has had as a newsman, twenty-some years telling Baltimoreans their stories. Alvarez picks through the city's detritus like a pack rat at a flea market, snatching up objects no one else noticed, holding them to the light for others to wonder at, weaving words around them with vaudeville timing and an artist's eye. From the most mind-numbingly routine of assignments — the ones that cause reporters to avoid eye contact with editors when the temperature soars or snow falls — he sometimes comes up with poetry.

You pluck your paper from the snowdrifts one February morning, and you read:

While the rest of the city was doing rush-hour cartwheels trying to get from here to there yesterday morning, a lone cross-country skier traced the silky perimeter of Baltimore's great star fort.

The pointless frenzy of morning traffic, deftly captured in a few words, is contrasted with the meditative solitude after a snowfall, conveyed in a single image. Ordinary Fort McHenry gets a "silky perimeter," is ennobled as the city's "great star fort."

Not a hack in a hundred can write like that. So it may be no surprise that *The Sun* is losing Alvarez not to some other newspaper, but to the distinguished realms of literature. Already, many of his newspaper fans are acquainted with the sensuous imagination of his first two books of fiction, *The Fountain of Highlandtown* and *Orlo and Leini*; and readers of his fiction may have dipped into *Hometown Boy*, his first collection of newspaper stories. In *Storyteller* the two genres are seen for the first time side by side, with some noticeable crossover. You read the short stories in this book and you understand their roots in a two-decade discipline of local journalism: devotion to truth, an eye for detail, an ear for speech, a shoe-leather acquaintance with the streets.

In "Wedding Day," a complex emotional dance is played out among the great monuments of city life: the Basilica of the Assumption, the Enoch Pratt Library — and Miss Bonnie's Elvis bar. "Pilgrim Reluctant" situates its magic on the insistently real turf of a hot dog joint and the Maryland Penitentiary. "The Fountain of Highlandtown," newly revised for this book, alternates deftly between three points of view — the elderly immigrant, the eligible young doctor, and the young artist who bridges their two worlds. But the fiction could not ring so true if the author had not spent so much time with his pen and reporter's notebook.

There is no kind of newspaper story Alvarez has not written, and along with exotica this book celebrates some of the daily short-order cooking of news. There's the life sentence for the oh-so-Baltimore guy who stabbed his uncle to death over a debt of $4.75; the small drama of the usher pleading with fans to leave Memorial Stadium on the Orioles' last evening in residence ("Five times I've asked you now to leave, five times"); the day folks flocked to post offices to get their hands on the Elvis stamp. This last story illustrates Alvarez's knack for finding a zinger of a lead for a ho-hum subject: "There was one line for Elvis and another line for everything else." Ditto, on a court ruling permitting total nudity on the Block: "From their heads to their toes," he wrote, "anything goes."

Newspapers are the natural habitat of officialdom, and county executives and housing chiefs fill too much of their pages. Alvarez has long combated the Bureaucrat Said Yesterday syndrome by inviting into ink some of the most striking characters to gather on or near the Patapsco. He'd bring 'em back alive (the heir to a Kentucky newspaper dynasty who drank his way to a janitorial job, the 300-pound bar bouncer who talks about maintaining "my decorum," the artist who drives a load of Baltimore crabs to New York, New York). Failing that, he'd give them a good write-up when they died: "'Pistol' took his last ride in a horse-drawn a-rab's cart yesterday, his flag-draped coffin rolling west from stables near the Hollins Street Market, a cavalry of mourners behind it." You read that lead, and you wish Pistol was still around to read it, too.

Especially in recent years, the griot of Greektown has often left the staid confines of the Maryland section for the personal voice of the features section or the op-ed page. There he has paid homage to musicians; interrogated writers; recorded in picaresque installments a summer-vacation driving marathon with his son. My personal favorite *Sun* story in this book is his op-ed tribute to the Royal Farm store on Key Highway — "the court of the kings and queens of Locust Point who run in for lottery tickets while the roof-deck yuppies of Federal Hill pull up in jet-black Jettas to buy cat food." In that most ordinary of settings, the chain convenience store, he finds life so vivid and diverse he makes you wonder what you might notice if you would just slow down and pay attention.

Another writer who began with newspaper work has eloquently described what it gave him. William Kennedy, who has set *Ironweed* and other novels in his hometown of Albany, N.Y., wrote in 1990 in the *New York Times*: "For a time I was a true believer in journalism, lived it passionately, gained entry to worlds I had no right to enter, learned how to write reasonably well and rapidly, was never bored by what I was doing, found the work an enduring source of stimulation, met thousands of the crazy people who populate the profession and learned madness from most of them. I loved the tension, the unexpected element of the news, the illusion of being at the center of things when you were really at what approximated the inner lining of the orange peel."

That last phrase is a knife-thrust at the perceived self-importance of journalism. You can quarrel with it, but that is an argument for a different day. For now, we can soak up stories true and imagined and wish Rafael Alvarez an interesting journey towards the juicy center of the orange.

— Scott Shane

Scott Shane, a reporter at *The Sun* since 1983, edited this book as well as *Hometown Boy*, a 1999 collection of newspaper stories by Rafael Alvarez. A former Moscow correspondent, he is the author of *Dismantling Utopia*, a book on the collapse of the Soviet Union.

Something Made

"The first Roman Catholic cathedral in the United States..."

Wedding Day

"What was the name of that love song you played?
I forgot how it goes . . ."
— Michelle Shocked

SICK TO HIS STOMACH ON THE COOL MARBLE ALTAR, BASILIO BOULLOSA WAS dressed like a million bucks and dreaming of green bananas.

Bananas that rot before they ripen.

Green with envy. Green with promise.

Green, straight to black.

From his spot on the altar of the Basilica of the Assumption of the Blessed Virgin Mary in Baltimore, the young painter could see everything. The happy couple, the priest before them, and 300 of their guests.

He saw his parents, his baby daughter and a tear — for him — in his mother's eye.

Opposite Basilio, at the head of a row of bridesmaids, sweet icing on a bitter cake: Roxanne.

They'd been introduced just before the curtain went up on this cold, bright afternoon in late December, their conversation limited to which way to turn and when to do so; instructions for a parade route.

(The night before, since Roxanne hadn't yet arrived from out-of-town, Basilio had rehearsed with the bride's widowed mother.)

All he had pledged was to bear witness to love's great pageant, yet the young man who made his money painting signs was more spooked today than when it had been his turn, not so long ago.

You don't get a view like this when you are in the barrel, he thought, when it would be bad form to turn around to see what's behind you.

Joseph loves Mary.

And Mary loves Joe.

They do.

They do.

They do.

Basilio's best friend was marrying the girl of his dreams before God and family in the first Roman Catholic cathedral in the United States.

And Basilio, who had not picked up a sincere brush in more than a year, who'd moved in with his parents after his marriage had died like an infant in its crib and had tried and tried and tried again to paint his daughter and attempted a portrait of Joe and Mary for their big day only to duck flying shards and crusty glue from his shattered sugar bowl; the same shit that rained down when he tried to capture Trudy the way he remembered her back when she wanted him: riding a bicycle through her parents' neighborhood; Basilio who every week sent Trudy a small support check by drawing crabs and fish on the sides of refrigerated trucks — this young man had agreed to testify to the power of love.

High Mass incense wafted over the 90-proof shot of courage in his stomach as Basilio managed to smile for the good things before his eyes; wondering why people say things they can only hope to be true.

Paint or die, that was Basilio's good news and hard truth.

The altar glowed in the warmth of 300 faces bathing Joe and Mary in beams of joy, but it was a dim bulb next to the flood lights of devotion the betrothed poured into each other. Basilio's wedding ring tumbled through nervous fingers in his tuxedo pocket and while he wasn't sure at age 26 that if your search is true you will happen upon another heart of contradictions that feels as you do, he still wanted it.

He'd rid himself of the ring today. Leave it on the altar.

Or drop it in the poor box.

When Basilio was a boy and his family drove into the Holy Land for Sunday dinner at his grandparent's house on Macon Street, he'd lead the younger kids in make-believe Mass down by the bottle cap factory, consecrating sugar wafers into Hosts; all of the children kneeling together on the sidewalk to watch him scratch wedding cakes like flying saucers onto the sidewalk with rocks, the smart alecks teasing him that he wanted to marry his cousin Donna and torturing him that he couldn't unless he wanted to go to jail. In the Catholic church, matrimony is the only sacrament in which the priest is merely a witness; in truth, the man and woman marry themselves. You make believe the way you make a painting. The way Basilio had not for so long.

"Joseph and Mary, have you come here freely and without reservation? Will you love and honor one another until death? Will you accept children lovingly from God?"

Basilio tried to catch Roxanne's eye.

"All the days of my life," promised Mary.

"Each and every day," said Joseph.

The priest asked for the rings and Basilio had to think for a moment so he didn't pass his bad luck onto Joe.

He'd taken the dive before any of his friends.

"I love her, Dad," he told his father, arrogant in his youth. "That's why."

His parents were merciful when Basilio came back to the same kitchen table to tell of the collapse and ask for his old room back.

Taking the ring from Basilio and placing it on Mary's finger, Joe prayed that he would never take his wife for granted, as his bride asked God to remind her to always give her husband encouragement.

As they exchanged rings, Basilio washed the cathedral with the busy brushes in his head, his real ones dry and brittle on a windowsill of the house he'd shared with Trudy and a red and gold umbrella behind him on the altar.

Red and gold: the colors of Spain.

Basilio's grandparents' marriage had been arranged in a basement kitchen in Highlandtown by people who knew better and it had lasted for 57 years.

Basilio glimpsed his face in the golden chalice held aloft by the priest and he began whispering to his reflection: Take it easy. No big deal. You're just helping out a friend.

Not only had Joe done the same for him — best friends and best man — his old buddy from Transfiguration High spent a long evening trying to persuade Trudy to give it another try.

"What'd she say?" Basilio had pestered. "What'd she say?"

"She just said, 'Joe, I gotta go . . .'"

The bridal party was turned out in verdant shades of Eire with accents of orange in homage to Mary's dead, Protestant father; green and orange in tribute to the troubles her parents had overcome. In Basilio's row: Emerald bowties and matching cummerbunds.

In Roxanne's: Kelly green and black velvet. Satin sculpted and scalloped along white flesh and freckles and in each pretty head, fragrant blossoms of orchid: trellised, Dreamsicle petals of comparettia.

A wedding's worth of just-this-morning blooms had not come cheap, but Joe had paid the cost with the surety that it was money he'd never have to spend again. Mary hadn't needed to grace her head with orange for it was a natural, coruscating copper, a crown trimmed in white lace.

The flowers took Basilio back to his childhood, back when Grandmom was living and Grandpop still slept upstairs in their bed; back to summer vacations painting flowers in their small backyard, adolescent easel built from grape crates and set beneath the clothesline, the alley behind Macon Street exploding with roses in May, tomatoes in July, sunflowers and figs as the summer wore on, the vegetable man idling through the alley in a pick-up with a scale hanging in the back.

If any of his juvenalia survived, Basilio didn't know where.

The Flowers of Highlandtown.

How to get back there?

Basilio traced Roxanne with desire dipped in paint; green satin and black velvet hugging plump curves; hair barely tamed around a pale, oval face from another country, another age; the kind of eyes that peered over golden fans at bullrings before her people were expelled from the land of Basilio's ancestors; and a mouth like a baby's heart.

"I do . . ." said Joseph.

"I will," said Mary.

- o -

Two great Baltimore temples stand face-to-face on Cathedral Street: the Basilica of the Assumption of the Blessed Virgin Mary and the Enoch Pratt Free Library.

Joe and Mary strode from one to the other with the promise of spring in their hearts, applause in their ears and the bite of December at their backs. It was dusk, a few stars and a pale moon showing as a cop held back traffic for the bridal party to cross over to the reception.

Basilio wanted to say something to Roxanne — something new — but he couldn't think of anything and now the library was in front of them, its doors dividing a dozen display windows inspired by the department store palaces of the 1920s, windows dressed with the Story of Joe and Mary.

Baby pictures side-by-side, First Communion portraits and posters of them at pastel proms.

The street lamps came on and flurries of snow danced in their margarine glow. Basilio breathed in the winter air, close enough now to dust Roxanne's every pore. Glancing down at his shoes and the thick white lines of the crosswalk, he said: "Just like Abbey Road."

In her best Liverpudlian, Roxanne thanked Basilio for taking her hand as they stepped over the curb and he took it as a good sign.

The lobby of the library was crowded with long tables covered in white cloth, a ballroom walled with books, and Basilio and Roxanne stood together behind their chairs at the head table as Joe and Mary were introduced as man and wife for the first time. Scanning the crowd for his parents and daughter, Basilio spotted a sign on a shelf above the bride and groom.

"Look," he said, touching Roxanne's elbow. "New Fiction."

What kind of good luck speech can a best man give when the thought of marriage is turning his stomach? The one he has rehearsed.

"GERONIMO!" shouted Basilio before tossing back a glass of champagne.

Taking his bride's hand, Joe took Mary out onto the floor for the first dance of their marriage, arms around each other, whispering and laughing, eyes locked.

Roxanne scanned the shelf at her elbow and pulled down a fat book of paintings by Chagall. Flipping through the pages, she happened upon a bride in a white gown wandering through a sapphire canvas of cocks and fiddlers.

"What do you think?" she asked Basilio.

"Nice colors," he said, moving an index a finger across the lavender bridal canopy. "I'm going to find my family. Want to come?"

"I'll wait," said Roxanne, squinting past Basilio for a glimpse of his daughter; beginning to ache — not again, she thought, not here — the way Basilio had ached on the altar.

At his parents' table, Basilio kissed his mother, put his hand on his father's shoulder and knelt down before India.

"Hey baby," he said. "Hey pretty girl."

"Da-da!"

"Baby doll," said Basilio, pressing his forehead against his daughter's stomach, making her laugh.

"Isn't her dress pretty, Daddy?" asked Basilio's mother, picking up the plate before her, looking for her reflection in it. "Did I ever tell you about our wedding? The reception was downstairs on Macon Street. Those old Spaniards drank and sang for three days and the Polacks half-killed themselves trying to keep up."

She ran her finger around the gold leaf along the edge of the plate.

"We ate off of your grandmother's wedding china. It's still down there. Now that would make a nice picture."

"It's only a pretty dress on a pretty girl, Ma," said Basilio, kissing India on the top of her head and going back to his seat when the bridal party was invited to join Joe and Mary on the dance floor.

Basilio and Roxanne danced near the bride and groom; Joe winking at them over Mary's shoulder and Mary doing the same when they turned.

"Look at them," Roxanne said. "Complete happiness."

(Not that long ago, with no hope of any happiness, Roxanne had sent the father of her child-to-be away.)

"Complete happiness?" laughed Basilio.

"Looks like it to me."

"Ever hear about Elvis' wedding?"

"No."

"They had a six-tiered cake — five feet tall," he said, holding his hand above the ground to show the magnificence of it. "Priscilla got pregnant on their wedding night."

"So why'd she leave him for her karate teacher?"

"Not right away she didn't," said Basilio. "Not at first."

Moving in time with the music, Basilio saw India bouncing in her chair and glimpsed a wisp of Trudy in his daughter's face.

"Have you ever painted her?" asked Roxanne.

"Priscilla?"

"Your daughter."

"Not yet," said Basilio. "Elvis took 'obey' out of the vows but only if Priscilla dyed her hair black and and piled it up high in a beehive. Just like the old ladies up in Highlandtown."

"Highlandtown?"

"The Holy Land," said Basilio.

Late in the party, Mary asked the band for "Daddy's Little Girl" and walked out onto the floor to greet the melody alone. Her mother joined her after the first verse, their arms around each other's neck as Joe stood on the side and watched his bride grieve on her wedding day.

Roxanne's gaze was drawn to a far corner where Basilio danced with India in his arms.

"What are we gonna do, baby?" he whispered, running his lips over the curve of the girl's ear. "What we gonna do?"

The song faded and it was time to go. Basilio handed India to his mother — "Be good for Grandmom . . ." — and Joe grabbed his shoulder.

"Thanks a million," he said, a little drunk.

"It was all you, man," said Basilio.

"Take a walk?" said Joe

"Where's Roxanne?"

"She's still here," said Joe, pulling Basilio into a back hall, past rooms dedicated to Mencken and Poe and Zorzi, the two friends side-by-side and quiet; Basilio guessing that Joe wanted to catch a little buzz the way they used to in high school, Joe about to roll one up when they heard laughter rolling down the hall.

"Manners," said Joe.

"Manners," agreed Basilio and they crept down the hall to a reading room where Seth Manners, another mug from Transfiguration High, was pitching woo on a red leather couch with one of Mary's married cousins. Joe and Basilio held their breath on each side of the door.

Manners had a hand up the woman's dress. She'd come to the wedding alone because her husband was working overtime to pay the mortgage on their dream house, the one they'd promised themselves, the one they deserved. Manners was single for the same reason Mary's cousin would be one day and as he worked his way into the woman's panties, Joe inexplicably whispered: "How's Trudy?"

Basilio turned his back and headed for the reception.

"Sorry," said Joe, catching up. "Everybody misses Trudy."

"There he is!" cried Mrs. Boullosa, standing with Roxanne and India as Basilio walked into the nearly deserted lobby. "Where've you been?"

Basilio fastened the top button of his daughter's coat and hugged her until she cried. Roxanne took the orchids from her hair and set them on the baby's head.

"I'm ready," she said.

- o -

Basilio drove east with Roxanne for a rendezvous in the shadow of the King; east into the Holy Land toward Miss Bonnie's Elvis Grotto. It was almost 11 p.m. when they pulled up to the corner of Fleet and Port.

"Where are we?" asked Roxanne, scooting up to a plate-glass window where a bust of the King stood in a carpet of poinsettia leaves, lights twinkling around his neck.

"We're here," said Basilio, holding the door open. Roxanne stepped inside, her pupils opening wide in a poorly lit sanctuary for people who have nowhere to go on days when everyone is supposed to have a place to go.

Three solitary regulars looked up from their drinks to give Basilio and Roxanne the once over: a wrinkled dwarf in white face; a woman who couldn't hold her head up; and an old foreigner who needed a shave falling forward on an aluminum walker.

A cold cut buffet was set up against the wall; behind the bar, goldfish floated in and out of a white mansion sunk in a long aquarium; 45 rpm records spray-painted silver and gold hung from the ceiling and Elvis crooned: "The hopes and fears of all the years are met in thee tonight . . ."

No one spoke until Miss Bonnie — deep in an easy chair at the back of the bar, savoring a voice that came to visit but not to stay — noticed her visitors.

"Why darlin'," she said, putting down a movie magazine. "I was wondering if my boyfriend was gonna remember me on Christmas."

Basilio blushed and stepped over the threshold with Roxanne.

"Miss Bonnie," he said. "This is Roxanne. Roxanne, my sweetheart Miss Bonnie."

"Why hello, honey," said Bonnie, giving Roxanne a hug. "Don't you two look gorgeous."

Roxanne gazed over Miss Bonnie's shoulder to a life-sized creche in the back, a manger of limbs from trees that grew along the waterfront before the piers were poured from cement trucks; tall plaster figures of beasts and blessed.

She had never been this close to one before, never one this big — not figurines behind glass, but life-size statues out in the open and she slipped Miss Bonnie's embrace to get a closer look.

She crouched for a lamb's eye view, her satin gown stretched tight across full thighs and wide hips, knees up against her chest as she peered through wooden slats to see the infant.

"She's a keeper," whispered Bonnie to Basilio.

Closing her eyes, Roxanne asked the universe for forgiveness, a clenched fist between her breasts. Stand up, she said to herself.

You better find a way to get up.

Reaching through the slats, she plucked a stalk of hay from the manger and with swift elan, used it to gather up her great mane before returning to Basilio and saying: "You like?"

It was too much.

The last straw.

Basilio took Roxanne's shaking hand, stood in front of Miss Bonnie and said: "I can't keep it in anymore."

"What?" asked Roxanne.

"What, honey?" said Bonnie.

"We just came from the priest!" he shouted. "We're married!"

Roxanne flinched.

"It's true," said Basilio, pulling her hand to his lips. "By God, it's true!"

"Hallelujah!" cried Bonnie, coming in for hugs.

Roxanne smiled at Basilio over Bonnie's shoulder, mischief replacing guilt as she waved a naked ring finger before him with a look that said: "You didn't think of everything, Mr. Smarty Pants."

"Lock the front door," said Bonnie. "We got us a wedding here."

Fussing over every little thing, she smacked Basilio's fanny and said: "Honey, you shoulda gimme some notice."

"Wasn't any notice," said Roxanne.

"Oh Christ, one of them," said Bonnie. "Two of mine were like that."

And then she turned a cynical eye on Basilio.

"Catholic?"

"Of course."

"How the hell did you get a priest to say the magic words without jumpin' through all them goddamn hoops?"

Basilio rubbed his thumb and forefinger together.

"The usual way," he said.

"Well, well," laughed Bonnie. "It's good to know they didn't change everything in the church."

"Didn't all go smooth," said Basilio, his bride's hand in the air. "No time to get a ring."

"Stores closed," said Roxanne.

"Wedding rings?" said Bonnie as though they'd asked her for a bag of chips.

"That's it," said Basilio.

"That's all," said Roxanne.

"Shit," said Bonnie. "Come here girl."

Roxanne walked behind the bar to the 100-gallon home of a submerged Graceland and three generations of Holy Rosary Spring Carnival goldfish floating in and out of the mansion's empty rooms, the path to the King's front door paved with bands of gold.

"Ever been fishin', honey?" said Bonnie, reaching behind the cash register for a toy rod with a paperclip hook.

Basilio hopped up on the bar, his head over Roxanne's shoulder, and the regulars followed: Ted the Clown, still in make-up from a nursing home gig; the drunken

Carmen; and Mr. Voliotikes, leaning in hard solitude upon his his walker.

"Fish?" said Roxanne, taking the rod.

"Don't wanna stick your hand in the muck," said Bonnie, pointing to five rings nestled in slime.

"Go fish," said Basilio.

Ted scurried around the bar to stand alongside Roxanne, and Carmen twirled on a barstool like a kid.

"Don't hurt the fish," said Carmen, twice divorced.

"You can't hurt them fish," said the clown.

"Don't crowd her," yelled Bonnie.

"Which one?" asked Roxanne, dropping the line into the tank.

"Any one," said Bonnie as the hook dragged gravel.

"Got one!" squealed Roxanne.

"So quick," said Carmen.

"Lickety-split!" sang the clown.

"Told you," Bonnie said.

Roxanne turned to Basilio with the dripping ring, but when he reached out for it, Bonnie snatched it away and wiped it clean.

"Not yet," she said, passing the rod to Basilio. "Your turn."

Oh boy, he thought, hopping down from the bar with the ring Trudy had once slipped on his finger deep in his pocket.

Holding the rod over the bubbling water, Basilio asked Bonnie which ring came from which husband; if, he wondered, one was any luckier than the others.

"You see where they wound up," she said.

Basilio let the hook sway above the tank until the crowd was hypnotized, lowered the line and slipped a hand into his pocket.

"Bingo!" he said, pulling a fast one.

Turning to Roxanne, Basilio stood with a dry ring on the end of his hook, unsmiling, four others still in the drink.

Such dexterity, at turns charming and nauseating, had ultimately convinced Trudy to leave, a truth that Basilio would try to stuff into poor boxes and sewer holes for years to come.

Bonnie led the couple out from behind the bar, handed Basilio the ring Roxanne had plucked from the aquarium, gave Roxanne the ring Basilio had reeled in and ordered them to trade.

Roxanne's ring was too small, stopping at her knuckle and she slipped it on her pinky. Basilio's moved along his finger without a hitch.

"Now kiss her," said Bonnie.

"Yeah!" said Carmen.

"Right in the kisser!" said the clown.

"Show some respect," said Mr. Voliotikes.

Their lips touched and a current passed between them to light every bulb in the bar and run the ice machine.

"Love . . ." marveled Bonnie before turning for the stairs that led to her apartment above the bar. "You kids enjoy yourselves. I'll be right back."

In Bonnie's absence, Ted the Clown took over, guiding Basilio and Roxanne to a table against the wall as they stared at their rings.

"We're married," said Basilio.

"What now?" asked Roxanne.

Ted slipped behind the bar to tipple a little of this and some of that before bringing Basilio a beer and a glass of white wine for Roxanne in a goblet from which no customer had drank.

With the goo-goo eyes of the regulars bearing down upon them, the newlyweds could not enjoy themselves or leave without saying goodbye to Bonnie, whose absence had changed the room.

"This was just another neighborhood gin mill selling boiled eggs and pickled onions until Bonnie's last husband died," said Basilio. "When he dropped dead Bonnie started putting up pictures of Elvis to make herself feel better."

Roxanne shifted to take in the massive collage that was Miss Bonnie's Elvis Grotto and was particularly taken by a Graceland postcard of the tux and gown that Elvis and Priscilla had worn on their wedding day, an exhibit of empty clothes.

"And then Presley died," said Basilio. "And everybody began loading the joint up with the King, but none of it made Bonnie feel any better."

Feeling ignored, Ted leaned across the table so far that his rubber nose nearly poked Roxanne in the face, his head bobbing on a pencil neck.

"You don't think people marry clowns?" he said, smacking himself on the back of his head until the red ball popped off of his nose. "Happens every goddamn day."

Ted stuck the rubber nose on Basilio and lamented: "But all them gutter balls. Maybe that's the way it oughta be. That's the way it is."

"Dog shit!" shouted Carmen, drunk on gloom and schnapps, edging her way to the table with Baby Jesus in her arms, tripping toward Roxanne when the clown grabbed her ass.

Carmen dropped the infant and it shattered on the floor. Roxanne screamed.

"Oh my God," said Basilio, picking up the pieces.

"Ted, you mental patient."

"I didn't do it," shouted the clown. "I had nothin' to do with it."

Carmen stood over Roxanne like a runaway, tangled hair in her eyes as the lights blinked on and off across the stucco paste of her face.

"Goochie-goochie goo," she warbled. "Goochie-goochie goo . . ."

"Oh Christ," said Basilio, on his knees. He hurled the rubber nose at Ted and held Roxanne's ankle as she cried. Ted polished off everyone's drink and slipped out the side door as Mr. Voliotikes lumbered toward the head of the table.

"Out of my way," he roared, kicking Carmen with his good foot.

"Why," he asked, taking Roxanne's hand. "Why you do this without your mother and father."

Roxanne wiped her eyes on the cuff of her gown and blew her nose in a napkin.

"It's my life," she said, pulling her hand away as Bonnie came down the stairs with a sheetcake in her hands. Stopping halfway down, she saw Basilio piling pieces of Jesus on the table, Roxanne in tears, Carmen passed out on the floor, the old Greek preaching and no sign of the clown.

"What the hell's goin' on here? I can't leave for five goddamn minutes without you smokehounds turning a wedding into a wake? For Christ's sake, this is the best thing that's happened here in years and you rumpots ain't gonna poison it with your goddamn war stories.

"Carmen? CARMEN! Get the hell off the floor. What's wrong with you? Somebody help her up. Mr. V, wipe your eyes and sit down. That girl don't need no Daddy. She's got a husband now."

Walking the cake over to the table, Bonnie rubbed Roxanne's shoulder and told her not to mind the others: "They ain't right."

Putting her arms around the guests of honor, she assured them, "We're making our own happiness here," and brought over a fresh pot of coffee to go with the cake.

"Okay," she said. "Mr. V, say a nice grace for us. Something for a Christmas wedding. In English." The old man closed his eyes, bowed his head and was just starting to get warmed up — "Forgive us, Father, for the vows we could not keep" — when Bonnie shouted "Amen" and began cutting the cake.

The caffeine and sugar gave Roxanne and Basilio new strength and when Bonnie started clinking a spoon against her coffee cup for them to kiss, he put his lips next to Roxanne's ear and said: "Let's get out of here."

"Miss Bonnie . . ."

"I know, you gotta go," she said. "Let me give you something first."

From a shelf behind the bar, she took down a bust of Elvis made into a lamp and handed it to Basilio at the front door.

"Works on batteries," she said, flicking the switch on and off.

He thanked her with a kiss on the cheek and said: "You made this a special night for us."

"I didn't make it special, hon. It is special."

And the heart-shaped clock on the wall said it was time.

"Now out with you," said Bonnie. "Out you go."

- o -

The cold slapped color into Roxanne's cheeks and bit through Basilio's pants as they hurried to the car.

Basilio put Elvis between them on the front seat and waited for the engine to warm up.

Stuffed with their rich lie and too full to speak, a young man and a young woman who'd never met before that day drove through the Holy Land with rings on their fingers and wedding cake in their pockets; the city as silent as the bride and groom as Roxanne stared through the darkness at rows of narrow brick houses and Basilio drove south to the water's edge at the end of Clinton Street.

The road was unpaved and the moon made silhouettes of coal piers and cranes, fuel barges and corrugated fertilizer warehouses. They drove past the hulk of the S.S. John Brown Liberty Ship and Schuefel's, the saloon where a monkey named Dinky drank beer from a can.

Gravel crunched under the tires until the road stopped at a wooden pier jutting out from the front yard of a house with "SALVAGE" painted across its side.

Basilio parked in front of a twisted guard rail as a red tugboat with a white dot on its stack pulled a barge across the harbor, the flag over Fort McHenry starched in a stiff breeze.

Engine running, heater on, he pushed the seat back and closed his eyes, fresh out of script until Roxanne opened her door and a blast of winter air accompanied her command to get out and bring the lamp.

Basilio sat up to see her walk down a warped pier beneath a feta moon, high heels steady on the splintered boards, black hair flying in a nocturne of ebony and cream.

Hurrying to catch up with Elvis in his arms, he found Roxanne sitting on the edge of the pier with her legs over the side. Basilio set the lamp down and sat beside her. It was freezing.

Roxanne turning the switch on the lamp and a pink halo floated up from the pier into the night.

She asked: "Have your fun?"

"Didn't you?" said Basilio, numb fingers struggling with the ring on his hand when Roxanne kissed him with an open mouth, her saliva freezing on his chin.

"We'll die out here," said Basilio, sliding his palm across the front of Roxanne's gown to her left hand, tugging the ring free from her pinky and shaking it with his own like dice before tossing them into the harbor.

Opening her coat, Roxanne pulled the velvet gown from her chest, her breasts snug in a strapless bra.

"What are you doing?" said Basilio, laying his head against her chest, no room of his own to set up an easel, much less rattle a headboard.

Defiant against the cold, Roxanne freed her breasts one at a time, looked down at Basilio and said: "Paint my portrait."

"Nude?"

"With India on my lap."

"When?"

"Let's go," said Roxanne, and, as Basilio began buttoning Roxanne's coat, he remembered the good morning light that came through the window near the sink in his grandfather's kitchen and took aim at work that had been vexing him since he was a young boy.

"The steel pyramid of Baltimore..."

Pilgrim Reluctant

GET UP, SAID THE ANGEL.
And Ruthie did.
Grab your baby.
And she did.
Now run . . .
Run, run, run.
Run away.
"Where?" the girl whispered.
"Home."
Ruthie lifted a lamb's wool coat from a hook in the hallway of the Mercy Hospital maternity ward and slipped through a side door into a brutal January night in Baltimore.

Struggling on the icy sidewalk, Ruthie stutter-stepped a half-block down the steep incline of Saratoga to Calvert Street and, with radar not her own, charged north against the wind with her unnamed child fast to her chest. Two blocks up, beneath the viaduct that canopied Bath Street, the recovery that began the instant Ruthie did what she was told — love, honor, obey and run like the wind that froze her ears to the sides of her hard head — was complete.

The Caesarean incisions and the cuts into her chest, as many stiches as the nut brown hairs upon Ruthie's head, every follicle counted and catalogued, healed without scars and dissolved into fairy dust.

A new aortic valve, the contribution of a man who'd lost his life trying to keep a neighbor from beating a child, fused with the heart the 15-year-old had been born with like the smooth and silent seal on a zip-lock sandwich bag.

The weather was raw and with each lash, Ruthie felt like a rockfish being scaled on a bed of crushed ice, one gray and jellied eye staring blind into a world ready to eat her alive.

In her nightgown and gym shoes, she ran past the Sunpapers, where the biggest news in two millennia would go unnoticed and unreported; she turned right at Centre Street and made a move for the train station on the corner, rain freezing like needles on her nose, her cheeks; rain freezing beneath her feet.

She ducked into the abandoned rail station and slumped onto a cold wooden bench near broken windows and a chalk board still bearing arrivals and departures — the 2:12 Oriole Wing to New York City — under the scrawl of graffiti vandals.

The baby opened its mouth in a twisted oval of pink, eyes flush with tears and tight with the shudder of a wail, but no sound accompanied its cry.

Only silence.

This telephone, thought Ruthie, does not ring.

Unbuttoning her nightgown to nurse, Ruth saw no cuts on a chest that hours before had been hacked open like a cantaloupe; nary a mark where her heart had been lifted from its cage like crippled Communion; and she wondered, through chattering teeth, about the logic of a deity that could do such a thing while neglecting to give a voice to Its chosen.

The infant took a frigid nipple and where there had been a silent cry there was now the sound of suckling as Ruthie walked the filthy building in fear that her baby's lips would freeze to her breast; warm milk flowing through a small haze of steam, the strain of shivering and feeding and walking about to deplete the teenager.

Ruthie's hunger took her back to meals she'd grown up eating on a WASP lane in Roland Park; back to catered seders and Thanksgiving dinners and ready-to-cook chicken filets stuffed with croutons and slices of apple that her black nanny made on weeknights, the tender traif of bacon and cucumber sandwiches that Ruthie ate alone in front of the TV long before her parents came home from work.

Pacing to stay warm, Ruthie found a package of stale crackers in the pocket of the soggy coat. Tearing the cellophane with her teeth, she wondered where her parents were now; wondered, as she shoved the brittle wafers in her mouth, if they'd remained married, who was getting paid to clean up after them and if they cared that they'd become grandparents.

"Who's the boy?" was her father's chant the day that Ruthie left home, homeward bound.

Her mother had screamed: "WE WANT THE BOY, RUTHIE!"

And the lonely girl replied: "There is no boy . . ."

There is only me.

Only me, she thought, staring at the dark lashes feathered across her baby's heavy eyelids.

And this.

Who, she thought, tracing the child's lips, is this?

The rain tapped out a G upon the roof.

It spelled G-L-O . . .

G-L-O-R-I-A!

The pigeons in the rafters cooed: Gloria!

The wind howled: Gloria!

And Ruthie, aware that this child and the clothes on her back were all she had — that the ripe teat of the world the angel had promised was nowhere to be seen — called her daughter by name for the first time.

In excelsis Deo!

Beyond the arch of a broken window, Ruthie glimpsed THE DOG HOUSE lunchroom across the Fallsway, a Greek spoon that catered to prison guards, cops and public defenders, its menu painted in big red letters on the side of the white building.

Squinting through the rain, Ruth licked crumbs and salt from her fingers and sang her way through a lullabye of links: Ostrowski's kielbasa, Roma's Italian, Polack Johnny's, Esskay franks, Blimpie's Bratwurst and Jose Pepper's chorizo.

Drawn to the sign — Babka's Blood Pudding beckoning and the promise of Parks' Patties — Ruthie buttoned up, wrapped the coat tight around Gloria and walked across the street to lean her small frame against the diner with a hunger so great she could have eaten everything on the menu with room left for pie. Standing with her back against the diner, not a nickel to her name, Ruthie waited for the next cue while staring at an 18th-century castle across the street that served Baltimore as the oldest functioning jailhouse in the United States. A light burned in a room on the left and a man stirred there, looking warm and content on the other side of the window, enough serenity in his gait for Ruthie to race across the street with Gloria and bang her head against the front door in the freeze. A sacred heart?

Ruth had survived a difficult, seven-month pregnancy on the streets without divine instruction; she'd rarely missed a meal and often had a bed.

She cried: "WE'RE GOING TO DIE OUT HERE!"

Laying her body against the heavy door, Ruthie felt locks tumble on the other side, rushing in when it opened.

"Whoa," said the man she'd seen through the window. "Hold up."

A redeemed murderer in his mid-50s — a lifer who'd never met a guilty man in prison — the man was trim and neat and wore green work pants, a prison-issue sweatshirt and a Jinnah cap. He put his hands on Ruthie's shoulders and took a long look at her. In all his years on kitchen duty, Petush-El had ignored a million wails at the door without opening it for anyone — not ever, not once and certainly not because a runaway was cold and wet and hungry; certainly not for something as common as that. Shivering before the man, Ruthie opened her coat to show the tadpole between her breasts. The man took Ruth's wet coat, led her into a kitchen built to feed a few hundred people at a time and set a scalding cup of coffee before her.

"Food?"

"Yes."

"Eggs?"

"Sure."

Petush-El found a blanket and draped it around Ruthie's shoulders. He nodded at the baby and Ruthie said that she was fine.

"She?"

"Gloria."

"Petush," said the man, extending his hand. "Petush-El."

Petush in penance and El for Allah. Petush the name of the Polish baker whose face the convict had blown away in a fit of adrenalin and arrogance and anger at Greenmount and North on the day of Martin Luther King's assassination; a hard-working Polack whacked for three dollars and two doughnuts and the right to say you were there when the shit went down.

He had waves of gray in his thinning hair and no angels to tell him what door to knock on and when; he'd had to take a life and think about it for a couple of decades before finding the confidence and calm that earned him the run of the warden's kitchen.

"Ruth," said Ruthie and Petush dropped to his knees to untie the laces of his guest's soggy shoes before laying them on a radiator to dry. He grabbed a skillet from a hook on the ceiling and whipped up a plate of egg sandwiches on white toast.

"Got some good sausage. Fresh from the Dog House."

"Yes," said Ruth, draining a glass of milk. "Please."

Ruthie ate slowly with her right hand while cradling Gloria in her left. As the links simmered in the skillet, perfuming the large, sterile kitchen with the sweet pork, Petush-El scurried for everything his guest would need for a long bivouac. She sipped juice and started on the sausages as Petush-El grabbed a canvas laundry bag, walked behind Ruth to size her up and began stuffing the sack with everything from first-aid kits to tins of creamed corn and a can opener, all courtesy of the State of Maryland.

"Here," he said, offering long johns and coveralls. Ruthie slipped behind a rack of roasting pans with Gloria and changed into the warm clothes. When she came back, Petush led her down a tiled hallway lined with storage shelves, told her to take what he pleased and began talking about Mohammed and the mountain.

"Solitary used to be above the top tier, in the space below the steel pyramid," he said, dropping items Ruthie had selected into the laundry bag. "They had me up there for more than a year after I got here, with a little window looking out on Eager Street. "I used to watch a man across the street who had no legs. He'd sit in the front doorway in a wheelchair, good weather and bad. And one day I got it in my mind to throw him a pitch."

"A pitch?" said Ruthie, marveling at racks of dried apricots.

"A fastball," said Petush-El. "Like Jim Palmer. Those were the glory days — four 20-game winners: Palmer, Cuellar, McNally and Dobson."

"Like what?"

"Like this," said Petush, setting his feet together for the wind-up before sending an imaginary pitch down the hallway. "He caught it and tossed it back."

"Across the street?"

"Back to me," said Petush-El, pretending to play catch while leading Ruth past gallons of bottled water and pearl onions. "Then I threw another pitch and then another. Full wind-up, over the top. I was bringing heat."

Petush explained how the game evolved between a guy who couldn't get up and a guy who couldn't get out; how the cripple took to wearing a catcher's mitt and a backwards baseball cap long before it was fashionable; how one day a man stood behind him like an umpire to call balls and strikes and then a kid started to score the games in chalk on the side of the house and before he knew it, Petush was pitching a nine-inning game every day.

"Stamina," he said. "Some weeks, I'd pitch both ends of a double header."

"How long were you in solitary?"

Petush was now a calm man, a trusted inmate with privileges and a simple routine; a man who worked to protect a hard-earned contentment that would evade Ruthie and Gloria in every neighborhood in Baltimore until they reached home.

"Long enough to play all 162 games. Sometimes I'd stare through the bars on the window for 20 minutes before delivering a pitch. It became my prayer and my meditation. The week the crippled guy died, they put me back in population."

Petush-El set the bulging laundry bag outside a narrow door and Ruthie wondered what more she could need for a life on the street. Her benefactor unlocked the door that led to a cramped cupboard where a 15-watt bulb threw off more shadows than light and Petush-El became a showman.

"You've got your wall of bread stuffing and a mess of potatoes," he said, as if surveying a field awaiting harvest. "Stacks of spice, rows of macaroni and over here . . ."

Reaching for the ceiling, Petush unscrewed the small bulb and replaced it with a thick ceramic screw that set a wall of shelves turning to reveal a secret annex and in it a large sheet of plywood on which Petush had built a Holy City from Popsicle sticks, dried mashed potatoes and spent bullet casings smelted in the prison boiler room. Mecca.

"Goodness," said Ruthie.

Petush-El circled the platform, holding a palm above the buildings to feel the heat they gave off. With a handkerchief, he wiped a smudge from one of the ivory turrets and told Ruth, without complaint, that he'd never get there in this lifetime.

"I moved the mountain one shovel at a time," he said. "But you . . ."

Staring over the glory of Islam as Gloria squirmed at her bosom, Ruthie remembered the one time that her mother had taken a day off from work to chaperone a class trip: third grade, Smithsonian Institution.

Somewhere in the labyrinth of the great museum, Ruth separated from the group of children her mother had been assigned to chaperone and then, wandering through hordes of schoolchildren in search of them, found herself talking to an eight-year-old boy who'd also lost his way. They stood in awe

together before the crinkled foil magnificence of the THRONE OF THE THIRD
HEAVEN OF THE NATIONS MILLENIUM GENERAL ASSEMBLY. And for
nearly an hour, as her classmates looked at mummies and dinosaurs, Ruthie and
the boy tried to figure out a piece of junk found in a derelict garage.

"What is it?" asked the boy, a kid from public school.

Ruthie stepped up to the sign to recite.

"It's the THRONE OF THE THIRD HEAVEN OF THE NATIONS
MILLENIUM GENERAL ASSEMBLY" and the smitten boy — who'd come up
behind Ruthie to smell her neck — knew he was in the presence of the smartest
kid he would ever meet.

"I have to go," she told Petush.

"You are going," said Petush, throwing a sheet over the model and putting the
wall back in place. In the hall, he picked up the laundry bag and led Ruthie to the
front door of the jail. Peeking outside, he saw that the rain had stopped, dawn
was near and January 8, 2000 had turned to January 9. Staring into the gray sky
splintering above the DOG HOUSE, Petush knew that today, like every other since
his change had come, he could have walked away.

With a thick black scarf drawn around her head and tucked it into an Army
jacket Petush had found, Ruthie stood before the sculptor like a janitor from
Palestine. Gloria slept inside her mother's clothes, swaddled in clean aprons, and
the laundry bag sat heavy upon the virgin's small shoulder.

"I can't even tell you where to go," said Petush, slipping $40 into Ruthie's hand.
"It's not my town anymore."

He wanted to guarantee her fair weather and wished he could call her a cab but
cabs never came to the neighborhood; he wanted to say that everything — every
little thing — was going to be all right.

"Can I hold her?"

Ruthie unzipped her coveralls and brought forth her child.

In Petush-El's cupped hands — hands that had fired five slugs into the wide,
simple face of a family man who sold pies for a living, which had pitched 162
complete games with a legless man for a battery mate, fingers that had shaped
Mecca from scraps of food — the sovereign Gloria lay mute and alert; a living doll
like the ones that boardwalk carnies give to sports who know that nothing
ventured is nothing gained.

"A surreal octagon of Confucius..."

The Fountain of Highlandtown
(2001)

BASILIO

I LEARNED TO LIVE IN THE DARK THIS YEAR WHEN I QUIT MY JOB, SOLD EVERYTHING I owned, and moved in with my grandfather.

This new life makes the simplest things complicated, even for a sharpie who decides to quit his job, sell everything he owns and go live in the dark.

But that's my problem.

Grandpop would tell you that.

It's a fine summer night in Baltimore and I am walking from Grandpop's house to meet Katherine, who is young and beautiful and smart and almost completely unknown to me.

I haven't told her much about myself, hardly anything except that my grandmother died in the hospital where she works, that my grandfather stopped sleeping in their bed on the day she passed and that it would be better if I met her where she lives than the other way around.

I said all this last week when I found myself next to her in line at the Broadway market. I was picking up fresh fruit for Grandpop and she was buying scallops and shrimp and filet of rockfish for a dinner party.

No, she said, you can't come.

Yes, she said, I'm sure.

But maybe . . . maybe we can do something and I borrowed a pencil from the fish man to scratch her number across Grandpop's bag of peaches.

And so I am walking from the narrow Highlandtown rowhouse where my father was born and raised, passing bakeries and record stores and coffee shops, on my way to Katherine's apartment a few miles away near Johns Hopkins Hospital.

It's early (I had to get out of the house) and there's a creamy wash of pink across the early evening sky as I pass Jimmie's Grocery on my way to Eastern Avenue.

The street jumps with kids on new-wave scooters, Saturday shoppers coming home with carts of detergent and bundles of frozen chickens and toilet paper. Fat women in short pants squirting down the sidewalks and middle-aged sports with slick hair and brown shoes wait for the word.

I hit the Avenue and Greek men who haven't shaved for three days stand in front of stag coffee houses telling lies and ogling American women going for kabobs at Samos. Packs of black and white hip-hoppers graze for drugs and kicks and young girls walk by, dressed up for each other.

My eye swims through the heart of the canvas but the margins are crowded with Katherine.

What will she wear?

What won't she wear?

What hangs in her kitchens?

I think: How will our time pass?

And, if all goes well, will we find our way back to Macon Street?

Fat chance.

My world is ruled by Grandpop and he is driving me crazy.

Right up the wall.

I am afraid that my time with him won't last long enough for me to get my work done.

Every morning at breakfast he says the same thing: "Why are you here?"

It's like he forgets that I am living with him between the time we go to bed and the time we wake up. All night, Grandpop tosses and turns on the sofa bed downstairs, like he's being chased. At daybreak he asks: "Why are you here?"

And then: "Turn off that light. You think I'm a millionaire? How were you raised?"

Grandpop was so poor growing up in Chapela that one summer he carved an entire bicycle out of wood, wheels and all, so he would have something to ride besides an ox-drawn plow.

It doesn't matter that he's had it good in this country for 60 years; that, in his own words, we "eat like kings" and he can lock the front door to a warm home he has owned for twice as long as I've been alive.

Nope, it don't matter that he's got a good pension from the shipyard and Social Security and more money in U.S. Savings Bonds deducted every week from his Bethlehem Steel paycheck than I have earned in 28 years on Earth.

Don't mean shit if you are foolish enough to leave a light on in a room you aren't in or care to read or draw or scratch your ass by electric lamp before the sky outside has turned to pitch.

And there is no reason to use lights after dark because at night you sleep.

Electricity, says Grandpop, is money and a poor man can not afford to waste either of them.

Bent over and angry, pointing to an offending 15-watt bulb, he says: "You think I'm a millionaire?"

When I try to tell him not to worry, that it's only pennies anyway — when I smile and say: "Hey Grandpop, we got it pretty good in this country" — he says

I can go live with somebody else if I want to waste money.

He demands: "Why are you here?"

But he doesn't charge me a dime to sleep in his bed and eat his food and he doesn't say a word when I do the things I need to do.

Just as long as I don't turn on any lights.

God Bless America.

God Bless Grandpop.

I cross Eastern Avenue and dart between traffic into Patterson Park, where Grandpop used to play soccer with other expatriates from around the world.

It's hard for me to imagine his legs strong enough to kick a ball the length of the park; he's barely able to climb the steps in the middle of the night to make sure I'm not reading under the covers with a flashlight. But up on dusty shelves near the sofa where he talks in his sleep like he's trying to make somebody understand, there are trophies to prove it.

"Grandpop," I say. "Tell me about playing soccer in the land of baseball."

The Pagoda sits on the highest hill in the park, a surreal octagon of Confucius bordered by the first rowhouses in Baltimore with indoor bathrooms. When you stand on the top tier, you can see all of the Holy Land, all the way past Fort McHenry to freighters in the harbor and the Francis Scott Key Bridge in the mist.

I would like to take Katherine to the top and present her with the view, but it's only open on Sunday mornings when the Friends of the Park are around to let you in.

Grandmom and Grandpop used to walk me up here when I was a kid; they'd stay on the ground and wave up to me and I can see them now like it was yesterday, smiling through their broken English: "Doan breaka you neck."

After a while Grandmom couldn't make the walk anymore; other things became more important to me and I didn't care to visit Macon Street so much.

The city let the Pagoda rot while punks and drunks and whores and glue-heads did things inside of it that made the girders rust. One of our failed mayors tried to tear it down a few years ago when the mother of some goof who jumped off and killed himself sued the city but good people saved it and now you can only go up on Sunday mornings.

I tried to paint the Pagoda for three years before I moved in with Grandpop and never got it right. Tonight I stare up and fix its scale in my head.

Does Katherine know any of this stuff? Does she care? Will she want to know once she sees how much I care?

What I know about Katherine you could suck into an eyedropper with room to spare. She is young and beautiful and smart and gives dinner parties with scallop and shrimp.

I don't even know if she's from Baltimore.

Leaving the Pagoda, I walk out of the park onto Pratt Street, passing families of Lumbees and Dominicans, black folks and hillbillies, the neighborhoods changing as I get closer to downtown.

I hit Broadway and turn north on a wide stretch of asphalt that rolls beyond the statue of Latrobe and the housing projects named in his honor; up from the harbor a good two miles to Johns Hopkins where my grandmother died 20 years ago, leaving Grandpop all that time and how much more to lie in the dark, conserving kilowatts to save pennies he doesn't count anymore.

Katherine's apartment is in the shadow of the hospital's great dome.

The neighborhood used to be called Swampoodle before Hopkins started gobbling it up, back when Bohemians lived there, in the days when Grandpop played soccer in Patterson Park and Grandmom sat on a bench with her girlfriends to watch.

I tried to paint the Hopkins dome too, in the last days before I moved in with Grandpop, but all I could think about was what we lost there.

I smeared the canvas with vinegar and vowed that I would not paint pictures of buildings anymore.

KATHERINE

I didn't know what to expect with this guy.

I haven't dated much lately because it's all been the same, but I said yes to this guy (yes masquerading as maybe) in the market. I knew it would be different, but I didn't know how. Certainly I didn't expect to be picked up for our first date on foot.

He knocks on the door, comes in with a polite hello, and looks around.

 "I walked over," he says, "because I sold my car when I moved in with my grandfather."

But he doesn't say what one has to do with the other.

He tells me that my dress reminds him of the flowers his grandmother used to grow in her backyard until the summer she passed away "right there," he says, pointing through the window to the hospital.

"That perfect pale yellow," he says, staring just a little too long.

He's cute, in a funny way, like a kid; younger than me and a nice change from the clever men with tasseled loafers and Beamers, so suave and witty until they find out that I'm a doctor and then they really start acting like kids.

I don't mind walking and out we go, strolling south toward the water.

I'd bet you anything that we're headed for the bars in Fells Point, where every man I've dated in this town goes sooner or later, like its the only place in Baltimore that sells beer.

But he doesn't mention any destination, just pleasant chatter about things you can't imagine — wooden bicycles and chestnut trees and the Rock of Gibralter (I've seen it, he hasn't) — and now we're cutting across the side streets and through the alleys, moving east toward the neighborhoods where my patients live and die.

He doesn't say what he does for a living and I wonder if it's anything at all, if maybe this lassie is out with the unemployed. He must do something because his shoes and pants are speckled with smudges of paint.

Maybe he's the Cartographer of Baltimore, so well he knows these cobbled paths crowded with dogs and kids and garbage cans.

"You know what I love?" he says.

"What?"

"I love to walk through the alleys and look in peoples' houses. Especially at night when the lights are on and the blinds are up. You can look right in and see people eating and listening to the radio. Just living."

He doesn't ask me what I do and it's a relief not to answer all the questions, a blessing not to feel the evening turn when it finally comes out. It seems enough for him just to know that I work in a hospital.

How odd, I think, gazing into the tiny concrete yards of kids splashing in wading pools, their Moms watching from lawn chairs with their feet in the water; old men listening to the ballgame in their undershirts; how comfortingly odd not to talk about what you do for a living.

I extend the same courtesy for as long as it lasts.

Our walk is slow and evening falls with a warm breeze from the harbor At the end of one alley we stop in front of a corner bar called Miss Bonnie's and he points out the green and blue neon oozing behind block glass.

He talks about colors as if they are alive and he talks about his grandfather.

"Grandpop won't let me turn on any lights. He sits at the kitchen table all day circling crime stories in the paper with a red pencil. Nothing bad has ever happened to him here, but he says America is going to hell."

An Indian girl on a tricycle zips between us and he talks about the shades of red and brown — "like autumn leaves" — in her cheeks.

He says that American Indians are the only minority his grandfather has any sympathy for because they had no New World to run to when things went bad at home.

Now we're in the park, the sun going down as we walk quietly toward the Pagoda. He shakes the gate on the iron fence around it but you don't have to shake it to see that it's locked.

"Grandpop forgets that I'm living with him between the time we go to bed and the time I come down for breakfast. Every day we start from scratch."

"So why do you stay?"

He turns away and we walk east across the park toward Eastern Avenue and Greektown.

Just beyond the railroad trestle marking the incline that gives Highlandtown its name, he spies a sidewalk stand and says: "Wanna a snowball?"

I get chocolate with marshmallow and he asks for grape, fishing out a couple of dollars from the pockets of his white jeans.

We pause at a bus stop and I wonder if maybe we're going to catch one to God knows where.

Holding out his palm, he invites me to sit down and I think: This bench is the sidewalk cafe in Paris that the dot.com jerk wanted to take me to last month until he found out that a ticket to France would get me across the ocean and wouldn't get him anywhere.

We sit and start enjoying the snowballs. I put my head back on the bench and see that right above us hangs one of the most bizarre landmarks in a city filled with them.

Up against the sky: the Great Bolewicki Depression Clock.

Bolted to the front of Bolewicki's Appliance store, it has a human face and crystal hands filled with bubbling water — the little hand bubbling lime and the big hand bubbling orange — and around the numbers are lights shaped into words: "It's not too late, it's only . . ."

And then you read the time.

Like right now. It's not too late for anything: It's only ten past seven.

"I've been to Germany and Switzerland a half-dozen times," I say, "and I've never seen a clock like this."

"Pio Talle's grandfather made it," he says. "And I tried painting it for three months."

"Bolewicki's hired you to paint their clock? How many coats did it take?"

That does it!

He starts laughing and can't stop; a wild, crazy screech from down in his throat and I start to laugh too because he sounds like some strange bird.

Tears come to his eyes and he spews crystals of purple ice.

And somewhere inside of this ridiculous laugh I decide that I like this man and surrender to whatever the night may bring as the No. 10 stops to let people off beneath the Great Bolewicki Depression Clock in the middle of Eastern Avenue and my date with a guy named Basilio whose tongue is the color of a plum.

He catches his breath and says: "I wish old man Bolewicki would let me paint his clock. It would be the first money I've made with a brush in a long time."

He looks me dead in the eye.

"I'm an artist."

"I see."

"This thing was so hard, Katherine. You see the water bubbling in those hands, like bubble lights at Christmas? Did your tree have bubble lights when you were a kid? Loved those things. Don't see 'em anymore. But I couldn't get the water right, I couldn't make it look like it was really bubbling."

He loses himself in the clock, the big hand bubbling orange and the smaller one pumping green — "It's not too late, it's only . . ." — and he catches me staring at him and gets up.

We walk deeper into the neighborhood and he points out things I know and things I don't.

"That's a great little place," he says as we pass Garayoa's Café Espanol, where, he informs, they serve squid stuffed with pine nuts and tentacles and cooked in a sauce made with the ink.

I don't tell him that I have eaten there with an investment banker, a screen writer and a car dealer.

"The ink turns into a thick sauce that shimmers on the surface," he says. "I tried painting with it once — thought it would be perfect for a sweet night sky. But it was ugly when it dried."

At the next corner, Basilio hands our empty snowball cups to a short man selling produce from the trunk of a gigantic Pontiac and in return the man gives each of us a soft brown pear.

"Lefty," says Basilio, shaking the guy's hand.

"Señor," says the man with a thick Greek accent, looking me over and winking at Basilio. "How is your old *abuelo* my friend?"

"He's good, Lefty. I'll tell him you said hello."

"You do that and enjoy your evening."

Walking away, we bite the fruit as the sky turns dark and pear juice drips down the sides of my mouth. Basilio pulls a spotless white handkerchief from his back pocket, wipes my chin and then his own and it is all so very simple and nice . . .

Until we come upon a narrow lane paved with brick and identified by stained-glass transoms as the 600 block of South Macon Street.

Basilio points down the street of identical rowhouses, white marble steps before each of them and says: "I live down there with Grandpop."

He pauses as though trying to decide if he should go home and it makes me feel like I am no longer present.

Beyond the next bend in the Avenue, past a cluster of Greek restaurants painted white and sky blue, I see the Ruth Tower rising up from the University of East Baltimore and since there is no agenda and Basilio's verve faded at Macon Street, I point up to it and say: "Let's go."

It is night and we move through the dark campus toward a granite spiral that is the Bambino's only gift to the city of his birth.

Great moments from his career are carved into the stone and bolted to the tower's base is a plaque that quotes the slugger on the day the monument was dedicated: "Let the poor kids in free and name it after me."

We walk inside and start climbing to the bar at the top.

I tell Basilio that when I first came to Baltimore — Good Lord, it seems like 10,000 dead children ago — the top of the Ruth Tower was *the* spot: Espresso and Delta blues; black olives, crusty bread, cheap beer and young people from around the world shouting at each other about what it's all about.

He tells me that he was stuck in the suburbs back when he should have been going to college.

"Did you ever try to paint this?"

"Grandpop brought my old man here to see the Babe when Dad was a kid and Ruth was half-dead with termites."

We head for the bar and I can feel Basilio behind me, looking around.

I hand him a draft and steer us to a table with a window facing west, toward downtown where Baltimore's money finds Baltimore's art in chic storefronts along Charles Street.

The docs I work with write big checks for paintings that probably aren't any better than the ones Basilio destroys, but I really don't know if he has talent or not. All I know is what didn't turn out: half the buildings in East Baltimore.

I sip my beer and think that maybe I can help this guy.

"Tell me about the paintings you're happy with."

He drinks and ignores the question.

Over there is the National Brewery, he says, home of the One-Eyed Little Man; and the Esskay slaughterhouse used to be there before they razed it, they had some great stainless steel letters out front; and way over there, beyond the rooftops, is Orlo's Salvage House where you can get things you can't get anywhere else.

He's a fraud, I think, and for a moment I am sick.

Turning his dark head with an angry finger, I direct his gaze toward the Hopkins dome.

"And over there is where I fish bullets out of 14-year-old boys on Saturday nights just like this before I have to tell their 27-year-old mothers they didn't make it."

And still this hard-head gives me words instead of pictures.

Grandpop skinning squirrels at the stationary tubs in the basement for dinner; Grandpop lecturing a little boy at those same tubs that a man really hasn't washed up if he hasn't washed his neck; and Grandpop making love to his bride on Macon Street, conceiving the man who would seed the artist.

"Those," he says, "are pretty good."

"Take me to see them," I say. "Or take me home."

At the front door to 627 South Macon Street, just before turning the key, Basilio tells me to take off my shoes and leads me into a dimly lit room where shadows from the street light fall across a small figure sleeping in the parlor.

"Grandpop," he whispers as we creep toward a staircase along the wall.

No one answers and as I move up the stairs, the old man stirs in his bed and the hem of my dress rustles around my knees.

Basilio keeps moving and I am right behind him, shoes in my left hand, my right against the small of his back. When we reach the top, he whispers "Hallelujah!"

He says: "I've never done this before."

Neither have I.

A door in front of us creaks open as Basilio turns the knob and I slip in behind him.

We stand still just inside the door and my nose stings from the turpentine. As my eyes adjust to the dark, I sense that this is the biggest room in the house, that there is only one room on this floor — that it is as long and as wide as the house itself — and I am in it.

Basilio escorts me to a saloon table against the side wall and sits me down at it before crossing to the other side of the room.

"Ready?" he asks, holding a cord.

"Ready," I say, and he pulls it.

A tarp whooshes to the floor, night fills the space where the roof ought to be, the light of a nearly full moon and a sky of stars floods the room and in one clear instant I am in this man's world.

There's no roof!

My head spins as I try to take in the sky, the paintings, the smile on Basilio's face and the colors.

"I told you Grandpop won't let me use the lights. I cut the roof out a little bit at a time and paint with what it gives me. I never would have thought of it if I didn't have to."

Dumbfounded, I stand.

"You can't turn on lights but you can saw the roof out of his house?"

"As long as I don't use electricity or bring women home, he pretty much leaves me alone."

I move close to the work, silver light from the sky giving each painting a glow I've never seen in any gallery in the world. On one canvas after another, I read the narrative of his grandfather's life.

Grandpop as a boy, sitting on a rocky hill, carving a pair of handlebars from the limb of a chestnut tree; Grandpop shoveling coal on the deck of a rusty freighter, Gibraltar bearing down in the background; Grandpop kicking a soccer ball, his right leg stretched out in front of him as the ball sails past the Pagoda; Grandpop strolling down Eastern Avenue with his wife on a Sunday afternoon, the Great Bolewicki Depression Clock bubbling to beat the band.

And then, running the length of a single wall, a huge canvas of a bedroom cast in moonlight and pearl.

In the bed is a young man who looks a lot like Basilio, a white sheet draped across his back, arms strong and taut as he hovers over a dark-haired beauty.

Transfixed, I wonder if there is a cot in the room.

"What do you call this one?"

"The Fountain of Highlandtown."

GRANDPOP

Suenos. Siempre suenos. Dulces suenos y malos suenos.
Suenos de amor.

I can feel it.

Basilio must be making a *pintura* upstairs. A woman. I feel it in my sleep, like she is in the house.

He must be getting good.

"Grandpop," he says at my kitchen table every morning, up before me, coffee ready for his *abuelo*; this boy is a man, doesn't he have a home?

"Grandpop," he says while I'm still trying to figure out what day it is and why he is living with me. "Grandpop, do you remember what Grandmom looked like the first time you saw her?

"What did her skin look like?"

I say: "Basilio," (he was named for me, two Basilios in one house is one too many); I say: "What are you doing, writing a book?"

"Something like that, Grandpop."

Last week it was questions about the shipyard, before that it was Patterson Park, now it's about Mama and I don't have the strength for it.

Questions and questions and questions as he marks up a napkin with a pencil.

"Grandpop, tell me about Galicia and the corn cribs on stilts and the baskets your father made."

"Grandpop, tell me about the ox and the cart and the *cocido* your mother stewed over the fire."

"Grandpop, tell me about the first time you went down in the belly of a ship."

Why does he want to live with an old man who is so mean to him? He is good company, this boy with the questions, even if he has to turn on a light to scrub the floor in the middle of the afternoon.

"Grandpop," he says to me on his way out tonight — where he was going in the shoes with the paint on them, I don't know, he should get dressed and go out with a woman before he gets old — "Grandpop," he says: "What did Grandmom's hair look like on your wedding night?"

I told him: "Turn off the light and lock the door when you go out."

This is what I didn't tell him: It was black, Basilio, black like the coal I shoveled out of ships at la Roca; black like a night at sea without stars and it fell down around my shoulders when she leaned over me; *que linda Francesca, que bella Francesca, que guapa Francesca para me y solamente para mi.*

He asks in the morning while we eat our bacon and eggs; eggs he makes like I made for him when he stayed with Mama and me when he was a little boy (even then he wouldn't listen); bacon fried crisp into a circle and the egg in the middle, grease spooned slow over the yolk.

I say: "Basilio, what are you doing here?"

And he says: "What did Grandmom's eyes look like when she told you she loved you?"

After all these years, the thought of her kiss (I can feel it at night, on nights like this, Basilio you must be painting upstairs), just the thought of it makes me excited, *un caballo fuerte*; and it makes me ready, so sad and ready, and I get mad to answer this boy with skinny brushes and silly paints and goddammit why doesn't he go live with his father in their big house in the suburbs?

My house is small and life here is finished.

I get mad and tell him he's too much trouble. You don't turn on lights in the daytime and a boy doesn't ask an old man so many questions.

But he doesn't get hurt or angry, he just touches my arm and gets up to wash the dishes.

"I know, Grandpop," he says. "I know."

What does he know?

By the time I was his age I spoke good English, was supporting three kids, had a good Chevrolet and seniority down the shipyard.

What does he have?

My electricity and no *trabajo*; pennies he saves for paint (where his pennies come from I don't know, maybe he finds them in the street, he takes so many walks); and a loaf of bread he puts on the table every day before supper, one wheel of bread fresh from the Avenue in the center of my table 4 o'clock every day without a word.

I should go easy on him.

He's the only one who really talks with me; the only one who comes to see his old *abuelo*.

But when did he move in?

How did that happen?

That's the question you never asked, Basilio: "Grandpop, can I live with you?"

Suenos. Dulces suenos.

He must be painting upstairs.

I can feel it.

I remember when his father was just a baby and I called her Mama for the first time and she became Mama for all of us — *Mama de la casa* — and his father would wake up in the middle of the night and scream in his crib and nothing would make him stop and Frances would get so exhausted she would turn her back to me in bed and cry.

I would smooth her hair — it was black, Basilio, black as an olive — and I would turn on the radio — electricity, Basilio, in the middle of the night — to try and calm the baby and listen to something besides the screaming.

Mama liked the radio and we listened while your father cried — *cantante negra, cantante de almas azules* — and it helped us get through.

I had to get up early to catch the streetcar to the shipyard, but when the crying stopped sometimes the sun was coming out and Mama's breathing would slow down and her shoulders would move — sleeping but still listening, like I listen for her now on this no good bed, and Basilio — *Mira, hombre,* I will not tell you this again — if I lay very close and kissed her shoulders, she would turn to face me and we would have to be quiet Basilio, under the music . . .

So this I want to know, Mr. Picasso.

This, if you want to live on Macon Street for any longer.

Can you paint an apple baked soft in the oven, an apple filled with cinnamon and raisins?

Can you paint such a woman?

Are you good enough yet with those brushes that she will step out of your pictures to turn on the radio in the middle of the night?

Will she visit an old man on his death bed?

If you cannot do that, Basilio, there is no need for you to live here any longer.

"Measuring wealth through food..."

NEWSPAPER WORK

The New World: From the hills of Spain to the tables of Baltimore

LIKE MANY WHO CAME TO AMERICA FROM THE OLD COUNTRY, MY GRANDFATHER has a way of measuring wealth through food.

"We eat like kings in this country," is a line it seems I heard as I was growing up at almost every meal eaten in the company of Rafael Alvarez, my 79-year-old namesake.

While this boast was an immigrant's way of paying respect to America's bounty, it was never more true than on Christmas Eve.

For my family, Christmas Eve is a holiday feast of such magical proportions that it dwarfs all other special days of the year combined.

This is the story of that tradition, tracing an assimilation of palates and a parade of food from the rocky hills of Galicia in Northwest Spain, across the Atlantic to the long, narrow basement of a Highlandtown rowhouse, and finally, out to the wood-paneled basement of a suburban ranch house in Linthicum Heights.

It is a story of an American family who would like to think that on one night at least, they eat like kings.

"On Christmas Eve, not even a millionaire eat like we eat in my house," said my grandfather recently, in English that remains broken after more than a half-century in the New World. "Eat, eat, and eat, eat and drink."

In Spain, as in the rest of the Catholic world which honored the eve of Christ's birth by fasting from meat, eat, eat, eat meant fish, fish, fish.

In the countryside surrounding the port province of Galicia, "empanada" is a specialty — a thin pot-pie filled with bacalao (dried salt cod), merluza (known in Baltimore as "whities"), onions, green and red peppers, and other seafoods.

On Christmas Eve, empanada was the centerpiece of a table laden with 13 different dishes representing Christ and the 12 Apostles. The meal, with everything set out at the same time, began about 6 p.m. and ran to the other side of midnight.

The food lasted three days.

"Jeez oh my," said my grandfather, thinking back to his mother and sisters' all day chore. "They make enough for two families."

As the oldest of eight children, he was responsible for cutting up pine trees and their stumps, and was expected to bring home enough wood chips to keep pace with the feast.

While he cannot remember the names of each dish, my grandfatiter also recalls smaller pot-pies made of sardines, stewed fish, baked fish and fried fish.

But like children everywhere, the richest memories my grandfather carries from the Christmas Eves of his childhood are of treats — a rice and milk dessert, and sweet bread made soggy with wine and sugar.

The son of a basket weaver who also ran a hauling business with a wooden cart and oxen, my grandfather remembers his mother making dessert from flat round dough "filled with figs, and raisins, and nuts, covered with chestnut leaves and left to cook in the hot ashes" of a heavy stone stove.

There were no presents.

"Who's going to give us presents?" he said. "Nobody leave no presents over there. Enough food for a couple days or more, but no presents."

As did many of his fellow "Gallegos," my grandfather left while still a teenager to find better work than farming the rocky soil around Galicia. Traveling to Gibraltar by train and covered wagon, he found work shoveling coal onto English ships.

His memories of Christmas Eves spent on ships docked at "the rock" are bleak.

"What you gonna celebrate?" he said. "No women, no family, nobody, just the men. To get to shore you had to get a rowboat and row yourself up."

After three years in Gibraltar, Rafael Alvarez became a merchant seaman in the United States in 1926. Three years later he married my late grandmother, an Italian-American named Frances Prato Alvarez, and the couple set up house in a section of Highlandtown now known as Greektown.

In the early 1930s, and for at least the next 20 years, he was one of a handful of Spaniards in a neighborhood teeming with Italians. Here, the foods in the melting pot began to mix, and new aromas were created.

Off the top of his head, my grandfather would tell his wife as best he could what his mother cooked, and Frances would approximate it.

"All you have to do is tell her once, and the next time she do better," my grandfather said.

My father, Manuel Alvarez, the second of three children, was born in 1934.

He said his memories of Christmas Eve on South Macon street go back to when memory begins.

"At that time there were a lot of relatives and friends in the neighborhood that celebrated the same way," he said. "Christmas Eve was a fast day for even the Slavic people."

To hear my father tell it, almost everyone in his neighborhood made their own wine.

The work began with the crushing of grapes in October, and by Christmas, red-stained corks were popping.

"The big thing was opening the wine the day before [Christmas Eve]. We took our wine from relative to relative, neighbor to neighbor, and they tried ours and we tried theirs, and everybody said how wonderful it was, even though it was all [just about] the same thing.

"As a kid I went with my Daddy from place to place. The women [my grandmother's sisters and aunts] didn't care much about the wine, they had all their special goodies," my father said. "All kinds of cookies, and treats, sweetmeats, and nuts, candies. We'd show up at Mr. So and So's house, bring a gallon of wine, try all his goodies, and drink his wine, and it just kept on going round and round like that."

Though the wine and the cookies — some aged in wine, some aged in anise, some aged in honey — remained tasty footnotes to the fish, they represent the Italianization of the Alvarez Christmas Eve.

Sometime in the week before December 24, for an entire afternoon, anise-flavored waffle cookies called "pizzelle" were made by holding heavy cookie irons coated with olive oil over an open flame.

Though some Italian families here still make their own pizzelle, many use electric irons.

We make them the old way.

That same week, my father and grandfather would travel to Broadway Market by streetcar to buy the fish. Squid — deep fried as an appetizer into chewy, tentacle crisps and called calamare — was so cheap then it was almost given away at the market.

Because my grandmother was legally blind, my grandfather cleaned all the fish — tediously separating and deboning anchovies packed in heavy salt — before she cooked it.

The primary use for the anchovies was to make Italian "alisce cakes" — anchovies wrapped in dough and deep fried.

To an American kid twice removed from the old country, doughwrapped anchovies deep fried in olive oil isn't exactly a Whopper with cheese.

For the light of stomach, plain dough was fried without the fish center. But with or without, these bite-sized, salty, golden brown cakes symbolize Christmas Eve.

As my grandmother's sight grew worse, a new tradition was created.

Beginning early in the morning, my father, his brother Victor, and my grandfather stood around a fry pan filled with olive oil, wine glasses in one hand, a fork in the other, frying pound after pound of whities, cod and smelts.

It is doubtful that many married men in Spain fry the fish for Christmas Eve.

At this time, empanada shared the spotlight with baked cod, and later, orange-hued red snapper baked with lemon, thinly sliced potatoes and onions.

Unlike cod and whities, red snapper was one of the more expensive fish in the market, and it wasn't until prosperity followed the end of World War II that it began appearing on Christmas Eve.

In the mid-'50s, my grandfather's children began to marry, and the tradition again responded to the influx of new blood.

Both my grandfather's sons married girls from Canton. My father married a Polish-American named Gloria, and my Uncle Victor married a German-American named Claire.

One of my grandfather's concessions to these young ladies was to remove the eyes of the squid before frying. Another change was the introduction of spaghetti cooked with clam or tuna sauce for those weary of fish.

By the late '50s and early '60s, my generation was sitting in high chairs around a table with celery sticks to be dipped in shallow dishes of black pepper and olive oil, salty "lupino" beans you pop out of their shells, fresh fruit and vegetables, Italian nougat candies called "torrone," and roasted chestnuts.

Seated with us were non-family members, mostly Spanish seamen, who celebrated with us because they had no families. Because it would be insulting to my grandfather for these guests to try to repay him for the invitation, these people always rewarded me, my brothers, and my cousins by stuffing large bills into our little hands.

Following a silent prayer by my grandfather that began the meal came the traditional toast — saluda — with dozens of arms extending glasses of wine high in the air.

About 8 o'clock other relatives would begin dropping in for a glass of wine, a drop of Spanish anisette, a bite to eat, some coffee and cookies.

At midnight the women and children went to Mass; the men would remain at the table, drinking and eating.

When my father was little, he says they also walked up and down the alleys separating the close rows of houses, drinking wine and singing songs.

After church, we would exchange gifts and my grandfather always sat apart from the ripping of wrapping paper, embarrassed by presents bought for him, finding it hard to identify with the trading of gifts on a night celebrated with food.

Pictures of these scenes from my childhood are firmly etched in my mind.

Growing up in the manicured suburbs, I always felt more special than my friends during the Christmas week.

I had two celebrations to look forward to — the American Christmas morning with stacks of toys wrapped beneath the tree like everyone else, and a feast of good food and good feeling the night before.

When my grandmother died in 1976, the tradition moved to my father's house in Linthicum. Fish began to give way, and meat — one year kielbasa and sauerkraut, no less — was introduced.

According to my mother — a woman whose ancestry goes back to Galicia, Poland; a woman who married and learned to cook the family foods of a man whose family goes back to Galicia, Spain — this year's menu will be:

Two large trays of lasagna, one large cod empanada, shrimp and rice, fried squid, fried cod, fried whities, fried smelt, about 150 alisce cakes, celery with oil and pepper, lupino beans, a glazed ham set on the side for family neighbors who drop by, fruit, crackers, cheese, olives, chestnuts boiled in salt water and anise seed, torrone candy, pizzelle, raisin squares, pineapple cookies, chocolate chips, assorted nuts, kielbasa and sauerkraut, salmon dip, wine (now supplied by Cribari of California), coffee and anisette.

My wife sometimes pokes fun at me for repeating it to our children in our home, but it's true: "We eat like kings in this country."

A MELTING POT OF RECIPES FROM THE ALVAREZ FAMILY

Here are a few Alvarez family favorites for cooking up during the Christmas holidays:

Empanada de Bacalao

5 cups flour
$1/2$ cup butter (melted)
2 eggs
1 teaspoon baking powder
1 teaspoon salt
1 cup cold water
1 pound dried salt cod (soaked for 24 hours)
$1/2$ cup olive oil
$1/2$ pound onions, chopped
2 large green peppers
1 tsp. paprika

Put flour on table, making a hole in the center for baking powder, butter, salt, water and eggs. Blend well with hands until it makes a cohesive mass which does not stick to the fingers. Let dough rest in a warm place in a bowl covered with a damp cloth while preparing filling.

Soak dried salt cod for 24 hours, changing the water several times. Rinse thoroughly and dry. Put the cod in a pan with enough water to cover it, bring to boil, then take the fish out immediately. Bone and cut into small pieces. Heat the olive oil in a deep frying pan. Add the chopped onions. Sweat gently, then add paprika and seeded chopped green peppers. Let stand a little while to gather flavor, then add the fish.

Divide the dough in half and roll it into two rounds, $1/4$ inch thick. Arrange the fish mixture on one round; a small amount of raisins can be added, if desired. Top with the second round of dough and pinch down along the edge. With pieces of dough left over, an outside border can be formed. Prick all over the top with tines of a fork and bake in a warm (300 degrees F.) oven for 45 minutes. Brush top of dough with beaten egg and return to oven for additional 3-5 minutes.

Fried squid (kalamaria)

2 pounds squid
flour
salt and pepper
oil for frying
juice of 1 lemon

Wash squid, remove inside bone, eyes and ink bag; peel off skin. Dry squid and sprinkle with salt, then roll in flour until well-covered.

Heat oil and fry squid at high heat until nicely browned. Remove from heat. Place squid on a platter and sprinkle with salt and lemon juice. If used as appetizers, cut into small pieces.

Salt cod with potatoes and onions

1 $^1/_2$ pounds salt cod
$^1/_4$ cup olive oil
6 medium-sized potatoes, peeled, cut lengthwise $^1/_2$ inch thick
4 medium-sized onions, sliced
2 large green peppers seeded and sliced
dash of saffron
$^1/_2$ teaspoon finely chopped garlic
2 tablespoons finely chopped parsley
2 cups boiling water
1 teaspoon paprika

Starting a day ahead, place the cod in a glass or stainless steel bowl. Cover it with cold water and soak for at least 12 hours, changing the water three or four times. Drain and pat dry.

In a large skillet heat oil over moderate flame; add garlic, onion and green pepper; cook until soft. Add saffron, paprika, potatoes and cod.

Pour on boiling water to cover entire contents.

Simmer covered about 30-35 minutes. Add parsley, salt and pepper to taste.

Anchovies wrapped in dough and deep fried

1 (2-pound) can anchovies, packed in oil, drained
2 cups warm water
1 package active dry yeast
1 tablespoon sugar
2 teaspoons salt
flour (about 3-4 cups)

Pour water into large bowl. Sprinkle on yeast and stir until dissolved. Add sugar, salt and 1 $1/2$ cups flour. Stir to mix, then beat until smooth and shiny.

Stir in additional 1 $1/2$-2 cups flour until soft dough is formed. Let rise until double in size.

Taking small amount of dough, flatten with hands and place one anchovy in center of dough. (Keeping hands oiled helps in the handling of the dough.) Twist to form a small ball. Repeat procedure for rest of anchovies, then deep-fry pieces in oil at 375 degrees F. until golden brown. Drain on paper towels.

These treats are delicious warm, but can also be good days later after they've cooled and hardened, accompanied by a glass of wine.

Torrijas (fried bread dessert)

Soak sliced, stale bread in sweet wine about 5 minutes.
Fry on both sides in half butter, half oil until golden brown.
Sprinkle with cinnamon and sugar and enjoy.

"Ten thousand miles..."

CHAPTER 1

Summer Vacation 2000

On a cross-country quest
from Atlantic to Pacific, the sightseeing
promises to be terrific. And away we go ...

THREE DAYS AGO, MY 17-YEAR-OLD SON AND I LEFT BALTIMORE FOR A 10,000-mile journey through America. Up, down and sideways we will go, in a counter-clockwise road trip from coast to coast, Great Lakes to Gulf.

This morning, we should be in Cincinnati. By midnight, the St. Louis Arch should be in view. We are making the trip in a 1999 Volkswagen Beetle with a five-speed stick that Jake learned to drive for the expedition. The trunk is packed with clothes and books, dry cereal and peanut butter. Our bright blue buggy's dashboard vase holds ballpoint pens. The tape deck is cued to rock and roll.

"I'm so glad," sings the prophet. "I'm living in the USA!"

Beyond the Midwest lie the Badlands of South Dakota, the Great Salt Lake, the coast of California and, as the trip curves southeast toward home, the deserts of Nevada and Texas before New Orleans emerges from the swamps.

Two-thirds of the way into the five-week trip, Jake and I will part company. He'll fly back from Las Vegas to spend the last weeks of summer with his buddies. By Labor Day, I will be back home in Highlandtown.

Between now and then, there will be overnight stops in more than two dozen cities and cups of coffee in a hundred towns along a 22-state route selected on three criteria: places with friends or family, things we had never seen, and the mystery that shimmers between the two.

The lure of things not yet experienced was best articulated for me on a less ambitious trip in 1994 when my daughter Sofia and I visited the Andy Warhol Museum in Pittsburgh.

Amid huge silk screens of Marilyn and Mao, walls of cows and movies in which nothing moved strolled an old man who looked as though he'd lost his way from an American Legion bull roast.

After watching him eyeball the art, I asked why he had bothered. He said: "I want to see everything before I die."

So do I.

The Badlands — alive in my imagination since 1991, when I saw the Terrence Malick film of the same name at the Orpheum Cinema on Thames Street — was the first piece of the puzzle. The rest fell into place one phone call at a time.

"Do you know anyone who lives in Minnesota?"

(I want to walk by the boyhood homes of F. Scott Fitzgerald and Robert Zimmerman.)

"Anybody you know live in Montana?"

(I have to see the mythical crops of dental floss.)

"What about Austin, Texas?"

(The university there has the private library of Evelyn Waugh.)

Between South Baltimore and South Dakota, where we will look forward to seeing Mount Rushmore but will be almost giddy in anticipation of the monument to Crazy Horse, is the Chicago home of my Aunt Dolores.

Dolores Alvarez Kelly, my father's older sister, grew up in the Macon Street rowhouse where I now live. We have traded visits for years. She comes to Greektown, admires her mother's rosebush and sleeps in her parents' bed. I go to Chicago and chase the blues.

This time around, we will take the El from downtown to Northwestern University, so Jake can get a glimpse of a major-league campus before deciding on a college after his senior year at Mount St. Joseph this fall.

Jake's impending commencement — from the Xavierian halls of Irvington to the world at large — was a big reason for taking this vacation now. His older sister, Amelia, now considers Manhattan home. It won't be long before he gets his mail outside the 21224 zip code as well.

At first he was somewhat reluctant. Not because he didn't want to be with me (we've taken many trips together, from Smith Island to the Grand Canyon) but because he didn't want to be away from the neighborhood. In a teen-ager's mind, the month of August represents one-third of the disappearing pie called summer vacation.

I did what my parents always did (and sometimes still do) with me. I sat him down at the kitchen table and started preaching.

"Jakey," I said, "after next year, you'll be too busy for your old man."

"No I won't, Dad."

"Trust me," I said. "Things change when you leave the house. By the time we have this opportunity again, if ever, you might be pushing me in a wheelchair, trying to find a nice spot to park me in the shade."

A deal was struck: Jake would go along if I promised to fly him back from out west. My mom found a one-way ticket from Vegas to Baltimore-Washington International Airport for about $230. I'll put him on the plane after we search for the ruins of the old Aladdin Hotel, where Elvis married Priscilla in 1967.

In the thousands of miles to come, Jake will pass time with a portable Game Boy and I will groove to the Fleshtones. He will read *Shogun* for the second time in a year for pleasure, and I will continue a months-long trudge through Melville's *Confidence Man*, trying to learn something.

There will be spirited discussions and long silences. Home-cooked meals and junk food. We will take turns driving, get on each other's nerves, miss everyone back home, capture 21st-century America on a digital video recorder and share the adventure with you every Sunday for the next five weeks.

July 23, 2000

Surprising tastes of home

ST. LOUIS — IN PITTSBURGH I ATE A GRILLED KIELBASA AT A PLACE CALLED Wiener World, a gnarled little dog that Ostrowski's would not have sold to the Soviets.

The Skyline diner in Cincinnati offered up an abomination of spaghetti topped with chili and enough grated cheddar to make grilled cheese sandwiches every afternoon for an entire adolescence. It is called, I kid you not, a three-way.

Oh, baby.

When the homemade pasta and tomato-canning spirit of my Italian grandmother protested, the waitress said: "Oh, you want real spaghetti. With Ragu."

My son Jake whispered: "Let it go, Dad. We're strangers here. Let it go."

I ordered a chili dog.

Perhaps this is what Robbie Robertson was talking about in "The Last Waltz," when he said the road was "a [expletive] impossible way of life."

You travel a thousand and one miles from home to see things you've never seen and meet folks you didn't know.

You take a fine room in a hotel at one of the most spectacular rail stations in American history — the 1894 Union Station on St. Louis' Market Street — stow your bags and set out.

A sweet, unseasonably cool breeze blows through the old fur-trading post on the Mississippi, and the stainless-steel curve of the Gateway Arch — far more impressive than expected — shimmers against the sky.

Ducking into a neighborhood bookstore along a gentrified lane called Euclid, you lay your fingertips on the wrist of the city like a Chinese doctor divining the pulse of someone with a will to live but more past than future. And who do you meet?

A guy from Highlandtown wearing a "Joe Bonvegna for State Senator" T-shirt.

Peter Genovese, City College class of 1963, left the 200 block of South Highland Avenue some 30 years ago to teach college English. The son of an Italian barber, Pete told his family he would have to leave home to find work.

A politically connected uncle — in those days, this meant that Mimi DiPietro often stood behind you in the Communion line at Our Lady of Pompei — told his nephew not to rush off.

Let me work on it, the uncle said. I'll find you a teaching job around here. After putting in calls to Johns Hopkins and Loyola and the University of Maryland, the uncle said: "No luck with the teaching, but I can get you a good job down the Civic Center."

That was three decades ago. Now retired from the Meramec campus of St. Louis Community College, Genovese publishes poetry under the Garlic Press imprint and grinds the patience of his wife with tales of East Baltimore.

For dinner, he took Jake and me to a neighborhood joint called Hodak's on Gravois in the LaSalle Park neighborhood, an ethnic enclave of "scrubby Dutch," the local term for German immigrants.

Hodak's, promised Genovese, is a place like Gunning's or Webb's, but with fried chicken — $5.10 for half a chicken with coleslaw and mashed potatoes — instead of steamed crabs. Jake pointed out that chicken is unlikely to make the endangered species list, while his grandchildren may never taste a Chesapeake Bay blue crab. However common, though, the chicken was splendid, easily the best neighborhood meal we've had so far.

From Genovese, I learned that sometime between the world wars, there was a place on Lombard Street near the recently razed Esskay plant called the "Christmas ball" factory.

A Christmas ball factory! Is anybody alive who worked there?

When Genovese was a kid, he and some friends climbed through a broken window and found an empty safe and a floor littered with dead pigeons but no Christmas balls. A half-century later, he is grateful that no one thought it would be fun to lock somebody in the safe.

For dessert, Genovese took us to Ted Drewes on Route 66 for frozen custard that has delighted St. Louisans since 1929.

Before we left, he gave Jake a book on the Tao of watercolors for his birthday and me a book of poems about Jack Ruby by David Clewell. I returned his kindness with a T-shirt from Matthew's Pizza. And I told Genovese that if he didn't visit us for steamed crabs in our basement kitchen on Macon Street, I would be mad.

Some other notes from the road:

• To Alice McDermott: Just south of Columbus, Ohio, I rescued eight copies of your novel *That Night* from the 20-cent bin outside a Methodist Church turned used-book store and have been giving them to good homes.

• To Mark Pietrowski: Don't forget to bring in the mail.

• To Mom: Don't be alarmed by this next paragraph. No one was hurt.

In St. Louis last Tuesday, I was in a car accident.

As a friend drove around the city following morning Mass at the Cathedral of St. Louis — after we visited the site of the 1904 World's Fair — an older woman rear-ended his car at 40 mph on Forest Park Avenue near Spring Avenue.

We had no cuts or bruises, but the car was wrecked and my friend accepted a medic's offer of a ride to the hospital.

I got my journal out of his smashed-up Geo Prizm and began walking toward downtown, stopping for an ice cream cone along the way and counting blessings.

I could have been killed on my son's 17th birthday. Was I saved because I went to Mass? Was Jake, who would have been sitting in the back of the car, saved because he didn't go?

Saved nonetheless, I walked along a ribbon of St. Louis highway like Woody Guthrie — "THIS MACHINE KILLS REPUBLICANS" written across my notebook — licking ice cream, giddy with gratitude.

And willing, if necessary, to eat a plate of pasta defiled with brown chili and fluorescent cheese every day for the rest of my life if that were the price of remaining on the planet.

July 30, 2000

Looking for character in great stone faces

BLACK HILLS, S.D. — THE DIFFERENCE BETWEEN THE CRAZY HORSE monument and Mount Rushmore is the difference between the quick and the dead.

I can't prove it, no more than Einstein could prove that imagination is more important than knowledge. But it's true. Some patriots may disagree, violently perhaps, yet the red man is alive and the four white guys are dead.

I am no noodle-brained new-ager, but a good Catholic boy, grateful to be a second-generation American. And I am here in South Dakota to tell you that something is present at Crazy Horse and absent at Rushmore.

"The difference," said a 14-year-old boy selling ice cream in these sacred hills, "is what they represent."

It makes you think about winners and losers and how they often switch places over the long run.

The Rushmore carvings are among the largest on the planet, on a par with the mighty Sphinx of Egypt. The incomplete Crazy Horse — 565 feet high by 641 feet long — is the biggest of all man's sculptures.

With nearly 9 million tons of granite already carved — and dynamited rock free for the taking — the three-dimensional memorial to the Lakota chief will not be finished in my lifetime.

Mount Rushmore was unveiled in 1941, six years before a Boston Pole named Korczak Ziolkowski began blasting granite nearby. A relief made with the removal of 450,000 tons of rock, Rushmore would fit across the Sioux warrior's brow.

These monuments to mortal enemies — settlers and the resettled, Americans all — loomed before us on week two of our 10,000-mile summer journey across the United States.

Before hitting Rapid City, the coolest thing we'd seen was a vintage log cabin near the Fox River in Wisconsin painted lime green.

Imagine a log cabin on the parking lot of the Harundale Mall.

Taking the suggestion of those who had made the trip before, my son, Jake, and I visited Rushmore first to avoid being disappointed by the difference in scale. George, Thomas, Abe and Teddy exude the cold, gray and formal feel of our nation's capital and capital — despite all the talk of liberty and democracy — they represent. It was like staring at portraits carved from hard cash.

Still, the tourists I spoke to during an afternoon hail storm at Crazy Horse, which was created without a dollar of government money, were more moved by cowboys than Indians.

Rushmore, said Joyce Hall of Garland, Texas, "is what we have today, it's our freedom." Her husband, Robert, a transplanted Okie who drills for water in the Lone Star State, allowed that before last week, his wife would not have known Crazy Horse from Crazy Glue.

"It's interesting," he said of the testimonial to the man who vanquished Custer. "But Rushmore takes my breath away."

From Graceland to Memorial Stadium — "Time will not dim the glory of their deeds ..." — monuments fascinate me.

I am interested in the ego that builds objects that honor others, and Crazy Horse is as much a tribute to the passion, diligence and beautiful lunacy of its creator as it is to the man emerging from the mountain.

Korczak's name, his progeny and his creations — including a Polish eagle carved from Tennessee marble that would look swell on the bar at the Polish National Alliance on Eastern Avenue — are everywhere.

The sculptor, who died at age 74 in 1982, is buried in a self-built tomb on the mountain where he labored for the last half of his life.

Above him, upon a colossal steed, is Crazy Horse, his arm outstretched forever across the Badlands, declaring in granite: "My lands are where my dead lie buried ..."

The fun of a loosely planned road trip, knowing you will get from A to B but not always sure by which route, is stumbling upon things along the way.

Jake and I knew we would encounter a monument to a people who have survived to see brethren from Mexico and South America flood into a nation built atop their dead ancestors.

But there has been much we did not anticipate.

In downtown Sioux Falls, S.D., we discovered Zandbroz Variety, an old-fashioned store where the soda jerks still make Coca-Cola with syrup and fizz water and, in addition to crime novels by Charles Willeford, you can get one of those wind-up robots made of tin that Beaver Cleaver would have traded Whitey a stack of baseball cards for.

A dozen or so miles east of Sioux Falls on Interstate 90, I was reeled in by an improbable billboard advertising a Fatima shrine.

There, in the cornfields of Alexandria, stands the National Fatima Family Shrine in honor of the appearance of the Blessed Virgin Mary to a trio of Portuguese shepherd kids in 1917.

The statues and open-air chapels came with a blessing you can't get in cities like Baltimore anymore: the church, built from local granite between 1905 and

1907, was unlocked even though there wasn't a soul around.

My son and I were able to sit quietly in the sanctuary, thank God for our good fortune, remember our loved ones and move on to the next monument.

The Corn Palace!

Where else but in Mitchell, S.D., can you see a building that looks like a Kremlin made from ears of corn upon which mosaics depicting Martin Luther King Jr., Elvis Presley and the raising of the Stars and Stripes on Iwo Jima are fashioned from kernels of maize?

Inside they sell trinkets and baubles, corn in all its forms and glory and, in the winter, play high school basketball.

Which gave me an idea for the guitar-strumming mayor of my beloved Bawlmer.

Why not keep your hands off Howard and Eutaw streets and erect the Crab Palace instead?

You could build it from the shells of steamed blue crabs in the wastelands of Fairfield and sell Old Bay, chips of white marble from all of the rowhouses Danny Henson demolished and life-size portraits of Barbara Mikulski on black velvet.

And decrease our property taxes with bingo games!

Oh, Martin, they would come by the busload.

You know they would.

August 6, 2000

Traveling companions

FOR 5,600 MILES, MY TEEN-AGE SON AND I HAVE BEEN TWO PEAS IN A Beetle-shaped pod. Close enough to tousle his hair in good moments. Or get our hands around each other's throats with no escape.

From Baltimore to Baker, Calif. — where a "Mad Greek" and his wife in the Mojave Desert sell lamb kabobs nearly as good as the ones at Samos — there has been plenty of good and enough of the not so good to keep it real. A hundred times, Jake has expressed awe at the natural beauty of North America, from the forests of Montana to the moonscapes of Nevada.

And twice he has let me know that three weeks alone on the road with his hard-headed father is no picnic.

When I insisted on pulling off the road to film Catholic chapels and giant ice cream cones on the top of vintage hamburger joints, he said: "You love that camera more than me."

When I was determined to wash the VW in the middle of fire-driven water restrictions in Montana, he said: "I can see that my opinion means nothing to you."

Oh, Jakey. *Au contraire*, my son.

I once thought my father liked my younger brother more than me because he let Danny use the good shovel to clear our walk of snow.

And now that I have more influence in the world than my old man — his connections, like the union guy who got me a job on a ship when I was Jake's age, are dead or dying — he often seeks my counsel.

Time sorts out these things, more time than it takes to chase the setting sun at 80 mph across the breadth of the United States.

What took us 21 days to travel by car, Jake covered in a few hours by plane on Thursday, jetting home to what remains of the Baltimore summer from this mirage of bad clothes and buffets in the desert.

For the next two weeks, as I move through Texas toward New Orleans and the sacred delta of Mississippi, a road map will lie in the seat where my navigator used to be.

We agree on Tom "I'm Big in Japan" Waits and what to eat for dinner, which is nearly anything. Of the Ramones, Jake says: "It sounds like these guys are always begging for medical help."

We disagree on whether it is OK to stare at strange folks on the street. (I argue that staring and eavesdropping and stealing from the narrative of other people's lives is the privilege of the artist. He says it is rude.)

For every Bobby Dylan reference I lay on him — there was something especially poignant about hearing "My Back Pages" with the Donner Pass in our sights — Jake comes back with five Homer Simpson references.

Not only is Homer funnier than Bob, he's deeper.

I scribble notes for short stories atop the coffee-table-sized dashboard of the Beetle and Jake sketches and inks original comics about the "Senator" and the "Non-Voter" as the nation zooms by.

The toothy Senator is the hero, with miles of sticky red tape as his weapon. The fat-bellied, baseball cap-wearing Non-Voter is the villain who spreads the "scourge of indifference" through the land.

The comedy turned serious in Helena, Mont., when we read an open letter to America's 100 million non-voters tacked to a pay phone that Jake used to call his mother.

The letter was from some guy named Mike. It argued that there is no difference between Democrats and Republicans at the level of Gore and Bush, insiders who both support the death penalty and NAFTA and the rich getting richer.

Then it exhorts all of the disgusted electoral dropouts to give corporate America its worst nightmare and vote for Ralph Nader. A heroic act, it says, tantamount "to that Chinese guy in Tienanmen Square standing in front of a moving tank and stopping it."

Mike encouraged people to take the letter, make copies of it, and spread the word for a candidate who supports universal health care. I helped Jake take the letter off the telephone pole before he folded it into his pocket.

Jake turned 17 on this trip, in St. Louis. At the Union Station mall there, I bought him a Peruvian chess set in which the Aztecs battle the Conquistadors of his great-grandfather's Espana.

We finally got down to a game in Rapid City, S.D., and although I taught him to play a long time ago, he beat me. He always does. On the night Manuel Jacob Alvarez was born — July 25, 1983 — my brother Danny (who got the good shovel) and I bought a six-pack of National Bohemian on Dillon Street and sat in a vacant lot in Canton that now sparkles with luxury townhouses.

We drank and made toasts to an infant named for our father; a kid who, to this day, remains the only male Alvarez of his generation.

Sitting on the ground, drinking in the moonlight over Boston Street, I asked Danny to be Jake's godfather, and he accepted with a smile and a nod.

Danny and Jake are much more alike in their interests — Japanese science-fiction movies, computer games and taking things apart — than Jake and his father.

I wonder what Jake would have learned if he'd taken this trip with his Uncle Dan, who vacations in Ocean City and doesn't leave Linthicum if he doesn't have to, instead of me.

I know they still would have made fun of people on the street.

Here's one of the 10 million things I like about my kid.

On Antelope Island in Utah's Great Salt Lake, I attended a reading by Natasha Saje, a poet who moved west from Baltimore to teach poetry at Westminster College.

Jake has suffered through hundreds of readings in his lifetime but was a good sport about supporting a friend who put us up for the night and served pork chops on the grill.

The scenery at Antelope Island is magnificent, making up for the relative lack of beauty in the city named for the lake. While Natasha read poems about white marble steps and a-rabbers to Salt Lake residents who knew not of such things, Jake busied himself behind a bank of craggy rocks.

As we left Salt Lake for the Golden Gate (if travel is education, Jake learned from his feet more than any book about the hills of San Francisco), I asked him what he'd been doing.

Writing a plea for help, it seems, on scrap paper.

Jake buried the note under a rock in the hope that someone might find it before his father pulled off the road to photograph a highway sign that said: "Feely — 12 miles."

That Jakey.

What a card.

August 13, 2000

Road rules learned on the drive to survive

LET'S PULL OFF OF ROUTE 6 NEAR THE SHACK WHERE ELVIS WAS BORN — IT WAS 23 years last Wednesday that we lost him in Memphis — and sit on the porch a spell.

I want to rock on the swing as the sun goes down and talk to you about driving. By the time you read this, depending on when you got to the paper today, I will have passed some 8,600 miles with a good 1,500 to go.

In the past four weeks, I have driven more than I have stopped to look at things. (Exceptions made for Sixth Street in Austin, Texas, and the midnight lamp burning at the Goodrich Avenue house in St. Paul, Minn., where Fitzgerald wrote "The Beautiful and the Damned.")

I have driven more than I have stuffed my face. (Topping the lip-smacking list are a beef barbecue sandwich in Durant, Miss.; an *al fresco* lunch of fresh fruit and summer sausage at the adolescent Wisconsin home of Baltimore's crab-selling poet Ingrid Ankerson; and shrimp broiled and buttered in Houma, La.)

More than anything else, what I have done for the past month is drive.

Drive, he said.

There is nothing especially Herculean about the effort, although I did pass by a city named for the Greek god of strength outside of San Francisco.

But it is no small thing either.

In his new book of essays called *Roads*, Larry McMurtry writes of driving 800 to 1,000 miles a day to meditate upon his life from the mighty interstates of America.

I stopped into his warehouse of 500,000 used and rare books in Archer City, Texas, a week ago to talk about literature and the highway. As I rattled off my itinerary the way Danny Aiello calls out station stops from his past life as a rail conductor, McMurtry alighted on the Black Hills of Dakota.

"Crazy Horse Mountain is one of the most amazing things in America," he said. "But I don't really like that part of the country. Pine Ridge — scary country. A rough, violent place."

I don't know what spooked Lonesome Larry about the Badlands besides the bloody history of the place — he says he reads history for five hours each night before bed — but I sure liked it.

There's nothing like seeing two dozen bikers take a wide mountain turn on their hogs with a town called Deadwood behind them.

Where I felt uncomfortable was west of Houston in the Sealy, Texas, public library, where a middle-aged woman and the desk clerk spoke in stage whispers about a book that proves how the Vatican rules the world.

And all this time I thought it was Hollywood. On days when I manage to nap in the car on a Wal-Mart parking lot — great places to sleep, plenty of cars for camouflage and people too busy looking for sales to notice anything — I manage about 500 miles.

While rain has soaked Baltimore for weeks, the rest of the country has been hotter than usual, with daily temperatures well above 100 in numerous states and heavy smoke from western wildfires wafting as far east as Tennessee.

Speeding through the summer, I have learned a neat little trick. When the air-conditioner vent is tilted a certain way, if I cup my right hand just right, I can direct air to the back of my neck between shifting gears.

Not as cool as being able to turn your eyelids inside out, but cool.

And while my 1999 Beetle has been a champ (if you want smiles from kids from 1 to 92, buy a Bug), I have a question for Valley Motors on York Road, which serviced the car before I left Maryland.

When I pulled into a Jiffy Lube in Gallup, N.M., for an oil change, the grease monkeys said I was more than two quarts low with no sign of leaks.

What's up with that?

And here's Ralphie's recipe for squeezing the last hundred miles out of a long day when all the motels in Nowheresville are full — Lord help you if there's a church convention or an interstate softball tournament — and you don't think you can take another step:

Pull into an all-night gas station attached to a good convenience store.

You'll know its the right place because the clerk will either be a very heavy woman or a very skinny man. Except when the clerk is a very skinny woman or a very heavy man.

Order animal fat on a bun that's been sitting under a heat lamp for 14 hours. Cheese helps. Wash this down with a Mountain Dew. Quickly. Eat two or three Tums. Pour a cup of coffee that looks like the oil struck by Jed Clampett and grab an ice cream on the way out.

Back behind the wheel, scream, "I'm comin', Mama!" into the silent night and throw "Gimme Shelter" in the tape player.

Jet fuel, baby — strong enough to rocket you from just north of Idaho Falls to just south of Pocatello. It only works once a day, however.

When it's gone, you're done.

And your next purchase may be a bottle of Pepto Bismol and a vial of Excedrin, as it was for me in San Pedro, Calif., after eating day-old anchovies and capers on toast after a party on Greenwich Street in San Francisco.

But as my son Jake said when I hobbled into a 7-Eleven willing to pay any price to be healed: "You can't go wrong with Pepto and Excedrin. They're the kings in their fields."

I washed them down with coffee.

When I was a kid and the Beatles would talk about not knowing what city they were in during worldwide concerts in 1964 and 1965, I found it hard to believe and hoped they had noticed something special about Baltimore.

How could you not know what city you're in? How could they all look alike?

You can and they do.

Spending less than 24 hours in dozens of small towns and big cities across the United States reminded me of what the legendary Mad Dogs & Englishmen tour must have been like, except that too many Americans resemble Joe Cocker and the only beauty I found that compared with the young Rita Coolidge was a deli clerk in Alzada, Mont. (Ever try to tell a teen-ager about Rita Coolidge?)

This is the way it is when there are more miles behind you than in front of you.

You claim a clean, cool room on the far side of midnight and are happy if it cost you less than $100. You unlock the door and find fresh sheets on the bed and a remote control.

You flop down, face forward, and mumble into the mattress: "I'm home."

Blasphemy.

August 20, 2000

Road ends, and memories stir

BLESSED BY ST. MOSES, KISSED BY SALT AIR, A 10,000-MILE ROAD TRIP ENDS IN a reverie.

Singing to the ocean, I can hear the ocean's roar. Somewhere inside the roar — the sound a conch shell pours into the ear of an innocent kid — this song of myself takes me back ... way, way, way back to the Maryland shore in the years when Lyndon Johnson showed us the scar where his gall bladder used to be and Louie Armstrong blew the Fab Four from the top of the charts with "Hello, Dolly."

Ah, Satchmo and the Beatles on the jukebox at Captain Tom's crab house in the basement of the Rideau Hotel in Ocean City. It is 1964 and my parents drink beer and eat steamed shrimp and crab cakes with Simone and Agnes Garayoa, friends from Karcz's Cafe on the South Broadway waterfront who, through the alchemy of love, became blood to us. Miss Agnes, her back and shoulders burned red, slips me enough quarters to play "I Want to Hold Your Hand" 10 times in a row and we kids can order anything on the menu. I see Mr. Simone give his son Mark a $20 bill — remember, this is 35 years ago — and my shaved little head spins at the amount.

At night, Mark's sister Kathy would baby-sit my brother Danny and me while our parents went "nightclubbing" at the Carousel. We would shout stupid things out the window to people strolling the boardwalk and duck down under the sill, laughing until our stomachs hurt.

A week down the ocean — sand and sea, the crabs, the beer, cheeseburgers and Coca-Cola in 8-ounce bottles tinted green — this was middle-class prosperity for a working family. We did it year after year throughout my childhood and, as best as my 6-year-old intuition could make out, everyone was happy.

This summer — when Paul McCartney is the same age that my grandparents were during Beatlemania — I have been nearly everywhere in these United States. From the birthplace of Jack London on the coast of California, to the grave of Thomas Wolfe in the hills of North Carolina, nearly 10,000 miles in five weeks.

I have eaten the day's catch off of Louisiana shrimp boats, gawked at the largest collection of mosaic in the world on the ceiling of the Cathedral Basilica of St. Louis, seen water slides in the desert and enough motor homes to shelter the town of Aberdeen.

But nothing will ever define vacation more for me than sitting in the sand while Atlantic waves — Neptune's hypnotic winding of this mortal coil — pound a beach speckled with bubbles from burrowing sand crabs.

It means the world to me, more now, as nostalgia does its odd math on my memory, than when I was living it. If only the people who are no longer with us could walk out of the surf and sit next to me on this towel. One more time. Just for as long as it takes the tide to go out.

One year, the course of our family's summer vacations took an abrupt change. Instead of going back to Ocean City for one week, we flew across the sea in a nearly straight line to spend six weeks with our relatives in Spain.

It was 1970, the summer between my last year at Linthicum Elementary School and my first year in the parochial halls of St. Philip Neri, and there was a girl back home that I liked a lot.

Within 10 minutes of being seated at the dining room table of my great uncle's house in the small Galicia town of Chapela outside the port city of Vigo, I was asking for a pencil and a sheet of paper to write a note to my sweetheart as I write to you now.

Why would someone use up all of their vacation to drive 10,000 miles in five weeks?

It was hectic, at times insane — an average of 18 hours or less in every town — and it wasn't cheap, costing more than $700 in gas alone. These moments I share with you now, on the beach between the Tar Heel villages of Duck and Corolla, is the only time I had the luxury of sitting and doing nothing.

Yet after hundreds of hours in a speeding car, the psyche doesn't immediately know what to do. The body is restless, and the sirens that once lured me to every roadside barbecue pit between west Texas and eastern Tennessee — the chorus which wailed at the Mississippi gravesite of Elmore James — now pester me to get back on the road, promising that the next exit will be O'Donnell Street off of the Baltimore Harbor Tunnel Thruway.

I had several reasons for taking this trip: to spend time alone with my 17-year-old son, Jake, before his senior year of high school. To see as much of the country as possible at one time. To get some sense of what a low-budget rock and roll tour must be like.

To see if I was up to it and glimpse the one thing that you won't always remember but will never forget: a face, a front yard, the golden orange of a late afternoon sun as it sets across a bayou.

In Louisiana, a foreign land that welcomes your arrival in French, I happened upon a sign that shed light on a discussion I had years ago with a Talmudic scholar, something humorous to put a few knots in his beard.

Back in 1994, when I began a cautious journey into the world of Baltimore's Orthodox Jews, one of the first things I did was request a meeting with Rabbi Moshe Heineman, one of the community's major players.

I asked simple questions and in my naivete wondered whether Jews, for all of their great sages and leaders, held any human in the same deified light that Catholics revere saints.

"No," said Heineman.

"Nobody?"

"No one."

"What about Moses?"

The rabbi shrugged his shoulders and said: "Just a man."

So imagine the thrill as I tooled through the small town of Jeanette, La., and passed a clapboard church on Route 182 with this sign on the front door: Saint Moses Baptist Church.

Redeemed!

In these travels, I may have passed more Baptist churches than McDonald's, many with exotic names, but this one was singular in bridging the law of the Torah with the gospel of Jesus Christ.

Turning off Route 182 for the swifter Route 90, I stopped to take a picture of a highway sign that read "Amelia, 2 miles" for my oldest daughter of the same name.

Walking back to the car, I happened to look down to see a turtle by the side of the road, its head stretched toward the yellow lines, trying to cross.

Kneeling down for a closer look, I saw that it wasn't a turtle at all but what remained of a turtle. The poor thing had run out of gas and weeks in the summer sun had baked it so completely that the shell was empty — just a leathery head and four feet sticking out from a diamondback.

I put the specimen in the back of the Volkswagen and here, on the Outer Banks, used it to thrill the vacationing Lichtenberg children — Sammy, Regan and Spencer — the way watching my father make blowfish puff out their bellies thrilled me as a kid on the fishing piers in Ocean City.

And that's how it ends after a long month of crossing highways, making it from one side to the other and back again with better luck than that Louisiana turtle.

Sometime this week, when you see my name on a story about a tanker-truck overturning on Pennington Avenue and spilling thousands of gallons of detergent, we will both know that I am home.

August 27, 2000

"I've seen many a lighthouse..."

CHAPTER 2

Characterus Baltimorensis

Baltimore Oblivion Marching Band, Three Mile Island and other disasters

THE MAN IN THE SILVER SUIT YOU SEE ON PAGE 1 OF THE SUN'S APRIL 4 EDITION was photographed by the Associated Press in the middle of a performance.

It was a quick performance given without notice or explanation at Three Mile Island during the nuclear crisis — a stage which already had the world captivated.

Though the wirephotos the AP transmitted to newspapers around the world identified the man as everything from a nuclear worker in a decontamination suit to a nuclear protester and prankster, only one newspaper, the *New York Post*, correctly described him as an entertainer from BOMB — the six-member Baltimore Oblivion Marching Band.

The man inside the silver suit, 25-year-old Baltimore art graduate Doug Retzler, was giving the biggest performance of his young career.

More people read about his presentation than the entire TV audience for Roots.

"I started working on the suit about 11 the night of April 2 and finished it in an hour and a half. We left Baltimore at 3 a.m. the next morning," explained Mr. Retzler (known to intimates as Sumu Pretzler), a seamstress of limited ability.

"We went to Three Mile Island with no expectations," said Mr. Retzler, who made the suit out of Mylar, a trade name for an aluminized acetate used in food packaging, recording tape, and electrical insulation.

Richard Elsberry, a video tape technician who films CETA applicants so they can prepare for job interviews, remembers planning the trip on the eve of the performance.

"There was a long period of conflict and tension as to whether our intentions were valid and if it was safe," said Mr. Elsberry from behind a strip of black cardboard that covered his eyes and nose (his "Mary Avara censor board").

Mr. Elsberry, who became hysterical with fear and had to be slapped when the Volkswagen Bombmobilebus came within sight of the nuclear plant's towers, played a plastic toy saxophone during the performance.

His biggest fear was, "getting arrested for breaking the crisis curfew and not being evacuated when the plant exploded."

The only female member of BOMB, free-lance photographer Grace Zaccardi, was more concerned with the group's principles than the possibility of a nuclear demise.

"I didn't want as to be going up there for the same reason people chase ambulances," she said.

But Mr. Retzler, Mr. Elsberry, and the remaining members of BOMB — Bob Dorsey, Mr. Elsberry's brother John, and the incredible Michael Tolson (a man who once had his entire head shaved except for 11 strategically placed moustaches and two very long pony-tails) agreed that they went to Three Mile Island for exactly the same reason people chase ambulances, to find out first-hand the truth about something terrible that has happened.

"We were just as much in the dark at Three Mile Island as we were watching at home on TV — just as uninformed as the press," said Richard Elsberry. "It was something you couldn't see, smell, or feel."

During hour 16 of a recent party hosted by BOMB (a 66-hour media orgy billed as "Sleep Deprivation Therapy") Mr. Retzler said that aside from being a fact-finding mission, the Three Mile Island Show was an exercise in manipulating the media.

While an educational film about pigs played on the north wall of BOMB's mangy Mount Royal art studio, Mr. Retzler revealed that he has always been drawn to extrovert behavior. He likes being able to alter public situations. And above all he has a "definite, all-consuming fetish for manipulating the media."

When told this, photographer Martha Cooper, a former Baltimorean who covered the nuclear crisis for the *New York Post* and the reason that the *Post* was the only newspaper in the world to get the real scoop on the Baltimore Oblivion Marching Band, said that BOMB failed.

"I felt they were not successful," responded Ms. Cooper over the telephone from New York.

"The suit was right. But they failed because they were disorganized. If they really wanted to manipulate me, they would have done what I wanted.

"At Three Mile Island at that particular time there was very little to get. I was looking for anything unusual since the press was kept on the fringes during most of the crisis anyway."

Ms. Cooper dismissed BOMB's manipulatory objectives as, "An emphasis of something that already exists and is well known."

Simply, the press is manipulated every day.

Doug Retzler ripped a slice of French bread in two with his teeth and vigorously dunked the bread into a bowl of creamed mushrooom and spinach soup.

On bringing a heaping spoonful of the thick broth to his lips, half the contents of the spoon fell on and into his beard.

He picked up the other half of the bread, wiped his beard clean with it, and popped it into his mouth.

Without missing a beat (or a creamy splotch from his brown beard), Mr Retzler tried to explain in a trendy South Baltimore restaurant what he and his associates had difficulty explaining on Mt. Royal Avenue.

Why?

"We don't consider any of the things we do art, although they all work from an art motif. We don't know what to do with a word like art," said Mr. Retzler who also said that going two days in a row without food is not unusual for him.

All the things BOMB does can be boiled down to modes of self-expression that cost little to perform and nothing to observe.

Always there is motivation. Seldom is there organization. Purpose is optional.

Next to the Three Mile Island Show two of BOMB's more notable projects are TESTES-3 and VD RADIO, two telephone-related schemes designed to get the entire Baltimore metropolitan area to express itself.

"We couldn't afford a radio station so we decided to use the telephone," said Mr. Retzler.

By dialing TESTES-3, merely an answering service, people could listen to messages from everyone who had called the number the day before and leave their own message to be broadcast the following day.

For five months, TESTES-3 got calls from lonely senior citizens, winos, intrigued sociologists, partying high school students and bored housewives. At its peak, TESTES-3 was receiving 150 calls a day.

The number was replaced almost two months ago by VD RADIO, a more demanding version of the same idea. To listen, all one has to do is dial VD RADIO. But to participate, listeners have to create their own tape and mail it in for broadcast.

Nowhere near as successful as the instant gratification of TESTES-3, VD RADIO receives about two tapes every three weeks. All kinds of recorded creations are encouraged and accepted.

Although the two telephone projects are considered BOMB's most ambitious undertakings, neither one is Doug Retzler's personal favorite. The performance he's most fond of took place the first week of July during a New Theatre Festival parade.

"We persuaded this whole troop of Cub Scouts to mutiny against their leader and lay down on the street," recalled Mr. Retzler warmly. "Then we made body tracings of the entire troop. It looked like one massive accident had taken place. The scouts had a lot of fun and the street wound up looking pretty neat."

Because BOMB doesn't consider what it does art, the members certainly don't consider themselves artists. Critics have accused the group of merely being a bunch of eccentrics (or bums) trying to outweird each other.

"That's not a valid criticism," responded Mr. Retzler with indifference. "If we weren't a group 'out-weirding' each other, as we've been dismissed as, we'd be individuals trying to 'out-weird' ourselves.

"We're trying to provide alternatives. People don't have to accept them. The fact that a person is totally different from you does not have to pose a threat to your own identity."

Michael Tolson ("the weirdest guy I've ever seen" remarked a local rock photographer) is one member of BOMB most observers believe would try to out-weird the Bromo Seltzer Tower if he could get it to pay attention.

Dressed in a clear plastic shower cap, Spider Man gloves, an inflated water wing around his mid-section, a plastic zip-up suit holder used by travelers with holes cut out for his arms, and blue dots that started at his left temple and worked their way down his chest, groin, and thighs, Mr. Tolson bluntly stated that everything he does should be taken as a joke.

"I deluded myself into thinking I was an artist for about a year," said Mr. Tolson, who changes his identity for each performance (he was known as MT at Three Mile Island and Tentatively A. Convenience during TESTES-3).

"But I discovered there was nothing worthwhile in art so I made the transition to mad scientist."

A man who was dedicated to graduating from Woodlawn Senior High School with a 1.00 average ("I wasn't slick enough and wound up with a 1.18"), Mr. Tolson said he's only worked two days out of the last month and if he wasn't dependent upon eating, wouldn't work at all.

He doesn't even want to be paid for expressing himself.

"The system that makes stars out of those who express themselves for a living perpetuates the delusion that only certain people are talented," said the 25-year-old.

Highlighted against BOMB and their various performances, it is a delusion most people people safe in believing.

August 14, 1979

Mr. Mack recalls the life he threw away

AMID THE BICYCLES, BIKINIS AND ADOLESCENT BOPPERS THAT CROWD THE walkways of Coastal highway, you may have seen an old man cutting a brisk pace between 37th Street and the U.S. 50 bridge.

The sun has wrinkled his skin into deep lines of tanned parchment, and a black lunch pail tied shut with clothesline sways in his hand. His pants, which carry a timepiece tied with string to a tattered belt loop, are worn and baggy, and he walks the 8 miles to and from his dockside home in West Ocean City in heavy work shoes and no socks.

Just after dawn, the black pail holds the old man's lunch — four raw eggs and a single fig newton. He carries it home empty in the afternoon.

At age 81, Watterson (Mack) Miller is the most fabled character among the cavalcade of eccentrics who found their way onto this boomerang-shaped sandbar and never made it off.

"I came here in the spring of 1942 and was going to leave right after Labor Day," he explained. "My Labor Day never came."

A one-time newspaper heir born into a prominent Kentucky family, Mr. Miller was a world traveler in his youth, a Dartmouth-educated rake who fancied himself "a famous drinker" until the demon spirits left him broke and miserable.

"I saw quite a lot of Europe from the bottom of alcohol glasses," he said. "Finally the men in the white coats were whooping off in the near distance. A girl I was with told me, 'Mack, you're the most unhappy S.O.B. I've ever seen. I don't see how you could be more unhappy if you were sober.'"

Although he hasn't had a drink since that day in 1937, a life of squandered opportunities (dropping out of Dartmouth, drinking away his trust money and failing to follow up on a letter of introduction that would have landed him a reporter's job on the *New York Times*) has led him down the social ladder to the position of janitor at the Castle in the Sand motel here.

Few people outside of his employers know much about Mr. Miller's private past, but it has been at the motel that his public legend grew among a generation of vacationers in the last 20 years.

Every summer, thousands of tourists come back to the 37th Street motel asking if "Mr. Mack" is still around, curious to see if he still takes his famous swims.

In late June, Mr. Miller begins a daily ritual he started a year after he quit drinking. At lunch, he wades out into the surf before diving under a breaker, swims out straight for a half mile or so, until you lose sight of his bald head bobbing in the current, and turns north or south to swim a few hundred yards before free-styling his way back to shore.

"The guests ask me how I manage to go out the same distance every day," Mr. Miller said before his maiden swim of the summer this past Monday. "I say, 'Madam, I'm a garbage man. I go out just far enough to wash off half the garbage and come back.'"

For many years after he walked to Ocean City from Virginia Beach in 1942, broke, sober and looking for work, Mr. Miller swam the choppy waters of the inlet that separates the resort from Assateague Island, crossing from West Ocean City to the beaches here.

"There's a story around that I'd swim the inlet in the winter, come over here to get my groceries and then swim back with them in a waterproof bag," he said. "It's not true."

In the old fishing shack where he lives without running water, Mr. Miller prepares a typical dinner he says gives him strength and is easy on his stomach. Tonight's meal is a huge, lean hamburger, browned on the outside, raw on the inside, a half-box of frozen lima beans, applesauce topped with evaporated milk and plenty of cold water to wash it all down.

He putters around the two-room shanty furnished with a refrigerator, sink, stove, a makeshift bed and boxes upon boxes of newspapers, magazines and books on all topics.

He has lived here for the past 22 years, and for 20 years before that called an abandoned lunch wagon home near the same spot.

Sitting down, he places a piece of cardboard on his lap, puts the iron skillet with the undercooked hamburger on the cardboard, and begins illustrating his storied life and personal beliefs culled from reading, hard labor and living alone.

"My grandfather was Henry Watterson, editor and founder [in 1868] of the *Louisville Courier-Journal*," he began, breaking up the hamburger with a spoon and eating as he talked. "Before Prohibition, my father [William A. Miller] made and sold Old Charter whiskey."

His grandfather, who guided the *Courier-Journal* editorially for 50 years before selling out in 1918, wanted his namesake to enter the business while still a teenager. The day young Mack was supposed to show up for work, he decided to go swimming instead.

"That night I heard my grandfather tell my mother, 'Milbrey, that boy is incorrigible.' And they sent me off to boarding school in Massachusetts."

There, he continued drinking, escalating the habit at Dartmouth before dropping out in January, 1924.

Thirteen years later, Mr. Miller said, he was able to quit and remain sober through prayer and faith in God. He says he has tried to help a handful of waterfront drunks near his home quit drinking by using his own life as an example, but after a few months or years of sobriety, they fell off the wagon.

Many of them, he said, ended up killing themselves.

Over the past 40 years, after much reading and thinking about the subject, he has come to believe in reincarnation of the soul, and views all earthly sickness and woe as punishment from a just God.

"How do you account for babies suffering so horribly when they're too young to sin?" he questions. "If there's a just God, they must have sinned in another life.

"I must have been one mean S.O.B. in my past life to have had it as hard as I have," he said, recalling the backbreaking waterfront labor he did on oyster boats and the fishing docks after an early life of intoxicated ease.

"I wouldn't want to do any of it over. Anybody who says they want to be a child again is either a damn fool or doesn't have much imagination.

"I'm kind of ashamed of my life, but the one thing pleasant about old age is you get a lot of smiles from young girls. They look at you as a grandpappy type. I didn't get a fourth of the smiles from pretty girls when I was young as I do today.

"When you get to be my age, that's about all you want, a little smile."

June 29, 1984

Ministry from a westside basement

A RADIO IN THE BASEMENT WINDOW SENDS GOSPEL MUSIC INTO THE 1900 BLOCK of West North Avenue, a hard stretch of Baltimore known for drugs and violence and not so much for the quiet good work of residents like Keith E. Bailey. The gospel choir sings from a radio in Mr. Bailey's basement florist shop. On a table in front of him is a table crowded with ten homemade cakes. Behind him are two dozen pork-on-whole-wheat sandwiches alongside a vase of fresh roses in a refrigerated case.

Every Saturday, from noon until dusk, Mr. Bailey gives away food to anyone who asks for it as he makes up bouquets of carnations, lilies and mums.

It's his own little ministry, a little bit of God in the pink basement of a westside rowhouse flower shop.

"I come from a family of six children, and my mother was the kind of person that didn't have nothing when we were growing up in the Lafayette projects," said Mr. Bailey, a 36-year-old Polytechnic Institute graduate. "People gave to us, and I never forgot that."

To give back what was given to him, he feeds people on Saturday afternoons: The hungry, the drunks, the homeless, the addicts, the poor, friends, strangers — even people who have food at home but take advantage of a good thing.

"Some people don't need it, but I don't turn them away," he said. "If they want to take something they don't need, that's between them and God."

It's all worth it, he said, if he can get someone's ear for a moment before they run out the door with a slice of cake, a chopped pork sandwich or a cup of bean soup.

"Most of the time these people need somebody to talk to," he said. "They can come in here and say, 'Keith, I've been put out on the street.' Sometimes, if you just tell them to go back and apologize to whoever put them out it gives them the lift they need."

Carrollton Lee, a mother of three who says she doesn't work because of high blood pressure, is a regular beneficiary of Mr. Bailey's kindness. She was one of about 20 people who stopped by yesterday for free food.

"I'm just a little ghetto girl ... I was a bag lady once, but then I went on social service," said Ms. Lee, who said her only income is a monthly $205 government welfare check. "Mr. Keith put a sign in the window one day that said 'Soup Kitchen,' and the word got out and everybody started coming around. He helps anyone with anything. He even gave me a free yellow ribbon for the troops."

Mr. Bailey, who lives atop his florist shop and counts on a small group of friends to help supply the food, has allowed homeless people to sleep on a sofa in the basement and sometimes gives away clothes.

His goal, he said, is to open a counseling center in the neighborhood to help people get off the hook of drugs, street corners, greed and alcohol.

Beverly Edgerton, who lives next door to Mr. Bailey's store, supports her friend.

"He helps everyone who walks up and down the street here, the junkies, the alcoholics, whoever. They all know Keith and ask him for something," she said.

"Keith really tries to make things better, but most of the lives don't change," Ms. Edgerton said. "They just run in to grab something to eat and go on about their business."

March 10, 1991

A boyhood on the block

FAMOUS TV SIBLINGS CHIP AND ERNIE DOUGLAS OF "MY THREE SONS" ARE THE real-life sons of a Baltimore Block stripper who performed during the Great Depression under the name Marilyn Primrose. This and other obscure and marvelous facts of Baltimore burlesque fill pages in the personal history of 81-year-old Bernard Livingston, lawyer, author, United Press International photographer, filmmaker, and favorite uncle of Stanley "Chip" Livingston and Barry "Ernie" Livingston.

"You got it," said Mr. Livingston, in Baltimore this past weekend to screen one of his documentaries in a film festival at the Orpheum Cinema on Thames Street. "Chip and Ernie's mother was a strip-teaser, and I'm their uncle."

And like two of his brothers, Mr. Livingston married a stripper from his old man's burlesque, the Clover Theater on East Baltimore Street known to clients from around the world as the Scratch House.

"Russell Baker told me he saw his first naked woman in the Clover Theater," said Mr. Livingston, remembering a conversation with the Baltimore-raised columnist for the *New York Times*. "I guess plenty of guys who grew up here could say the same thing."

The Clover Theater building, now home to the Club Miami, still stands at 412 E. Baltimore St. Nearby, a pawnshop continues to cast the Livingston name along what is left of the fabled Block.

But the family is scattered, and any connection to the decades when the Livingstons rubbed shoulders with the riff and the raff exists mostly in the memories of Bernard, author of *Papa's Burlesque House*.

His earliest recollections of Baltimore go back to the 1920s when he led his blind maternal grandfather, Philip Mogulevski, to an Orthodox synagogue.

"I'd walk him every Saturday morning to a synagogue at McElderry and Eden streets," Mr. Livingston said. "He didn't speak much English, and I didn't speak Yiddish but he taught me two words on our little walks: *arif*, which meant step up, and *aruf*, to step down.

"One Saturday morning I said 'arif' when I should have said 'aruf,' and he stumbled and fell. He got up and belted me. He was furious, shouting: 'What kind of Jew are you? Your father runs a theater with naked women and dirty jokes, and he doesn't teach his children Yiddish.' "

Mr. Livingston's father, who spent six months at the Maryland House of Correction in Jessup for sending strippers to private parties around the state, didn't always run a strip joint.

He was an out-of-work accountant during the early Roaring '20s while his Uncle Isaac was doing a good business as a Baltimore Street pawnbroker. Isaac held the mortgage on the Clover Theater and was looking for someone to run the business after a previous owner failed.

"My Uncle Ike told my father there was nothing to it, all you do is sit in the booth and sell tickets," said Mr. Livingston. "My father planned to stay six months and he stayed almost 30 years. He hated it but made good money, the place was always packed. My mother came from a 'respectable' Jewish family and didn't like the idea at all. But she always said: 'Children, don't say bad things about the place that feeds you.' "

The place that fed them changed the Livingston family forever.

"My older brothers were pretty much grown when my father got the business and they married neighborhood Jewish girls from Park Heights," said Mr. Livingston of his brothers Harry, a salesman, and the late Dr. Sam Livingston, a well-known Hopkins doctor specializing in epilepsy. "But the three boys who were youngsters when Dad got the burlesque all married strippers. I guess you could say we were 'exposed' to these girls," he said.

The stripper he fell in love with was named Nina Slovik, a nice Polish girl from Eastern Avenue, to whom he was married for about eight years.

"These were wonderful women ... ," he said. "Many of them were poor girls from the hills of Kentucky and Tennessee who took the first job they could get and sent money home to their families."

When Benjamin Livingston first took over the business, he forbade his family even to visit him on Baltimore Street.

"But he dropped that, and we were down there all the time," said Mr. Livingston. "If we wanted to see our father, we had to go down to the Clover."

Soon, he said, the entire family was all but living in the ticket booth to the burlesque theater.

The family spent so much time there, Mr. Livingston said, that his mother hung a mezuza — lines of Scripture directed by Jewish law to be displayed in all homes — on the wall.

"It was essentially our home," he said. "My mother would bring a kosher Sabbath dinner to my father on Friday night while he was selling tickets to the burlesque show — roast chicken and potatoes, sour pickles, barley soup."

After a while, he said, even his mother and sisters began to work the ticket booth.

"Mom even devised a method for fooling the police. She had a button under her feet that buzzed backstage, and the girls would start putting their clothes back on until the cops left."

The Livingston family owned the theater from about 1922 until 1948, four years after Benjamin Livingston died. In 1948, his widow, Bertha, and most of the children moved to California, where Bernard's brother Hilliard and his wife had their sons Chip and Ernie.

By then, Mr. Livingston was already established in New York, where he worked as a news photographer before making documentary films about thoroughbreds and writing books on his childhood, America's horsy set, and zoos around the world.

"I had a childhood experience that most young men didn't have. I was a bag man for my father's bookie operation, and I saw nude women day after day from the time I was 12 years old and I was the envy of all the boys at Forest Park High School," said Mr. Livingston. "But I was also estranged from my peers. I came from a family of criminals, and there was a stigma to the Block. To compensate for coming out of this raunchy porno background, I turned to intellectual pursuits. I began to read Keats and Shelley and hang out at the Pratt Library downtown."

"Eventually," he said, "I made it from the infamous Scratch House on the Block to rubbing shoulders at cocktail parties with the Whitneys and the Vanderbilts … "

August 3, 1992

Baltimoreans I can't forget

IN THIS YEAR OF HONORING ALL THAT IS IMPORTANT TO OUR CENTURY, I WENT fishing for local legends in the Baker-Whitely tugboat company file cabinet beneath the stained-glass windows of my Greek Town rowhouse.

I offer good-hearted goofs, thin-skinned merchants, passionate collectors, unsung angels and pains-in-the-neck; a Pikesville Rye barrel's worth of flawed and beautiful eccentrics who didn't waste a breath aiming for fame. Soft touches like corned-beef king Seymour Attman and a sleight-of-hand sorcerer called the Great Dantini.

Bernard Livingston — the real-life uncle of Chip and Ernie Douglas of "My Three Sons" TV fame — who grew up backstage at the Clover Theater strip joint on The Block and wrote a book about it called *Papa's Burlesque House.*

Lou and Judy Boulmetis, the mom-and-pop pixies who run one of the last haberdasheries in town — Hippodrome Hatters — and have resigned themselves to finding new happiness if the Westside renewal plan devours their block of Eutaw Street.

Evelyn Butterhoff, who played the piano at Rickters in Hamilton, cleaned houses for a living and declared from the stool behind her rollicking upright: "I got a story that never ends."

Good people.

People like "Miss Mary" Portera, the rabbit cacciatore-cooking "mother superior" of the St. Jude Shrine on Paca Street.

If you ran the numbers on Mrs. Portera's salary over the past half-century as chief cook and bottle washer at St. John the Baptist Roman Catholic Church, where the Shrine is housed, you'd tally up a Third World paycheck.

"I cooked so much the priests used to call it St. Jude's kitchen," she laughs. "All my life I did everything but hear confessions and say Mass and loved every moment of it."

The accents and hairdos and what's hidden in their shopping bags may be different, but there are spiritual siblings of Mrs. Portera in every neighborhood of the city.

She explains: "You've got to give so much charity in this world."

The gifts of Mrs. Portera will be honored at the shrine at 10: 30 a.m. Sunday, with a party celebrating her 85th birthday.

What she shares with pilgrims seeking hope from St. Jude is matched by sharp memories of a vanished city: The Italian enclave that surrounded Lexington Market, 25-cents-an-hour piano lessons from "Miss Maggie" Winters at 314 S. Poppleton St., and the Joseph S. Hoffman tailor shop at 12 S. Hanover St., where Mrs. Portera worked as a seamstress.

The former Mary Cannatella was born at 638 Dover St. near Camden Yards. Her father, who drove a mortician's flower wagon, ran a movie house and sold fruit, grew up at 222 S. Eutaw St. and played street ball with Babe Ruth.

Her grandfather ran a produce market from the front parlor of a rowhouse at 402 S. Paca St., which was torn down for a highway. The big house the family lived in at 11 N. Pearl St. was razed by the University of Maryland. The site of another home, 505 W. Mulberry St., is now a parking lot.

What Mrs. Portera lived, John Schulian tasted in the 1970s as a reporter for the Evening Sun.

So strong is Mr. Schulian's nostalgia for Crab Town that two decades of screen-writing success in Hollywood — where he created Xena, Warrior Princess — have not dimmed it. Asked to name his favorite Baltimore people, he began rattling like a windup Easter chick from Herb Rosenberg's Light Street bargain store.

"Absolutely Abe Sherman," he said, enthroning the crotchety Park Avenue newsstand owner at the head of the class. "Ellis of South Broadway who would sell you a comb for 15 cents and tell you never to come back. Dantini doing magic at the Peabody Book Store and Beer Stube. Is that place still around?"

Getting his answer, Mr. Schulian despairs: "Why do I even ask?"

After a respectful pause, he rolls on: "Polock Johnny, who was really Bohemian. Mr. Diz trying to make a living at the track by selling balloons and parking cars. Eli Hanover in the gym he ran above a bar on The Block and, of course, [burlesque queen] Blaze Starr."

In his native Los Angeles, Mr. Schulian encounters all manner of freaks, but never characters who remind him of Baltimore.

"It all comes down to soul, which is absent from most of American life. It would be more fun to have Abe Sherman bitch at you than it would be to do whatever Bill Gates does for fun," he says. "Everyone I wrote about in Baltimore enjoyed life in the weird little worlds they created for themselves."

Weird little worlds inside the weird little city that struggles forward along the banks of the Patapsco.

As "Miss Bonnie" Hunt filled her bar at Fleet and Port streets with the smile of Elvis Presley, "Aunt Mary" Dobkin, who ran Little League teams, taught poor kids how to bunt and chided Earl Weaver that the big boys didn't do enough of it.

Belnord Avenue's Virginia S. Baker, the city recreation department's Queen of Fun who preached: "If it ain't decent and it ain't right, stay the hell away from it."

George Figgs, the impresario of the Orpheum Cinema who commands more minutiae about unheralded Baltimore than the Maryland Room at the Enoch Pratt Free Library. Rudolph Handel, the earnest picket who logged thousands of hours outside of *The Baltimore Sun*'s Calvert Street building with a two-edged sword that said: "Sun Lies/Sun Errs."

Christopher Jensen, a plumber who often fixes pipes in exchange for artwork, lives in a house at Howard and 28th streets, which his great-grandmother bought not long after the turn of the last century, and risks his life asking motorists not to throw trash on the streets of the city he loves.

Singing Sam the Watermelon Man who bellowed "red to the rind," throughout the city's 10th Ward during the 1940s and 1950s; Paul "Hots" Watkins, an A-rabber barn boss in the days before H&S bakery razed the Aliceanna Street stables; Louis "The Hawk" Hawkins, a barroom tap dancer who performed in gin mills from Dundalk to Pennsylvania Avenue.

John Steadman, now a *Sun* columnist, who brought horses of a different color — like the Fallsway fisherman Balls Maggio and screen painter Johnny Eck — to the larger world through his columns in the old *News American*.

Civic leader and consummate gentleman Walter Sondheim — one of the few people successful, genuine and kind enough to make anyone's list — nominates Marie Oehl von Hattersheim Bauernschmidt, a Roaring '20s crusader for school reform.

"Because of Mrs. B," says Mr. Sondheim, "politicians stopped selling school principalships for $150 apiece out of the lobby of the Rennert Hotel."

Cops like Charlie Smoot who taught generations of rookies how to be "good police," and friendly Phil Farace, chief of the old chicken-wire lockup at Memorial Stadium.

Allan and Susan Tibbels, who traded suburban comfort to bring hope, ingenuity, elbow grease and a "New Song" to Sandtown-Winchester; Viva House's Brendan Walsh and Willa Bickham who have given away more meals to the poor than Tio Pepe has sold to the rich.

Veronica "Miss Fronie" Lukowski of Thames Street who in the early 1990s was still doing her wash on a scrub board long after her grandchildren had bought her a washer and dryer.

Stan Schneider, who sells custom-cut foam out of a carnival house of bric-a-brac on Conkling Street, has lectured scores of youth about the spread of AIDS since the death of his son Jay.

Ella Thompson, who after the 1988 murder of her daughter Andrea devoted her life to the children of West Baltimore through recreation and gardening projects. "Coach" Herman Johnson, who for 30 years has done the same at the Bentalou Recreational Center. Talent agent Irv Klein who brought Tiny Tim to town in 1968 and his wood-scavenging, cabinet-making son, David "Blue Skies" Klein.

William D. McElroy, a Johns Hopkins biologist who paid schoolchildren a quarter for every hundred fireflies they collected for his research. And the 14-year-old boy who turned over more than 37,000 lightning bugs to Mr. McElroy in the summer of 1952.

Sowebo's dynamic, hydroponic duo of Richard Ellsberry and Gary Letteron.

"I started planting trees because it needed to be done and it felt good," says Mr. Letteron. "And then people patted me on the back for it and that felt good, too."

It feels good to do the right thing without expecting anything in return and although the old tugboat file cabinet is fat with notes on folks who have worked toward that ideal, this list falls far short of celebrating all of them.

It is redeemed, however, with the inclusion of Amrom Taub, the peacemaking rabbi of Park Heights Avenue who shuns recognition out of modesty while helping thousands of people rediscover joy in their lives.

All in Baltimore, where thanks to Abel Wolman, a pioneer in water purification, something extraordinary in our taps nurtures an endless parade of characters, with a new generation of apprentices always bringing up the rear.

July 1, 1999

And then he got the idea ...

Over long years of studying the once-abundant species of "Characterus Baltimorensis," in its native habitat along the Patapsco, I have discovered sewing machine repairmen who thought they were Franz Liszt; charity clowns who spent all contributions on blackberry brandy; and collectors of antique fire sprinklers.

Now, as sure as marinas have replaced manufacturing, I am confident that Baltimore will never produce another character like Chester Rakowski. There may be a few like him swearing in nursing homes, but there ain't none squawking in nurseries.

Times have changed. People have changed. And Chester — who created and destroyed more enterprises with a seventh-grade education than most people do with an MBA — is dead.

On Jan. 25, while shoveling the first snow of the new millennium, Chester fell like a cold bag of hammers in front of his South Baltimore rowhouse, his heart shot through with 72 years of schemes, greed, ingenuity and sea salt.

"I've been in more gin mills than I've seen lighthouses," he said a dozen years ago. "And I've seen many a lighthouse."

This is a man who built a 26-foot cabin cruiser — one section at a time — in the parlor of his East Gittings Street rowhouse but kept the ceilings from caving in by propping them up with 2-by-4s.

Who could butcher a pig and turn it into souse — whose sour beef and dumplings were the rival of any German from Sacred Heart of Jesus — but subsisted on bologna sandwiches, cheap beer and cigarettes.

Who treated underprivileged kids to Halloween pumpkin rides on his beloved work boat, the Gertrude, but was hard-pressed to name all of his grandchildren.

Who used the Gertrude to spread the ashes of barroom comrades across Inner Harbor swells but was not afforded the same courtesy when it was his turn to depart this mortal port of call. Looking around the wrecked and ransacked house on Gittings Street where he and his four brothers grew up sleeping in the unheated attic, Gary Rakowski said: "We don't understand it, but this is how Dad lived."

I didn't discover Mr. Chester, he came as a birthright. One of my earliest memories is watching him paint the metal garage behind my family's house on Daisy Avenue in Lansdowne in 1961.

A good bunky of my father's on the old Baker-Whitely tugboats that tied up at the Recreation Pier on Thames Street, Chester was an around-the-world seaman who survived Japanese torpedoes in World War II and sailed the Baltimore harbor as cook and deckhand on the tug Progress.

My old man begins most stories about Chester the same way.

"And then he got the idea — "

When such visions took hold — like ferrying divers to the North Atlantic to scavenge treasure from the Titanic — Chester would quit or be asked to leave secure jobs. Upon completion of more realistic work, building a deck or finishing a club basement, he'd sometimes take payment in a side of beef, a freezer or both.

The namesake son of a Castle Street crabber, Chester Michael Rakowski was an accomplished mason, carpenter, plumber, welder and roofer.

He built boats, piloted them, used them to drive piles and build piers and let the vessels sink when he had no more use for them. A photographer and amateur filmmaker specializing in images of modest boats and immodest women, Chester captured honky-tonk scandals and old-world delicacies brought to Mobtown by his Warsaw-born mother.

In the end, slowed by bad legs, ulcers and colds that clung to his nicotine habit, Chester was reduced to tending lines for a derelict hospital ship and repairing supermarket shopping carts at a small yard he kept on Towson Street in Locust Point.

When a can of his ashes was placed upon the grave of his brother Frank at Holy Rosary Cemetery, none of his countless drinking buddies, few friends or the priest hired to say the magic words showed up. Only four of his sons, a sister and the cold wind of January.

He left behind debts, regrets and an unmended friendship with my father that broke over words chosen unwisely in a South Baltimore saloon.

His house was a jumble of meat slicers, plastic cups, a few hundred dollars in pennies, marine fuel pumps, welding rods, barrels of rusted nails, primitive darkroom equipment and broken radios.

The house itself is now worth more gutted than it was when Chester built his wife a beautiful kitchen in penance for the many months their narrow nest was clogged with the ribs of a boat named in her honor.

He took with him a brilliant mind, a great hardy-har-har laugh and more untold stories than Studs Terkel could have preserved with 20,000 leagues of audiotape.

March 1, 2000

A man of letters and leather gloves

NO ONE WRITES LIKE THIS ANYMORE, NOT WITH A STRAIGHT FACE.

"I just got back from Tijuana ... went down with King Tut and a couple of broads in his car ... gee, boy — talk about me getting a thrill! All the booze you want ... gambling and each bar had a four-piece jazz band ... I guess you read about me stopping Eddie Mahoney with a punch in the second round. I might box Mushy Callahan or Jackie Fields in a few weeks."

Written in 1927, the letter was sent by one Baltimore-born Italian-American who changed his name to get ahead in the United States to another local Italian-American boy who changed his name to make it.

Posted from the Chelsea Hotel in Los Angeles to a Fawn Street rowhouse, it is one of a hundred or so handwritten letters surviving a correspondence spanning the Roaring Twenties, the Great Depression, World War II and a gone but golden age of boxing.

Though only one side of the correspondence has surfaced, the dispatches from hotels, taverns and gyms around the country detail a friendship struck at the Grand Theater on Conkling Street during the Coolidge administration.

It is the story of Vince and Paulie, a couple of Mobtown mugs with big ideas in their heads and olive oil in their veins.

Born in Palermo, Vince Lazzara grew up a fruit-vendor's son near the Belair Market to become Vince Dundee, a lean but savvy boxer who charmed crowds, won 40 amateur fights in a row and claimed a middleweight crown in 1933.

Nicola Mugavero, from the 900 block of Fawn St. in Little Italy, was nicknamed Paul and took the surname Baker in deference to his family's trade.

Vince's route to the ring — where he won 89 bouts, lost 20 and fought to 13 draws — was paved by his older brother Joe, who became the world welterweight champ in 1927.

While Vince traveled through Europe with his fists, Paulie rarely wandered beyond Irvington, where he bought a home with wages earned selling tickets at Penn Station and cashing tickets behind a mutuel window at Pimlico.

Vince's letters and anecdotes of his childhood friendship on the streets of

Baltimore have been preserved by Paul Baker's namesake son, whose only memory of his prizefighting godfather is sitting on the ex-champ's knee as a young boy.

Mr. Baker has read the letters as much for clues about his father as news about the rise and fall of Vince Dundee.

"I would say that my father idolized Vince, and my dad wasn't the type to idolize anybody," said Mr. Baker, a former college basketball coach. "My father was negative toward everyone, particularly toward strangers. He always used the word stranger."

Asked if he and his father were strangers upon the older man's death in 1995, Mr. Baker choked and said: "Somewhat."

Mr. Baker hoped the letters might bring him closer to his father, whose presence he still feels. But while the Penn Station ticket agent is mentioned in them often, he remains silent.

Only Vince speaks.

In 1932, as Dundee chased the middleweight crown in the teeth of the Depression, he wrote:

"It's tough when your money's not safe even in a bank ... all in all, I had $2,500 of blood money in there, all the cash I had. ... I've been pretty busy the last three weeks, boxing Bucky Lawless [and two others]. I won all very easy, well, I won't say easy because no bout is easy."

He captured the crown on Halloween Eve in 1930, beating Lou Brouillard in 15 rounds in Boston. In 1934, he lost the title but took a $25,000 purse in a brutal 15-round decision to Teddy Yarosz in Pittsburgh. A year later, after hurting his knee in training camp, Dundee was knocked down 11 times, had his jaw broken and suffered a concussion in a Seattle fight against Freddie Steele that was stopped after three rounds.

After this, Dundee began to have chronic pain in one of his eyes and was operated on to save his sight. By age 27, he was finished. He started to distance himself from the boxing world and began signing letters to Paulie as "Vince Lazzara."

In 1941, he wrote Paulie from his last home in Glendale, Calif., where he'd bought a tavern.

"It's an old, old story, but it hits the spot — when you're on top, everybody is right with you. When you're through being the champ and [out of] the limelight, they forget you damn quick. I can count on one hand the real, honest-to-goodness friends I do have in this world."

Buddy Ey taught several generations of rookie cops to box at the Baltimore police academy. Now 72, Mr. Ey saw Vince Dundee ringside at the old Coliseum on Monroe Street in 1942.

By then, Dundee — who'd fought all the great middleweights of his era — was suffering from years of hard knocks, injuries from a traffic accident with a freight train and amyotrophic lateral sclerosis.

"It was like a great man revisiting his glory," remembers Mr. Ey. "He'd been a master boxer but the poor guy was in a wheelchair and in real bad shape — terrible, pitiful."

Vince Dundee died in 1949 at the age of 40, his life chronicled in letters written to a childhood friend. In our era of abracadabra e-mail and cheap long distance phone calls — an age when it seems only writers write and everyone else goes about their business — the Dundee-Baker correspondence is a treasure.

A few years before his death, while reminding his "long-life friend" Paulie not to forget him, Vince wrote: "I don't correspond with anyone in my family anymore since my dear mother went to heaven. See, I don't have that feeling to write as I used to ..."

April 26, 2000

Flagging down a patriot
on a Greektown street

THERE IS ONLY ONE AMERICAN FLAG ON MY BLOCK.

Cut from the morning paper, it is taped to the parlor window of a Macon Street rowhouse in Greektown. By this morning — Flag Day — this modest Stars and Stripes may be joined by billowing patriotic pennants hung from second-floor windows. Maybe not. But since Memorial Day, the small paper flag on the west side of the 600 block of South Macon Street is the only evidence of Old Glory in a once-pristine neighborhood strewn with trash.

The flag belongs to 79-year-old Walter Simancek, a decorated veteran of World War II. Mr. Simancek has lived in the same house for 48 years. He is a widower who, like my namesake grandfather who was his neighbor, began sleeping on the living room couch after his wife, Eleanor, died; whose legs — which once carried him across North Africa and Italy to lay phone wires in the fight against fascism — are no longer strong enough to climb upstairs to hang a proper flag from the side of the house.

But there it is, taped with pride beneath eight medals — including the Legion of Merit — that Mr. Simancek earned while an infantry communications expert.

"It was my flag, and I fought for it," he said. "In those days, we had a different attitude. It meant a lot. It still does."

Mr. Simancek, a native of Scranton, Pa., was living in Highlandtown when the war broke. He tried to get into the Navy, but bad teeth kept him out. His choppers were good enough, however, for the Army, which drafted him as a 22-year-old cable worker for the Western Electric Co. on Broening Highway. Today, the 223rd anniversary of our flag's adoption by the Continental Congress, Mr. Simancek will finally have the rest of them pulled. He wishes he'd taken better care of his teeth and his medals, which are replacements issued by the government after the originals were lost "somewhere between here and Scranton."

This is the first year Mr. Simancek has displayed his Bronze Star and the others — "some of them I didn't think I deserved." And he's not sure why he put them in the window facing a street where other East Baltimoreans once celebrated the Blessed Mother and FDR, except that they seem more important as he grows older.

"At one time, I was the only person who had communication with advancing troops in Africa," said Mr. Simancek, who saw combat for 15 months. "I think that had a lot to do with me getting the Legion of Merit."

Do kids care about war stories anymore? When my father was growing up across the street from Mr. Simancek's house, World War II was the defining event of his childhood, even though that experience was limited to radio broadcasts and trading war cards with grade-school friends the way children exchange Pokemon cards today.

Macon Street, considered a low-class section of Greektown by some folks who live closer to St. Nicholas Greek Orthodox Church a few blocks east on Ponca Street, is busy with curious kids and delinquent adolescents; darlings who drop boxes of half-eaten french fries in front of their own homes and have broken nearly every branch off a pair of young dogwoods that struggle to grow in front of mine.

These kids have seen plenty of guns on television; some, I'm sure, in their kitchens. Perhaps they even dream — nighttime, rapid-eye-movement dreams — of firing weapons.

Would two modest rows of medals from the most important war in the Earth's history — simple decorations not much bigger than a quarter — attract their attention in a digital world?

Would Mr. Simancek's peers even care?

"A few people stopped and asked if they were mine. Just a few," said Mr. Simancek, who was never wounded. "But I'm no hero. I consider it a blessing that I got home with the decorations."

His brother, Edwin, was not as fortunate.

"We went off together. He was in a bomber squadron and his wife was going to have a baby," said Mr. Simancek. "You had to fly a certain number of missions before you could come home, so he started taking all the flights he could get. I guess he pushed it too far."

Edwin Simancek was shot down over France. His widow named their son Edwin Jr. The youngster's Uncle Walter came back from the war in 1945, was paraded around a Florida boot camp in a crisp uniform and medals for the benefit of new recruits, and settled down to a 40-year career at Western Electric. In Mr. Simancek's time at Western Electric, the preferred vehicle for carrying the human voice moved from wire to threads of light.

"I wasn't needed anymore," he said of his 1982 retirement.

Mr. Simancek sort of feels the same way today, sitting out on his front steps on hot summer nights alongside a paper flag.

"The people who move here now, it looks like they're finding freedom from something, but they have no regard for the neighborhood," he said. "We used to call it Rose Alley around here. Everybody had roses. Everybody had pride. Not anymore. You can tell where the old people live just by looking at the houses."

June 14, 2000

Crabs turn Manhattan into an isle of joy

HE STOPPED FOR ICE ABOUT AN HOUR AFTER THE BARS CLOSED FRIDAY NIGHT; A couple of bags from the Royal Farm Store at Ponca and O'Donnell streets just two red lights away from the ramp to I-95 north and Gotham.

The convenience store clerk, who'd seen and heard just about everything on the late shift, had never witnessed this: A middle-aged man asking for tongs in the middle of the night while a posse of Chesapeake Bay blue crabs scuttled along the sidewalk outside.

Nope. No tongs for Peter Walsh, artist, self-taught scholar and long-time Baltimorean with two bushels of live Chesapeake Bay blue crabs in the trunk of a rented Toyota.

A pair of white work gloves would have to do in Walsh's effort to keep the crabs alive — pulling off the New Jersey turnpike every so often to drain the Jimmys of melted ice and keep them cool with fresh cubes — until he could get them to the roof of a Wall Street office building, where he planned to steam and serve them.

"I wanted to exchange a classic Baltimore communal and democratic meal with others in the center of the global capitalist juggernaut," said the 38-year-old Walsh, who now splits his time between New York and Baltimore.

"I wanted to take something out of my own backyard, recognize how exotic it is, transplant it somewhere else and invite people who have never experienced it to eat and talk."

To drive home his point of preserving regional culture against the onslaught of homogenized consumerism, Walsh covered wooden tables with copies of the Wall Street Journal on which his guests could crack their crabs.

Walsh's Wall Street Crab Feast — a long Saturday afternoon of work masquerading as a performance called "Trafficking in the Vernacular" — took place in the stone and glass canyons of lower Manhattan's financial district.

The crab feast's locale, 16 Beaver Street, is home to an arts organization of the same name, a group of young people determined to find a middle ground between starving and selling out a few blocks from the New York Stock Exchange.

The exhibits at Saturday's open house orbited the notion of exchange, in the spirit of goods once traded around Manhattan's Bowling Green; commodities from which some of the oldest streets take their names: Gold, Pine, Stone and Beaver.

"We selected the neighborhood deliberately and built the organization around a corporate model," said Cincinnati native Colin Beatty, 28. "We wanted to be self-sustaining and we wanted accountability."

With colleague Rene Gabri, 27, Beatty secured 2,600 square feet of office space and use of the roof for $3,108 a month, divided it into eight small studios that rent for $500-to-$600 a month and went to work building a community.

The exchange project, curated by art historian Carrie Lambert, was the first major event for the fledgling Beaver group. Amid personal confessions broadcast via video cameras, the gold-leafing of a section of Wall Street and a kiddie pool in which tossed coins symbolized reinvestment in childhood dreams, Walsh steamed and served Maryland crabs, corn on the cob and homemade potato salad to some 40 people from around the world.

Along the way, he explained the process from bay to belly.

"These crabs were caught yesterday morning in the Chesapeake Bay near Gibson Island," said Walsh, holding an especially lively one aloft. "They cost $90 a bushel and I bought them out of the back of a truck parked on the side of the road in Baltimore."

Parked throughout the summer in front of Mercy High School on Northern Parkway, the truck belongs to middleman Eric Nehus. Walsh traded cash for the crabs to Ingrid Ankerson and Megan Sapnar, $12-an-hour "crab girls" who work for Nehus.

"You have power when you sell crabs," said Sapnar, 25. "You can give people a deal."

This weekend, a dozen crabs were going for $12-to-$19 a dozen, depending on size. If the girls like you, an extra heavy crab or two may find its way into your bag. If you are arrogant or nasty, you can get your crabs somewhere else.

Said Ankerson, also 25: "People always say they can get 'em cheaper down the road."

About 200 miles up the road in New York, Walsh culled three dozen corpses from the bushels, emptied a small bottle of apple cider vinegar into the bottom section of a steam pot and squirted brown mustard into it. But because the guests were drinking Rolling Rock and not National Boh, he passed on adding beer.

Though he held up a can of Old Bay seasoning to give an old favorite its due in the finicky approach to spicing crabs, Walsh actually used a combination of J.O. red, black pepper spice and dry mustard Nehus gives to customers.

To this Walsh added a touch of kosher salt, then invited people to begin putting live crabs in the pot. The crabs were combative and the guests were hesitant.

Abel Yee, a New York architect from Japan, went first, admiring the pincer reflexes of a creature that would rather eat than be eaten. People squealed. In a gallery busy with electronic gadgets, the crabs provided electricity. Painters knelt alongside the bushel to admire the color of their armor: violet and white and olive and the piercing blue along the claws.

After 20 minutes atop a propane flame, the shells turned a Halloween orange and Walsh began instructing folks on how to break through to the meat. They caught on quick, learning not to eat the lungs and to suck juice from the fins.

Where Walsh had hoped his project (in which he invested about $700) would spur talk of parochial pleasures lost in a changing world, there were oohs and aahs of gustatorial delight as delicate backfin slipped into mouths.

As the sun set over Manhattan, no one budged for hours. A video artist from Milan was happy to have another image of Baltimore besides beauty parlors. People talked of foods from their homelands — crabs stewed with vegetables in a yellowish broth in Belize was one — and remembered favorite dishes from childhood.

Michael Loveland, a Miami-born sculptor living in Brooklyn, N.Y., remembered hunting for blue crabs with his uncle on the gulf side of the Florida panhandle.

Theirs was a curious method: using flashlights to follow blue crabs through shallow water during tide changes, Loveland and family would chase the crabs into a chicken wire net and then dump them in floating buckets tied to their waists with rope.

"We'd boil them in a colander with a curry broth," said Loveland, remembering his Florida crab feasts while eating them Baltimore-style in the Big Apple.

"In a place like New York, where it's a major feat just to invite someone over for dinner, this is a huge success," he said.

In the end, fun won out over theory. As any good Baltimorean would tell Walsh: To hell with art, let's eat.

June 19, 2000

"I would buy buildings and keep them safe..."

CHAPTER 3

The Spell of a Place

Baltimore's polished statues

It appears that the Marquis de Lafayette is riding a bit higher in the saddle over in Mount Vernon Place. Baltimore's 72-year-old bronze statue of the legendary French general — a hero of the American Revolution and confidant of George Washington's — is the same size as always. But a soldier can't help but look better after the kind of spit and polish job he got the other day.

The horse the general rides determinedly on Charles Street and 13 other pieces of outdoor sculpture around Mount Vernon were cleaned, waxed and buffed to a deep, lustrous blackish green. Conservationists also worked on two statues at the Johns Hopkins University as part of the adopt-a-sculpture program, a project of the Mount Vernon-Belvedere Improvement Association.

"I lived in Mount Vernon Place for years and have a romantic attachment to the square. The sculptures sort of become like your children," said Bob Pringle, an art conservator now working out of Manhattan.

Pringle has been treating Baltimore sculpture for 15 years and, with a couple of helpers, cleaned all of the Mount Vernon bronzes and the Lanier and Hopkins statues in Homewood, in five days last week.

He likes the expressionistic quality of sculptor Andrew O'Connor's Lafayette, the way his face is almost a caricature of intensity, the way the tail on the general's horse flies in the air.

By comparison, he said, the John Eager Howard monument near Madison Street looks like a piece off a chessboard.

"After years of working on the pieces, you see characteristics and depth you didn't see the first time," he said. "The [Antoine-Louis] Barye lion always strikes me. It's simple and strong, but the expression on the face is incredible — one of the greatest pieces of animal sculpture I've ever seen."

Believed to be nearly lost to the elements in 1980, works such as Barye's depictions of war, peace, force and order near the Peabody Institute were found to be structurally sound but in need of cleaning and maintenance. In a city that can barely afford to keep its public libraries open, benefactors were sought to adopt the sculptures and pay for their care.

Thus, the Time Group ponied up half of the $10,000 it takes to maintain the Lafayette statue for five years. The rest comes from the city. Other benefactors include Maryland Art Place director Suzi Sinex, who put up $1,250 for Grace Turnbull's 1932 statue of a water nymph known as "Naiad," and Agora publishers, who adopted the Boy and Turtle fountain.

"In 1980, we found out that the pieces were not falling apart but needed ongoing care," said Kathleen G. Kotarba, director of the city's Commission for Historical and Architectural Preservation. "The method we chose was the hot wax treatment."

This traditional process, dating back to the Roman era and the same technique applied when bronze is cast at a foundry, involves washing the statue with conservation soap and a little detergent. If the surface is not absolutely clean, the wax seals the dirt.

The bronze is heated with a torch, which helps old wax sink in as new coats of synthetic and natural waxes are applied while the sculpture is still warm.

The torch is repeatedly passed over the bronze with the heat reduced each time, allowing the wax to cool. The next day, the newly waxed sculpture is buffed with brushes. Now protected by a shield of cold wax, the statues are good for another year. Without public and private benefactors, Baltimore could not afford the job's cost every year.

"We were advised not to start this if we couldn't keep it up," said Kotarba. "We've done all the outdoor bronzes that the city owns from the Pulaski Monument in Patterson Park to the Union Soldiers and Sailors monument in Wyman Park. The tough part is doing it annually. The Recreation and Parks budget is limited, and there are more pieces [about 45] than we're able to do."

Steven Tatti owns the conservation company that employs Pringle. In past years, Tatti has done some of the Mount Vernon work himself.

"Baltimore is very densely populated with sculpture, on a par with Philadelphia, Boston and New York," Tatti said. "Most of these monuments were executed from the turn of the century through the 1940s. People tended to ignore these pieces for the first 50 years. You can't do that anymore with our corrosive atmosphere. They look cared for now. They look solid."

June 25, 1996

Digging the raw edges of Mobtown

DERELICT BUILDINGS ARE UNBURIED CORPSES AND BALTIMORE IS LITTERED with the dead.

In a tune about aging American cities — in which the middle doesn't hold and momentum moves toward ghetto or gentrification — the songwriter John Gorka sings: "I just want to make enough to buy this town and keep it rough." I drive through my hometown and daydream about the resurrections I would perform upon the ruins of Mobtown if I had the money of a Peter Angelos, an Ed Hale or even my buddy Willie Mattricciani and his booming fence business.

I would build the Muddy Waters Memorial Library of American Music in the rubble on either side of Attman's Delicatessen on East Lombard Street.

I would save Memorial Stadium from the teeth of the maul — "Time Will Not Dim the Glory of Their Deeds" — and let old people play softball and grow vegetables in the outfield.

I would buy buildings and keep them safe until they told me what they wanted to be.

I swear to squander a fortune to do these things.

The things that the sculptor Marc Braun is struggling to achieve in a 19th-century funeral home carriage house at 1008-1010 Hollins St.

I first met Mr. Braun in 1989 when he and friends were reciting "Frankenstein" in a candlelit series of midnight readings at a West Baltimore Street loft.

Since then, Braun has traveled through South Africa and Morocco, the Middle East, Spain and a thousand cafes in between.

"I left the United States knowing I was going to Israel to live forever," says Mr. Braun, who earned his keep on a kibbutz by making a huge swinging gate leading to the fields. "When you leave Baltimore, you take a [compelling] illusion of the city with you. And even though you know its going to evaporate when you return, you come back anyway."

Braun came back to the defunct stables and warehouse of the old Joseph Cook Funeral Home, which, along with its black and gold sign that rattled in the wind, was razed not long ago near the corner of West Baltimore and Schroeder streets.

The Cook warehouse — where wood from coffin crates lines the ceiling along with bridles for horses that pulled hearses on carriage wheels — runs 150 feet deep by 28 wide with sloping, 9-to-16 foot ceilings on each of the two floors.

The oldest identifiable date is "1871" stamped into an elevator wheel cast by the Bates Co. on President Street.

"I can't stop digging the raw industry of Baltimore," says the 36-year-old Beltsville native. "The raw age that has settled over everything."

Mr. Braun purchased his raw slice of Hollins Street for the price of a new Cadillac Eldorado.

"This building will live again, and I will live richer because of it," says Braun. "When you revitalize something, you gain the life that it's had, plus the life you're giving it, plus the life that results from that combination."

Inside the Cook building, Mr. Braun envisions a stage for performances, a coffee house, a modern-day blacksmith's studio to bend remnants of the industrial age to his artistic will, and in time, room to live.

"I don't know how I'll do it," he says, an answer that hardens the hearts of loan officers when poets show up with unrevealed business plans. "I don't have any money and I don't expect anything from anyone. But when you commit to something good, someone good always comes along and says: 'I want to help.' "

Mr. Braun's neighbors in Sowebo are a combination of working class, poor and weird. They are good white people and bad white people. Black folks, good and bad. He is surrounded by the insane, pigeon breeders, butchers, puppeteers, and a gay guy who plays Cher records at high volume.

The area is trying to regain an artistic footing knocked loose by crime and the loss of the Cultured Pearl and Gypsy Cafe restaurants. Mr. Braun senses a recent decrease in brazen drug dealing and lauds city cops for caring.

"But the wrong element is always trying to insinuate itself," he says.

Before leaving, I kneel at a low table on the second floor — where Mr. Braun has made a room out of Libyan carpets, washtubs turned into flower pots, and a big plastic hose that pulses warm air into the freezing warehouse — to sift through sketches of nudes he has drawn over the years.

Doors from a thousand demolished buildings line the walls, and I can see the roof atop the B&O Railroad Museum roundhouse.

I select a sketch of a woman at rest before a vanity and tell him: "This is our Paris. This is our Jerusalem."

January 26, 2000

Dredging up the past

WHAT DO YOU THINK LIES ON THE MUCKY BOTTOM OF A 2.5 MILLION-GALLON POND in the middle of Patterson Park in Highlandtown?

Engagement rings hurled into the drink by disillusioned lovers? Handguns with hot fingerprints?

Or maybe a Stingray bicycle, the kind with a banana seat and butterfly handlebars?

"It's like cleaning out your freezer," said Charlie Gougeon, part of a city and state team that has been pumping the 136-year-old "boat lake" dry this week. "You know something's at the bottom, but we don't know what it is."

The man-made pond is being drained to allow for $1 million in park renovations to begin in the spring. Officials decided to get rid of the water while the weather is still mild enough to transfer the fish, frogs and snapping turtles that live in the pond.

While a state Department of Natural Resources truck stood by yesterday with an oxygenated tub to haul away whatever crappie, catfish, carp and bluegill have survived the park's annual "fishing rodeos," locals strolled by to watch the water drop by nearly imperceptible degrees.

Gougeon, a DNR fisheries manager assigned to Central Maryland, said whatever fish and other wildlife that are saved will be transferred to local waterways, such as Herring Run and a man-made lake in Lansdowne.

"You get a lot of 'Johnny Appleseed' fishermen stocking the pond," said Bob Wall, the city's recreation programmer for Patterson Park and a Highlandtown native. "They catch a fish, bring it home, show it to somebody and throw it in the boat lake."

Wall, who used raw dough from John's Quality Bakery on North Kenwood and Fairmount avenues for bait when he went fishing in the park as a kid, said his father tells tales of angling for bluegill in the pond during the Depression with a safety pin attached to a thread.

Yesterday, as the 3- to 6-feet-deep basin was drained for the first time since 1984, families of ducks took advantage of the shrinking water table to gorge themselves on insects and algae, a rusted 55-gallon drum appeared, and Randy Cashion used a crab net to scoop up a bulky Polaroid camera from the early 1970s.

"I know there's some reptiles in there, some turtles that people have let go, but I haven't seen any fish yet," said Cashion, a city public works employee who brought pumps from the Back River Waste Water Treatment Plant for the job. "Mostly it's just normal junk — soda bottles and plastic milk crates."

The typical junk of East Baltimore culture included an empty bag of Utz cheese curls, a deflated soccer ball, and three broken fishing rods. The unnatural included a pair of shoveler ducks, a species that is notoriously skittish in the wild.

"In East Baltimore [the pond] is an oasis for birds that aren't attracted to the city, especially for migration," said David H. Pardoe, chairman of the Maryland and Washington chapter of the Audubon Society. "You see shovelers at the Blackwater Refuge on the Eastern Shore, but they aren't normal around here. You never know what's surviving in an enclosed pond."

Or not surviving.

On the off chance that the pond would give up the dead — or clues to how someone ended up dead — the Southeastern District sent over a couple of police officers to monitor the draining. But they didn't have much to do but sip coffee and chat while the water gushed out of the pond, through a couple of big hoses and down a storm drain.

Middleton Evans, a local photographer known for his wildlife photos, has traveled from Alaska to Mexico in search of subjects for his coming book on North American waterfowl. But he found the perfect shot for the book's cover — a wood duck with its wings spread wide — near the spot where Luzerne Avenue heads down toward Eastern Avenue at the pond.

"Someone told me there were wood ducks here, and I didn't believe them," said Evans. "I've shot 600 rolls of film here this year of 15 different types of birds. Every day there's something different."

At 8 last night, with pockets of the pond still 4 feet deep with water, the pumps continued to slurp away at the mystery.

They will start running again about 7:30 this morning. Until then, curious East-siders will wait to see what's on the bottom of the pond where their grandparents did the court and spark in rowboats.

Waiting along with them will be the immature Black-crowned Night Heron, which roosted all day yesterday in the willow tree at the north end of the pond.

The lower the water gets, the easier it is to snag lunch.

October 20, 2000

Saving Highlandtown's Grand

BEYOND THOUGHT AND GREATER THAN REASON, I AM A PRESERVATIONIST.

When I see wrecking balls cracking the hides of buildings whose likes we will not see again — the old Horn & Horn on The Block torn down for a parking garage or the current crime at Redwood and Light streets — a spirit older than my 42 years cries out at the stupidity. The desire to save people and things, be it my grandmother's dented spaghetti pots from the Depression or the ice-eating homeless man named Bruce who lives behind *The Sun*'s building, is keen and often overwhelming.

Nostalgia, as any literate Greek flipping eggs in Baltimore can tell you, comes from *nostos*, a longing for home so strong it can lead to a severe and sometimes fatal form of melancholia.

The home I long for has sheltered all of us, and it was here, it seems, just the other day ...

I don't know how to fix stuff that breaks the way the dead and gone old-timers from the city's factory days once did: a broken handle riveted to a sauce pan or wire twisted between the legs of a wobbly chair to keep it tight and straight.

But I dream a lot; save nickels to buy any rowhouse within a fig's throw of my own and try to honor local customs and architecture slain by the greed that hides behind expedience and progress.

Which brings us to the Grand Theater off the corner of Eastern Avenue and Conkling Street in the heart of the Highlandtown shopping district. For years, I hoped that the long-vacant Grand, built in 1913 on the site of a German slaughterhouse, would become the Senator Theatre of the east side. Alas ...

Recently, the City Council passed legislation to acquire all but one property on the east side of the 500 block of S. Conkling St. To make way for a state-of-the-art regional branch of the Enoch Pratt Free Library, the grease-stained cottage that was the Little Tavern, the Phyllis Beauty Salon and a few other remnants are set to tumble with the Grand.

Naturally, the one building so ugly that it should be torn down, the suburban-styled Carrollton Bank at Conkling and Fleet streets, gets to stay.

After years of covering public protests to keep neighborhood branches of the Pratt open, I find it odd to be criticizing a move to add a jewel to the library's crown. Still, I must side with nearly 1,000 of my neighbors who have signed a petition of the Grand Theater Preservation League asking Pratt chief Carla Hayden to incorporate the building into the design of the new library.

While activists have commissioned a number of strong, creative blueprints from Gant Hart Brunnett Architects showing ways in which the entire theater could be used, they may find themselves lucky to save the Art Deco facade.

Having seen efforts fail to build the new library on the site of a rather run-down supermarket a few blocks away, the Pratt is making no promises.

"Keeping the facade would be the easiest thing to do," Ms. Hayden said last week. "We've always said that."

"The entire building is less likely," said John Sondheim, the library's manager of planning. "It's in dreadful shape on the inside and, as a neighborhood theater with a balcony, it's not very adaptable."

Salvatore Zannino, who grew up above his family's funeral home a few blocks away from the Grand and heads efforts to save the landmark, doesn't buy it.

Holding a sheaf of Gant Hart Brunnett documents the other day over coffee at DiPasquale's deli on Gough Street, Mr. Zannino showed how the theater's sloping floor could be used for wheelchair ramps. He envisioned the stage as the centerpiece of a children's auditorium and argued that the whole place could be preserved if somebody in charge made it his or her business to do so.

Ms. Hayden says she won't know what is possible until she gets inside the old vaudeville palace with her own architects.

Mr. Sondheim was skeptical of salvaging anything beyond the facade but welcomed all ideas at a community meeting to be scheduled in late February or early March.

The biggest thing the folks who want to see the building saved have going for them is that no date has been set for demolition.

If you never held hands with a date at the Grand or got treated to a screening of "Pinocchio" by an olive-skinned grandmother who shared the same heritage as Geppetto, you can glimpse the theater in "Cecil B. Demented," John Waters' last film, or stop in Louie's on North Charles Street to see a watercolor by Carol Offutt.

Ms. Offutt never saw a picture at the Grand, but the beautiful show that is the building itself stopped the artist one day as she drove along Eastern Avenue.

"It's very dramatic and romantic looking," she said. "And the colors are wonderful — pale green and ochre — especially in certain light. I was there late in the day with the sun setting on it and pigeons roosting in the marquee."

January 17, 2001

"Thomas Wolfe: died in Baltimore Sept. 15, 1938"

CHAPTER 4

The Writer's Life

Library salutes determined founder

SOME KIDS GET IN TROUBLE FOR FIBBING. SOME FOR PLAYING WITH THEIR FOOD.
Ted George used to get punished for reading too much.

"I wouldn't stop," says Mr. George, 78, a life-long resident of Towson. "When I was supposed to be in bed sleeping, my parents saw light coming from under my bedroom door, so I put a towel there. When the light came through the keyhole, I hung a shirt over the back of the door. After they caught on to that, I'd make a tent out of my covers and sit under it with a flashlight. Then they gave up."

But young Ted the bibliophile — the kid who learned to read before he went to school — never gave up on books. "I worked in my father's candy store and every little bit of money I made, I spent on books," he says.

Yesterday, his love of the printed word was feted at the Greek Orthodox Cathedral of the Annunciation in a 40th anniversary celebration of the church's Theodore J. George Library, a first-rate collection of about 11,400 volumes on all things Greek and Byzantine.

"Outside of my family, it's the only thing in my life," says Mr. George, a parishioner who was the 137th infant baptized in the congregation. A retired Baltimore County teacher, he still reads for an hour every night before bed because, "Reading unwinds me, no matter what I've been through."

The library that bears his name at 25 W. Preston St. began in 1954 when Mr. George happened upon books in distress and rushed to their rescue.

"They were tearing down part of the Cathedral to expand the Sunday school program, and it started to rain as I was walking by," he remembers. "I saw a pile of books the workers had put atop some rubble. I ran through the rain, threw them in the trunk of my car and took them home. These 13 books had to do with the history and dogma of the Orthodox faith. I thought to myself: 'Here's the beginning of a parish library.'"

That modest, soggy beginning was nurtured with a pair of typewriters still in use (one in Greek and one English) and $300 seed money. It has since flowered into one of the finest Greek and Byzantine libraries in the United States, open to the state's estimated 35,000 Greek Orthodox believers and any sincere soul who knocks on the door. (The library requires a $25 security deposit from nonparishioners.)

"I lectured there once and tried to come up with the most obscure book on Byzantine history I could think of," says Gary Vikan, medieval curator at the Walters Art Gallery. "I went over to the shelf, and there it was. They have set a very high standard."

The jewel of American libraries on Byzantine culture is Dumbarton Oaks, an organ of Harvard University in Washington with about 120,000 volumes, according to Dr. Vikan. Second best is either Holy Cross Greek Orthodox Seminary in Brookline, Mass., or St. Vladimir's Russian Orthodox Seminary in New York. The Theodore J. George Library is often mentioned next.

"Watching Ted in that library is such a pleasure because of the pride he takes in the books — he knows where he got every one of them," says Dr. Vikan, who has enhanced the Walters library with copies of hard-to-find titles on the Annunciation's shelves. "I watch him and think: 'Geez, what a lucky guy to be able to do what he loves and do it so well.'"

On Saturday, as his wife Gloria and library volunteer Joanne Souris Dietz set up the church ballroom for the anniversary banquet, Mr. George took a visitor through his elegant room of books.

Amid original artwork and Hellenic statuary, he points out *Greek Heritage in Victorian Britain*; boxes of Sunday bulletins published by the cathedral since 1935; and *The Genocide of Satellite Croatia 1941-to-1945*, before picking up a heavy black volume with gold script on the cover.

It is obviously a holy tome.

"*Gone With the Wind* in Greek," he says, smiling.

With a staff of 14 fellow volunteers, Mr. George operates the library with an annual budget of about $15,000 provided by the cathedral.

Most of the patrons are students from local high schools and colleges. Some have asked Mr. George if Greeks still worship gods and goddesses.

"I ask them to take a little walk with me and I show them the title page of the New Testament," he says. "And I point to where it says 'translated from the original Greek.'"

Chrisoula Kakavas Carlesimo, who grew up waiting tables at her father's old Mount Vernon Restaurant on Charles Street, used the George Library to write a paper for her master's degree at Loyola College.

"I was doing research on second-generation Greek-Americans in Baltimore, told them what I needed and walked out with an armful of good books," says Ms. Carlesimo. "I learned that the earliest Greeks in Maryland arrived in 1670, that the largest influx occurred between 1890 and 1914, and the first Greeks in Baltimore were nine young men escaping a Turkish massacre in 1820."

Many of the books, which cost between $10 and $500, have been donated by parishioners in honor or memory of loved ones, and carry inscriptions about the gift. Paperbacks are sent out to be hard-bound. The most valuable volume was printed in Greek in 1570 and is about Demosthenes, the father of oratory.

The reference books and archives — including baptismal, marriage and death records of thousands of local Greek Americans and their ancestors — is growing so quickly that the congregation recently bought the old Preston Hotel next door to the library with plans to expand.

"I never expected to see anything like this," says Mr. George, who credits the Very Rev. Constantine Monios, dean of the cathedral, for helping to lift the library to its current status. "When Father Monios came here 17 years ago he told me: 'Ted, we're going to give you the kind of library you deserve.' "

April 11, 1994

The beat goes on

LOWELL, MASS. — I AM A GRAVE ROBBER.

Jack Kerouac died a drunken mama's boy 30 years ago today in St. Petersburg, Fla. I found his grave at Edson Cemetery after seeing highway signs for this old mill town in northeastern Massachusetts. The simple marker, flush to the ground and littered with liquor bottles, reads: "He honored life."

Jack did, as the tender stenographer for the ants-in-my-pants soul of America.

And he didn't, drinking himself to death by 47, denying his daughter and urinating on the gift that produced *On the Road*, *Vanity of Dululouz*, and *The Dharma Bums*.

Along with bottles, notes and letters are left on Kerouac's grave. They arrive regularly with visitors from around the world. In deference to the life he honored and in defiance of the one he destroyed, I took the notes and left the bottles.

A cat named Charles Brown wrote: "If only I could remember the things you said to me last night in my dreams."

Another dreamer asked: "Where have you been all my life?"

And Paul drove his family — wife Geri, children Julian and Zoey — from Detroit to say: "This is just a stop in my life, my family's life. I leave these words for your life. For your death, I leave a can of alcohol. It consumed you faster than words did."

More than 40 years after hitting American literature — about the same time that Elvis kamikazied pop music — *On the Road* is consumed by more readers than ever.

The book was lived by Kerouac between 1947 and 1950 — with a pass through Baltimore to practice driving in traffic! — written in New York City in April 1951, published by Viking in 1957 and will be in print forever.

Reading it is a common rite-of-passage not confined to the toll road that bridges adolescence and adulthood. Wherever you are in life, Kerouac's yearning for "all that road going ... all the people dreaming in the immensity of it ..." can take you to the next stop on the way.

Read it at the wrong time, and it might kill you.

Or set you free if the time is right.

"Nobody," Kerouac writes, "knows what's going to happen to anybody."

When I was 18 and sailing between Baltimore and Beaumont, Texas, on a merchant ship, I banged out primitive stories on the steward's typewriter and studied Dickens to learn structure.

Had I been reading *On the Road* that summer, I might have jumped ship in New Orleans and never found my way home.

A dozen years later, without knowing why, I started reading a beat-up paperback copy at stoplights as I drove my kids to school. I disliked my life enough to be seduced by Kerouac's descriptions of things that no longer existed in America.

At every crossroad, he claimed in verse worthy of Robert Johnson: "There were mysteries around here."

The year I read *On the Road*, my marriage collapsed. I went to live with my grandfather in Highlandtown and settled down for a self-imposed apprenticeship in fiction.

And, through a grace that eluded Kerouac in this world, gave up some things that he never did.

On the edge of downtown Lowell is a park honoring the town's most famous son. On upright slabs of polished granite, Kerouac's words reveal his true self: "I am actually not a beat, but a strange, solitary Catholic mystic."

And I am an unrepentant grave robber.

October 21, 1999

Terkel records winners, losers on stage of life

THE MAN WHO HAS SPENT HIS LIFE HELPING AMERICA REMEMBER BELIEVES THAT the country has succumbed to "national Alzheimer's" disease.

All information, little knowledge. And scant wisdom.

"We don't remember anything. There's no yesterday in this country, and I want to re-create those yesterdays," says Studs Terkel, the dean of oral historians whose adventures with a tape recorder have secured the life lessons of hobos, soldiers and losers for all time. "The free market is God now, but we forgot what happened in the 1930s — that people were crying for the government to save their asses and that the people who condemn government [regulation] always cry the loudest. You see, we forget."

To stem our forgetting, the 87-year-old Chicagoan, in Baltimore today for a pair of appearances, has interviewed thousands of people and written a dozen books. Among them is *The Good War*, a 1985 volume that won the Pulitzer Prize for its first-person accounts of World War II; *Hard Times*, about the Great Depression; *Working* and *Race*.

In these books shimmer the great and silent trick of journalism that Terkel has perfected: the interviewer who makes himself invisible.

We talk, Studs listens.

"Sometimes when I'm talking to the so-called ordinary people, those who are capable of extraordinary things, every once in a while there's a great moment," says Terkel. "Once, I interviewed a woman at a public housing project. I can't remember if she was white or black, but she was pretty and had bad teeth.

"She's talking and her little kids are jumping around — they want to hear Mama's voice. When I play it back, the woman puts her hand to her mouth and says: 'Oh, my God, I never knew I felt that way before.'"

That, says Terkel, is the jackpot.

Not gossip or titillation — which sicken him — but the simple things that move people through an accumulation of days called life.

Terkel's latest book is *The Spectator: Talk About Movies and Plays With Those Who Made Them* (New Press, 1999), 364 pages of memories from the stage and screen.

Culled from more than 9,000 hours of interviews he has donated to the Chicago Historical Society, *Spectator* covers everyone from Moms Mabley to Marcel Marceau.

"I got on my knees and prayed to God to open a way," says Mabley, the late comedian, in an interview from 1960. "And something said to me: 'Go on the stage.'"

And Terkel was waiting backstage with a reel-to-reel.

Reading Terkel is like thumbing through a set of World Book encyclopedias in which every volume is an index of interesting people.

In *Spectator*, you will find Buster Keaton, Eubie Blake, Yip "Over the Rainbow" Harburg, Zero Mostel and Tennessee Williams.

A typical chapter concerns the writer William Saroyan and Bill Veeck, legendary baseball executive and friend of the little man. In it, the author of *The Time of Your Life*, and the former owner of the St. Louis Browns, Cleveland Indians and Chicago White Sox both address the dignity of life's losers.

Said Saroyan: "[The play implies] that the only winner is the loser who knows that he's a loser. Who the hell else could possibly win unless he was self-deceived? We're all losers."

From *The Time of Your Life*, Veeck told Terkel, he got the idea to erect an exploding scoreboard at Chicago's old Comiskey Park, an electronic gadget that launched fireworks every time one of the Sox hit a home run, which, when Veeck owned the team, wasn't often.

Said Veeck: "We're losers in a country where winning means you're great, you're beautiful, you're moral. Saroyan was saying something. You keep trying and trying and you finally do hit a winner. You hope, you dream, suddenly the rockets go off, the bombs burst in air. The loser has his day."

"I interview the incomplete people," is how Terkel describes his work. "What's it like to be a certain person in a certain circumstance? I connect with Geraldine Page in Tennessee Williams' *Sweet Bird of Youth*, and discover her fear of growing old, a beautiful woman, long in the tooth. It's through the art that we know these people, and here I am — 87, with a new book out and another on the way.

"The difference in this book from all my others is that instead of celebrating the non-celebrated, I'm celebrating the celebrated," he says. "But I talked to Jimmy Cagney the same way I talked to the parking lot attendant. We're losing the passion of these people without even realizing it."

February 22, 2000

Where (book) lovers settle in between the covers

WHO DO YOU LOVE?

Ralph Ellison?

Kate "Please Wake Me" Chopin?

Or that dirty bird genius, Philip Roth?

There is a man running around Baltimore who wants to bring you closer to the storytellers who make your blood sing.

But Clifford Panken is so busy schlepping books from one end of the city to the other — out of people's basements and into his three used bookstores — that he doesn't have time to organize love-ins between readers and the stories they crave.

Still, he wants to.

"I wanted a meeting place for people interested in books; that's why I named the business Rendezvous Books," says Panken, a 40-year-old South Baltimore resident who quit a government job in Washington to sell books in Mobtown. "Maybe a 'Dorothy Parker Night,' where you bring in a local expert and charge people a couple bucks at the door. The next week we do somebody else and use the money to start a scholarship for young writers in Baltimore."

Panken, who holds a degree in economics, puts in seven days a week "buying books, doing paperwork and looking for cheap wood for shelves" and doesn't have time to read, much less play match-maker for literary-minded Baltimoreans.

He didn't even know that Bukowski was dead, only that his books sell.

But if you have the gumption to get a scene started — even if it's a night devoted to UFO books, which fly off the shelves — Panken would like you to introduce yourself.

Of his 4-year-old business, he says: "I'm working like a dog. Maybe somebody can help me."

The best rendering of a used bookshop, whether in life or in art, I found in a novel by Cynthia Ozick called *The Messiah of Stockholm*.

"The mullioned door [and] skimpy vestibule — the narrow back room, a sort of corridor behind a fence of books — wares in nearly any language [from] the newest Americans [to] the oldest Russians — the shop window crowded with all of the alphabets — that funny lamp, the shade a crystal daffodil — a teakettle."

Here, on the other side of a window with BOKHANDLARE lettered across it in gold, the proprietress serves vodka to privileged patrons in a back room, much the way Abe Sherman would take anointed customers downstairs for a sip of brandy at his long-vanished book store on Park Avenue.

The shop owner sips her tea and tells her customer: "You think you're the only one with a story?"

Be it Stockholm or Swampoodle, this is the place you search for all your life.

This is not what you encounter at Rendezvous Books off the corner of Calvert and Baltimore streets, some 1,800 square feet of an old bank lobby where Panken envisions a literary salon amid the 15,000 volumes.

The Calvert Street store sits behind scarred glass that has been repeatedly broken during break-ins and patched with plywood. The shelves are made of cheap, unvarnished pine. And though Danielle Steele sells better than Daniel Defoe, I found a cheap copy of *A Guide for the Perplexed* by Maimonides.

Most of the customers come from nearby office buildings on their lunch hour or dash in before catching the bus.

A 23-year-old guitar player named Steven Menzer manages the store for $6 an hour. If there is vodka behind the counter, he's yet to share it.

"It looks like we're on the verge of going out of business, but that's not so," says Menzer. "We just got in a great shipment of nearly new cookbooks, and just the other day a guy came in named Darryl Croxton who does a one-man Shakespeare show and he bought a lot of books."

Panken has a two-year lease at 6 N. Calvert St. with a five-year option. Though his per-square-foot rent is about the cost of a medium pepperoni pizza, the planned resurgence of downtown would likely price Rendezvous out of the market.

Declining neighborhoods, it seems, are fertile soil for used bookstores.

"It's a business with very tight margins," says Panken. "The aesthetics simply drift."

The most fun I ever had with used books, besides reading them or using a slim tome to bring a crooked sofa into plumb, was Halloween in 1995.

Waiting to go to a Fleshtones concert in Annapolis, I sat in my own skimpy vestibule and greeted trick-or-treaters with battered paperbacks from the John Mason Rudolph collection I had recently inherited.

Shelly's *Frankenstein*, Stoker's *Dracula*, Leroux's *Phantom of the Opera*, and whatever creepiness crawled between soft covers went right out the door, hitting the bottom of goody sacks with a thud.

Although the kids of Highlandtown were not amused — "A book?" they cried, "Mom, that man gave me A BOOK!" — the Rendezvous chain has enough paperbacks to fill 10,000 Easter baskets next month.

As the spring chicks say: "Cheap! Cheap!"

Wednesday, March 22, 2000

Somewhere in the city,
a diary waits to be found

THE OLD PIRATE STEVE BUNKER TOLD STORIES OF WATERFRONT DIRTBALLS WHO'D show up at his Thames Street salvage shop to sell their grandfather's engraved pocket watch. Outside the family, the timepieces weren't worth much and Bunker, angry that someone would unload an heirloom for a few bucks, would try to talk the customer out of it. He lobbied in vain.

Unloved diaries don't even make it as far as the pawn shop. I was thinking about the title of this column — City Diary — while hiding out at the Kelmscott book shop on 25th Street.

As a novitiate in the priestly cult of J.F. Powers, I tracked a copy of his 1962 novel, *Morte D'Urban*, and found this epigram: "The life of every man is a diary in which he means to write one story, and writes another ..."

Where are such diaries, the private thoughts of ordinary Baltimoreans who thought they were going to experience one narrative but lived another? Grandpop's pocket watch may be worth a couple of beers, but what about cousin Theresa's memories of her girlhood?

I bet most wind up in the trash.

"The other day I came across one of those blank, hardcover notebooks you buy at stationery stores. A pregnant woman had started using it in the 1970s when she was having her first baby," said Al Cunniff, a local book collector who fishes "from the stream of life that flows through yard sales" and wrote about pop music for the *News American* back when Mott the Hoople was making records.

"I couldn't not read this diary — only the first four pages were filled," said Cunniff. "The very next entry was from the 1990s. The woman had rediscovered her own book 20 years later and the mystery of what her child would grow up to be was solved. I guess she lost it again. It saddened me."

I sometimes find notes written from one kid to another in the alley behind my Macon Street rowhouse; magical, urgent scribbling: "Amber, meet me behind the tree at the end of the block after dinner."

Once, when a neighbor and I let ourselves into a nearby vacant house to set off scores of bug bombs, I found a purple, spiral notebook from a previous tenant filled with hope and worry for her young children and alcoholic husband. The entries trailed off as eviction neared but at least the memoir was saved from the pile of the diarist's furniture that wound up on the curb.

And this past January, while cataloging the contents of Chester Rakowski's narrow roost at 130 E. Gittings St. in South Baltimore, I found two diaries in the attic written in pencil by an adolescent girl during the Carter administration.

One was a hardbound "Kahlil Gibran Diary for 1976" and the other a red plastic "pocket minder," used by traveling salesmen to keep their schedules straight.

The girl's name was Karen and on Aug. 27, 1977 — the 12th anniversary of the day the Beatles met Elvis Presley in Hollywood, an event apparently unknown to her — she wrote: "Today is Margie's birthday. We had cake and ice cream. She got five dollars from her mother."

What are such things worth?

Not much, apparently. I tracked Karen down in White Marsh to say I had found her childhood musings and she exclaimed: "Really?" I remember those!" But never bothered to come and get them.

I keep Karen's diaries on a small shelf next to the purple notebook of the young Highlandtown mother who couldn't make ends meet; the World War II memoirs of a born storyteller named Analeis and love notes to Jack Kerouac I stole last summer from the writer's grave in Lowell, Mass. Sometimes I write my own thoughts in their margins.

The Maryland Historical Society on Monument Street has hundreds of homespun diaries in its stacks, stuff like J.T. Wilson's 19th century reports of cholera and fire engines but nothing close to Mok Hosfeld's "visual diaries" of his pilgrimage to the Yucatan.

"I don't even date the entries except for the beginning of a notebook and the end," says Hosfeld, a Charles Village poet who'd like to read the diary of a guy he knows who fills aquariums with combs he finds on the street.

In a half-dozen years of cleaning out attics, basements and garages for books to sell at his Rendezvous shops around town, Clifford Panken stumbles on personal diaries every six or seven months.

"I'm just too busy to sit down and read these things, and I don't feel inclined to interpret somebody's handwriting," said Mr. Panken. "I pop them in an envelope and mail it back."

Last Saturday, the good people of Wilhelm Park in southwest Baltimore buried a time capsule in front of the neighborhood church at Cowan and Wilmington Avenues; a big plastic pill not to be opened until 2100. All sorts of things went down in the hole, but not, it occurred to me while staring at the crowd, a single diary of a citizen of Wilhelm Park.

The next time you hire somebody to clean out the basement, be sure to check the books first. If a diary is rotting among the pulp, photocopy the pages before burying it next to the goldfish in the back yard.

Wednesday, May 10, 2000

What the literary life has come to in Charm City

HAS THERE EVER BEEN A TRUE WRITERS' CAFE IN BALTIMORE? THE KIND YOU dream about in visions of 20th-century Paris, 19th-century Vienna and 18th-century London? The late Peabody Bookshop and Beer Stube on Charles Street served Gerald Johnson and F. Scott Fitzgerald and probably Dos Passos and James M. Cain.

If city planners can route their strategic stupidities around Martick's Restaurant Francais — which made a good Bohemian run at art and literature in the 1950s and '60s — the old speakeasy will endure at the corner of Mulberry and Tyson for as long as its namesake proprietor can light the stove.

And the Port Street poetry readings at Miss Bonnie's Elvis Bar in the 1980s were as short-lived as the King himself.

Into this breach, I nominate a joint where anyone with a ballpoint and bald ambition can linger for hours over a 94-cent cup of coffee, where a plot that emerges in a 4 a.m. nightmare can be hammered like a tin ceiling as you savor the pleasures of ice cream on a stick.

A clean, well-lighted place dead center in the heart of the city's past and future: the Royal Farm Store at Key Highway and Lawrence Street in South Baltimore.

In the glow of neon that spells Domino Sugars across the Patapsco, you can choose your desk from eight plastic tables, each with a bright overhead lamp. If you run out of paper or your pen goes dry, there are more in a middle aisle. If you forget to bring cash, there's a bank machine.

The booths hug a floor-to-ceiling wall of glass through which to ponder the passing world; the skyline of East Baltimore on the far side of the harbor and GENERAL SHIP REPAIR painted on a corrugated steel building across the street to remind you that the Port of Crabtown wasn't always home to boats that never get dirty.

Nearly two dozen pots of coffee are warming at all times; hot dogs roll on those hot-dog roller grills; there are bathrooms to flush the coffee after your body has flushed the coffee; and Southern District cops are constantly popping in with dispatch radios broadcasting the best in local drama.

And for 50 cents you can choke down a handful of aspirin if the stimuli of the Hair-Do Capital of the World starts microwaving your brain like a breakfast biscuit.

"In a restaurant one is both observed and unobserved," says David Mamet in *Writing in Restaurants*, a 1986 book of essays.

"Couples play out scenes in restaurants," he writes. "The ritual dissolution of the *affaire* in a restaurant is strong and compelling now [that] the marriage ceremony has become an empty form."

I'm not so certain about affairs of the heart — somehow its seems more appropriate to be served your walking papers as the appetizer to a $25 plate of pasta — but the Farm Store is an amazing place to observe affairs of the stomach.

While scribbling an early draft of this essay on Key Highway, I watched a middle-aged woman with pink toenails and white sandals demolish a chili cheese dog in two bites.

It brought to mind one of John Waters' favorite bits of eavesdropped conversation, the one in which a true daughter of Bawlmer waves off a dessert tray by announcing: "I'm bloated!"

Escorting such women, invariably, are men in tank tops with too much tank and not enough top.

And while any spot with a table, a chair and something to drink can become the private cafe of any writer, the convenience store of the 21st century attracts real people living real lives.

Here you will not find booze (what good did alcohol ever do for an American writer?) or timid coffeehouse poets scribbling in cloth-bound journals bought at Barnes & Noble.

To cast your shadow across the fluorescent-lit tiles of the Key Highway Farm Store is to enter the court of the kings and queens of Locust Point who run in for lottery tickets and cigarettes while the roof-deck yuppies of Federal Hill pull up in jet-black Jettas to buy cat food.

Between the cash register and the curb, people from across the country pump gas beneath a long awning equipped with enough high-powered lights to illuminate the landing strip in "Close Encounters of the Third Kind."

In these quick observations alone — we haven't even touched the Farm Store's wide selection of pornography geared to every fetish of anatomy, ethnicity and age — are enough details to fuel a first novel.

But most importantly, the Royal Farm Store is a place, like the vanished New York cafeterias of Isaac Bashevis Singer's beloved Upper West Side, where you can sit without fear of being hustled away by a manager making room for the next Joe with a dollar.

John McIntyre, an editor at *The Sun* and the rare modern newspaperman interested in conversations such as this, believes that the privilege of lingering is paramount to a legitimate artists' cafe.

"Most restaurants," says Mr. McIntyre, "are not designed for lingering."

And yet one of the contradictions of our era seems to be that the garish places hustling fast food are the same establishments willing to suffer people who live at a slower pace.

There's no better place in Baltimore to sketch the people of our time and place than the Royal Farm Store on Key Highway. And if you want to show up one night to watch the parade while arguing whether Tim O'Brien is the greatest writer of his generation, I'll be in the booth next to the motor oil and the M&Ms.

Wednesday, July 19, 2000

Hiking to Pratt's Canton branch

WHEN MY FATHER AND HIS SIBLINGS WERE GROWING UP ON SOUTH MACON STREET between the Great Depression and World War II, the only reading material in the house was their father's Bible — written in Spanish, it was sanctuary for a stubborn man who renounced the Catholic church because of Franco — and the *Evening Sun.*

If they wanted to read anything else, the children of Rafael and Frances Alvarez walked 1 $1/_2$ miles from what is now Greektown to the corner of South Ellwood Avenue and O'Donnell Street to one of the four original neighborhood libraries established by Enoch Pratt in 1886.

Known as old No. 4, the Canton branch is the last of the original quartet still in use as a library. Miraculously, each of the identical buildings still stands, the others enduring on Hollins Street, Broadway and Light Street in South Baltimore. (Hollins Street, where young H.L. Mencken ate books for breakfast, houses a nonprofit community planning group; the Light Street branch is a private home. Does anyone know what happened to original Broadway library? Body and fender shop? Pentecostal church?)

After my grandfather, who would read the newspaper to my legally blind grandmother as she prepared supper (potatoes skinned, cubed and boiled with rivulets of El Toro olive oil and salt for seasoning to complement cold bean salads and all the fish in the sea), my Aunt Dolores was the reader in the Alvarez family.

It was Dolores who turned my seafaring father on to Hemingway, who initiated the adolescent hikes to Canton from the corner of Macon Street and Foster Avenue, across a field just south of Oldham Street known as the Three Ponds and over the railroad tracks.

"We would cut behind an old barn we called the spook house — it had tons of pigeons in it. The farmer used to breed canaries in his basement and he had cows on his property," now an asphalt lot for trucking companies, remembers Dolores, who left Highlandtown for Chicago in the early 1950s after marrying a Windy City Irishman. "We went the back way until we got to the breweries on Conkling Street. Then we'd hit O'Donnell Street and go all the way to the library."

She claims to have made the trek with her cousins, Ernest Adornato Jr. and his sister, Theresa, but neither of them seem to remember it like Dolores does.

Ernest — whose father helped my grandfather replace a front window that Dolores broke with a wooden-heeled slipper hurled at my father for pestering her while she was reading — has more vivid memories of throwing rocks at the farmer's cows and killing rats by the train tracks.

In the brick cottage of books that sits in the O'Donnell Street median, the world would slip away as Dolores sat in a chair, swinging her leg with the fidelity of a metronome, enchanted.

"I was proud as punch when they gave me that library card. I started with fairy tales and then the Bobbsey Twins and Nancy Drew before I moved up to the English writers," she says. "You could sit and have adventures all over the world without leaving your chair."

In 1940s Baltimore, a city divided into strictly defined ethnic villages, it was rare for a kid to wander too far from home and for all of Dolores' love of books, she only remembers being taken to the Pratt's magnificent headquarters on Cathedral Street once.

Who needed a streetcar to go downtown when you could sit with a book down the street from your house and go around the world?

Now 70 and widowed, Dolores begins her days the way her father used to, with the Bible. In a not-too-pushy way, she tries to evangelize me by reporting the "fascinating stories" to be found in the good book.

How to tell this no-nonsense believer, who inherited her Spanish father's hard head and her Italian mother's kindness, that the stories she tells about growing up in southeast Baltimore are Holy Land enough for me?

During readings of my short stories about Orlo, the waterfront A-rabber, and Leini, his Greek lover, I am often asked to unmask the models for the characters.

It's a question that writers hate. From the Tim O'Brien novel *In the Lake of the Woods*, I found the following reply: "Magicians never discuss their tricks for the explanation, however clever, always disappoints."

But here I confess that in certain ways — not so much romance of the heart as the romance of books — the young Dolores Alvarez is the model for the beautiful Leini.

Leini wanted to be a writer, a scholar and failing that, a librarian. Like Dolores, she settled for the vocation of wife and a mother. Running this by my aunt, she dismisses it out of hand.

"Ralphie," she says, "I don't have too many skills. I just like to read."

Wednesday, August 30, 2000

A writer's search for an angel
sent homeward

THOMAS WOLFE, THE AMERICAN ROMANTIC WHO SPENT HIS SHORT LIFE TRYING TO cram the universe into a single sentence, had a big birthday last month.

On Oct. 3, the day the United States Postal Service honored the author of *Look Homeward, Angel* with a stamp celebrating his life and work, Wolfe would have been 100. Instead, he died two weeks short of his 38th birthday of tuberculosis that destroyed his brain.

In the late summer of 1938, Wolfe — having visited every national park in the western United States in two weeks — contracted pneumonia after downing a pint of liquor with a derelict on a ferryboat.

The illness reopened a TB lesion from childhood on the author's right lung, cells from which entered his bloodstream and traveled to his brain. A passenger train carried Wolfe from Seattle to Baltimore, where an operation to save his life was performed at Johns Hopkins Hospital.

An adolescent Walter E. Dandy Jr. watched his father perform the surgery. "I used to sit in the gallery and watch my father operate on Saturdays," said Dr. Dandy, 75, a retired anesthesiologist. "Wolfe was desperately sick. Everyone agreed that he had TB of the brain, but without the technology we have today, they couldn't be sure."

To be sure, the world's leading neurosurgeon drilled Wolfe's head at the base of the skull on Sept. 12, 1938.

What would Dandy find inside the 6-foot-6-inch man of letters?

Fear?

Certainly. Sick or not, the last place Wolfe wanted to be was Baltimore's domed hospital on Broadway, the place where his tombstone-carving father had been treated for prostate cancer before being sent home to die.

Unkempt rows of ambition, resentment and envy irrigated with Scotch?

Love?

"When they opened the skull," said Dr. Dandy, "tubercles were everywhere." Nothing, a medical report said, could be done.

And so the incisions in Wolfe's head were closed with silk sutures and three days later, the soul of a giant who had enough of everything to set our manifest destiny between hard covers — perhaps the 20th century's one lunatic up to the task of the Great American Novel — was sent homeward.

The man who tried to save him — who'd been dispatched too late to Mexico to relieve Trotsky's headache and was no good to the dying Gershwin for the same reason — didn't know much about the man-child under his scalpel.

"My mother had to tell Dad that Wolfe was a big shot," said the junior Dr. Dandy. "He was probably aware that he was famous, but didn't know why."

For all that Wolfe published — mountains and rivers and constellations of words and enough discarded prose to best any number of today's authors — he was just wetting his whistle when they buried him in his Asheville, N.C., hometown at an age when most serious writers are just starting to hit their stride.

I drove through the mountains of Asheville last summer on a 10,000 mile, do-it-yourself book tour that took me from Poe's grave at Fayette and Greene streets to Jack London's birthplace in San Francisco and back again.

Hustling my own books from the trunk of the family car, I stopped in Asheville long enough to give a reading (no one showed up so I went to the movies and fell stupid in love with Jennifer Ehle in the movie "Sunshine") and pay my respects to Wolfe's grave at Riverside Cemetery.

The hillside cemetery reminded me of the journey I took in the autumn of 1988 to the Blue Ridge Mountains, where Sherwood Anderson is buried. But winding through the hills of Marion, Va., to pay respects to the guy who wrote *Winesburg, Ohio*, all I heard about was Thomas Wolfe.

The mad bibliophile who couldn't stop yakking about Wolfe was a Baltimorean who had exiled himself to the hills of Virginia, a strange and foul-mouthed hybrid of uneducated novelist, racetrack sharpie and rare-manuscript hound named John Mason Rudolph.

"Wolfe unearthed the Earth," ranted Mr. Rudolph in the way I imagine Wolfe ranted about Tolstoy. "After him, no one had to write a word. He said it all." (Where are you reading your beloved Wolfe now, Johnny? Are you binging through *Look Homeward, Angel*, a la Fitzgerald in Paris, in an 18-hour marathon? Sweet obsession! I haven't seen you since you banged out your novel in that flophouse on Light Street. Is it published? Are you alive?)

It is widely assumed that Wolfe, like Saroyan and Kerouac and other writers unwilling to surrender their naivete, is the stuff of precocious adolescents — a great piece of caramel to suck on before setting out for the truer worlds of John Cheever or Richard Yates.

In an Oct. 2 story about the recent publication of *O Lost* — a restored version of *Look Homeward, Angel* that is faithful to the manuscript Wolfe submitted to Scribner's before Maxwell Perkins got out the long knives — the *New York Times* said that Wolfe's work, "if read at all, is usually the domain of college curriculums."

The guest book at the Thomas Wolfe Memorial in Asheville, a product not of journalists but readers, gives the lie to the *Times* report.

"They come as friends and strangers, a huge variety of 12-year-olds and people in their 90s from all over the world," said Ted Mitchell, a Wolfe biographer who has worked at the museum for a dozen years. "All of his novels are in print and in today's world, publishing houses don't keep titles just for prestige."

November 12, 2000

An author's vision for Vietnam

SAN MARCOS, TEXAS — TIM O'BRIEN WOULD LIKE TO BE KNOWN FOR HIS LONG and difficult labor to illuminate the one thing that William Faulkner believed worth writing about: the human heart in conflict with itself.

Instead, the heavily lauded author of *The Things They Carried*, *Going After Cacciato* and *In the Lake of the Woods* is known for stories of human beings trying to kill one another. Fate assigned O'Brien war as the great subject of his life. The anguish in these books is, in every case, traceable to the characters' having been in Vietnam, as their author was, or somehow having being marked by America's war there.

Vietnam was O'Brien's war and, for a time, his world, as it was for his generation. It has never seemed entirely past; it has remained as current as President Clinton's trip last week to Hanoi and Ho Chi Minh City, the first visit to Vietnam by an American president since the war.

"It's about time," says O'Brien. "I hope it eases the hurt on both sides."

Other writers have chosen Vietnam as a subject. But because no one has written more poetically in fiction about grunts in Southeast Asia than the former foot soldier who pulled duty in Quang Ngai in 1969-1970, O'Brien has been tagged as a Vietnam writer.

While he finds that label unfortunate — is Faulkner merely a Mississippi writer, Phillip Roth simply a narrator for Jews? — O'Brien knows that it's the mystery of art, and not the tyranny of facts, that "keep things alive." It is his sorcerer's gift for weaving war narrative in which the fight for love is more mythic than the fight for land that keeps Vietnam fresh.

"First though, there was Vietnam," says the narrator of *In the Lake of the Woods*, the 1994 novel about a man named Wade, known to his platoon as Sorcerer. Vietnam, "where John Wade killed people and where he composed long letters full of observations about the nature of ... love."

If America has a 51st state, one that is mapped with a million pins on the psyche of the country, it is Vietnam. Americans were there for two decades, suffered the deaths of 58,152 men and women, saw their own nation rent with fierce protest over those deaths, and left in humiliation.

Jimmy Carter's presidency began with a pardon for all draft dodgers and people criticized him for it. Ronald Reagan said the United States didn't really lose the war and found millions eager to agree. Some have said that the United States could have won if the country had only tried. And to this day, some veterans and their families wonder in pain and anger whether all soldiers missing or taken prisoner have been accounted for.

"It was a war of incredible ambiguity and confusion," says O'Brien. "It's the back yard where my generation spent its bad childhood."

Today, O'Brien shares what he knows about writing fiction with students at Lyndon Johnson's alma mater: Southwest Texas State University in this town a half-hour south of Austin. To be teaching at the old school of a president whose administration was crippled by Vietnam is an irony O'Brien finds "weirdly coincidental."

He is available to the apprentice writers on almost any subject — indeed, there's nary a subject that isn't broached when O'Brien holds court at the Red River Pub after class — but he doesn't talk much about Vietnam.

"People have asked him about the war outside of class, but it's his work as an editor that's most important to me," says student and aspiring novelist Chad Hammet, 28. "He makes you aware that a writer only has 26 letters and 10 punctuation marks to work with and has to use them well."

It is storytelling that O'Brien was lured to Texas to teach: all the ways to put something as limited as language around something as unlimited as the heart in conflict with itself.

"As a boy, I practiced magic but discovered it was trickery," the author tells the class. "Why not someday use my wand to wake up the dead? So I took up a new hobby — writing stories."

O'Brien is 54. Most of his graduate students are half that age or younger, born about the time Saigon fell, and the author suspects they know more about the Beatles — whose "Hey Jude" provided succor to him and his fellow infantrymen — than Vietnam.

"I travel to a lot of campuses," says O'Brien. "And I don't think the kids think about Vietnam at all. To them, it might as well be the Battle of Hastings." It is his hope that Clinton's trip to Vietnam will have begun to change that.

"We have to start treating Vietnam as a country and not a war. It'll take the old age and death of all the veterans before it stops being our 51st state," O'Brien says over pitchers of beer at the pub. "Vietnam is not an appendage of America. That sort of thinking got us into the mess in the first place. We're bound together by some painful history, but it's not our liver or our appendix — it's a country."

Clinton's visit came five years after the United States re-established diplomatic ties with Vietnam, and four months after Vietnamese leaders signed a bilateral trade agreement that was viewed as the last step toward complete normalization between countries.

Standing beneath a huge bust of Vietnamese patriot and war hero Ho Chi Minh, who counted Thomas Jefferson among his heroes, Clinton told his guests how moved he was by the friendliness he felt on the streets of Hanoi.

That friendliness, and the affection the average Vietnamese citizen carries for Americans and the stubborn individualism the United States embodies — that, not the war, should be the foundation for a new relationship, O'Brien says.

"More Americans should visit, that would help," he says. "They would get a sense of the physical beauty of the place ... of how forgiving they are. There's a magical quality to the Vietnamese that is undescribable unless you've been there."

The French, O'Brien says, were despised by the Vietnamese because they forced their language, religion and culture onto the nation for nearly a century while exploiting it for commercial profit.

The Soviets who poured into the country after the retreat of the United States, says O'Brien, were simply clods: foreigners without style or sass or dollars.

"But our tentacles were only war-deep," he said. "Despite the napalm, they had an incredible love for the pizzazz and sizzle of America, a shared love of freedom."

November 24, 2000

STORYTELLER

"Every man wants to work and to be loved..."

CHAPTER 5

Working-Class Heroes

Bouncer's fame is as big as his frame

WITH NEARLY 300 POUNDS PACKED ONTO HIS 6-FOOT-L-INCH FRAME, LAWRENCE David Jackson Statom carries quite a formidable resume for his job as a rock-and-roll nightclub bouncer. Yet Mr. Statom — named after Sir Laurence Olivier and known around town as "Big Bird" or "Tiny" — is not the kind of guy to throw his weight around.

Just nine credits shy of a degree in psychology from Morgan State University, Mr. Statom has never needed schooling to know how to deal with people. And when you earn your money clearing crowded dance floors of dames, dudes and drunks at 2 a.m., you've got to know how to deal with people.

"You need patience and a really high [expletive] tolerance," said the bouncer, just up from an early evening catnap on the second floor of the 8 x 10 club in Federal Hill where he works. "Alcohol has a way of changing people's attitudes, how they perceive themselves.

"Dealing with the guys is not too bad," he said, rubbing his eyes and arranging a scarlet beret on his head. "But women drunks are the hardest to work with. They have a tendency to be very belligerent. And because they're women they think they can get away with it.

"I've been hit [by patrons] before and maintained my decorum," he said. "You can't be as big of an [expletive] as the guys you've got to control. Once they make you mad, they've got you where they want you."

His gentle attitude, engaging personality, ability to talk knowledgeably on many subjects, a gift for whistling, a network of friends who cross all quarters, and of course, his size, have combined over the last 20 years to elect Tiny to the A list of Baltimore characters.

"He's definitely legendary," said Bart Haffner, who worked with Mr. Statom at No Fish Today on Eutaw Street, where the big man earned much of his notoriety. "It's his personality for one, his size for another. He used to wear this football jersey that said Michigan Shade Tree, which I always found fitting. And the girls seemed to like him, he could dance real well.

"Instead of trying to push a drunk out the door," continued Mr. Haffner, "Tiny would talk a drunk out. When he had to use his muscle he would, he'd just bear hug the guy and walk him out the door."

"He's an institution," explained Dickle Gammerman, the 8 x 10 owner who hired Mr Statom not only for his abilities, but for the legends that lumber through the door with him.

One of eight children, Larry Statom, 35, was born in West Baltimore, the son of a stevedore and a social worker. He attended public schools (weighing 200 pounds in the seventh grade), and worshiped with Southern Baptists.

"The preacher always said, 'It don't make no difference if you're poor, or if you're black, there's no excuses not to make it. If you believe, you'll make it.' I remember that through the tough times."

Growing up in the Harlem Park area, he considered his family somewhere between poor and working class, thought of it "as my job" to do well in school, and says he always tried to make his folks proud.

When the boy was 13, his father died. Later, in 1967, Tiny's football team at Edmondson High School won the Maryland Scholastic Association title (the year before they lost to a City College team led by Kurt L. Schmoke) and he dedicated the season to his dad.

"I was a tackle," he says, "the same position the Refrigerator plays."

"The Refrigerator" is William Perry, the mammoth rookie defensive lineman for the Chicago Bears who has become a media darling this year. Because they are both big, and black, Mr. Statom has been hearing a lot of "Fridge" wisecracks lately, but credits Mr. Perry with bringing big men back into vogue.

He generally begins discussing his weight the same way.

"When you're my size," he says, "people think you've got hamburger for brains.

"When you're my size, you really can tell when you're sick. You lose weight fast, you feel faint. If I'm sick I drop 15 to 20 pounds in a couple days.

"And when you're my size and black, people can see you all the time. I'm the first person they see when they walk in the door and it frightens some people."

Mr. Statom says that after serving briefly in the Army and gathering credits at a handful of colleges, he considered a career as a pro wrestler before falling in with a "pseudointellectual, pseudo-jock" crowd that spent a lot of time living it up. By the early Seventies his renown began to match his girth.

Living in Mount Vernon, his hangouts then were O'Henry's on Centre Street, and the Buttery, a 24-hour lunchroom at Charles and Centre streets, digging the downtown life "before the yuppies moved in."

The greatest image many people from those days have of Mr. Statom is one of him leaning against the Charles Street wall of the Buttery, 2, 3, 4 o'clock in the morning, giving breath to a whistle that carried for blocks.

"All you could hear," he remembers, "was my whistling and the sound of the buses going by. Wasn't no coffeehouses in Baltimore so that's where a lot of us hung out. I'd whistle walking home after parties when I was too drunk to see. I'd know where I was by the whistle bouncing off the buildings."

In 1977 he attended a blues show at the Marble Bar on West Franklin Street, back when Scott Cunningham owned the place in its pre-punk days. When Mr. Cunningham sold the bar in 1978, Mr. Statom latched on around the corner at No Fish Today, perhaps the town's best-known music bar before arsonists destroyed it in 1981.

The bouncer says that through this club work, he learned much about the cross-pollination of American music, realizing that if the musicians were on target, white boys could play blues and black boys can rock and roll. Such thrills, which he continues to savor at the 8 x 10, have given him a goal beyond the college degree that continues to dangle just before his nose.

One day, he said, maybe in five years, maybe never, he hopes to open his own music bar "somewhere on the fringes of downtown." And he's already got the name.

"I'm going to call it," he said, "The Tiny Fish."

January 8, 1986

Skills — and blades — honed over century

NILO VIDI'S OLD MAN COULD MAKE A MEAT CLEAVER SING.

The dean of Baltimore's grinders, Nilo Vidi is the 63-year-old edge between two generations of Vidi knife men, and he remembers the days before monotone stainless steel, when a carbon-steel knife would throw out a range of notes as well as sparks when you held it against a sandstone wheel.

"Every position has a sound," he says. "The sound will tell you if you have the right bevel. You learn to grind by the sound and the feel."

That's the way Frank Monaldi learned the trade. At 39, he is one of the family's current crop of grinders — his mother is Nilo's sister — and he began fooling with knives as a kid on visits to his uncles' row house in Little Italy. "While they were watching us, they'd put us to work on the grindstone," said Mr. Monaldi.

Unable to find work after his discharge from the Navy in 1975, he decided to join the family business and apprenticed with his uncle, the late Pio Vidi.

"Uncle Pio would be in the other room when I was starting out, and he'd yell at me without even looking at what I was doing. He could hear that I was messing up. He'd say: 'Put that knife on straight!' It takes about two or three years to get good at it."

The Vidi family has been putting knives on straight against grindstones in Baltimore for almost 100 years. They began beveling blades and honing edges in a row house on Trinity Street in Little Italy and continue today in a pair of "sharp shops" in Hamilton.

It started with a letter.

A grinder named Collini had found success in the New World and wrote home to Pinzolo, Italy — one of Europe's knife-grinding capitals — to his friend Bartolo Vidi.

Explains Nilo Vidi: "Collini told my Uncle Bart: 'Come over to America, this is the place to grind knives.' So my uncle took his pushcart, put it on a boat and came to Baltimore in 1904."

Brother followed brother: After Bartolo in 1904 came Pietro (father of Nilo and Pio) in 1907, David in 1909 and Lino in 1912.

The brothers brought their wives and kids and made more kids in the old Italian neighborhood just east of the Inner Harbor, and soon the Vidis were established in the busy commerce of Baltimore's alleys. Among the men selling fruit from the back of carts, scavenging rags and junk with a horse and wagon, and collecting pennies for grinding an organ while a monkey danced on the end of a leash, were the Vidis.

"My father traveled Baltimore City on foot with a cart for years," said Nilo Vidi.

The Vidis repaired umbrellas, fixed pots and put an edge on any hunk of steel brought to them — sharpening knives for housewives, chefs, carpenters and butchers from Dundalk to Pennsylvania Avenue.

In an old newspaper interview, Nilo's late brother, Pete, said he last pushed the cart in 1937. He remembered it this way: "I push [the cart] down the street and maybe I cover 20 miles in one day. When a lady hollers for me I stop, set [the cart] upright like this and I work the pedal. Like a sewing machine. The wheel goes around, you're in business. I walk those streets summers and winters. On a good warm day I make maybe $3. I charge 10 cents a pair of scissors, sometimes less."

One of Nilo's uncles was a specialist: "He wouldn't touch a knife, he was strictly a razor and scissors man. All he had was a tiny grinding stone. It was finer work. Everybody had a straight razor back them."

The grinding business changed along with America. Safety razors began replacing straight razors, fewer women were using scissors to sew at home, and a horse and wagon replaced the heavy wooden pushcart that the Vidis pushed through the narrow streets and alleys of Baltimore before World War II.

Nilo Vidi looked back on those times the other day, admiring a postcard his father had mailed back to his parents in Pinzolo in 1913. The picture shows Pietro Vidi, a big pipe in his mouth, standing in front of a horse-drawn grinding wagon.

Mr. Vidi squints at the faded script and translates his father's Italian. "I show you my horse," the card says. "This is the way we work here in this land."

In 1927, the year Mr. Vidi was born, the horse and wagon was replaced by a truck. That was the end of foot-pedaling; the truck's motor made the wheel turn.

Today the Vidi and Monaldi families rely almost strictly on restaurants and butchers for their business. Corner grocers who cut their own meat began fading during the 1960s, and few modern American families seek a professional edge for their kitchen knives.

Nilo Vidi's oldest client is Attman's Delicatessen on East Lombard Street, owned by Seymour Attman. "My father used to sharpen knives for Seymour's father, Harry," he said.

The families say they are not in competition, that the Monaldis have their routes and the Vidis theirs.

What eateries and other businesses are actually doing is renting knives from the families, who own them and keep them sharp. The rates are $1.25 to $1.50 per blade per week. Customers are all over, from Bertha's in Fells Point to Marconi's downtown and even down to the guys who filet fish at the Jessup Farmers Market. The families also sharpen lawn mower blades, the occasional pizza cutter and utensils you wouldn't think need sharpening, like spatulas from the Sip & Bite diner on Boston Street.

Mr. Monaldi expects his 12-year-old son, Steve, to take up the family business, hoping that he will grow up to sharpen carving knives for the next generation of Attmans. And Nilo Vidi expects his son David to give him another grandchild any day, perhaps a boy.

"Once again," he says, his eyes sparking, "there will be the Vidi brothers!"

February 18, 1991

Immigrant grocer went first class
in Roland Park

IN THE OLD DAYS, THE WEALTHIER PATRONS OF VICTOR'S MARKET IN ROLAND PARK only accepted fresh money.

"We'd cash checks for the richest people in Baltimore — judges, doctors, bankers, lawyers and little old ladies who pulled up to the store with their chauffeurs," remembers longtime dairy manager Morris Lipsitz, who used to run to the bank for crisp currency. "They all wanted clean, new bills. They didn't like dirty money."

Victor's Market, now celebrating 50 years in business, became Eddie's Supermarket of Roland Park. And through those years, the money of North Baltimore's Roland Park allowed an immigrant Jewish grocer named Victor Cohen to become the high-class merchant he always wanted to be.

In Roland Park — an enclave of wealth and social prominence where the average price of a single-family house was $246,732 last year — people were willing to pay for premium quality and pampered service.

Upon that logic, a man folks know as "Mr. Victor" built his success, using prime cuts of meat and fresh produce to lead the way.

"The way to hold good customers is to do everything for them," says the semi-retired Mr. Cohen, 81, from his winter home in Florida. "You stand at the front door and give them a smile, say hello, find out their names. At check-out, you unload the basket, bag it, and take it out to the car. You can't do it all by yourself, so I made sure every employee in the store was exactly the same way."

He says: "To be pleasant is not a false thing."

Today, that legacy rests on the shoulders of Nancy Cohen Kaplow, his only child.

"When I get an idea, I won't let go of it," says company president Ms. Kaplow, whose earliest memory is of looking at the world from Victor's front window while nibbling oatmeal cookies.

Ms. Kaplow, 44, joined the business in 1981 and opened a second store at 6213 North Charles Street in 1992. With a staff of 75 employees at the Roland Avenue store alone, she plans to run Eddie's into the 21st century using her father's devotion to service — combined with an in-store bakery, natural foods, and take-out gourmet dinners for the upscale and harried.

In the segregated Baltimore of 1944, when Mr. Cohen established Victor's Market in the Morgan Millard shopping center at 4800 Roland Avenue, it was unlikely that a Jewish family would have desired or been permitted to live in Roland Park. The Cohens lived in Pikesville.

Fifty years later, Mr. Cohen marvels that his daughter sold 162 Passover dinners out of the old neighborhood store this year.

He says: "That is something I never thought I'd live to see."

Born in Kiev on May 2, 1912, Victor Cohen landed in Baltimore from the Ukraine at age 12, graduating from City College in 1929. Working his way through the ranks of the A&P grocery chain — known as 'grandma' to employees — young Vic learned to cut meat during the Depression and made store manager at 19. By 1940, he owned small markets under his own name on Park Heights Avenue near Pimlico and in Windsor Hills.

In those neighborhoods, Mr. Cohen was beholden to the bargain. Yet he longed for a store where customers wouldn't mind paying more for fresh raspberries, good chocolate, aged beef, home delivery, and ultra-attentive employees.

He found it while taking a Sunday ride along Roland Avenue.

"In no way could Park Heights Avenue and Windsor Hills support what I had in mind. Roland Park could afford it, so I decided to have the best," says Mr. Cohen, who became friends with the likes of Ogden Nash and Milton Eisenhower along the way. "Oh, it was exciting. Our sales nearly doubled every year."

Even if they can afford it, not everyone will pay Eddie's prices for everyday items.

"We use Eddie's to entertain," says Vivienne Wilson, a longtime resident. "But the Giant is cheaper. It's that simple."

Compared with Pimlico, Roland Park was uptown.

And compared to the Kiev of the Bolshevik Revolution, it was the Garden of Eden.

Mr. Cohen remembers: "My father was a successful lumberman but that went in the revolution. Then he became a baker, but there was terrible hunger. One day I had to go home with a loaf of bread and all of a sudden there was a mob of people chasing me for it. I hung on to it for life, running like crazy. Finally I made it to our apartment house — like a fortress with big iron gates. I slipped inside, safe with the bread."

Victor's Market, a small grocery specializing in fresh meats, remained next to Morgan Millard from 1944 until 1976.

In 1953, he expanded by buying Eddie's Supermarket a few blocks north at 5113 Roland Avenue. In 1976, Victor's left its original address for an honored spot inside Eddie's, where discriminating palates find Leo Denisuk behind the meat counter.

"The average American can't recognize a good cut of meat anymore," says Mr. Denisuk, who began his apprenticeship in 1939 at age 10 in Dundalk. "Everything is wrapped in plastic and forced on you.

"I'd say more than 60 of our old customers have died in the last couple of years. The new generation doesn't know how to cook, but if you show them and it works out, you've got them for life."

To ensure there will always be a good man with a blade behind the counter, Ms. Kaplow intends to apprentice young people to Mr. Denisuk and his colleague, Charlie Hatfield, 76, who recently returned to Eddie's after a 10-year retirement.

Forty years ago, Mr. Hatfield taught newlywed Margaret "Lou" Pine, a Roland Park native, how to prepare meat. Years later, she helped organize an in-store retirement party for Mr. Hatfield that included a $2,500 check from customer contributions.

"He literally taught all of us young brides to cook," says Mrs. Pine. "I think he's the one who put up the sign: 'Our meat is aged, our fish is fresh and our butchers are both.' "

March 31, 1994

Days of burgers, 'Towerettes'

ROSE SUIT LOOKED AT THE 1940S JUICER WITH TEARS STREAMING DOWN HER cheeks. It was just an old-fashioned juicer, the manual type with a handle you yank down hard.

But to Rose Suit, it is a touchstone from the best years of her life.

"Many a time I squeezed that durn orange juice out at Park Circle," said Mrs. Suit, 71. "You squeezed them oranges, you didn't get them out of a can. People wouldn't drink juice out of a can."

Park Circle was home to Baltimore's first White Tower restaurant and the juicer is now behind glass at the Peale Museum downtown, where Rose Suit and about a dozen of her retired "Towerette" colleagues gathered last night for a reunion.

The women brought their families, their cameras, their youth, and their memories.

"Hi hon," said Velma Bosley, laying eyes on Rose Suit for the first time in many a year. "I've been wanting to see you for a long time. We was working in Randallstown, remember?"

Rose remembered.

And it is the hope of the Baltimore City Life Museums that everyone who ate a White Tower hamburger in this town or cast a shadow against one of the restaurants' gleaming white facades will remember.

For those born too late — only one of the original nine Towers still exists, surviving on Erdman Avenue — curators will reassemble a 1948 Tower inside a new museum building next year.

At the Blaustein City Life Exhibition Center, now under construction near the Shot Tower, a visitor will be able to sit down at the counter of old White Tower No. 8 from Howard Street and listen to waitresses tell their stories on tape. Last night, you could watch them hug, laugh and cry with one another, and remember the good old days in person.

"I got divorced in the 1950s and I needed a job," said Mrs. Bosley, 72. "I made out like I had experience, but I didn't. They put me to work in No. 5 on Pulaski Highway and I wound up working in every one. You had to go fast. You wouldn't believe how fast I could go taking orders, making the food, and serving it, all by myself."

Under a glass cabinet lay a pay stub from 1959: $39.55, including $1.20 overtime, for a week's work.

When Bob Donnells started working part time as a "Towerman" while a high school student in 1960, he made 45 cents an hour. He kept his Dundalk Senior High School homework under the counter and kept up with his studies between customers.

After two years, he saved enough money to buy his first car — a gray, 1955 Chevrolet for $200. He also found time to fall in love with Rose Suit's daughter, Betty Jane.

"Right in the back room of No. 8 he said he was going to marry my daughter," said Rose Suit, who in turn urged her daughter "to go out with that nice Bob Donnells."

She did, and has been married to him for 26 years.

Looking at the 51-year-old Mr. Donnells today, said some of the ladies who remembered a fresh-faced high school kid, made them feel old.

To remember when she was young — and as a memorial to her late husband — Cora Hegege keeps Baltimore's last White Tower open on Erdman Avenue. Joe and Cora Hegege met on the job at a Washington Boulevard White Tower in the 1960s. Mr. Hegege died in January.

"Joe worked for them for something like 35 years and he couldn't see them closing the last one down," said Mrs. Hegege. "It was Joe's dream to keep it going and when he passed away I decided to keep his dream going. It's holding its own with minor changes."

Most everyone got along swell, the workers said, and no one was more loved than Betty Ackerman-Donaldson, one of the White Tower's first female supervisors.

Mrs. Donaldson's first husband, Bruce Ackerman, was a supervisor.

Her current husband, Melvin Donaldson, was the one-time national chain's first customer in Baltimore when he ate a burger in 1936 at Park Circle.

And her daughter, Shirl Ross, remembers traveling to Atlantic City as an adolescent to help her mother polish up a new White Tower.

"You had to scrub those white tiles inside and out," said Ms. Ross. "I did my share, maybe mom gave me a milk shake or something, but you didn't get paid. You did it because you were White Tower people, you were White Tower family."

Betty Donaldson, remembered by one and all last night as the prettiest of all the Towerettes, joined that family at age 16 and in time became supervisor of all nine of the Baltimore stores.

Her first $10.50 pay check for 48 hours persuaded her not to return to Western High School in 1940.

"I wish we could relive some of those days," Mrs. Donaldson said. "I could check out of the old No. 8 on Howard Street and walk down to No. 2 on Liberty Street at 11 o'clock at night and not be afraid."

July 20, 1994

Blowing glass in tune with creation

GIANNI TOSO BELIEVES THAT GOD WAS THE FIRST GLASS BLOWER, AN IDEA THAT fascinates Mr. Toso, a master glass blower and Orthodox Jew. "Sixty-two percent of the Earth is silica," said Mr. Toso of the compound used to make glass. "God [gathered] Adam from the Earth. How we are alive is because God blew into the pipe."

For 1,000 years, natives of the Italian island of Murano near Venice have been making the finest colored glass in the world. Mr. Toso is one of them, part of a large family of chemists, artists and craftsmen who have been working with glass for 500 years.

Mr. Toso, 53, began working in the glass factories near his home at age 10. It took him until he was 38, however, "to become a full-time Jew."

And it is his Jewishness, as much or more than his world-renowned sculpture, that six months ago landed Gianni Toso, his wife, Karyn, and their four children in the intense Orthodox community of Northwest Baltimore. He hopes to spend the rest of his life on his big estate on Bancroft Road, turning out huge, surreal masks of glass and tiny, delicate figurines of pious Jews getting married, exulting the Torah, and carrying the fruits of harvest.

He works with a small blow torch to melt, fuse and shape colored glass rods into bodies, heads, hands and feet. Using dental picks, steel clamps, butter knives and tools favored by the average welder, he puts humans together with glass.

The small figures, some of which sport eyeglasses with lenses half the size of a shirt collar button, start at $300. Larger, complicated pieces have sold to private collectors for as much as $30,000.

And his secular work includes a glass arena for Jews and Christians to face off: a chess set that pits 16 rabbis against 16 Catholic priests.

Of Baltimore, he said: "People listen here. It's impossible to define any human being, but if I can categorize the people I've found in Baltimore — Jewish and non-Jewish — it would be people that care. Because they care, life is better. In New York and New Jersey, people don't have time to be human. In those places, I missed Venice. Life is more civilized in Baltimore. You are not lonely anymore."

About 17 years ago, in Venice, a city with a vanishing population of Jews, was without a rabbi. A new rabbi arrived from Morocco and was making the rounds one Sabbath when he came upon Mr. Toso, who was then loosely observant, working in his studio.

The rabbi was incensed to find a Jew desecrating the day that God has set aside for rest. Mr. Toso explained that he was doing nothing wrong, that he did no work for profit Saturday. "I use Saturday for myself," he told the rabbi, explaining the spirituality between himself and his work. "I use [the Sabbath] for my best creating."

The rabbi screamed even louder.

"I turned off my flame and said: 'Stop screaming at me and teach me why I am wrong.' "

The rabbi talked and Mr. Toso humbly listened, thinking: "If I obey all the limitations, what kind of Gianni will I become?"

He became Orthodox — a Jew who believes his work is nothing compared with what God has done.

"When you limit, with your own free will, the creativity given to you by God, then you understand who is the Creator," he said.

In his passion, exuberance and humor, Mr. Toso is a pure reflection of his homeland. In his observance of laws given to Moses on Mount Sinai, he represents a Jew who believes the purpose of his life is fulfilling those laws. Mix it together and you have a warm, philosophical and very funny man, most likely the only Orthodox Jew from Italy in Baltimore.

Pointing to the long tassels that Orthodox men wear under their shirts — fringe that hangs down from their waists — he said: "I'm Italian, that's why I wear my spaghetti." Every Orthodox home has a Biblical scroll called a mezuza on the doorpost. The one leading to Mr. Toso's studio is encased in glass.

Around the studio are shelves of figures he calls "my children," work displayed in museums from Jerusalem to Japan and available at the Zyzyx! store in Pikesville. Mr. Toso will be at the store the evening of April 6 to meet people and hold court. He hopes people will pay as much attention to him as they will his work.

"Your work must have some kind of dignity, but I am the typical human creature," he said. "Because of the intensity of life, I sometimes lose contact with the Creator and that is my tragedy."

March 29, 1995

Grimm portrayals

ROBERT WANG STAYED HOME FOR EIGHT YEARS PAINTING PORTRAITS OF PEOPLE who had plucked out their eyes, children with spikes through their heads, a bearded, naked woman nailed to a cross and (his personal favorite) a father chopping off his daughter's hands while a goblin offers her a rosary.

Wang is not an illustrator for some sick heavy metal band.

From 1988 until this year, he obsessively brushed oil on canvas to depict all 242 fairy tales collected by the Brothers Grimm.

The feat took seven hours a day, five days a week for eight years and is believed to be an accomplishment without precedent. All the paintings have been hand framed by Wang, and the biggest measures 3 feet by 4 feet. Most are about the size of a small television. Others, based on the shortest of the tales, are the size of a snapshot.

"I grew up listening to the stories, and I had these images in my mind, visions of magical creatures under stairs. In my mind, I was hearing them from a 14th-century grandmother," says Wang, surrounded by scores of Grimm images crowding the walls of his Columbia townhouse. "My visions weren't always what other people think of."

Indeed, these are far from Disney's sanitized versions of Snow White and her darling dwarfs.

Except for a few of his own ideas painted into the margins — like the goblin with the rosary — Wang's intense pictures are faithful to the dark side of the original stories first brought together in the 19th century by Jakob and Wilhelm Grimm of Germany. The tales go back more than five centuries and are rife with murder, cannibalism, mutilation, incest and baby killing.

In Germany, to this day, the Grimms sell second only to the Bible.

"I didn't make any of this up. The medieval people thought this stuff was hilarious," says Wang, a 58-year-old doctor of art history. "I'm the first person willing to take the words of the Grimms and really show it instead of painting around it. Only a few are really cruel, but when the Grimms are cruel, they're cruel."

Among the cruelest is "The Maiden Without Hands," in which the devil bullies an impoverished miller into severing his pious daughter's wrists. Wang, who has no children, jokingly calls the painting "You're Grounded."

Although there's a happy ending when God rewards the maiden's faith by allowing her hands to grow back, this is not what Wang has chosen to paint. He ignored most of the happy endings.

"I would think that kids today, who are so much into brutality and violence and everything they see on MTV, would be able to understand the Grimms," he says. "But I've had young people come in to see these who didn't know who they were."

To Wang, ignorance of the pioneering German lexicographers is more disturbing than a portrait of a man eating his son's head from a bowl of blood, as occurs in the tale of the juniper tree. He wants the paintings to be exhibited by a major museum to reward his years of work and generate new American interest in the subject.

"I didn't do this as a crusader, I did it because I love the stories," he says. "If I could possibly bring a new generation to Grimm's fairy tales, that would be very nice."

Wang used *The Complete Fairy Tales of the Brothers Grimm* by Jack D. Zipes as his text for the paintings. The 1987 edition includes many stories omitted in earlier versions. The author was amazed to learn what Wang had done so quietly.

"Oh my God, this is an astounding feat," said Zipes, a professor of German at the University of Minnesota Twin Cities. "If he painted every one in the book, he's the first to do it — a great accomplishment."

When Zipes goes into elementary schools to recite some of the tales he loves so much, he first asks the children if they know any of the stories.

"What they know is a hodgepodge of ideas, and, if they know anything at all, it's through Disney," says Zipes. "I retell them because it's important to go back to the source. The tales are still popular, even on the Internet, but most people don't pay attention to the historical tradition."

Bob Wang — whose passions range from the cabala of Jewish mystics and tarot to power tools, bookbinding, French cuisine and antique furniture — pays close attention to tradition.

The books he's written, including a 1988 handbook for tarot based on the psychology of Carl Jung, are meticulously researched. Royalties for *Tarot Psychology*, published in more than a dozen languages, helped sustain him in the eight years he labored over the Grimm project.

His next ambition?

"I want to paint all 68 short stories of Edgar Allan Poe," he says. "I feel strongly about people who love things and stick with them. How can you know anything without knowing all of it? I like to see things complete."

June 9, 1996

"Lose the accordion..."

CHAPTER 6

Don't Try to Lay No Boogie-Woogie on the King of Rock and Roll

Nils Lofgren

A FUNNY THING HAPPENED TO NILS LOFGREN WHEN HE DROPPED OUT OF HIGH school, ran away from his Bethesda home and hit the streets of Greenwich Village to look for rock 'n' roll success. The kid found it.

In August of 1968 the shy, determined teen-ager from the suburbs was mesmerized watching Jimi Hendrix coax blue devils from his guitar at Washington's old Ambassador Theater. A little more than a year later Mr. Lofgren's band Grin had gone from coffee house gigs at the Club Bluesette on North Charles Street to opening concerts for the fabled guitar hero.

Experiencing Jimi Hendrix provided Mr. Lofgren with the vocational guidance he couldn't get at Walter Johnson High School, where battles with the administration over his clothes and the length of his hair speeded his exit.

"I think Nils said, 'I have a right; I'm going to get an attorney,'" remembered Dr. Donald H. Reddick, the principal of the Bethesda high school at the time. "I think he combed his hair back rather than getting it cut. At the [junior] prom it became obvious that he had not cut his hair. I think he even had some jewelry attached to it."

So while his peers worried about scoring well enough on their SATs to get into good colleges, Nils Lofgren studied ways to enter the world of his rock 'n' roll idols.

"When I was about 15 I saw the Beatles," he said, an event that torpedoed a decade of accordion lessons. "And I picked up the guitar as a hobby. When I was 17, after seeing Jimi Hendrix, I realized I wanted to be a professional guitar player. Before that I didn't know what I wanted to be."

In the 17 years that have passed since the morning he left a long goodbye note to his parents and walked from Bethesda to National Airport for a flight to New York, Nils Iofgren has taken part in enough prime-time rock 'n' roll for a dozen careers — all without the benefit of a badly wanted hit record.

The ride began in 1969 when Neil Young asked him to play piano on his classic "After the Goldrush" album and picked up speed most recently when Mr. Lofgren played to millions around the world as a member of Bruce Springsteen's E Street

Band on the "Born in the USA" tour.

In between, the 34-year-old has persisted in a solo career, snaring flickers of the spotlight with fresh songs, the pastel voice of a mannish boy, hot razor guitar work and a true believer's sense of what is, and what is not, rock 'n' roll.

The combination of these credentials — particularly his sweet stiletto guitar style, and high spirit for rock camaraderie — landed him a spot in the most successful band in the world today.

"He fit like fingers in a glove, man," said E Street drummer Max Weinberg. "Right from the first beat of the first time he played with us. He really became a member of the E Street band, not just a guitarist for the tour."

But while Mr. Lofgren's own career has had more downs than ups — Grin disbanded deep in debt, none of his nine solo albums has made a dime, and most critics, while sympathetic, believe he failed to realize his early promise — he has never betrayed the teen-age optimist who'd knock on any door to see if opportunity would answer.

This is a guy whom guitarist Keith Richards respected enough to offer a tryout for a guitar in the Rolling Stones when Mick Taylor quit in 1974. (Before Mr. Lofgren could fly to England for the audition, Ronnie Wood changed his mind and took the job.)

Neil Young remembers Mr. Lofgren finagling his way backstage at the Cellar Door in mid-1969, screwing up the courage to ask one of the biggest, most enduring artists of the hippie era for advice.

"He was about 17 and he had his guitar with him," said Mr. Young in a recent telephone conversation. "He was like a fan, a groupie. But he played a couple of songs for me and he was great. His [guitar] technique was wonderful and his songs were really good — real emotional, very alive.

"He was not," said Mr. Young, who actually handed Mr. Lofgren one of his own guitars for the impromptu audition, "the kind of guy you forget."

He didn't, and a friendship was born under a promise from the established star to produce Grin's first album. Rock 'n' roll, it seemed, was beginning to deliver the goods.

To Nils Lofgren, the kind of kid who didn't have many close friends, or much luck with girls, rock 'n' roll was more than just music, although he's always been smart enough to know that without the beat the rest of the scene is pointless.

"Rock 'n' roll was just a great release, something that made me feel a bit useful," said Mr. Lofgren, who still considers himself "mellow," if not shy — a trait outsiders have described as aloof. "At least it was something I could do OK, and get the payback of audience acceptance."

He began paying his dues as a high school "roadie," hauling equipment for a band of hotshot older boys called the Renegades. "Before I knew how to play guitar I carried their stuff in a black Ford station wagon my dad had," he said. "They kind of used me, but not in a bad way, although it destroyed Dad's car."

With practice, applying his disciplined musical gifts to the wop-bop-a-loo-op vitality of rock, the young tag-along began to eclipse the talents of the older guys he hung out with.

"I grew up very slowly," he continued. "I was about two or three years behind all my friends when it came to girls, beer, cars. I was kind of a loner, kind of lost. Until I started playing music I was an ugly duckling, I wasn't real popular with the girls.

"But when I started playing music all of a sudden they started coming around. It bothered me because I hadn't changed. I had all these dreams to make records, hit the big time and all that, escaping the responsibilities of the normal 9-to-5 reality."

To capture that dream, he was convinced he had to run away, to flee an environment where he made the varsity soccer team but wasn't allowed to play because he wouldn't cut his hair, to sneak out of America's wealthiest county and pitch a tent in the daring rock carnival of the late 1960s.

"I was very shocked that I realized I was going to do it," he said of the morning he finally left, two weeks into his senior year. "And I was very worried about my parents misinterpreting it.

"I tried to hitchhike to National Airport, but wound up walking. I was in a daze — scared that someone would see me. I'd never skipped school in my life. I just got on a plane for New York, got off, got in a taxi, and said take me to Greenwich Village. I kind of lived in the street with the runaways. During the day I'd take the subway uptown, sneak into record companies and ask for a record deal.

"I remember calling my parents from a pay phone around from the Fillmore East about five days later. I didn't have it straight how I could explain how important it was. [In the note] I was acknowledging a love that we had, that I was running away from a situation, it had nothing to do with them. That was an impossible thing to do on a piece of paper, but I tried.

"Back then if you dropped out it was like you were a juvenile delinquent. I thought if I was old enough to make a decision not to go to college, I should be mature enough to support myself.

"I wasn't running away from my parents. I love them, they're my best friends. I just felt like ... I don't know, I just felt like it was something I had to do."

"We were naturally upset," said Nils Lofgren's father and namesake. "We were disappointed that he didn't discuss it with us before he left. But I think he concluded that he couldn't put up with high school anymore. He was convinced that he could make a success in music."

"It was very disruptive to our normal family routine," said Tommy Lofgren, a former Grin member, and the second of four Lofgren boys behind Nils. "My parents were confused. Trying to find the right solution was difficult."

As it turned out, Nils was forced to come home and talk it over. After a week in the Village — having spent the $150 he had made mowing lawns the summer before — he arrived home broke and sick.

"I was only there about a week and a half before I got pneumonia," said Mr. Lofgren. "It was [fall], the time of year where you're hot and sweaty during the day and get the chills all night. I'd stay with runaways on doorsteps, someone would stay awake while the other guy tried to sleep. I was lucky; I didn't get jerked around or messed up. I'd sip on tea at a HoJos in the Village all afternoon to keep warm."

Back in Bethesda, his parents suggested music school as an avenue to success. Their son wouldn't hear of it.

"I had my heart set on pursuing a career immediately," he said. "It was something I didn't know anything about, and I felt like I had to start jumping into it quick."

In 1918 a master carpenter named Hilmer Lofgren came to America from Lyseik, Sweden, looking for work. He settled in Astoria, Oregon, and after getting established sent home for his wife Frida, and their four children, the oldest a boy named Nils Adolph Lofgren.

About the same time in Chicago, Frank Gaglione and Mary Lagreco arrived separately from Sicily. They met as young adults, got married, and had three children, one of them a daughter named Josephine.

After flying warplanes in World War II, Nils A. Lofgren studied liberal arts at the University of Chicago on the G.I. Bill. He met "Jo" on the dance floor of a ballroom, and they fell in love and married.

The couple settled in an Italian, South Side Chicago neighborhood near Midway Airport, and Mr. Lofgren began working as an assistant editor for a National Safety Council publication.

On June 21, 1951 — the first day of summer — Nils and Jo Lofgren were blessed with a 4-pound, 12-ounce baby boy. They gave the youngster the first name of Nils, a Swedish nickname for Nicholas, and the second name of Hilmer, after his paternal grandfather.

The boy, called Lefty by his friends through adolescence, wanted to play music by the first grade.

"In Chicago in the '50s, in strong ethnic neighborhoods, the accordion was a very popular instrument for young people," said the elder Mr. Lofgren. "Nils was very anxious to take lessons. We wanted him to wait a year, but he insisted he was ready.

"I bought a small accordion from someone at work, and arranged for lessons. Nils showed a very strong aptitude for it; it was something he seemed to need. There was never any difficulty getting him to practice. The lessons became more advanced, we got a full-sized accordion for him, and he began to get into semiclassical music."

In 1959, when Nils was almost 9, his father landed a job with the Insurance Institute for Highway Safety and the family moved to Bethesda.

"He continued his accordion here, and his teacher put him into classical music, overtures," said Mr. Lofgren. "When Nils was about 14 there was a graded competition among accordionists here. He came in second and immediately began preparing for the next year, when he won first place. I think he felt, 'Well this is it,' he more or less achieved his goal with the accordion.

"At that same time a group came here from Europe known as the Beatles. He wanted to go, so I took him to see them at [D.C.] stadium," now called RFK.

As it did for tens of thousands of other American teen-agers, the group from Europe known as the Beatles forever changed the direction of Nils' life.

"I had an old acoustic guitar in the house, and he began playing it," said the elder Mr. Lofgren. "A friend taught Nils what he knew, then Nils went to professional teachers. From that point on the guitar was his principal interest."

Said Gilbert Muir, Nils' high school music theory teacher: "He caught on to traditional forms very quickly. He was ahead of the rest of the kids because he was disciplined."

Unlike the many parents who lashed out against the rock 'n' roll youth movement that blossomed around outrageous music, far-out fashions, illegal drugs and the anti-Vietnam war movement, the Lofgrens weren't threatened by the scene that had captivated their son.

"We didn't approve of everything that was going on," said the elder Mr. Lofgren. "But we saw that music was a great interest for him, and he was improving. He went through a half-dozen bands, becoming more proficient and beginning to compose music on his own.

"We had a lot of confidence in Nils."

Their son says: "My parents were rare. Most of my friends would just matter-of-factly tell you that they didn't get along with their parents."

Less than a month after he met Neil Young, with Grin already established as the biggest rock band between Washington and Baltimore, Nils Lofgren flew to Los Angeles to "pave the way" for bigger success while drummer Bob Berberich and bassist George Daley, formerly with a local band called the Hangmen, drove cross-country in a Volkswagen van to join him.

"We were all young and stupid," said Mr. Berberich, now a carpenter.

Mr. Lofgren immediately began looking for his mentor after landing in L.A. "I knew Neil [Young] was serious because he had been calling me from other cities," he said.

Soon Mr. Berberich and Mr. Daley arrived. Anxious to see what kind of magic Mr. Young could weave, the band lived in a house under the freeway in East Hollywood and found work as the house band at a Topanga Canyon club called the Corral. Taj Mahal regularly played there, as did the Flying Burritto Brothers, with Mr. Young occasionally sitting in with Grin.

When Mr. Lofgren and Mr. Berberich, with prompting from Mr. Young, fired

George Daley, a call went out to Bob Gordon, a neighborhood friend back East who'd played in several Lofgren bands.

"I asked Nils how much he could pay, and he couldn't promise anything," said Mr. Gordon. "He said we'd make a buck and get by."

But instead of Neil Young producing the first Grin album, he passed the job onto his own producer, David Briggs.

"One day Neil said he was joining Crosby, Stills and Nash, and was going to Woodstock," said Mr. Berberich. "But Briggs made things happen for us. He got money [$20,000] together, we cut the first record and then he shopped it around and got us a deal" on Spindizzy, a now-defunct subsidiary of Columbia Records.

Simply called Grin, the first record was sweet, tough and to the point. A dozen songs in all, the cream of Mr. Lofgren's writing between adolescence and young manhood, they remain some of his best. Although Columbia supported the album with full-page magazine ads hawking an unknown guitar whiz named Nils Lofgren, few people bought it.

November 25, 1971, a *Rolling Stone* review of the debut: "Lofgren can not only play guitar, piano and organ extremely well, he also writes beautifully simple songs and has a gift for composing exuberant melodies and choruses.... Grin is a band with no pretensions and its first record stands head and shoulders above every debut album released this year. Thanks to Nils Lofgren, 1971 will not be devoid of hope."

The word was getting back home that good things were happening for the band that played teen centers and junior high schools all over Baltimore.

Paul G. Gregorzak, a Ramblewood-area guitarist, remembers older kids in his neighborhood crowing about Mr. Lofgren and turning him onto Grin. "I modeled all my guitar stuff after him," said Mr. Gergorzak during an acoustic Lofgren show last month at Back Streets Cafe in Towson.

"He plays the guitar the way Fred Astaire dances: agile, very agile and sensitive. He's subtle with his volume knob, he kind of emulates a violin or an organ. Also he's a romantic with all his boy-girl lyrics, and there I am, a teen-ager, looking at girls and getting inspired. Nils is important as a true rocker, a guitar hero," said Mr. Gregorzak. "And he's relentless, been at it a long time."

Two Spindizzy albums, "1 & 1" and "All Out," followed the debut, and a fourth album, "Gone Crazy," was released by A&M Records. Each album contained some good and some great rock 'n' roll, but the reviews became increasingly negative, and the attention given Mr. Lofgren continued to dwarf that given to Mr. Gordon and Mr. Berberich.

Although the gigs became a bit more prestigious — Mr. Lofgren was now doing his show-stopping, mini-tramp back-flips while playing the guitar to open Carnegie Hall shows for Van Morrison — Grin never broke out of opening-act status.

"We weren't able to get across on record what we could do live," said

Mr. Gordon, 35.

Regardless, said Mr. Berberich, 38, who still bowls a game of ten-pins now and then with Mr. Lofgren, "the fact is we weren't successful. We had four albums out and weren't going anywhere.

"We were always living for when we would make it. The day-to-day enjoyment of life was passing us by," Mr. Berberich continued. "I got $7,000 cash for signing with Spindizzy — thought I had made it. I bought a '55 Cadillac, the best drugs, and ate in the best restaurants. Then I was put on a $150-a-week salary. We played the 'Midnight Special' [TV show), were touring the country and I was broke. I made more money when Grin was a local band in Baltimore.

Feb. 28, 1974, *Rolling Stone* reviewing "Gone Crazy," the last Grin album: "On the strength of his first three albums it's unbelievable that [Mr. Lofgren] has not yet achieved commercial success. ... It's sad to report that Nils and Grin's fourth album is substandard. Although all the tunes are pretty, a pervading melodic ordinariness robs them of any memorability. Even with its manifold failings, 'Gone Crazy' is superior to the general run of rock product. Clearly Grin can do better. Lofgren is a major talent."

Later that year, Grin would play its farewell concert at the Kennedy Center.

"I feel fortunate," said Mr. Gordon, now working for a federal government contractor. "You take it as it is because you still have to get up in the morning every day."

In 1975, about a year after Mr. Lofgren disbanded Grin and, against advice once given by Neil Young, reluctantly sold half his publishing rights to cover the band's debts, Mr. Lofgren recorded his first solo album.

Known as "the Fat Man" because that's what is shown on the antique circus poster reproduced on its cover, the "Nils Lofgren" album generated more excitement than any work since his accordion-styled "oompah-oompah" piano on Neil Young's "Southern Man."

Included on the album that should have put Nils in the major commercial category (*Rolling Stone* predicted the Fat Man would end Mr. Lofgren's status as "a cult figure in search of a mass audience) was an autobiographical, career-theme piano ballad, "The Sun Hasn't Set On This Boy Yet."

Mr. Lofgren played the song three weeks in a row early last month during his "intimate living room" acoustic concerts at Back Streets Cafe in Towson.

"I dropped out of high school, it bored me to death. They taught me a dress code, and lost my respect. I fled up to New York, and learned from neglect — that the sun hasn't set on this boy yet."

For the better part of the last two years, the nova-bright rays of Bruce Springsteen have kept the sun shining over Mr. Lofgren at high noon.

"Until Nils played with Bruce he was a friend," joked pro basketball's Mitch Kupchak, the former Washington Bullet who got to know Nils when he wrote and recorded the "Bullets Fever" theme song for the 1978 NBA championship team. "Since he joined Bruce he's been 'my best friend Nils.'"

More to the point, Mr. Lofgren had been living with his parents for about three years before he played with Mr. Springsteen — whom he'd befriended years ago at a Fillmore East audition night — back home after "being broke for many, many years, sleeping on people's floors and couches" because of a chronically unprofitable solo career.

Because of the Boss, Mr. Lofgren can now afford to live in a new, upper-middle-class thicket of woodsy suburbia, not too different from the neighborhood he ran away from in 1968.

"Actually I bought a loan," he said. "Thirty years to pay it off, like most people." Mr. Lofgren shares the house, and much of the expenses, with his youngest brother Mark, a 24-year-old carpenter.

If Mr. Lofgren's house is conservative, his dress remains rocked out, owing more to the casual hippie scruff of the early '70s than the calculated schlock of the '80s. His stage dress is neater than his house attire, but in the same thrift-store spirit.

From his toes — 5 feet and almost 3 inches up to his tousled black hair — he is dressed in a pair of knitted, olive green ankle slippers, somewhat linty black Nike athletic pants, a faded, bone-hued tie-dyed shirt, an embroidered denim "Born in the USA" tour vest, commemorating Mr. Springsteen's shows at the Los Angeles Coliseum, and a trademark knotted scarf around his neck, loaded down with thumb picks.

He continues to follow Yasser Arafat's shaving schedule, and politely but firmly tells a photographer that he does not smile for the camera, explaining that he has never been comfortable smiling for photos, even as a kid.

This past St. Patrick's Day, sitting in the basement of the 2,800-square-foot, four-bedroom "traditional Colonial" built by Pulte Homes on the fringes of Gaithersburg — "the kind of place when I was a kid I told myself I'd never live in" — Mr. Lofgren explained how the good fortune came about.

"There were all these rumors about Bruce getting a new guitar player, months before Steve [Van Zandt] left," he said. "I told him if he ever needed a guitar player, I wanted an audition — just a passing statement, but he knew I meant it.

"A few months later in May [1984], about five weeks before the first show, Bruce called me up to jam. I knew that meant they needed a guitar player. I stayed up all night writing out chord charts of all the songs I knew Bruce would have to play — he's got to play 'Promised Land,' and 'Born to Run,' and rightfully so; they're what he's about.

"The day I got to Bruce's we stayed up all night, [Bruce] telling me how to approach it, talking about philosophies. The next day at rehearsals, I was like, 'God I hope they like it,' and focused on nailing the songs. We spent about three hours going through the hits. The second day we did the same thing.

"Bruce had said he might need the weekend to decide; but as soon as we got on the street, he asked me to join the band. I asked him if he really meant it. I didn't just want a job for 16 months, I wanted to join the band. And he asked me.

"It was one of the greatest moments in my professional life," said Mr. Lofgren. "Right up there with playing piano on 'After the Goldrush.' I was in heaven. The first people I told were my mom and dad. Nobody was happier than them, except maybe me."

Yet with all the attention he's garnered through Mr. Springsteen's tour — getting to play a pickup basketball game at Boston Garden with Kevin McHale and Larry Bird, and meeting stars as diverse as Keith Richards and Bob Dylan, Don Rickles and Elizabeth Taylor — Mr. Lofgren continues to ache for a hit record.

There is a song on "FLIP," his latest album, released last summer, that addresses his frustration, a tom-tom rocker that would appear to have replaced "The Sun Hasn't Set on This Boy Yet" as his career theme.

Called "King of the Rock," it has Mr. Lofgren pleading, "If I could just get a start, man, I would never stop ... the screams you hear come from a wounded warrior, bent on recovery, bent on discovery ..."

Mr. Lofgren talks of the elusive radio hit through yawns of exhaustion, feeling "so fried" that his head drops down for a nod here and there near the end of a three-hour interview.

When the year-and-a-half-long "USA" tour finally ended last October — played across 11 countries, through 156 shows for 5 million fans — Mr. Lofgren played large electric gigs with his own band in support of last summer's "FLIP" album, then booked a month of small acoustic shows in Washington and Baltimore.

"I want a hit record," he said, "and it's frustrating. This next album [to be recorded next month at Sheffield Studios in Baltimore County] has to be a hit or I'll probably be out in the street again without a record deal," he said.

"Certainly more people know me as the guitar player in the E Street Band than as a solo artist, but I'm not trying to be a cult artist. I haven't had that one hit that gets you to the next step.

"But I'm a survivor. I just hope that sometime I'll make a record that's not only good, it's good for the times. I may never have it, or I may have it this year."

April 27, 1986

Mississippi, Part I:
Deep blue music, vast green fields, and the
Elvis Presley Heights Bar and Grill

WE ENTERED THE GREAT MAGNOLIA STATE WHERE THE KING WAS BORN AND EIGHT days later we left it where he died.

And in between Tupelo and when we crossed to Memphis, we saw a whole lot of Mississippi.

I traveled to the land of deep blue music and vast green fields with my buddies Tyrone Crawley and Art Lien, and a pound of Old Bay seasoning.

Before we left Baltimore, friends took turns telling me to be careful. One advised me to put on some reverence and take off my bangle-bracelets; another said that two white men driving through the Deep South with out-of-state plates and a black man would be risky. Others warned that a quick mind is conveniently mistaken for a smart mouth, and we all know what a smart mouth is an invitation to.

More than anything, I was reminded that Mississippi just ain't East Baltimore.

To which I replied: Tell me something I don't know.

Having returned safely, the trip reminds me of my childhood. It was genuine and wonderful and the only trouble I had was trouble I courted.

Believe it or not, it is 1988 in Mississippi. At least it seemed so in the way we were treated in the dozen-and-a-half specks on the map we visited. East Baltimore should be so friendly.

Passing into Mississippi from northern Alabama, we cruised into the fabled city of Tupelo, a town of red clay and 23,905 people that is known around the globe as host to the cradle from which Elvis Aron Presley first cried out.

We stayed at the All-American Motor Inn, whose marquee boasts "Owned and Operated by Americans." Directly beneath that assurance is a sign for a Chinese restaurant. Because of its proximity to the whitewashed shack where the King was born in 1935, the motel is in a part of town now known as Elvis Presley Heights.

The beer we brought back to our room after the town closed up at night — a room whose balcony looked out on an endless cotton field that reminded me of a beachfront room down the ocean — was purchased at the Elvis Presley Heights

Bar and Lounge.

Tupelo, also home to the very first Motorola television set, knows a good thing when it explodes in its municipal face.

We visited the Elvis Presley Lake and Campground; the Elvis Presley swimming pool; and the Elvis Presley Memorial Chapel — where after meditation we noticed that the only stained glass panel donated from somewhere other than Mississippi or Memphis came from a fan club in Baltimore. We drove along Elvis Presley Boulevard; swung on the Elvis Presley swings; and watched dust blow over the infield at the Elvis Presley sandlot.

All of this took 20 minutes, about 18 minutes longer than a walk through the two-room house that Elvis' old man Vernon built for $180 in borrowed money in 1934. It took considerably longer to make it through the Elvis gift shop.

What did they sell? Look around your house, put Presley's image or name on any item that catches your glance, and that's what they sell.

To unwind from the overload we walked downtown, to City Hall and the county courthouse. We made our way past a store that had 8,000 pairs of used shoes for sale and bought unroasted peanuts — they taste like raw lima beans — and juicy red tomatoes from a fruit shack next to the Court Street Lounge and Recreation Hall.

A converted auto repair garage, the rec hall had 20-foot ceilings; brick walls painted brown 4 feet from the floor and dirty beige the rest of the way up; century-old pool tables inlaid with mother-of-pearl and whose side pockets were little woven sacks of rawhide; a jukebox; high-legged benches; cheap beer and cheeseburgers; a map of the United States to settle bets; used clothing hanging in the front window; an integrated group of men playing dominoes — including one who called himself "The Mad Man of Rockabilly" — and, behind the bar, a woman named Carol.

Carol's father, a farmer who owns the pool hall and the fruit shack, has spent his summer driving to Alabama every morning to buy produce because the drought, according to Carol, "has burned up his crops."

"Who's the mayor of Tupelo?" we asked her.

"Don't know," said Carol.

"Do you care?" we asked.

"Hell no," she said.

Bruce Springsteen advised from the jukebox to "learn to live with what you can't rise above," and Carol pulled out a photo album to show us mug shots of the regulars. When she opened it, four dozen baby roaches scurried from the laminated pages. She brushed them to an early death, and we took a quick Polaroid of Carol and Art to add to her collection.

No doubt millions of roach eggs are being laid on Artie's face as you read this.

Back at the All-American Motor Inn, we drank up the rest of the Elvis Heights beer, filled an empty juice jug with sandy orange dirt from the town that gave the world a King, and rested for the next day's event: the 4th Annual Chunky Rhythm and Blues Festival near Meridian, just about three hours south of Tupelo.

We never did get to see that first Motorola set.

Mississippi is a writer's daydream illustrated with creeping kudzu and roadside churches set up in trailer homes, and the Route 45 ride south to Chunky confirmed a hunch that it is also the land of a million datelines: Leotis, Okolona, Golden Triangle Airport, Tibbee, Artesia, Sessums, Noxubee County, and Scooba.

When we stopped for an early lunch just below Tupelo in Shannon — $7.95 for deep-fried frogs legs — we were declared the friendliest Yankees ever to stop for a bite. Our charm was rewarded with a 30-pound watermelon that all the waitresses signed in magic marker for good luck.

Chunky was the dateline that called out to us, and before long we were being directed into a pine-studded former cattle field for a long day of barbecue and blues.

At these wide-open gigs of 2,000 people or more you expect to meet bluesmen driving Gran Torino station wagons from the early 1970s with no shocks and Sears latex paint jobs; you take it in stride when you bump into a young writer named Martha Foose who lives in wrecked railroad cabooses on Pluto Plantation, and you don't bat an eye when she tells you her latest work is called "Darlin' It Hurts My Heart To See Your Trailer Rockin' in the Night" and that her heritage is "common Delta trash."

But it does give you pause to see a pair of brand-new, burgundy Cadillacs parked on a hill, a combined value of $60,000, to be raffled off for literacy.

That's right. Cadillacs for literacy.

The raffle was run by a group calling itself the "Human Emphatic Redevelopment Organization," or H.E.R.O., run by director Rick Williams.

Mr. Williams told us that more than 400,000 adults in Mississippi are functionally illiterate and that his group was about to set up nightly bingo games in Hattiesburg. The games will finance afternoon tutoring projects at the bingo hall, he said.

As the day turned to night — and the Ed the Blues Imperials rocked the crowd with the "Car Wash Blues" — people began filling out the $10 raffle tickets by the light of a small bulb in the Cadillacs' glove compartments.

By 1 a.m. most folks began trudging out of the cattle field, and those in tents, sleeping bags and recreational vehicles stayed over to be awakened by the sun coming up over the pines and a breakfast wagon serving up sausage, eggs and biscuits.

It was the first time, said co-organizer Fred Richardson, that the Chunky festival has turned even a modest profit.

"There are more BMWs down in the parking lot than any dealer has in this whole county," he said. "I wouldn't call this a blues Yuppie festival but it's something that people with an education will travel great distances to be a part of. We have a show that gets the crowd up on its feet. That's why we're growing while the local opera company is sinking.

"If it's a boogie lick," he explained, a breakfast Budweiser in hand, "then it's spontaneous combustion."

August 14, 1988

Mississippi, Part II:
Shrimp steamed in Old Bay and a not-for-sale souvenir from "Mr. Bill" Faulkner

OUR PATH HAD CUT A BIG SQUARE OUT OF THE MIDDLE OF MISSISSIPPI. ALREADY behind us were Flora, Canton, Jackson, Vicksburg and Greenville. We had genuflected in Tupelo at the Elvis Presley birthplace, had danced in Chunky with thousands at an all-day blues festival, and had seen some of the lowest Mississippi River water levels on record along the Delta.

With three days to go, Oxford and, just over the state line, Memphis, were still before us. We had yet to turn any Dixie folk on to seafood steamed with Old Bay seasoning and away from boiling it bland, and the car was filling up fast with junk.

One friend, Tyrone Crawley, bought used records, books and clothes at every roadside flea market we passed; and the other, Art Lien, was going nuts for fishing equipment.

Somewhere along the line, Artie bought four Huck Finn fishing poles: long pieces of bamboo with a line, a bobber and a simple hook. We had to step over them every time we got in the car. About the same time, he bought a wild turkey call for $5 and practiced from town to town.

And we hadn't even made it to the Graceland gift shops yet.

We left the river and Greenville in a dusky deluge celebrated by every farmer there — including plenty who had boogied the night before at a classic country juke joint in the middle of nowhere called the Tin House — and headed northeast on Route 6 to Oxford, home to 9,982 people, the University of Mississippi and Rowan Oak, the sleepy estate of William Faulkner.

If you think Baltimore has capitalized on H. L. Mencken, spend some time in Oxford to experience the cottage industry built around the ghost of the man they called Mr. Bill.

We arrived in Oxford well after midnight and took a room down the street at the Ole Miss Motel, where the doors are decorated by pink hearts with room numbers written on them. Our little Valentine was No. 32.

The next day, I had to file a story on the great drought of 1988 and all-time-low water on a river called mighty, and settled down at a computer in the Blues Archives of the university's Center for the Study of Southern Culture.

Suzanne Steele runs the quiet show at the archives, which hold the largest collection of blues documents — sheet music, records, books, articles, posters, interviews and videos — in the world. There's even a clay head with real hair on display of late bluesman Sam Chatmom — he of the fabled Mississippi Sheiks — sculpted by Delta slide guitarist James "Son" Thomas.

Just a night or two earlier, back down in Leland off Highway 61, Son had welcomed us and a tub of chicken into his home and hospitality.

"He loves another woman, and I love you," he sang in his fluid, eerie falsetto, accompanying himself on slide guitar. "But you love him, and stick to him like glue. Oh, when things go wrong, so wrong with you ... it hurts me too."

A former grave digger and sharecropper who has been a guest of Nancy Reagan at the White House, where his sculpture was honored, Son put down his guitar and stared at a poster of a toddler Elvis Presley we had brought him from Tupelo. The baby picture was unmarked, and Son had never seen it before.

Tracing his fingers around the child's face, particularly the lips, Son declared: "That's Elvis. I can tell by the mouth."

In between the songs, the chicken and a can of orange soda he asked us to bring along, Son played with his dog Snow, waved around a pistol he says he takes "to be prepared" every time he goes to Greenville's Nelson Street nightclub ghetto, and returned to the sad theme of never having anything to show for his labor.

"Money," said the man with the thin, creased face, "never comes to a poor man."

At the archives, Ms. Steele goes about her work in the shadow of dozens of T-shirts from blues societies across the nation that hang on the wall. Before we left, one from Baltimore looked down on her, too.

While I wrote about Mississippi "river rats" like *Vicksburg Evening Post* maritime reporter Fred Messina — "That big mean sucker just absolutely fascinates and scares the daylights out of me," he says — Tyrone and Artie searched Oxford for fresh shrimp.

Not only was the Old Bay still uncapped and waiting, but earlier, while browsing a bookstore in the town square where Mr. Bill squints at you from postcards, bookshelves and posters, we received an invitation to an evening cocktail party.

And we were determined to bring the flavor of the Land of Pleasant Living along with us.

Tyrone says the seafood store he found just outside Oxford was manned by college kids who followed the slow tradition of Southern hospitality. They wouldn't wait on more than two customers at a time and gave each person their undivided attention.

After boasting that he was going to "introduce a new sensation to the state of Mississippi," Tyrone, humbled, was directed to a nearby shelf lined with Old Bay. Apparently it doesn't move all that well, but the counter clerk was more than willing to steam our 5 pounds of shrimp on the spot.

Using our can of Old Bay, the guy decided to "try something new," according to Tyrone, and put the shrimp into an industrial steamer that looked like a refrigerator-sized oven. Using just a little bit of the Old Bay, he slopped a mess of butter on top of the shrimp and slid them into the steamer on trays, cooking a pound of the store's shrimp first as an experiment and then cooking all 5 pounds of ours at once.

The trick was a hit, with the butter taking an edge off the Old Bay and making for sweet shrimp with a faint sting. The help at the seafood store loved it, we loved it, and our new friends at the cocktail party, including students from France and a young scooter-riding woman masquerading as Zelda Fitzgerald, loved it.

By dawn, time was running out. The Faulkner home was our last and only Oxford stop before leaving Mississippi for Memphis and the gates of Graceland, but the big white house wasn't open when we got there. The only people around besides the three of us were an old guy driving a University of Mississippi tractor (the property is maintained by the school) and a couple from Ireland on a literary tour of the United States.

They were awfully nice, so we overlooked the slight — later apologized for — that they had skipped Baltimore, and along with it the grave of Edgar Allan Poe, the home of Mencken and the central branch of the Enoch Pratt Free Library.

Also in Baltimore is one very special writer who, as hard as this is to believe, made it very clear that she did not want a souvenir of Mississippi bearing the name, likeness or aura of Elvis Presley. I remembered this as I stumbled upon a little oak seedling, just about 4 inches tall, while strolling the Faulkner grounds.

While Tyrone engaged the tractor driver in conversation, I took a pen, used it for a shovel and worked fast to dig the thing up without killing it. I won't rationalize this act. I stole a tree from Mr. Bill's back yard in broad daylight with a felt-tipped pen and my bare hands. It's one of those things you just can't buy in a store.

Walking back to the car parked out front, I put the seedling in a plastic foam coffee cup, packed it with black Mississippi soil and used my hands to scoop rain water from a pothole to keep it moist. Setting it in an empty National Boh beer case surrounded by used books, I propped it up in the black window of the station wagon, and for the next 1,200 miles or so home we were a mobile greenhouse.

The little oak made it back to Baltimore in fine shape and the writer I gave it to, my wife, was wild about it. My 5-year-old son Jake and I dug a small hole in the back yard, carefully planted the tree and then, for good luck, sprinkled some orange "Magic Elvis Dirt" from Tupelo around it.

All was well until a few days later when I came home to find the prize on its side, uprooted, brown and brittle. My always innocent children, eyes wide and palms upturned, put the blame on a neighbor kid. I believed them.

Elvis might be alive, but the oak from Rowan Oak appears to be as dead as dead can be. After Oxford, it was on to Memphis and the big show at Graceland that is experienced by an average of about 4,500 people a day, 6,000 or more last week during the 11th anniversary of his death.

Meredith Phillips is the spokeswoman there, having worked her way up from a tour guide at the mansion, where she once escorted big-time Elvis fan Muhammad Ali through the house, to the front office.

This summer Miss Phillips has handled such luminaries as the heavy metal bands from Van Halen's "Monsters of Rock" tour, and the endless talk — neither officially confirmed nor denied by Graceland officials — that the King is still with us, somewhere.

"If you're a tour guide and you believe he's alive," said one of the estate's employees, "then you're allowed to say, 'I believe he's alive.'"

Talking to the guides and the other tourists was more fun than looking at all the Elvis stuff. When a guide announced that Elvis "died upstairs," a man from Texas turned to us and declared, "That's a crock. He died on the john and everybody knows it."

Another guide told us that the only people ever to be formally invited never to come back to Graceland were the Beastie Boys, juvenile New York rappers who had the gall to sit their beastly butts on the King's furniture.

"We believe they were drinking," the guide whispered. "No one who comes through here is more famous than Elvis. They should have more respect."

Finally, before being driven out of the gates to hop in our car and make the 20-hour drive back to Baltimore, we asked one of the guides what was the most unbelievably absurd question they'd ever been asked by a tourist.

"One lady," she said, "wanted to know if the bird noises in the trees outside were real or if they were piped into the trees."

It sounded reasonable to us.

August 21, 1988

A trip through the South shows
there are all kinds of monuments

IN NASHVILLE, PEOPLE ARE MOVING TO BUILD AN INVISIBLE MONUMENT TO AN invisible man. The friends of Otis Blackwell, the largely anonymous composer behind many of Elvis Presley's early hits, are moving fast here in Music City to complete his memorial before the great writer passes from this world to the next.

If they are successful, their tribute to the stroke-debilitated author of "Don't Be Cruel," "All Shook Up," and "Return to Sender," will be unlike any of the monuments I saw on a road trip of 3,200 miles through the American South this summer.

On that trip, in the mountain town of Marion at the far end of southwest Virginia, I waded through the book-cluttered apartment of John Mason Rudolph, a hustler of great literature, bad horses and his own legend.

The legacy of this native Baltimorean is scribbled on countless thousands of sheets of paper under the title, "Notes to Myself," a scrap collection amassed over the last quarter-century.

"I don't even know of a case history like mine that is on record. ... If there is, I'd sure like to read it," reads one of the notes, written, like the others, on napkins and the back of coffee stained envelopes and filed in any crack that will hold them. "Thomas Wolfe tried to unearth the Earth. He ate the world, spit it up, and ate it again. What am I unaware of?"

Just outside of Marion in the hills of Troutdale I went once again to see the stone and timber mansion of Sherwood Anderson, author of the enduring *Winesburg, Ohio* and a kindly inspiration to Faulkner and Hemingway. The house by Ripshin Creek is marked with a bronze government plaque claiming it for the historical register, but the plaque doesn't say why.

Read *Winesburg*, and you will know.

From Virginia, it was west to Tennessee, home of the twin rhythm cities of Nashville and Memphis.

Nashville boasts the Parthenon, an exact and mighty replica of the principal temple on the Acropolis in Athens and one of the most stunning sights in all of the New World: a monument to Nashville's centennial above modern highways and gas stations on 60 columns, housing a statue of the Goddess Athena 41 feet and 10 inches tall.

It is in Nashville where Otis Blackwell fights for his life every day and it is to Nashville I will shortly return to tell you about the monument without mortar being erected to the 59-year-old Blackwell.

A quick 210 miles away to the west, the river town of Memphis sits at the crown of the Mississippi Delta. There stands a besieged monument known as Graceland, generator of big tourist dollars and the former home of Elvis Presley, who is buried under the lawn.

The man who supplied Presley with so many million-selling songs had repeatedly refused to meet Elvis before the King died in 1977, believing it would break the spell. "Elvis and I both had a thing going that was super," Otis said in 1982. "Call it superstition, but I wanted to keep it."

From Memphis the tour headed south on Highway 61, the blues gateway immortalized for middle America by Bob Dylan, and I stopped in Clarksdale, Miss., to rattle the locked doors of the Delta Blues Museum and pick through records at the Stackhouse on Sunflower Avenue, buying a copy of "Negro Fife and Drum Music of the Deep South" for $7.99.

Steadily rolling south down the double-lane of 61 through Leland, birthplace of Johnny Winter and home to James "Son" Thomas, I took a little turn to pass through Rolling Fork, where on April 4, 1915, a boy named McKinley Morganfield was born. He grew up to be a man, a son-of-a-gun known from Baltimore to Tokyo as Muddy Waters.

The clerk at the convenience store didn't know, and the desk sergeant at the local police station didn't know, but I kicked around the deserted Sunday streets of Rolling Fork long enough to find a sign that the sleepy town at the crossroads of Highway 61 and Highway 14 had given birth to a monumental American artist.

On a little scrub of land near the corner of China and Ash streets stands a pathetic, unfinished wooden gazebo, the kind you might see in a suburban back-yard, unmarked and lopsided, a make-shift testimonial to the man who informed the world: "The blues had a baby, and they called it rock and roll ..."

Staring at the gazebo, I thought of Graceland and thought that even Elvis would have been shamed by the inequities of fortune.

Farther south I toured the vast Civil War battlefields of Vicksburg, where the monument to Illinois war dead alone has enough marble to duplicate every set of white steps in Baltimore; and several dozen miles below Vicksburg I stumbled upon the remote splendor of the Windsor Ruins.

Out beyond Port Gibson, in the green and lush middle of nowhere, tower Greek Revival columns rising to support nothing, a void conjuring wonder.

So beautiful was the Windsor Plantation that it moved the Union Army to spare it the wrath of victory; it burned to the ground a decade later during a grand ball. The columns and a historical marker remain.

No matter where you go you will discover such sites, arrogant and humble monuments of mystery and decay that stand or fall in testimony to man's deep pride.

But from Baltimore to Mississippi and back, I didn't see anything like the effort in Nashville to immortalize Otis Blackwell, who, when he wasn't writing for Elvis Presley found the time to pen "Great Balls of Fire" for Jerry Lee Lewis and "Fever," covered most notably in 1958 by Peggy Lee.

The Otis Blackwell Foundation intends to benefit composers and performers who have not had it quite so good as the man for whom it is named. If established, the foundation will serve as a benevolent health insurance fund for musicians.

Now being put together by the friends Blackwell has made over the years, the foundation is to be vested by money raised in a big "We Love You Otis" concert planned for the last week in March at the Ocean Center in Daytona Beach. Stars lined up to perform include B. B. King, Jerry Lee Lewis, Junior Walker, the Beach Boys, the Shirelles, Ronnie Dove, Freddie "Boom Boom" Cannon and Ray Peterson.

Once the revenue from the concert and albums and videos that result from it are invested, it is hoped that dividends from the trust will be enough for the foundation to give annual grants to old-time rock and rollers down on their luck.

"We hope to have money to help writers and artists of the old school who need help," said Mr. Peterson, who scored in the early 1960s with "Corina, Corina" and "Tell Laura I Love Her."

"We'd like to help anybody who needs hospitalization or medical care or who needs to eat," he said.

Otis Blackwell once told me that while he grew up poor in Brooklyn, every family had a piano.

"Even if you didn't have nothing to sleep on growing up, you had a damn piano," he said. "Everybody had an upright."

Now far removed from the health and poverty of his youth, Otis Blackwell's talent has given him little need for money. But there remain few people, even among the legion of Elvis Presley fans, who know that from his imagination sprang some of the primary planks in the foundation of rock and roll.

Said Mr. Peterson: "It's time now to do something for Otis."

It may not be seen, but it should be felt.

October 6, 1991

'You don't think it's going to be a hard life for a long time'

MY WILLINGNESS TO FOLLOW THE BLUES WHEREVER THEY LEAD HAS TAKEN ME down good roads and bad, from the rough end of Baltimore's Clinton Street to tin shacks in the distant fields of Mississippi. Not too long ago, I was drawn to a tiny apartment on the Lower East Side of Manhattan where my path would cross once again with New York slide guitarist Robert Ross.

I took the night train to Manhattan as autumn began its fade toward winter. Folded between layers of underwear in my suitcase lay a newly written short story about miracles and a mythical bluesman named Fat Hatted Ned, and in a chill box at my elbow were five pounds of Chesapeake crab meat picked in the kitchen of my Highlandtown rowhouse.

I was ready for anything, despite knowing that every time I travel to New York I leave with gratitude for a safe exit, despair for the future of humanity and a note to myself that Gotham does not represent all of American civilization.

Says the bluesman Ross: "If you can't get the blues in New York then you're immune."

On this trip I would not, as I had on previous trips, be tracking people intimate with the Bronx killers of a Maryland state trooper or sneaking into the Helmsley Palace hotel to interview maids who might have watched the top aide to a Maryland Congressman leap to his death from the 24th floor.

This time around, Robert Ross would entertain a dinner party with music he learned the hard way, and I would follow him by reading a fable of truths gleaned from the kind of life Mr. Ross chose for himself while still a teen-ager.

Non-spiritual nourishment was provided by 29 lump and golden cakes of *callinectes sapidus*, delicacies shaped and bound with bread crumbs, eggs, Old Bay seasoning, mayonnaise and the sweet meat of end-of-the-season female crabs bought back home on Highland Avenue.

On the street below the apartment where the gig was held, down off the corner of Stanton and Orchard Streets, people born in lands from around the world celebrated a sunny Columbus Day weekend buying and selling luggage and pork chops and neckties and chorizo; a colorful bazaar in daylight, but a deserted and frightening place after dusk when merchants bring down steel security doors and the shoppers retreat.

On this Sunday it was warm enough to throw the windows open, and the sounds of the street wafted into the party as Mr. Ross plugged his 1969 Gibson SG guitar into a parlor stereo, sat in a corner, and began to pick the Elmore James classic featured on his new compact disc "Rockin' the Rails."

"When things go wrong, so wrong with you, it hurts me, too," the bluesman wailed, his voice rough and pliant and booming through the $700-a-month closet of an apartment, no more than two postage stamps and a kitchen in a neighborhood that would pass for a slum in most other cities.

In a quarter-century of playing the blues for love and money, more than a few things have gone wrong for Robert Ross on his way to becoming a respected but largely unknown practitioner of the art.

On the good end, the 42-year-old has performed with some of the biggest names in the history of blues: Muddy Waters, Willie Dixon, Big Mama Thornton, Sam "Lightning" Hopkins, Sonny Terry and Brownie McGhee, Jimi Hendrix, Bo Diddley, Big Joe Turner, Sunnyland Slim, John Below, John Brim, Homesick James, Johnny Winter, Louisiana Red, Otis Rush, Wilbert Harrison, Memphis Slim and a one-armed harmonica player named John Wrencher.

Mr. Ross has jammed for spare change in the Paris subway, taken the blues to shut-ins committed to nursing homes, been flown by big-shots to Switzerland for one-night stands at private parties and gigged in countless "amazing dumps" between Maine and Florida.

I first met him in April of 1981 when he accompanied the great J.B. Hutto at No Fish Today, the defunct and legendary Baltimore club on Eutaw Street destroyed by arson in January, 1982.

"There were nights when I was doing my own gigs and wasn't getting anything, a buck or two bucks a night," said Mr. Ross, recalling one road trip when a van's steering wheel came off in his hands while approaching a toll booth. "We slept in that van in Boston in the middle of the winter. It was a lot of fun, but mostly I remember being on the road and being cold, six degrees in Rhode Island and no heat, and we were dying. It's been a lot of disappointments, a lot of back-stabbing, a lot of embarrassment, and a lot of humiliation.

"When you're young, you think this isn't going to last long," he said. "You believe that any day now you're going to be rich and famous, and people are going to realize how wonderful you are. You don't think it's going to be a hard life for a long time."

The hard road remains his way of life, with his biggest payday in 1980 when a $793 royalty check arrived as payment for writing "Sitting in the Jailhouse," a rocking blues recorded by Johnny Winter on an album titled "Raisin' Cain."

He isn't rich or famous, but the dozen or so people who heard Mr. Ross at the literary blues gig on Stanton Street thought he was most wonderful; they bought a few copies of his new record and now follow him to performances in Manhattan and New Jersey, another handful of supporters on the long haul.

While the blues are a constant part of what it means to be human, they remain a cyclical fad in public taste. A minor blues revival has been under way in New York City for a little more than a year in the midst of the Great Bush Recession and perhaps Robert Ross' career will be helped by it.

I followed Mr. Ross to a spot at the front of the party and read "Nine Weeks With Saint Jude," an unpublished story about a Mississippi Delta bluesman who travels to Baltimore to make a Novena at the Saint Jude shrine on Paca Street.

The story is for me what the blues are for Mr. Ross: devotion to protracted labor without any assurance of reward.

When the reading was over, the crab cakes all but gone and most of the guests on their way home, Mr. Ross and I talked about the kind of faith it takes to travel unguided roads.

"Since I was 16 years old, I've been hoping and praying and working toward getting more recognition than I have, and I've always thought it was right around the corner," he said.

"It hasn't worked out that way, but the most important thing is you have to enjoy the process. I suspect it to be real easy to enjoy success, but if you can enjoy the gradual process of getting there and not take the disappointments too hard, life is a lot more entertaining."

December 1, 1991

The Richard Manuel Indulgence Tour

LATE LAST MONTH, I TRAVELED FROM MY HIGHLANDTOWN ROWHOUSE TO THE Grotto of Our Lady of Lourdes in Emmitsburg; a Catholic Worker house in Cleveland; and on to Champaign, Ill., to write and deliver the Prayer of the Faithful at a Roman Catholic wedding.

At every turn, I carried prayers for Richard Manuel alive in my heart.

By the time I made it back to Macon Street, it was Nov. 2: All Souls Day.

Although educated Catholic from grade school through Loyola College, I don't ever remember celebrating or understanding All Souls Day, which honors the eternal spirits of the faithful departed.

This year, for the first time, I consciously observed the 1,005-year-old custom and dedicated it to the soul of Richard Manuel, a rock and roll piano player raised Baptist in Ontario and known throughout the world as one of the voices of The Band.

Gentle, gifted, supra-sensitive and alcoholic, Manuel tightened a belt around his neck in a motel bathroom in Winter Park, Fla. on March 4, 1986, hooked the strap to the shower curtain rod, and sat down hard.

I did not take much notice of the death because I had not yet begun to pay much attention to The Band.

Best known for songs like "Up On Cripple Creek," "The Weight," and "The Night They Drove Old Dixie Down," The Band helped Bob Dylan cross Electric Avenue from folk to rock and toured the world with him in 1974.

In the last year, the beauty of The Band has been revealed to me the way America's cornfields first spoke to Sherwood Anderson. Before leaving for the wedding in Champaign, I held a small party to watch "The Last Waltz," Martin Scorsese's documentary about The Band's 1976 Thanksgiving farewell concert.

Before the film rolled, my old friend Michael Reeb from *The Sun* sports department asked if he could say a few words. Reebie, who witnessed the music of Levon Helm, Robbie Robertson, Rick Danko, Garth Hudson and Richard Manuel 18 times before the Band's demise, opened a new book he'd just bought.

Quoting Levon Helm in *This Wheel's On Fire*, the drummer's story of his life with The Band, Mike read a passage about Manuel's funeral:

". . . Garth played, 'I Shall Be Released,' which Bob Dylan had written for Richard to sing. . . . I had a funny experience while Garth was playing. I was thinking about Richard and asking myself why, when I clearly heard Richard's voice in the middle of my head. It came in as clear as a good radio signal. And he said, 'Well Levon, this was the one action I could take that was gonna really shake things up. It's gonna shake 'em up and change things round some more, because that's what needs to happen.' "

Shake 'em on down.

Near the middle of the movie, Scorsese pulls his camera from the magnet of Robbie Robertson's ego for a moment to consider Richard Manuel — supine on a couch, eyes deep, brown and glazed. He is explaining how The Band got its name.

"It was right in the middle of that whole psychedelia and Chocolate Subway and Marshmallow Overcoats, those kind of names, you know," says Manuel. "And we started out with the Crackers. We tried to call ourselves the Honkies. You know, everybody kind of backed off from that, you know. It was too straight, you know. So we just decided . . . just to call ourselves The Band."

With his long, shaggy hair, thick black beard and liquid eyes, Richard Manuel looked to me like an original disciple of Christ.

"He looks like John the Baptist," said Glenn Donithan, a friend at the party.

In that moment I was struck with the notion that if Manuel could shake things up from the other side by robbing the world of his talent, then perhaps I might do the same for him from this side of the Jordan.

Something told me to pray for this poor man.

The sensation reminded me of Naomia Stiers, an 87-year-old woman from Hot Springs, Ark., whom I interviewed at Graceland during the annual observance of Elvis Presley's death in 1991. Celebrated as the world's oldest Elvis fan, Miss Naomia explained what drew her to a teen-age heart throb in 1956 when she was 52.

She said: "The first time I saw him on television, it just seemed to me that he was pleading with me to love him."

Something like that passed between me and the sad, addled visage of Richard Manuel.

And it told me to pray.

Two days later, through plans made long before "The Last Waltz" played in my parlor, I was at the Grotto of Our Lady of Lourdes in Emmitsburg.

There, on a wooded hillside where Elizabeth Ann Seton prayed to the Virgin Mary, a shrine has been erected for believers to give thanks and ask for help. Near a statue of the Virgin and a small stream were instructions on gaining a "plenary indulgence."

Plenary indulgences are something like Catholic parole for the souls of the living and the dead. Ritual prayers, they seek deliverance from punishment for sin, even if the sin has been confessed and forgiven.

Plenary indulgence wipes the slate clean; partial indulgence achieves freedom by degrees. Pilgrims to Emmitsburg, a shrine sanctioned by the Vatican, may take advantage of either. But since I wasn't there on one of Mary's feast days or a weekend, the only option was a partial indulgence — a process by which you can earn relief for yourself or others in increments of 500 days.

To do this, signs instruct you to recite a "Hail Mary" along with prayers for the pope and the invocation: "O Mary, Virgin and Mother of God, pray to Jesus for me."

But instead of praying for myself, I prayed for Richard Manuel and, without thinking, I failed to pray for the pope. Could the omission negate the effort? Did Manuel's soul only benefit from a mere 250 days of grace?

I have no idea what Richard Manuel believed (from day to day I am often unsure of what I believe), but certainly this man with a voice like sweet air had fallen to an awfully bad place upon drinking one more of his innumerable bottles of Grand Marnier before hanging himself.

If, as I have seen painted on the side of a Smith Island crab shanty, "Prayer Changes Things," how could a sincere petition on behalf of a suicide fail to do something?

As I knelt in the Grotto and prayed, my mind wandered to Manuel's fragile falsetto as it moved through the verses of his signature song, the one that Bobby Dylan wrote just to hear him sing it.

". . . any day now . . . any day now . . . I shall be released. . . ."

The next day I was in Cleveland, knocking on the door of the Catholic Worker house on Whitman Avenue to trade my dish-washing skills for a bed and a meal.

Part of the legacy of the Catholic social worker Dorothy Day, Whitman House gives away food and shelters the mentally ill.

During my short time there, I met a Quaker environmentalist and a young woman who joined the community right out of high school only to find herself without faith after giving away eight years of her life and thousands of meals.

A former convent, Whitman House sits behind St. Patrick's, an old stone church with a cobbled aisle to the altar. After a communal meal of noodles and cabbage, I helped with the dishes and wandered toward the church because the lights were on.

Inside, a priest lectured a group of older people about peaceful living in the modern world. When he finished, I paused at the statue of the Virgin and said a Hail Mary for Richard Manuel.

Two days later, I was in Champaign, banging out a list of petitions on a 1930s Remington Rand portable typewriter I bought for $20 two years ago from a storefront preacher at the corner of Baltimore Street and Central Avenue.

My good friends Allie Scott and Kathy Neal were home from Bangkok to get married before family, friends, and God and they wanted me to write and deliver the Prayer of the Faithful.

While soliciting prayers for the bride's deceased grandparents from the marble altar, I mentioned all the penitents in purgatory, adding a silent request of my own for the soul of Richard Manuel.

After Al and Kathy flew off to honeymoon in Ireland, I pointed my Subaru east for home. All Souls Day was drawing near, but I did not know it. Before this year, I could not have told you when it was observed.

Tuesday, Nov. 2, found me in a pew at Holy Redeemer Chapel on Oldham Street, the church where my father's mother carried me to Mass in the 1960s. At 35, I was the youngest person in the chapel by at least 30 years.

Advising the congregation that it was good and proper to pray for the souls of the dead — particularly those of family members — the priest quoted Saint Monica, mother of Saint Augustine. "Bury this body where you please," Monica is supposed to have said, "but never forget me at the altar of the Lord. . . ."

Her words reminded me of a lyric by Mississippi bluesman Robert Johnson: "You may bury me by the highway side ... Baby, I don't care where you bury my body when I'm dead and gone. . . . You may bury me by the highway side, so my ole evil spirit, can get a Greyhound bus and ride ..."

Walking back from the communion rail, it occurred to me that most certainly I was the only one there offering prayers for a dead rock and roll singer instead of a loved one. There was a twinge of shame, but that is where I stood.

The same day, I ferried an "All Souls Day" envelope with a dollar on the inside and Richard Manuel's name on the outside to the altar of the Basilica of the Assumption on Cathedral Street, where, every day this month, Masses have been celebrated for the souls of the Christian dead.

Reading an explanation of the ritual in the church bulletin, I could not help but picture Richard Manuel with a head full of booze, a heart full of soul and a belt around his neck.

The bulletin explained: "... at the moment of death, we are not always the kind of persons we should be for all eternity ... For this reason, we pray for the deceased that God may grant them a vision of His glory."

Any day now, sweet Richard.

Any day.

November 28. 1993

A musician who went to work every day

FRANK ZAPPA'S MOST VIVID MEMORY OF HIS EARLY CHILDHOOD IN THE 4600 block of Park Heights Avenue was watching the knife grinder roll through the neighborhood.

''Down the alley used to come the knife-sharpener man, you know, a guy with the wheel,'' he reminisced in 1986. ''And everybody used to come down off their back porch to the alley to get their knives and scissors done.''

In a long conversation ambling along 20 years of a global musical career, Frank's story about the man who pushed a grinding wheel through the alleys of Baltimore stayed with me the longest.

One day, on the obituary page, I saw a notice for longtime knife grinder Pio Vidi and telephoned his survivors for an article about the art of laying a fine edge on blades of steel.

Old Pio, said his relatives, could make a meat cleaver sing. And Frank Zappa could make an electric guitar do anything he wanted. Frank joined Pio in death on Saturday, succumbing to prostate cancer nearly 53 years to the day after his birth in Baltimore's old Mercy Hospital.

In all of music — from the do-wop he loved and parodied as a young turk to the orchestral complexities he composed in middle age — there was no one like Frank Zappa. In an adolescent letter to his "Aunt Mary" Cimino in Baltimore from his parents' new residence in the Mojave Desert, Frank wrote: "Could you find some space for me if I were to come and visit? I think I have invented something new in the way of music (probably not) which I would like to take to the conservatory back there for investigation."

Something new?

It wasn't Beatlemania.

The sounds that came from Frank Zappa's guitar were often sacred, the lyrics that fell from his lips were more often profane, and the intellect behind both was world-class. "I'll put my brains up against anybody," he said.

And often did, as Tipper Gore and the United States Senate found out in 1985 when Mr. Zappa testified against efforts to censor rock music or anything else

179

guaranteed in a free society.

After my story on the Vidi family's 100-year-old knife-grinding dynasty appeared in *The Sun*, I called Frank up to tell him about it. It was early in 1991 and he was already fighting cancer, which had caused him to cancel a 50th-birthday concert in his honor.

We talked pleasantly for a while about old-time Baltimore — even the fig tree behind his maternal grandparents' former home at 2019 Whittier Avenue — but it didn't hold his interest. Frank politely suggested that a good reporter might better spend his time digging up dirt on the crooks who run the country instead of chasing after dead Italian men who sharpened knives for a living. He talked about the endless absurdities and offenses he witnessed every day on C-Span.

"Geezy, Frank," I said. "Why do you let politics eat at you like that? Sounds like you're becoming Lenny Bruce in your old age."

This made him very angry.

"Lenny Bruce was a drug addict who ruined his talent and killed himself," he barked. "I'm a musician who goes to work every day."

It was our last conversation.

When Frank went public with his sickness, I mailed the knife-grinding story and a get-well card to his Los Angeles home.

Mud sharks and muffin men.

Jelly roll gum drops.

And penguins in bondage.

With a comic-book imagination, the spark and nuance of a virtuoso, a basement baritone and composing talent he credited to the public library, Frank Zappa made rock and roll like nobody ever made it before. He didn't fill a hole in rock, he carved a wild kingdom inside of it.

"Until I was 20 I never wrote a rock and roll song," he told me. "The only stuff I was writing was chamber music and orchestra music, but I couldn't get any of it played. So what do you do? You go where the action is."

In 1974, inside my tilted universe, Frank Zappa was action.

Every morning, while adjusting our minds to face another day of Catholic education at Mount Saint Joseph High School, my brother Danny and I listened to Frank while cruising to Irvington in our old man's yellow Mustang, with "Overnight Sensation" rolling inside the eight-track. I never got around to memorizing Eliot's "The Waste Land," but I could recite every orgasmic line of "Dinah-Moe Humm."

In "Camarillo Brillo," Frank ragged on the Earth Mother cool of the early Seventies: "Is that a real poncho, I mean is that a Mexican poncho or is that a Sears poncho?"

And in "Dirty Love," he simply asked us to give it to him.

Of all the insights Frank shared with hundreds of reporters and millions of fans in the last quarter-century, my favorite addressed the spirituality conjured when man coaxes sounds from inside of himself.

"Music," he said, "is the only religion that delivers the goods on Earth."

December 8, 1993

"I learned from my father..."

CHAPTER 7

The Groaning Board

Father's pizza secret stays safe with his son

WHEN MATTEO (MATTHEW) CIOCIOLO DIED 34 YEARS AGO TODAY, THE Highlandtown pizza maker left his baking secrets to his son, Frank, and apparently no one else.

If his heart stopped beating tomorrow, Frank Ciociolo says the recipe for Matthew's pizza — celebrated around the state and as far off as Florida and New York — would die with him.

"I learned from my father and we just kept it to ourselves," said Frank, who hoped to become a barber after his World War II Navy discharge but got caught up in the family business. "If my son was interested, I would have taught him the trade."

The trade stands without distinction in a former row house across from the Patterson Theatres. Clean, spare and modest, Matthew's Pizzaria at 3131 Eastern avenue is an east side landmark as genuine as the Pagoda, and as important to its patrons as the No. 10 bus downtown.

"I'm getting third generations in here," said Frank. "I remember their grandparents."

Many a wise father (like old Matthew Ciociolo, whose portrait hangs behind the counter) has taught his children to find one thing they enjoy doing, and do it well. The only food Matthew's sells, and has ever sold, is pizza — inexpensive "Italian tomato pies," made from scratch.

Matthew's success was publicly confirmed in 1983 when Baltimore Magazine named its pies the best in town. An editor there said the honor was awarded after several Baltimoreans of varying backgrounds and unassailable good taste urged the magazine to sample Matthew's fare.

Bill Stern, once a partner in Sascha's Cafe, was one of those people. (Another Matthew's booster was Sascha Woldhandler herself, now a respected local caterer.)

"I'm from New York and [after moving here] I went all over Baltimore looking for the definitive pizza," said Mr. Stern, now a public relations official for MCI Communications in Washington. "Some were very good, like Squire's in Dundalk, but then I homed into Matthew's. There's something very special about it. The crust isn't too thick or too thin, and their mozzarella has a little punch to it."

Asked for a more detailed description, Mr. Stern balked.

"I just like it, that's enough for me," he said. "Don't dissect it, eat it."

Matthew's small (9 inch) tomato and cheese pie is $2.55, with large adding an inch and 20 cents to the tab. Cheese comes in grated parmesan, somewhat of an oddity, or shredded mozzarella.

Onions (diced, not sliced) are 40 cents extra and the rest — Spanish anchovies, green olives sliced big as nickels, pepperoni, mushrooms, and green pepper — are 60 cents each. Frozen, take-out pies are $2.10 for small, $2.25 for large. Prices, the family said, have not changed in four years.

Matthew's petite sizes, another oddity in this day of 16-inch bicycle-rim pizzas, came long before Pizza Hut began marketing its "personal pan" pies.

"We started with 9 and 10 inches and never changed," said Jenny Perticone, Frank's 68-year-old sister, who began helping her dad when he first opened. "People are satisfied, we're satisfied."

Howard G. Myers, gobbling up a pepperoni pie on a recent evening, said he's had his pizza pangs regularly satisfied at Matthew's for over 20 years.

"I like the flavor of 'em, it's great," said Mr. Myers, a 54-year-old city worker. "The crust is better than all the others. A lot of places the crust is so hard you can't eat it. This is like bread."

"That's what everybody says," said Jenny, smiling wide.

The light airy bread crust rises high from the bottom of Matthew's pizza, forcing the owners to sell their pies wrapped in cardboard plates and paper. Boxes are too flimsy to hold them.

The bright sauce is subtly sweet with an even consistency, far from the dark red glop served up by lackadaisical pizza hucksters. It doesn't just sit atop the crust, it slowly seeps into the bread, lacing the pie with flavor.

As a student, East Baltimore Councilman John A. Schaefer (D, 1st) courted his wife, Joanna, over pizzas at Matthew's, eating his first pie there some 30 years ago.

"I like anchovies," Mr. Schaefer said, revealing the mark of a serious pizza man, "and their anchovy pizza is fantastic."

Many pizza joints are liberal with their pepperoni, but right stingy when it comes to the anchovy — you're often lucky to get a half-dozen on a large pie. Frank Ciociolo lays two full-sized fish on every slice, and sprinkles a hint of black pepper over the pie to complement the saltiness.

"I've been all over for a good pizza, even the ones in New York don't compare," Mr. Schaefer continued. "I can't say enough about it. Nothing but accolades from me."

Yet so protected is the decades-old key to this success that Frank Ciociolo says he cooks his sauce and completes most of the day's preparation before his help arrives. The 60-year-old Towson resident claims that he has not shared his father's recipe with his wife, his children, or sister Jenny.

An Italian immigrant who arrived in Baltimore at the turn of the century, Matteo Ciociolo began life in America as a baker, working in a variety of bakeries around Little Italy and specializing in Italian bread.

Having perfected the crust, the crucial foundation for any popularity-bound pizza, Ciociolo set out on establishing his first pizza parlor in 1943 at 3413 Gough Street near Highland Avenue.

Four years later, with son Frank beside him in a baker's apron, Ciociolo moved his business into the rowhouse where it operates today.

While Frank stands mum on the recipe — saying the only person who will find it out is the person who buys the place from him when he retires — frequent visits to Matthew's have revealed a few basic qualities of its pies.

Here is a recipe that should approximate, even if it can't duplicate, the legend left by Matthew Ciociolo.

Italian tomato pie with anchovies and onion

To bake a quality pizza pie, your sauce should be made from home-canned tomatoes and, as the Ciociolo family apparently does, with freshly kneaded Italian bread dough for the crust.

Pizza dough:
> 2 envelopes dry yeast
> $1/2$ cup lukewarm water (105-115 degrees)
> 1 3/4 cups water
> 7 cups bread flour
> 1 teaspoon salt
> olive oil

Stir the yeast into the warm water and let it sit for 10 minutes. Add one cup of flour to form a very soft starter dough. Cover with a cloth and let rest in a warm place for about an hour.

Add 1 $3/4$ cups water (olive oil can be substituted for $1/4$ cup of this water for a slightly softer crust) and the salt, mixing well. Start adding the flour, a cup at a time, until the dough becomes too stiff to stir. Turn it out on a floured board and continue kneading in the rest of the flour, using the heel of your hand to push forward and pull back. As you work (about 10 minutes to knead) the dough should become smoother and more elastic. Divide the dough into six portions, place them on a floured surface and cover with a cloth to let rise. They should double in size. Judge by eye. It should take one to two hours. Punch them down after risen, and knead until each can be worked into a circle.

When pizza sauce is ready, flatten into $1/2$-inch thick circular shell onto a pan greased with olive oil.

Fresh pizza sauce:

Begin with home-canned tomatoes. (If you haven't canned your own already and don't feel like waiting until next summer to try this recipe, substitute canned Italian plum tomatoes.)

To can tomatoes:

Check canning jars for nicks and cracks and sterilize. Wash a basket of ripe tomatoes and boil them for one minute in scalding water. Peel and cut in quarters. Wash fresh basil and put one piece basil in each jar.

Fill each jar with tomatoes one quarter inch from top of jar. Add 1 teaspoon salt to each quart of tomatoes, and a half-teaspoon salt for pints. Secure lids on jars.

Process canned tomatoes in a boiling water bath in large pot: 45 minutes for quarts, 35 minutes for pints. Remove, let cool on shelves. They are ready to use when cooled.

Use home-canned tomatoes as base for pizza sauce. In frying pan, saute a small onion and a garlic clove with two tablespoons of olive oil. Add one quart tomatoes and two tablespoons tomato paste to pan with $1/4$ teaspoon oregano, salt and pepper as desired, and pinch of sugar. Simmer 15 to 20 minutes. Ladle over pizza dough.

Spread grated mozzarella cheese (Stella's, 3815 Eastern Avenue in Highlandtown, sells a top-grade imported mozzarella, as do other Italian specialty food shops in the area) over pie, lay 6 to 8 Spanish anchovy filets (also available at Stella's) on pie, and dice a firm, medium-sized onion to sprinkle over pie.

Preheat oven at 400 degrees and bake for 15 to 20 minutes at 425 degrees.

February 6, 1985

Son regrets that he and father worked side-by-side, but never saw eye-to-eye

NICK FILIPIDIS WANTS TO KNOW: HOW CAN A GUY SPEND HIS ENTIRE LIFE WITH HIS father and never feel like he knew the man? It's not a question that vexes Mr. Filipidis simply because today is Father's Day.

It is something he thinks about all the time.

"I worked alongside my father every day for the majority of my life," says Mr. Filipidis, who grew up in Jimmy's Restaurant at 801 S. Broadway, the diner his Greek-immigrant father started in 1944. "But there's so much I just don't understand. I try to figure it out and get angry, sad or sentimental. I miss him."

The worst thing that ever happened to Nick Filipidis, he says, was his Dad's death in 1987.

To this day, the heavy Old World accent of his father's voice swims through his head.

"Always," said Mr. Filipidis yesterday, his eyes welling up in an office above the family business, tears of love and frustration for a tough old man. "I hear it all the time."

And they weren't even close.

Not like little Nicky always wanted them to be.

Or believes they could have been if his father hadn't worked himself to death becoming a success in America.

"He worked every day from the time he woke up until the time he went to sleep," said Mr. Filipidis, 47. "I was with him most of the time — near him physically, but I wasn't really with him, if you know what I mean. His mind was always on something else, always on work. He had something driving him, and I never found out what it was."

James Nicholas Filipidis was born on the Greek island of Andros in 1916.

He left the family village and went to sea when he was 16, eventually making his way to New York, where he went to work for an uncle who owned a diner in Hastings-on-the-Hudson in 1937. When World War II erupted, he joined the Army, which traded him citizenship for his service.

Discharged with chronic ulcers in 1942, Jimmy Filipidis came to Baltimore to work for another uncle, a man named Odesseos who ran a hot dog stall in the old Broadway Market shed.

After a few years with his uncle, Mr. Filipidis bought a candy store on the southeast corner of Broadway and Lancaster Street, renamed it Jimmy's, and ran it as a confectionery with his wife Helen.

The couple sold groceries, comic books, over-the-counter medicines, women's hosiery, breakfast, hamburgers, submarine sandwiches, milkshakes and hot dogs served at the counter or through a window that opened to the sidewalk.

The couple worked hard, had four kids, and made money.

In 1955, Uncle Odesseos died and left Jimmy Filipidis a restaurant on the northeast corner of Broadway and Lancaster, now a rock club called Max's on Broadway. In 1960, Mr. Filipidis turned the building into a nightclub called the Acropolis, a seaman's bar known for belly-dancers who did the shimmy-and-shake from table to table.

Running two businesses was not enough, and about 1962, Mr. Filipidis bought 64 acres in Harford County and made it a working farm of pigs, chickens, cows and sheep.

Whether at Jimmy's, the Acropolis, or the farm, the family was expected to work shoulder-to-shoulder with the head of the house, a man who simply could not stand idle.

Because the work never ended, Nick Filipidis grew to hate the restaurant and the farm. He joined the Army and later went away to college.

After a particularly bad argument in 1976, father and son didn't talk to one another for some time. Nick left the family business to work for the gas and electric company until the older man stopped his son one day and said he wanted to give him the restaurant.

The boy turned the gift down, offering to buy it instead.

Said Nick: "I never would have felt it was mine."

Although retired, Jimmy Filipidis stayed on at the restaurant to help. He didn't really slow down until early 1987, when a doctor said he had cancer of the stomach and liver.

He lived for six weeks and died on April 25, 1987, at the age of 71.

Looking back, Nick remembers a good man with a soft heart and a hard head.

He said: "My father was the kind of guy who only knew one way to drive a nail — grab a hammer and bang it."

Today is Father's Day, and Nick Filipidis has planned a picnic with his wife, his son and his in-laws.

And somewhere in the back of his mind, Nick will hear the voice of a stern man with a thick accent who never had time for such foolishness as picnics or ballgames or trips to the zoo.

"Father's Day was just another work day for him," said Mr. Filipidis. "If I had ever asked him to go on a picnic, he would have said: 'You want hot dogs?

Grill 'em here.'"

Mr. Filipidis nurses a lot of heartache, but he doesn't blame his father. He doesn't think his old man knew any other way.

But he does wish his Dad were around to witness how the old business has prospered.

Not to count the cash at the end of the day, but to see for himself that his only son is a success — a businessman who serves breakfast, lunch, and dinner to thousands of people every week; whose clientele includes U.S. senators and the governor of Maryland; who just this month was host to the First Lady of the United States when Hillary Rodham Clinton ate at Jimmy's on a visit to Baltimore.

Said Mr. Filipidis: "My father wasn't one to give praise. He never told me: 'You did good.' "

The father of a 17-year-old — a kid who just happens to be named Jimmy — Nick Filipidis is asked if he ever tells the boy that he's proud of him.

"All the time," he said. "A man's self-confidence doesn't just come from himself."

Sunday, June 20, 1993

Paczkis and sweet sacrifices

DON'T LET THE NAME FOOL YOU.

Marianna Frederick is as Polish as paczki, the doughy, deep-fried confection from Poland eaten with gusto today before the long and sacrificial season of Lent begins in the Christian world.

Pronounced "punchkie," in the local dialect, these globular goodies of sweet cream and yeast, good butter and sugar were once whipped up in kitchens throughout Polish Baltimore, particularly in Canton and Curtis Bay and especially at this time of year, when "punchkie parties" were common.

These days, many of the young people fueling the waterfront renaissance in southeast Baltimore happen by Marianna's store of Polish treats and trinkets — located across from Holy Rosary school on South Chester Street — and remember where they came from.

Today, they will stroll in to the aroma of fresh paczki, all lined up at 50 cents apiece.

"The old Poles are dying or moving out or dying and their families are selling the old houses," says Marianna, whose mother was born in Poland and whose maiden name is Groah, an American bastardization of the Polish word for peas.

"But when the weather breaks, the young people walk in and look around and say, 'You know, my grandmother was Polish —' "

And then Marianna — a self-proclaimed "true Polish citizen of Baltimore" — schools the youngsters on things they should already know.

My maternal grandmother, Anna, was Polish and lived her entire life in the shadow of St. Casimir's parish at 2729 Dillon St. A cannery house worker and industrial seamstress, Bushi didn't have the time or energy for the three-hour process of making golden brown paczki dimpled with raisins and dusted with powdered sugar.

But her daughter Gloria, my mother, had a best friend named Angie Hetmanski, and Angie's mother was a cook at St. Casimir's rectory who every year made paczki on the day before Ash Wednesday.

"When punchkie day rolled around, you could always count on Miss Hetmanski to do her thing, and I was always fortunate to be in her kitchen. She was a very gentle woman, and you knew it when you were in her presence," my mother remembers. "The raisins and sometimes minced nuts were added separately to each punchkie, never mixed into the dough. Then she deep fried them and let them cool before they were sprinkled with powdered sugar."

Whether it be Mardi Gras or Shrove Tuesday, the glee and gluttony that usher in Lent are practiced throughout the Christian world. Baked goods are common to the day, perhaps because the making of them helps clear the pantry of butter and eggs.

Goodbye to foods of comfort. Goodbye to plenty. Hello to carnival, which means "goodbye to meat."

"Have some jam with your tea," says a character in an Anton Chekhov short story about the start of the Easter season. "Tomorrow the great fast begins. Eat well today."

In England, they feast on pancakes. In New Orleans, gumbo is the fattening fare. Swedes savor semlor, cardamom-flavored buns with almond and whipped cream.

And in Venice, they gorge upon sweets that patrons of Vaccaro's would die for.

Here, in our own Poland along the Patapsco, it's paczki.

"You've got to eat them warm. If you don't, it's just a regular doughnut," says the former Elaine Fabizak, whose elderly neighbor on South Streeper Street makes paczki year-round. "The dough has to rise, and you punch it down and let it rise again. A lot of people just make a regular doughnut and put raisins in it and call it a punchkie. That's not a punchkie. By the time [a bogus] punchkie hits the bottom of your stomach, it's a stone."

Genuine paczki were plentiful at Holy Rosary church hall this past Sunday and Marianne Frederick makes them at her shop, Polish Treasures, year-round. Sometimes, says Marianna, the Safeway will carry a version of punchkie for a day or two, and Harry's Bakery at Fleet Street and Montford Avenue will be selling scores of them today at 59 cents each.

Tomorrow, the 40 days of Lent begin and the well-meaning will strive to give up sweets along with habits as harmful to the soul as tooth.

March 7, 2000

STORYTELLER

CALLIE LIPKIN 1999

"It's so hot the chickens are standing in line to get plucked..."

CHAPTER 8

Deadline

For final few, turning out lights isn't easy

DOZENS OF BALTIMORE ORIOLES FANS LINGERED ALL OVER MEMORIAL STADIUM after the tears and hoopla died down last evening; loyal fans savoring old memories and a ballpark the Orioles decided they didn't need any more.

As ushers asked, ordered, and pleaded with fans to go home, sisters Jackie Gordon and Janine Sheeler and their niece Elizabeth Johnson sat in seats behind home plate waiting for the lights to go out.

Sheeler had one picture left in her camera and she wanted to get one of the lights going out for the last time. As the trio waited for the place to go dark, Sheeler went hunting for souvenirs.

"I went up to get some bunting, but there were four ushers up there and they wouldn't even let me down in the mezzanine," said Sheeler. "And then I wanted to take a banner and a policeman told me it was city property."

"Five times I've asked you now to leave, five times," said an exasperated usher as they sat waiting.

Finally, after being told that the lights wouldn't go out until after clean-up crews were finished picking up trash, the women settled for having their picture taken together before walking out.

On the way, they brushed by Donna Beth Joy Shapiro, a local art deco expert who attended scores of ballgames with her mother and father while growing up in Baltimore.

"They just kicked us out of the upper deck," said Shapiro, who was dressed in black from head to toe and was wearing Victorian mourning jewelry to show her sadness at the passing of the stadium.

Her grief grew when she noticed that the stadium's memorial urn — a metal vase filled with a teaspoon of soil from every American military cemetery around the world — was missing from its perch behind glass inside the front of the stadium.

"The dead fly is still behind the glass, but where's the urn?" Shapiro asked.

At the end of a corridor outside of the players' clubhouse, fans stood around to get autographs from players. On the west side of the parking lot, Clarence

"Clancy the Beer Man" Haskett and other vendors held a tail-gate party for their regular customers.

"A lot of people don't want to leave," said Haskett, who met his wife while selling beer at the stadium. "I felt a few tears, I don't want to leave."

At least one fan couldn't leave.

Shawn Catayas, 23, of Carney, didn't get out of the stadium until a little before 8 p.m., six hours after the game started.

Catayas couldn't have left if he wanted to — his hands were cuffed behind him and he was locked behind iron bars in the police detention center at section 41 on the lower concourse, the last person to be arrested at an Orioles game at Memorial Stadium.

While 50,700 people cheered three generations of Orioles heroes, Catayas bolted from seat No. 21 of lower section 40 and ran through the outfield.

"It seemed like the thing to do at the time. I had two beers on the way to the game and four when I got here. I had a buzz, but I knew what I was doing," said Catayas, who streaked from right field to center and stood in the middle of the field taking pictures — including several of the mounted police — before being hustled away. "My buddy said, 'Come on, let's do it,' but then he didn't go. I got some good shots."

For the stunt, which occurred as Jim Palmer ran out to the pitching mound during a post-game tribute and tarnished an emotional moment for thousands of fans, Catayas was charged with trespassing.

He faces a $500 fine and/or three months in jail and may find his mug shot taped alongside a small bag of stadium infield dirt on the wall at the Northern District, a lasting tribute to all of the people arrested at Memorial Stadium before him since 1954.

"It was worth it," Catayas said. "It felt great."

Outside the stadium, Ed Stromberg was enjoying a different kind of satisfaction.

Standing beneath the towering stone face of the stadium, he stood with his neck craned up to the inscription on the front of the ballpark, words carved out of steel and dedicated to America's dead from the two world wars.

"I've read it before," said Stromberg, the father of three. "But it struck me today to see it one more time."

October 7, 1991

For snow lovers, it was a day to savor

WHILE THE REST OF THE CITY WAS DOING RUSH-HOUR CARTWHEELS TRYING TO GET from here to there yesterday morning, a lone cross-country skier traced the silky perimeter of Baltimore's great star fort.

With gulls and geese gliding through thick harbor clouds the hue of a derelict nickel, the solitary skier glided over virgin snow white as a wedding gown.

Round and round she went, reluctant to break her reverie with small talk, her face scarlet as poles propelled her around the sea wall of Fort McHenry.

She, and not many others, knew yesterday that the national landmark in Locust Point was a magnificent place to savor the snow.

By a little after 10 a.m., there were only a few cars in the parking lot, most of them belonging to employees; clusters of empty picnic tables; two people in the museum theater to see a movie about bombs that burst over the fort in 1814, prompting Francis Scott Key to write the Star Spangled Banner; and Lou Miller, as usual, taking it easy at his favorite spot in the world.

"You don't need snow for it to be good here," said Mr. Miller, looking toward a freighter docked across the channel at Clinton Street, the vessel's name and home port obscured by fine granules falling quick and steady.

"It's the tranquillity, the peace and quiet. You know, the hustle and bustle of the world gets nerve-wracking, standing in lines at the supermarket and all.

"But when you come through those gates, it changes," said the 64-year-old retiree who drives to South Baltimore from Lansdowne every morning to pass through those iron gates.

"People are more cordial, they take the time to say hello. And with this snow, the water is calm, the birds are settled down, and there's not much boat traffic. It's a good place to sit and meditate or for walks — no problems."

It's unusual that he's alone there, but Mr. Miller's fair weather cronies, a group of men who came of age during World War II and meet at the fort just about every morning, don't like driving in the snow.

But Mr. Miller loves it and, yards in front of him, down toward the sea wall where only the skier's smooth tracks and the webbed footprints of water fowl blemish the snow, a sign explains the port of Baltimore to tourists and unknowing locals.

It says: "Petroleum, iron ore, raw sugar, bananas, and lumber are among the port's leading imports. . . ."

But to read it you had to brush away an inch of snow and the only vessel plying the deep water port of legend at the moment was a city trash skimmer.

Far behind Mr. Miller, west toward the gates of the fort, is the huge statue of the music god Orpheus — bronze, nearly nude and towering over the park on a marble pedestal as snow collects on his broad shoulders.

Just about the time the snow stops around 11:30 a.m. it is time for Mr. Miller to go out into the world and do some shopping, to leave a place where "people come from all over town just to walk around and feed the birds," he said. "You can be all alone here and still have friends."

February 14, 1992

Pier sign shines in Fells Point

THE GLOW OF 410 LIGHT BULBS SHINING THROUGH A HARD HARBOR RAIN HAD Virginia Baker jubilant last night.

"Wow!" said the 71-year-old champion of fun and games in Baltimore when the lights went on at 7:15 p.m. "My heart's dancing."

Alone, each bulb burned no brighter than 11 watts. But together, they formed the words "CITY PIER BROADWAY," a legend once bright over Fells Point, but dark for almost 20 years.

The sign hangs on the back of the Broadway Recreation Pier, where it first beckoned sailors and harbor travelers in 1914.

Miss Baker, head of the city's Department of Adventures in Fun, decided years ago that the sign which brought her comfort in childhood would one day shine again.

"When I was a little kid, mama would take us down the bay for billy goat rides," she said. "And when I saw that sign coming home at night, I felt peace, I knew I was home."

By last summer, only seven bulbs were working.

Replacing them wasn't the problem.

The cost came to a little more than $200, all of it funded with donations from neighbors and local businesses.

What had the city stymied was a cheap way to install them.

Officials didn't want to spend the money to erect scaffolding and it was considered too dangerous to use ladders to reach signs that hang some 50 feet above the playground.

"People told us it was impossible, that you couldn't do it," Miss Baker said on the roof of the pier last night with about 30 neighbors and supporters.

"I said, 'If they went in one time, they can go in two times.' "

Miss Baker's wish to have the sign fixed spread around town and Troy Higgs, a man who had never even seen the Recreation Pier, came forward to help her.

Mr. Higgs owns Visual Sensations, a local window-washing business.

Hanging over the side of big buildings is an everyday thing for him.

"I looked at the building and what the community wanted to do," he explained last night. "And I said, 'Hey, I can do that.' "

He used mountain climbing equipment to suspend himself and local sea dog Stephens Bunker from the roof of the pier.

And he did it for free.

The first night they worked on the sign, Mr. Higgs and Mr. Bunker screwed in all the bulbs for the "B" and "R" in BROADWAY and the "C" and "I" in CITY.

"When we were done, we said, 'Let's light this thing up,' " said Mr. Bunker, who was lowered down from the roof by his ankles a few months earlier to unscrew one of the old bulbs. "We didn't light it up again until we were finished."

Still, five bulbs remained dark last night, the victims of bad sockets.

"OK, that's great," said Miss Baker, getting out of the rain after admiring the sign for a few moments.

"Now we can get to work on our next job."

November 13, 1992

For new Elvis stamp, a letter-perfect day

THERE WAS ONE LINE FOR ELVIS AND ANOTHER LINE FOR EVERYTHING ELSE.
The postal clerk bellowed: "Is anyone here for anything other than Elvis?"
No one answered.

Everyone was in the Elvis line.

By noon, it numbered more than a hundred, and had snaked out the door and into the parking lot.

This occurred at the United States Post Office in Brooklyn Park, where, at noon on what would have been the 58th birthday of Elvis Presley, postage stamps honoring the King of Rock and Roll were offered to an eager public.

The deal — one pink, first-class Elvis stamp in exchange for 29 cents — went down at a record pace yesterday at thousands of post offices across the country.

At the Richard Nixon Library and Birthplace in Yorba Linda, Calif., visitors were offered a limited series of first-day Elvis stamps canceled on king-sized postcards of the fabled photograph of Mr. Nixon and Presley shaking hands at the White House in 1970.

Elvis told Mr. Nixon he wanted to help fight the youth drug problem.

Mr. Nixon hoped Elvis might get him in good with Woodstock-era teen-agers who were making his life miserable.

And Presley wound up getting a stamp before the 37th president did.

About 300 million of the stamps went on sale at noon. They were the first of 500 million to be printed in the biggest sale of a single commemorative stamp in history — three times the amount printed for typical American heroes such as author William Saroyan.

Before the advent of the Elvis stamp, the biggest-selling U.S. stamp was one commemorating man's landing on the moon in 1969.

In Maryland, many post offices sold out in a few hours. The pace appeared to depend on Elvis demographics, an inexact science that dictates that Elvis stamps will sell out in working-class Highlandtown and Hampden, but perhaps not in Roland Park.

Yet even in the upper-class neighborhood of tree-lined streets and big Victorian houses, they came forward by the hundreds to buy Elvis stamps.

"We sold 6,000, and a lot of them to ladies I would never have guessed would want Elvis," said a clerk at the Roland Park post office. "A lot of people surprised me today."

Just as David Holmes wowed them at the 16th Avenue post office in Brooklyn Park.

A disc jockey when he's not selling stamps behind the counter, Mr. Holmes, 40, donned a whitejump suit, had his girlfriend spray his blond hair black, and jumped out in front of the throng with a guitar.

He lip-synced his heart out to "All Shook Up" at one minute past noon.Mr. Holmes wiggled and the crowd screamed.

"First time I've been Elvis in all my life," said Mr. Holmes, a good-hearted soul who rented the suit, sideburns included, for $55.

But he had to ditch the wig that came with it because it made him look more like a Beatle than the King. That sent Helen Mattatall, his girlfriend, running out at the last minute for a can of Colorama hair-color spray.

Relying on pictures of Elvis from books she borrowed from the library, Ms. Mattatall pushed Mr. Holmes' hair back from his forehead while laying the black hair spray on heavy in a back room.

"Careful not to get that stuff on the suit," Mr. Holmes said. "It's rented."

Observed station manager John Wojcik: "This thing has blowed way out of proportion. We wanted to promote it, then we thought: 'Hey, maybe we can talk Dave into being Elvis.'"

Why?

"Because he'll do anything," said Ms. Mattatall.

Said Mr. Holmes: "Elvis is the biggest thing to hit the post office since Express Mail."

January 3, 1993

Block bares it all legally

FROM THEIR HEADS TO THEIR TOES, ANYTHING GOES.

That has been the effect of a recent court ruling allowing full nudity on Baltimore's fabled Block and other city strip bars, a decision that has put the sound of ringing cash registers in the ears of business owners and sent Maryland legislators scrambling to cover it up.

Word of the decision reached The Block before it hit the news, and strippers wasted no time in shedding their pasties and G-strings. Visits to a half-dozen go-go joints last night — including the historic 2 O'Clock Club where Blaze Starr reigned — revealed completely nude dancers.

"I think it's great for freedom of expression," said Brittany Wilson, the manager of Club Chez Joey.

"It's a good thing," said Joe Chittams, a barker standing outside the Golden Nugget. "It will bring business back to Baltimore. Everybody was going to D.C., where they go fully nude."

In a decision issued Jan. 21, Baltimore Circuit Judge Richard T. Rombro struck down regulations issued by the city Board of Liquor License Commissioners that prohibited nude dancing and a variety of sexually explicit acts, ruling that the restrictions violated the "grandfather" clause in a 1993 state law.

Citing a 1996 Maryland Court of Special Appeals opinion, Rombro wrote that because the General Assembly had enacted a detailed set of rules on the subject, the board's usually broad rule-making authority was restricted.

More extreme forms of sexual entertainment would continue to be restricted by state criminal laws, Rombro stated.

The ruling reversed a city liquor board's guilty verdict against the Spectrum Gentlemen's Club in the 4100 block of E. Lombard St., where dancers fully exposed themselves onstage a year ago.

Rombro ruled that the Spectrum's owner, Reginald D. Krisher, was not subject to a 1993 adult entertainment law passed by the Maryland legislature because the business was first approved as a "Go-Go Girl" club in 1976.

The judge threw out liquor board citations against Krisher, who had been fined

$200 and had his license suspended for two days.

The ruling means that any strip club opened before May 31, 1993, is exempted and not subject to the law. At those clubs, wrote Rombro in an 11-page opinion, "neither the prohibitions nor the liquor board rules relating to nudity apply."

The legislature, Rombro ruled, specifically exempted the older establishments from a detailed list of prohibited behavior defined in the 1993 law. Reached last night, the recently retired Rombro said: "The legislature passed a law that superseded what had been in effect before."

Last night, state legislators met with liquor board officials in Annapolis to be briefed on the ruling and look for ways to resurrect the prohibition.

"They can display anything they want to display," said Sen. George W. Della Jr., the South Baltimore Democrat who sponsored the 1993 law in an effort to stop the spread of nude entertainment to city neighborhoods.

Della said he plans to back emergency legislation — already in the hands of the General Assembly's bill drafters — to put the restrictions back in place.

"I'm not going to question the judge's decision. The decision is his decision," said Della. "The legislature, if it chooses, can react to that decision There was evidently a flaw in the law that needs to be corrected post haste. When we did it, we thought we had done it right."

Liquor board chairman Leonard R. Skolnik told city senators last night: "Nudity is now allowed in the city of Baltimore, as well as a whole lot of other things."

Skolnik declined to specify what "other things" would be permitted, but referred to a state law's listing of acts prohibited at nongrandfathered bars. Those include a variety of sexual activity, including simulated intercourse, fondling of breasts and genitals and close contact between a nude entertainer and customers.

Block clubs have repeatedly been cited by police and the liquor board for violations that include dancing nude, prostitution, drug use and hiring teen-agers as young as 15 to strip.

For the past three decades, The Block has survived mayoral denunciations, grand-jury indictments and cleanup campaigns. It has bounced back after police raids, including one by 100 federal agents in 1971 and another by 500 state troopers in 1994.

After that raid, then-Gov. William Donald Schaefer proclaimed an end to the adult entertainment district, saying what had once been a city attraction had become a detriment to downtown revitalization.

Clubs survived the raid and charges of prostitution, drug running and gambling after it was revealed that undercover state police had engaged in corrupt methods by accepting bribes and sleeping with dancers during the investigation.

City officials passed new restrictions in 1997, prohibiting "barkers" from standing outside and beckoning potential customers. Two clubs lost their licenses for a brief time, and others faced penalties in the thousands of dollars for allowing dancers to entice customers with expensive drinks that served as propositions for sex.

Some club owners even promoted plans to recapture an air of respectability with gas lamps, brick sidewalks and 1920s-era facades. But many civic boosters made no secret of their desire to oust sex-oriented businesses from the city's downtown.

Sgt. Craig Gentile, a vice squad officer, said that there is far more crime on the streets directly outside the strip bars — including prostitution and aggressive panhandling — than inside.

"I'll go by what the law says," said Gentile about the new ruling. "It's not for me to interpret."

February 5, 1999

Heat wave Day Five

CELEBRATING HIS BIRTHDAY YESTERDAY AS MARYLAND SWEATED THROUGH DAY Five of the early summer heat wave, 34-year-old Van Wallace used a simple formula to stay cool as a cucumber on the streets of West Baltimore.

1. Fill plastic bag with ice. 2. Apply bag to top of head. 3. Repeat.

Keeping his bald head cool, explained Wallace as he hung out near the corner of Pulaski Street and Ridgehill Avenue, takes care of the whole body.

A cold front drifting southeast from the Canadian plains is expected to take care of Maryland by Sunday, returning temperatures to the mid-to-upper 80s — average for this time of year and a good dozen degrees cooler than the record heat that has fried the state since the July Fourth holiday weekend.

According to the National Weather Service, hot and humid weather will continue today through the end of the week. Forecasters are calling for highs in the low 90s with no chance of thunderstorms until Saturday. Temperatures at night should be close to 70 in Baltimore and in the mid-60s around the metro area.

The weather service reported a high of 95 degrees at 5:25 p.m. yesterday at Baltimore-Washington International Airport, four points short of the record set in 1993. The mercury hit 94 degrees at the Inner Harbor just before the evening rush hour.

The suffocating heat has led to 23 deaths on the East Coast and in the Midwest. Although no heat-related deaths have been reported in Maryland, the weather continued to exact a toll on the old and sick, and the state's agriculture, fish and poultry industries.

At Maryland Community Kitchen — formerly the AIDS support group known as Moveable Feast — the call went out for donations of bottled water. "We need to replenish our supply of bottled water and fruit juice," said executive director Jim Williams. "We're out."

To help the Baltimore-based group care for patients throughout the metro area, call 410-243-4604.

Yesterday, the Maryland Department of Environment issued a statewide drought warning and advised that chronic dry conditions could lead to severe water supply problems. Precipitation across the state has been below normal for six months, with the south and central areas of the state a foot below normal rainfall.

Officials are asking citizens to tighten dripping faucets, turn off water when brushing teeth, take shorter showers, use washing machines and dishwashers for full loads and curtail outdoor water use.

On the Delmarva Peninsula, more than 30,000 chickens have died in the heat since last week. Allen Family Foods Inc., a Seaford, Del.-based company, lost 33,000 birds between Saturday and Monday, according to a company official who could not recall such a spell of extreme heat in the past decade.

Salisbury-based Perdue Farms Inc., which bills itself as the third-largest poultry producer in the United States, said it had not tallied its losses. Grower Dwaine Bradley of Vienna in Dorchester County said he lost 1,000 of 42,000 broiler chickens on Monday.

Corn is entering a critical stage, in which the heat is exacerbating the drought conditions. The plants are beginning to tassel, and then must be pollinated if they are to develop kernels. The process fails during drought.

"When you have the hottest weather you could ever possibly have, on top of the [lack of] rain, it just makes the situation worse," said Bryan Butler, an extension agent in Carroll County.

In several creeks and coves off Middle River in Baltimore County, state environmental workers discovered yesterday thousands of yellow perch killed because of extremely high water temperatures.

"More fish will die until this weather breaks," said Quentin Banks, Maryland Department of Environment spokesman. "The water temperature in some of the more shallow sections of the creeks was 90 degrees Fahrenheit." He added that other factors probably contributing to the kills were changes in salinity and dissolved oxygen.

July 8, 1999

"No suspects, no witnesses, no motive..."

CHAPTER 9

Cops and Robbers

Man who killed uncle over debt of $4.75 gets life in prison

HENRY LOUIS BROWN WAS A LONGTIME ALCOHOLIC, DEFENSE AND PROSECUTION attorneys agreed in court yesterday — a man who talked too much when he was drinking and a man long in debt to his nephew for $4.75.

But all that, said Baltimore Circuit Judge Kenneth L. Johnson, was no reason to kill him.

"Everybody has a right not to be murdered," the judge said.

Refusing to hear pleas for leniency from the defense, Judge Johnson sentenced Mr. Brown's nephew and killer — a 37-year-old lifelong criminal named Robert Preston Howard, to life in prison yesterday with no chance of parole for at least 25 years.

The two relatives were drinking buddies who usually got along well, said Sharon D. Smith, the assistant state's attorney who tried the case and won a conviction from a jury April 19.

On the night of July 11, 1988, the men began arguing over $4.75 that Mr. Brown had borrowed from Howard more than a year before. Mr. Brown was drunk, according to testimony, and Howard was not.

They took their argument to the corner of Belgian and Elkader avenues in the Northeast Baltimore neighborhood where both men lived.

Ms. Smith said nasty words were exchanged, Mr. Brown slapped Howard, and the fight apparently ended when witnesses broke it up. Mr. Brown rejoined relatives on the front porch of his home and Howard retreated to his mother's house.

Howard soon returned — with a butcher knife.

According to Ms. Smith, Howard lured his uncle down from the porch, saying he wanted to talk.

Then he said they had to go around the corner of Belgian Avenue where they could talk privately.

"That's when [Howard] pulled the butcher knife from his clothes and lunged at Brown," Ms. Smith said.

"The blade went through a lung and severed the pulmonary artery, going in about 6 inches deep. Then he pulled out the knife and stabbed him again in the back," Ms. Smith said.

Howard testified in court — while weeping on the witness stand, Ms. Smith said — that he killed his uncle in self-defense.

June 2, 1989

Grocer fatally shoots son, mistaking him for burglar

AS POLICE STOOD OUTSIDE, A GROCERY STORE OWNER SHOT AND KILLED HIS
27-year-old son early yesterday after mistaking the young man for a burglar in
the family's Greenmount Avenue supermarket, homicide detectives said.

Neighbors around the row-house grocery in the downtrodden area just south
of Green Mount Cemetery said the father — identified by police as 55-year-old
Gil Nam Sung — began carrying a weapon after a relative was shot and killed
in the store more than a year ago.

Police identified the dead son as Moo Yul Sung, who lived in Woodlawn. The
younger Mr. Sung was shot once in the left side of the chest with a 9mm handgun
after 4 a.m.

He was declared dead on the second floor of the building housing Johnston's
Supermarket in the 1300 block of Greenmount Avenue, where he had gone to turn
off a burglar alarm believed to have gone off accidentally.

Investigators said the single shot was fired by the father, who had been sleeping
in a room above the store when the alarm went off.

Dennis S. Hill, a city police spokesman, said the older Mr. Sung — who apparently does not live above the store but was staying there Friday night — will not
be charged in the shooting.

At 3:57 a.m. yesterday, police and the younger Mr. Sung were alerted by a
security company that the supermarket's burglar alarm was sounding. The police
arrived within minutes and, after discovering that the business was not being
robbed, waited for Moo Yul Sung to arrive and turn off the alarm.

When Mr. Sung walked to the second floor, he was shot.

A family that owns a corner carryout at Greenmount Avenue and Preston
Street, adjacent to the supermarket, said the Sung family had owned the store at
least 14 months.

"One of the family was shot there before, about a year ago," said a woman at the
carryout, who did not know the earlier victim's name.

A friend of the family, Sue Kim, said that Mr. Sung's uncle had been killed
in the store more than a year ago. Ms. Kim also said the older Mr. Sung began

sleeping in a room above the store a few weeks ago after someone broke in and stole several small items.

Ms. Kim said the younger Mr. Sung had given his father the gun for protection.

Joseph Oh, a vice president of the Korean Businessmen's League of Baltimore, said Johnston's Supermarket has been the scene of frequent violence.

"That's a bad corner, a real bad corner," Mr. Oh said. "But [many] Koreans have the attitude that violence goes with the territory. I think they realize there's a risk involved when you run a grocery store, but this is so sad."

December 16, 1990

Not all the slammers at Memorial ended in runs

TODAY IS YOUR LAST OPPORTUNITY TO BE ARRESTED AT A MAJOR LEAGUE BALLPARK on 33rd Street.

And if it is your desire to take a little piece of Memorial Stadium with you as a keepsake of the Baltimore Orioles' last home game ever in Waverly, there will be 150 police officers — three times the normal detail — on hand to lock you up for theft.

The police expect a wisenheimer or two to try and get away with a chair or a brick or a slice of turf, and if they catch one, that person will experience the last big-league go-'round for an old, black prison cage known as "Farace's Condo."

That's Farace, as in Lt. Phil Farace of the Baltimore Police Department, the happy-faced man known around the ballpark as "Uncle Phil" and top officer at Memorial Stadium since 1975.

"In my 16 years here I've learned how to get along with people in large groups," Lieutenant Farace said. "I've learned how to deal with anything, from the man in the bleachers to the queen of England."

When the Orioles move to their new home in Orioles Park at Camden Yards for the 1992 baseball season, the police will move along with them, to new offices and a new detention area inside the stadium. Lieutenant Farace was asked for suggestions to make the new detention area better than the old one.

Now under construction at Camden Yards, just behind the main ticket windows facing southbound Russell Street are a pair of narrow rooms measuring 6 feet by 6 feet 8 inches and equipped with metal security doors.

This is where the police will hold the drunks who make trouble, the ticket-scalpers, the pickpockets, brawlers and bad guys who find themselves under arrest at the new ballpark.

Unlike most of the other offices at the new stadium, the walls of the twin holding cells will not be made of plasterboard; they are cinder block. "We don't want someone kicking their way out," said Stewart Ervie, an on-site architect at Camden Yards.

Lieutenant Farace, 63, said he will spend one more baseball season on the force, breaking in the new lock-up for a successor, before retiring.

"When I was promoted to lieutenant, the [police] commissioner gave me this job. I didn't ask for it," he said. "I didn't even know it existed."

Since then, Lieutenant Farace has met two presidents and Queen Elizabeth II, made close friends with some of the all-time heroes of America's national pastime — from Earl Weaver to Reggie Jackson to Brooks Robinson — and participated in scores of arrests.

He recalled: "I remember during a Colt game there was a real large gentleman using profanity like you wouldn't believe, so I decided to use some psychology on him. I said, 'Would you talk like that in front of your mother or your sister?' And he pointed to a woman on his right and said, 'I'd like you to meet my mother.'

"Needless to say, before half time they were both locked up."

People arrested at Memorial Stadium are held in the iron cage on the first concourse until a patrol wagon hauls them over to the Northern District in Hampden for formal booking. It is not lost on the officers at the station that their load will be a little lighter after today.

A little bag of dirt hangs on the wall behind the desk sergeant there and next to the dirt is this notice: "This bag contains authentic soil from the Memorial Stadium infield. It serves as a memorial to all the prisoners who have entered the portals of the Northern District cellblock after being arrested at Memorial Stadium over the years through the 1991 baseball season. We bid them and the stadium adieu."

"We're going to get the mug shot of the last guy arrested at the stadium," said one officer there, "and put it up on the wall next to the dirt."

The cause of most stadium disturbances, say the police and others, is alcohol.

"You see 'em getting carted out of the stands all the time," said Lou Beach, a novelty vendor at the stadium. "A lot 'em are drunk, just stone drunk. The cops gotta drag some of 'em because they won't walk. I don't think I've ever seen anybody other than a young male getting arrested, guys between 18 and 35. I've never seen them arrest a woman."

In the 37 years since Memorial Stadium was dedicated, a celebrity or two has have been arrested there, including R. Sargent Shriver III for scalping playoff tickets in 1983; Wild Bill Hagy for tossing a beer cooler onto the field; Donald N. Kroner for crashing a plane into the upper deck in 1976; and former Boston Red Sox outfielder Jimmy Piersall, who went after a heckler in the stands Sept. 14, 1962, while playing for the Washington Senators.

Now retired, Baltimore police Sgt. Walter Mina arrested both Mr. Piersall, known for his eccentric behavior and the subject of the movie "Fear Strikes Out," and the unruly fan, a 66-year-old official of the roofers union named Joseph Martin.

"I was walking around the stands during batting practice and I heard some guy yelling, 'Jim, you couldn't hit the side of a barn. . . . You and your whole damn family are crazy,' " Mr. Mina recalled. "And Piersall jumped over the wall and into the stands. He come over that wall like a bear. I think he would've torn that fan in half. I body-checked Piersall and knocked him down, and when I was locking up the heckler the guy said: 'Aren't you going to arrest him, too? He's disorderly same as me.' So I locked them both up."

Mr. Piersall was acquitted, with then-District Court Judge Robert I. H. Hammerman saying: "A fan has the right and privilege to heckle players, but like any other right and privilege, it can be abused. . . . Piersall should not have been subjected to this type of abuse. . . . He had the right to lose his temper, but he might have chosen other ways" to show it.

Officer Bob Brown, who arrested a man under the influence of drugs who had run down and killed his partner, Officer Richard Miller, in the middle of 33rd Street before an Orioles game in 1986, said he "can't ever remember having a problem from a sober person" at 1000 E. 33rd St.

And although the people who get locked up attract more attention that law-abiding folks, Officer Brown said they remain a small part of what has gone on at the stadium over the years.

"I've worked traffic at the corner of 33rd and Ellerslie [Avenue] for a long time," he said. "And I've watched this one kid grow up going to games, he must have been 7 or 8 when he started coming and now he's a teen-ager. And every time he comes out and sees me, he gives me a 'high five' if the Orioles have won. Things like that are what you remember."

October 6, 1991

Death of son gives new life to woman's fight against drug violence

IT WAS 8 O'CLOCK ON A SUNDAY MORNING AND OLIVIA "LIBBY" REID HAD JUST opened her eyes to the new day, a bright and sunny one in early October that she intended to greet by tuning in one of her favorite radio preachers, the Rev. Walter Thomas.

But before Ms. Reid could turn on her radio, gunshots rang through her West Baltimore neighborhood, modest cul-de-sacs of drug-riddled rental housing just across the county line from Woodlawn.

Gunshots, residents say, are as familiar in Forest Heights as birds singing in the trees, and almost immediately Libby Reid's phone was ringing with a call from a neighbor in her community association, a woman asking whether Ms. Reid had heard the gunfire.

She had, she replied, adding, "Let me call the police; it might be somebody's child."

"Somebody's child" turned out to be her own, 20-year-old Frederick Phillip Young, the only son of neighborhood drug fighter Libby Reid.

Children were soon at the front door of her house in the 4900 block of Carmine Avenue yelling, "Miss Libby! Miss Libby! It's Freddie that got shot!"

Ms. Reid ran down the street to the 1900 block of Beechwood Avenue. She found her son lying on his back, his eyes half-closed and his mouth moving soundlessly.

Before his mother's eyes, Freddie Young became murder victim No. 219 in Baltimore this year. (The toll is now closing in on 250.)

"I was whispering Jesus' name in his ear, and I said, 'Freddie, what happened?' but he didn't answer," Ms. Reid said the other day. "I put my ear to his chest, and it seemed to me he died right there."

And right there, under a utility pole at Beechwood and Clifton avenues, is where Libby Reid has left flowers and balloons since the Oct. 6 shooting. She has created a makeshift shrine to remind residents of the ceaseless toll of drug violence.

"It seemed like things just happened to Freddie, even though he was innocent," his mother said. "We knew something like this was going to happen in this community. We don't even sit in our family room because we're afraid of bullets coming through the patio door."

By all accounts, Freddie Young was a good young man. He learned how to cook through the Job Corps and worked in restaurants. He helped his mother distribute anti-drug literature and eluded the drug-dealing prevalent in his neighborhood.

"Freddie wasn't a criminal," said Detective Gene Constantine, who is trying to find the man who fired a half-dozen or so small-caliber bullets into Mr. Young's chest.

Detective Constantine's investigation has uncovered just about everything but a name to match a face.

Less than five minutes before Mr. Young was shot, Victor White, 19, was in a car with the man police believe committed the murder, offering to sell the man crack cocaine.

"At the time, I used to deal drugs," said Mr. White, who grew up with Mr. Young, went to the Job Corps with him and lives a few blocks away. "This guy drove by looking for drugs, and I was going to serve him some crack, about $50 worth. He was one of the white guys who come here to buy drugs, greaseballs and rednecks. He looked like one of those supremacists or something, in camouflage, but we get businessmen in BMWs too, all types," Mr. White said.

The potential buyer, according to the seller, drove a mid-1980s white Chevrolet Monte Carlo with a burgundy interior and a small stuffed toy hanging from the rearview mirror. He refused Mr. White's drugs because there wasn't enough, and the dealer became suspicious.

"When he turned it down, I started to feel funny about it," Mr. White said. "Usually, all you could have is a crumb and they wouldn't turn it down."

Mr. White said he got out of the car and that the man drove away. The car cruised by again moments later, he said. Freddie Young was walking down the sidewalk from a friend's house, where he had spent the night. The driver pulled over to the curb at Beechwood and Clifton avenues and motioned Mr. Young and a few friends to the passenger window of the Monte Carlo.

"The driver didn't say anything," said Detective Constantine. "He just started firing and drove away."

And that is how, in the middle of a neighborhood being shot up every weekend, one young man lost his life at 8 o'clock on a Sunday morning.

Victor White has a theory: A short time before Mr. Young's death, he said, a white man resembling the suspect tried to get away without paying for drugs and was pulled from his car and beaten severely.

Perhaps, Mr. White said, a friend or relative of the beaten man came back for revenge.

Detective Constantine doesn't care what the motive was. He believes he is one call away from making an arrest.

"It's a fairly simple case," said the detective, who has circulated a composite drawing of the gunman and is looking for the Monte Carlo. "I have four eyewitnesses willing to identify someone from really close up, but I can't put a name to the face."

Libby Reid wants someone behind bars for the death of her son, but an arrest won't keep her from trying to make Forest Heights the neighborhood it was when she moved in. That was when her son was little.

And an arrest won't make her forget about tying flowers and balloons to the utility pole near the spot where he was killed, or stop her anti-drug rallies, such as the one planned for Forest Heights Nov. 23.

"We've been trying so hard, but I knew somebody was going to die," she said. "There's bullets flying all the time, but I didn't think it was going to be my child."

November 11, 1991

Suspect's grandmother
follows her conscience

ALOMA SINGLE CRINGED AT THE THOUGHT OF VISITING THE DEAD GIRL'S FAMILY, but it kept nagging at her.

People told her it was a bad idea and that she would only be met with scorn, but she had to do it.

She had to go and give her condolences to the kin of Janet Paula Edwards, the 12-year-old West Baltimore girl whom Mrs. Single's grandson was charged with shooting to death last week.

"It was the hardest thing I've had to do in my life," said the 49-year-old restaurant worker. "But I had to say something."

Her 15-year-old grandson, Tyree "Haney" Paige, a boy she just about raised by herself, has been charged with manslaughter in the April 4 shooting. Witnesses told police that the boy was showing off with a handgun with a bunch of kids when the gun fired. The bullet cut the girl's heart.

Last Monday, less than a mile from Mrs. Single's West Franklin Street home, Beatrice Banks sat in the parlor of her own little rowhouse on Riggs Avenue off of Carey Street, mourning a grandchild that she raised pretty much by herself, a happy girl everybody knew as Paula.

She sat just one door away from the house where Paula died, wondering about how things could go so wrong in the world, when a frightened and grieving Aloma Single showed up.

"When she came I had my pain," said Mrs. Banks, 63. "But I was hoping to ease her pain, too."

"And you were comforting," said Mrs. Single when the women met again the other day. "I could tell by the way you treated me that you were Christian, loving people."

With tears in her eyes, Mrs. Single kept telling Mrs. Banks how bad she felt, over and over, repeating: "I'm so sorry."

Mrs. Banks patted her arm and said, "You don't have to keep telling me that."

The two women are raising extended families in bad neighborhoods. Mrs. Single is the mother of six, with 10 grandchildren. Mrs. Banks, who brought up

eight children of her own, said she has so many grandchildren and great-grand-
children there wouldn't be much point in listing them.

In Mrs. Banks' mind, the world could use more loving people and fewer guns,
more prayer and fewer drugs, more kids like Harlem Park middle schooler Paula
Edwards and not so many street-corner thugs.

And in the midst of it all she can find no hatred for Tyree Paige, the Hamilton
middle schooler who is being held in a state juvenile detention center.

"I've never seen the young man to know him, he's more or less a blank to me,"
she said. "I've had so much just trying to get through the loss of her, the waste. Her
life was a waste. God took her out of a hard cruel world and I have to accept that.
Accepting it is the hardest thing."

Mrs. Single tried to make amends with Paula's family the day of the shooting.
She rushed over before knowing how badly the girl was hurt, but only made it to
the front gate. "Someone said the child had died and I passed out right there," she
said. "A man from the house came out and put a wet towel on my forehead."

She succeeded on Monday, two days before the girl's burial at Kings Park in
Pikesville.

Both devout Christians, the women spent about 15 minutes together. Mrs. Single
said when she left she had the peculiar feeling of being forgiven but felt sadder
than ever.

"I felt a little more guilty for what happened because you all were so nice," she
told Mrs. Banks.

"I was hoping you'd be relieved," said Mrs. Banks.

"I was," Mrs. Single replied. "But I felt more hurt for your family, you were no
longer a stranger."

Today they're not strangers, but they aren't exactly friends, just a couple of
women thrown together by tragedy who probably won't see each other again
unless by chance. But they are grateful for having met, for the opportunity to cry
and talk about God's will for a hometown they see getting more violent by the day.

Mrs. Single said she hears teen-agers talking about buying and selling guns all
the time.

"I've always felt the Lord has your life planned out for you. Things happen," she
said. "But with this I had to go back to the things I learned in Sunday school for
some kind of understanding."

Fixing a gaze on her, Mrs. Banks said: "Jesus looked down on the city and wept
for it. I look on this city and I cry, too. My granddaughter and your boy are both
victims.

"Mine is a dead victim, and yours is a living victim," she said. "They are victims
of our time."

A Grandmother's Plea

Young people lay down your arms,
and open your arms to one another.
There is a storm brewing,
and we need each other.
You are our new beginning,
and if you do this we will be winning.
Life must go on, love must go on.
A gun is power, it's true,
but how would you feel,
when the gun is turned on you?

– Beatrice Banks

The grandmother of Janet Paula Edwards, who was shot to death last week, said she wrote the poem to stir the lost youths of Baltimore.

April 12, 1992

Man, 44, killed by thugs at bus stop

MICHAEL G. WAINWRIGHT — A WEST BALTIMORE FAMILY MAN WHO LOVED model trains and cooking out on the grill — refused to give up his knapsack to two thugs at a rain-swept bus stop near Johns Hopkins Hospital just after midnight yesterday. For trying to keep what belonged to him, a few dollars, his pipe and tobacco and a couple of books on toy trains, the 44-year-old grandfather of 10 was shot dead.

"He wouldn't have given it up, not without a fight," said Diane Wainwright, his wife of 22 years. "He didn't bother nobody, and he wouldn't allow nobody to bother him."

A member of the Hopkins housekeeping staff who lived in the 600 block of N. Bentalou St., Wainwright had just gotten off work and was making his way to a bus stop at Broadway and Eager Street.

The corner is four blocks north of the hospital, which is patrolled by private security guards.

Police said Wainwright was waiting across Eager Street from the bus stop, taking cover from the rain until the No. 15 bus arrived to take him home. He did not own a car.

"He went the same way all the time," his wife said. "I used to tell him to catch a cab, but he took the bus. That was his routine."

While Wainwright waited, two males — the shooter described as 15 or 16 and the other about 20 — approached and demanded his bag. "Without provocation, they shot him in the chest," said a homicide detective handling the case.

They fled, leaving Wainwright's bag behind. After a cabdriver called police, Wainwright was taken back to Hopkins, where surgeons tried to save his life.

He was declared dead at 2: 42 a.m.

Police knew of no suspects last night.

The teen-ager who fired the gun was described as wearing a dark blue sweat shirt, dark pants, and white athletic shoes, police said. His older companion was described as wearing a red and white shirt, blue pants and white athletic shoes.

The victim, fourth of nine children and a graduate of Forest Park High School, grew up in the 1900 block of W. Lexington St., spent 15 years hauling furniture for Shofer's on South Charles Street and inherited his love of trains from his father, Richard Wainwright. The elder Wainwright was too distraught to speak last night.

The victim's mother, Ruth, said services were being planned for Providence Inspirational Baptist Church, at Edmondson and Fremont avenues.

"He did love his trains, he used to have a beautiful display that my husband and my boys would put together and take apart," she said. "He was out there trying to make a living for his family."

At home, Wainwright was known as a baron of the barbecue.

"If it was cookable, it would go on the grill," said Michael Suggs, a family friend. "Even when it was raining, he'd cook on the grill."

At Shofer's Furniture, where he was known as Tony, Wainwright was remembered as a good guy who had the knack for maneuvering furniture through narrow doorways.

And he wasn't bashful about bringing in his latest model train layout to show what he was doing.

"We've been friends for about 20 years," said Ray Morris, a Shofer's worker. "I hate for something like this to happen to him."

May 10, 1996

Sad farewell for a slain little boy

KEITH CHASE HAD A BALCONY VIEW OF HIS YOUNG FRIEND IN THE WHITE CASKET the size of a small bathtub; he looked straight up the church aisle yesterday to see 3-year-old James Smith III with a wreath of flowers shaped like Mickey Mouse, a teddy bear at his shoulder and a dark cap covering the bullet wound in his head.

"In a way, you're scared that when you walk out your door you may never come back," said Keith, a sixth-grader at Northeast Middle School. "Now you got to be scared to go to the barbershop."

James "Boo Boo" Smith — who rode his bicycle on Keith's porch, loved cars and trucks and had been enrolled in the Malcolm X Head Start program — was caught in the middle of a barbershop gunfight on Jan. 2, his third birthday.

The afternoon shootout erupted in a crowd at Fresh Cuttz on South Carrollton Avenue, a shop known to some neighbors near the Hollins Market as a hangout for armed drug dealers.

Smith's mother, Cheryl Whittington, was shot in the arm while trying to protect her son. Two men charged with killing the boy remain jailed.

Boo Boo was remembered yesterday at Dalton Baptist Church before being interred at a donated site in an Arbutus cemetery.

The sad farewell on snowy Garrison Boulevard was another in about 30 funerals that Keith Chase says he's attended in 11 years of life and certainly not the first for a murder victim.

"My mother's boyfriend got shot by a group of guys last year and died," said Keith, who has decided that when he grows up, he wants to be an undertaker. "I like the way they fix up the bodies."

While the righteous anger, platitudes and frustration from politicians, clergy and family friends were too late for James, the eulogizers pleaded with African-Americans to come together to solve their problems before any more black children see the grave.

Said Mayor Kurt L. Schmoke: "Fighting evil is what we must do. We will fight the evil of guns, the evil of drugs, the evil of despair, of a misplaced sense of values."

Speaking directly to the black men among the more than 400 mourners crowded into the sanctuary, City Council President Lawrence A. Bell III said that if people cared enough to mourn a slain little boy they ought to care enough to work for change.

"For you to come and express your sympathy and that you're sad and then not leave here committed 100 percent to changing things, then you should not come here," said Bell to great applause. "Don't just go to the Million Man March if you're not going to work for change. I ask and I beg and I plead — I'm begging you — if you care, if you really care, let James' life not be in vain."

Bell was followed by City Comptroller Joan Pratt and Police Commissioner Thomas C. Frazier, who expressed regrets but didn't have much more to add.

Above the pulpit was a cross made of 12 red Christmas lights and a large sign bearing an Old Testament verse which read: "If my people, which are called by my name, shall humble themselves and pray and seek my face and turn from their wicked ways, then will I hear from heaven and will forgive their sin and will hear their land."

Below that piece of scripture, the Rev. Aggie Lee Brown of Dalton Baptist eulogized James as he has at least a half-dozen other murder victims in the past.

"The death of James Smith has tested the heart of the city ," Brown said. "Let us stop talking about what we're going to do. There really is no excuse if you are determined to get a job done that should have been done a long time ago. We must find ways to take the hurt out of our community."

After the three-hour service and before the cold ride out to Arbutus Memorial Park, Yolanda Griffin stopped to talk about what she had heard inside.

Griffin works with James' mother and grandmother at Liberty Medical Center, where the men's health center will be renamed in honor of the youngster. At the service, she sang a solo called "I Won't Complain."

"I think that we have to reach our youth," she said. "And we have to start not in the churches, but on the streets."

January 10, 1997

STORYTELLER

THE SUN 1920s

"In Baltimore boxing ... you always said Lee Halfpenny."

CHAPTER 10

The Dead

Boxing legend taught generations
of Baltimore boys to fight

LEE HALFPENNY, A LOCAL BOXING LEGEND WHO TAUGHT GENERATIONS OF Baltimore boys the pugilistic arts at the YMCA, died of a heart attack Wednesday night at Keswick nursing home. He was 87 and had Alzheimer's disease for more than a dozen years.

"He dearly loved being with kids, he loved teaching them to box and swim," said the former Norma Ege, Mr. Halfpenny's wife of 50 years. "He just loved it when the ones he had taught came back to visit him after they had grown up."

Mr. Halfpenny, a Hall of Fame boxer who fought his way out of Locust Point to become the amateur lightweight champion of the world between 1928 and 1931, was best known for his long association with the Central YMCA at Franklin and Cathedral streets.

His tenure at the Y — from learning to box there as a teen-ager to giving rub downs to politicians and teaching kids how to keep their guard up — lasted more than 50 years. Hundreds of people came through, looking to shed a few pounds or learn to defend themselves in an age when a man's heart and fists often were sufficient.

When he retired from the Y in 1972, he said: "Boxing is the greatest form of exercise in the entire world. It gives you confidence in life, as it does in the ring. You have to make quick decisions in life. You make them in the ring. You learn to always step forward. Never backward."

Born on Fort Avenue, the son of a U.S. Coast Guard employee at Fort McHenry, Mr. Halfpenny attended St. Jerome's Roman Catholic grade school. He dropped out of high school after a year or two.

In 1921, he began his life's calling by wandering into the YMCA, curious about fisticuffs. Except to go home at night or travel out of town with one of his fighters, he rarely wandered out.

"He was probably the most interesting personality ever to come out of the YMCA," said Richard Loebman, a chiropractor who worked at the Y with Mr. Halfpenny, while putting himself through school. "He taught many a kid how to box and worked many an overweight businessman into shape. Lee was an extrovert, a mingler. Every day he was just a happy person."

South Baltimore legend has it that moments before Mr. Halfpenny left home for his first professional bout, his mother begged him not to go. After some 130 amateur fights — including a finals tryout for the 1928 Olympics — Anna Halfpenny's boy decided to turn professional because his father had taken ill.

When he returned hours after his professional debut, he found his mother still complaining, swearing he would never fight again. He then spread 600 dollar bills on the kitchen table.

At Mr. Halfpenny's next bout, his mother sat at ringside.

He fought 47 professional bouts and compiled a record of 45-and-2 before retiring in 1931 because of a broken hand. More than once he recalled fighting six bouts in a single day, trying to earn a living.

In 1932, he helped coach the U.S. team at the summer Olympic Games in Los Angeles. Returning to Baltimore, he continued to work out at the Y, where he directed the health services program from 1947 to 1972.

The young men he taught were known as "clever" boxers, trained to wait for an opponent to make a mistake, then to exploit the miscue with smart punches.

"He was a very scientific boxer, what's called a counter-puncher. He would wait until the other guy moved and then counter it," said his son, Lee Halfpenny Jr. "He never encouraged people to box unless they were really good because it was a very tough business."

Mr. Halfpenny's namesake did not follow him into the ring.

Many others did. Mr. Halfpenny helped develop talent like Red Burman, who once fought Joe Louis for the title at Madison Square Garden; Harry Jeffra, a bantam and featherweight champion in the early 1940s; and Terry Downes, who held the British middleweight title in the early 1960s and once shared the world crown.

Mr. Downes, an Englishman who learned to fight in Baltimore, once introduced Mr. Halfpenny by saying: "Gentlemen, this is the man who knows more about boxing than anyone in the world."

Mr. Halfpenny even showed an actor a thing or two one day when the Thespian was in town to portray a boxer in a Center Stage production. During World War II, according to his son, Mr. Halfpenny taught soldiers hand-to-hand combat at Fort Meade.

"In Baltimore boxing, you never said you were training over at the Y, you always said Lee Halfpenny," said Johnny Marco, a local fight maven who took over the Y's health programs after Mr. Halfpenny retired.

A Mass of Christian burial will be offered at 11 a.m. Monday at the Shrine of the Little Flower Roman Catholic Church at Belair Road and Brendan Avenue in Baltimore.

He is survived by his wife and son, both of Baltimore.

The family asks that memorial contributions be made to the Alzheimer's

Association of Central Maryland, 540 E. Belvedere Ave., Suite 202, 21212; or Keswick nursing home, 700 W. 40th St. Baltimore 21211.

December 31, 1993

Louis Hawkins, dean of city's tap dancers

THE HAWK HAS "WALKED THE DOG" FOR THE LAST TIME. HIS "SHIM SHAM" WILL shake no more. And he's tapped his last sentence on "the typewriter."

Baltimore's Louis Hawkins is dead at 78.

The unrivaled dean of the city's small tap dancing community, "The Hawk" started hoofing in front of a Howard Street shoe store when he was 12 and ended up dancing for change in Fells Point bars.

In between, the longtime resident of South Carey Street danced with the Count Basie Orchestra, won a string of amateur night contests at the fabled Apollo Theater in New York, and worked with comedians Redd Foxx and Slappy White. Last year, he participated in an all-star tap revue in New York City.

"I'll dance as long as my legs hold out," said Mr. Hawkins in a 1987 interview.

His heart gave out first, taking him in a massive attack Wednesday afternoon at University Hospital, where he was operated on after a fall.

"Hawk was from that old school that could break down the wall between the performer and the audience," said Michael "Toes" Tiranoff, who performed with Mr. Hawkins in Baltimore for about 15 years. "He had that 'leg-o-mania' ability to throw his legs up in the air and do a twist in the middle of his routine — it was amazing."

Mr. Tiranoff, 43, said that his mentor in this American folk art would tell stories of tap dancing on roller skates, in a chair, on his back and against walls.

"He was a comedy dancer, with this great ability to mime — he could almost make it look like he was driving a car while he danced in a chair," he said. "He could stand on the chair and tap, fall down into the seat still tapping, bring the chair down on its back, lay down in it and keep tapping without missing a beat. As a showman, he was anyone's equal."

Louis Hawkins, who was raised on Gilmor Street, was the youngest of six children born to a pair of amateur dancers named Louis and Laura Hawkins. The boy learned tap from his father and went on to perform with a 10-piece family band called the Hawk Melody Boys.

"Years ago, they called it buck dancing, now they call it tap," said Marie Brown,

86, his only surviving sibling. "When my mother died she told me to take care of Louis, he was the baby, and me and him lived together all the time. It really hurts. He's gone now."

In the '30s and '40s, Mr. Hawkins performed regularly at nightclubs on Pennsylvania Avenue. In the 1950s, he was the doorman at Club Les Gals on Mount Royal Avenue, tapping on stage when the strippers took breaks. As he grew older, the only thing he enjoyed more than dancing was the race track, and he could be seen regularly at Pimlico.

"I bet Daddy taught about 20 young guys here in Baltimore to hoof and tap," said Mr. Hawkins' daughter, Rhonda Rogers.

"Hawk probably exposed more people to tap than anyone in Baltimore — hundreds of people saw him every night," said Megan Hamilton, a bartender at the Cat's Eye Pub and the organizer of a vaudeville troupe that included Mr. Hawkins.

"He hit all the bars and he had the bus schedules memorized," she added. "From Club Stabiles in Highlandtown to what was left of Pennsylvania Avenue, you could find Hawk dancing."

A Mass of Christian burial will be offered at 10 a.m. Monday at St. Peter Claver Roman Catholic Church, 1546 N. Fremont Ave., Baltimore.

Memorial donations may be made to the Music Department of Morgan State University, 4601 Hillen Road, Baltimore 21239.

May 20, 1994

Paul Swift, 'Eggman' in Waters' 'Pink Flamingos'

IF YOU WERE ONE OF THE ADVENTURERS WHO PASSED THROUGH LEDBETTER'S BAR in the early days of the Fells Point hippie era, you may remember Paul Swift. He was the guy dancing naked on top of the bar.

"Paul ended every night like that," said Mary Vivian Pearce, who starred with Mr. Swift in several of Baltimore director John Waters' early movies. "I guess he did it for the same reason he always wore 400 bracelets."

Mr. Swift, best remembered for his role as the Eggman in the Waters classic "Pink Flamingos," died of AIDS Friday at Francis Scott Key Medical Center. He was 60.

His other screen appearances included "Multiple Maniacs," "Female Trouble" and "Desperate Living."

It was in 1972's "Pink Flamingos" — in which he played the late Edith Massey's boyfriend — that Mr. Swift delivered one of his more famous lines: "Beauty, beauty, look at you. . . . I wish to God I had it, too."

In his own way, friends say, he did.

"I can't imagine Paul ever being normal," Mr. Waters said. "I wouldn't say he was an actor in the Shakespearean sense, but he was an actor people remembered. Paul always led his own life."

Susan Lowe, a former roommate, met Mr. Swift in the mid-1960s after he left the Navy and was relieved of a brief bar-tending job at Haussner's because of an LSD arrest.

"Day in and day out, Paul was a dramatic person, and Fells Point gave him his life," Ms. Lowe said. ". . . Paul wasn't ashamed of being gay, and that's why Fells Point was cool for him."

Or, as restaurant owner Frances Haussner put it, "The last time I saw Paul Swift he was wearing high heels, argyle socks, white shorts, and about 42 pounds of bracelets."

The son of the late Clyde and Dolores Swift, Paul Vincent Swift grew up in the Miller Island community near North Point.

Little could be learned about his early life; friends said they didn't even know where he went to high school. He apparently studied nursing for a while and was Catholic, receiving communion and last rites in the hospital a day before he died. He had lived next door to the Horse You Came In On Saloon since about 1980.

"He loved to cook for a bunch of people," Ms. Lowe said. "Big dinners of American food — meat and potatoes."

Mr. Swift befriended Edith "the Egg Lady" Massey when she owned her fabled "Shopping Bag" curio shop on South Broadway. For about 10 years before falling ill in 1992, Mr. Swift worked at "Oh Susannah's," another store on South Broadway.

Bob Adams has established a small memorial in the front window of the "Flashback" a store he operates at 728 S. Broadway.

"John's movies have a cult following all over the world, and fans would come into the store and ask: 'Where's the Eggman?' " Mr. Adams said.

"I'd say: 'You can meet him right up the street.' Paul always had photos to autograph and give away. He never minded meeting a fan."

Said Mr. Waters: "There's a lot of ghosts in those early films. Now there's another one."

Mr. Swift is survived by an aunt, Mildred Fowler of Baltimore.

A Mass of Christian burial will be celebrated at 8:30 a.m. today at St. Stanislaus Kostka Roman Catholic Church, 700 S. Ann St.

Contributions may be made to A Movable Feast Inc., Old York Road and 34th Street, Baltimore 21218.

October 10, 1994

City's queen of fun

BALTIMORE'S OLDEST KID HAS DIED AT THE AGE OF 76.

Virginia S. Baker — who began her career in fun and games as an East Baltimore playground monitor in 1940 and hopscotched her way up to City Hall in the silly-hat regime of William Donald Schaefer — died yesterday at St. Joseph Medical Center of complications from pneumonia.

"I've made a lot of kids happy," she said in a 1995 interview. "That's what I get paid for."

Never married, Miss Baker counted generations of Baltimore youngsters as her own special brood.

Her secret?

The girl who grew up as "Queenie" in her father's confectionary at Belnord Avenue and Monument Street — where she honed her childlike playfulness and steely resolve — never stopped thinking like a kid.

In a century that whittled an American child's idea of a good time down to pushing buttons on plastic gadgets, Miss Baker championed timeless fun: hog-calling contests, frog-jumping races, turtle derbies, sack races, beanbag tosses, peanut shucking and doll shows.

"And don't forget her annual Elvis salute," said Sue McCardell, Miss Baker's longtime assistant in the Department of Recreation and Parks. "We'll keep going with all the things Virginia started."

Bob Wall, a recreation programmer in Patterson Park — where the rec center is named in Miss Baker's honor — first met his mentor as an 11-year-old Little Leaguer in 1968.

"It was a Saturday and our game was rained out and we were walking past the rec center in our uniforms. I'd never been inside it before," Mr. Wall remembered. "This boisterous lady yelled out to us: 'You boys want to catch frogs for me today?'"

Of course they did. And that was Mr. Wall's initiation into a world he unexpectedly found himself eulogizing yesterday when the city's 58th annual doll show — launched by Miss Baker at the start of her career — coincided with her death.

"We had a moment of silence," said Mr. Wall. "And then we said the show's got to go on."

The Virginia Baker show started in 1921. Her father was a Czech immigrant who changed the family name from Pecinka to Baker. Her mother, Hattie, was a Baltimorean of Czechoslovakian descent.

"Daddy mixed the syrup for the sodas and milkshakes and Mama cooked the chocolate for the sundaes," she said of the family store, now a carryout restaurant and liquor store protected by iron bars and bulletproof plastic. "Boy, did this neighborhood smell good!"

Miss Baker had a voice so quintessentially Baltimore that Washington disc jockeys regularly put her on the radio just to let the nation's power brokers believe everything they'd ever heard about this city.

On the sidewalks of her beloved hometown, young Virginia learned the tricks she would turn into a career.

"We played every game you can imagine out here," she said during a 1995 visit to the old store that was her home from infancy until her father died in 1954.

Miss Baker rode scooters, shot marbles, made kites out of newspapers and sticks, played tag, spun tops, and made yo-yos sing and puppets dance. She collected matchbook covers and wagered hundreds of them at a time in card games of pitch, poker and pinochle down at Sprock's Garage on Lakewood Avenue.

And when she got black eyes from roughhousing — Queenie was a bruiser, she freely admitted — the local butcher put beef on them to keep down the swelling.

As a youngster, Miss Baker became a volunteer at the old Patterson Park recreation center. After graduating from Eastern High School in 1940, she made play her work, soon becoming director of recreation for the park.

From that time, she served nine Baltimore mayors, from Howard W. Jackson to Kurt L. Schmoke. She became best known during the 15-year tenure of Mr. Schaefer, who installed her at City Hall as perhaps the only civil servant in America in charge of an office called Adventures in Fun.

Miss Baker turned City Hall Plaza into a staging area for endless contests — marbles, pogo sticks, chess, checkers, Hula-Hoops, yo-yos, roller skates, bicycles, kites and tops.

She invented the Fun Wagon, a small trailer with a basketball hoop on back and stuffed with toys. Five of them toured the city. She started the Kid Swap Shop, where children traded toys, an event copied across the nation because of Miss Baker's knack for publicity.

"She was a great old girl," Mr. Schaefer said yesterday. "She initiated all sorts of hokey things and everybody loved them. I hog-called one year. I didn't have my own frog for the jumping contest, but she gave me one. He didn't win. But Virginia always had young people around her. She made them work hard and feel good."

For six decades, her motto never changed: "A kid is still a kid."

Miss Baker lived at the Marylander Apartments from 1954 until a stroke in 1992. She did not officially retire until 1995. She resided in recent years at a Towson nursing home and is survived by several nieces and nephews.

Services will be held at 10 a.m. Saturday at Church of the Nativity, Cedarcroft and York roads.

Donations may be made to the Virginia S. Baker Recreation Memorial Fund, c/o Friends of Patterson Park, 27 S. Patterson Park Ave., Baltimore 21231.

July 30, 1998

Irma 'Henny' Mooney, 84, decorator, advocate of city

IRMA "HENNY" MOONEY, A FORMER INTERIOR DECORATOR WHO WAS DEVOTED TO city life, died in her Bolton Hill home Sunday after a long battle with respiratory disease. She was 84.

Born Irma Elizabeth White Pointer in Ocean City in 1915, Mrs. Mooney was the daughter of George Pointer, a farmer, and his wife, Laura. As a young girl, she worked in Dolle's candy on the Boardwalk and later attended Buckingham High School in Berlin. She graduated in 1931, finishing first in her class at age 16. After graduating, she married a classmate, D. Collins Ayres. During the marriage, which ended in divorce in 1943, she had several houses built near Sixth Street in Ocean City and managed them as summer rental properties.

In the fabled hurricane of 1933, which cut the Ocean City inlet, Mrs. Mooney gripped a lamppost in the storm to watch the first ocean surges cross the beach and the Boardwalk.

Mrs. Mooney moved to Baltimore in 1942, settling on Cathedral Street near Chase Street. She went to work for the National Wallpaper Co. on Howard Street and enrolled in interior decorating classes at what is now the Maryland Institute College of Art. She completed the decorating program in 1945 and was awarded first prize for her work.

She took a position with the Louis Mazor Co., where she worked until 1950, when she married again. Her new husband, Joseph A. Mooney Jr., who was in the insurance business, died in 1977.

A staunch booster of the city who loved her neighborhood long before it was known as Bolton Hill, Mrs. Mooney remained in the area, with brief interruptions, for the rest of her life. Since 1956, she had lived in the 200 block of Lafayette Ave.

When many of her neighbors began fleeing to the suburbs in the 1960s, Mrs. Mooney remained an unwavering supporter of Baltimore. From 1978 until 1987, she worked at the warship Constellation in the Inner Harbor.

A past president of the Bolton Hill Garden Club, Mrs. Mooney also was active in the Mount Royal Improvement Association, the Mount Royal Democratic Club and belonged to the altar guild of Memorial Episcopal Church.

Memorial services will be held at 10:30 a.m. June 26 at Memorial Episcopal Church, West Lafayette Avenue and Bolton Streets.

Mrs. Mooney is survived two sons, John J.B. Ayres of Amherst, Mass., and Joseph A. Mooney III of Baltimore; four grandchildren; and five great-grand-children.

June 17, 2000

Francis Lukowski, 55, Baltimore ship pilot from waterfront family

A BALTIMORE BOY WHO WENT FROM PLAYING ON THE TUGBOATS OF THAMES Street to piloting huge ships on the Chesapeake Bay and Los Angeles harbor was remembered in his old neighborhood yesterday as the brash young patriarch of a waterfront family that has made its living from the port for three generations.

Francis Lukowski — who died of prostate cancer a week ago today at his home in Huntington Beach, Calif. — was given a final ride past his childhood home in Fells Point and the tugs at the Broadway Recreation Pier after a funeral Mass at St. Brigid's Roman Catholic Church. He was 55.

"Steering boats," said his brother, William Lukowski, a local shipping agent. "That's all he ever wanted to do."

A wake for Mr. Lukowski — laid out in the red bowtie and tuxedo he had hoped to wear to his daughter Kelly's wedding at St. Casimir's Church in July — was held at the Polish Home on Broadway.

There, family and friends enjoyed Maryland crab soup, ate kielbasa and sauerkraut, drank draught beer and listened to a Dixieland band while telling stories from the old days.

"It was everything he wanted," said his wife of 30 years, the former Beverly Zentz.

Mrs. Lukowski, who met her husband when he was a teen-ager hanging out at Doc Ollie's ice cream fountain at Eastern Avenue and Ann Street, wore white yesterday for hope.

The grandson of a longshoreman, Mr. Lukowski was born in the 800 block of South Ann St., close enough to the harbor to jump in. He attended St. Patrick's parochial school on Broadway and graduated from Mt. St. Joseph High School in 1963.

The Rev. Joe Bochenek, who went to school with Mr. Lukowski from the first grade through high school, celebrated his old friend's Mass of Resurrection yesterday.

After two years at Loyola College on Charles Street, Mr. Lukowski joined the Navy and was discharged in 1969 as a quartermaster second class. He then went to work as a deckhand on the old Baker-Whitely tugs on Thames Street in the footsteps of his late uncle, Jerome Lukowski, a longtime mate.

Mr. Lukowski was awarded his captain's license from the U.S. Coast Guard in 1974 and worked for Baker-Whitely, now McAllister Bros. Towing, until 1984 when he followed his younger brother Robert to the port of Los Angeles. He was a licensed docking pilot for vessels of unlimited size on both coasts.

"We gave Southern California a little taste of Baltimore," said Robert, also a harbor pilot in L.A. "We went for the economy, but our hearts were always here."

A computer enthusiast who loved all kinds of gizmos and gadgets, Mr. Lukowski once donned scuba gear for a dip in his backyard pool when he lived in Linthicum during the 1970s.

One of his best-loved memories was traveling down the Grand Canyon on a donkey with his second daughter, Kara.

Never one to shy away from a stiff drink, a hot party or his turn to buy a round at the Cat's Eye Pub and the Whistling Oyster, Mr. Lukowski was a hard working "good-timer" in a waterfront tradition that didn't put much stock in sleep.

A staunch union man, he died on his birthday and his wedding anniversary while wearing his International Longshore and Warehouse Union T-shirt.

Other survivors include his mother, Eleanor Lukowski of Fells Point; a brother, Thomas Lukowski of Ellicott City and a sister, Mary Anne Iwancio of Towson.

June 20, 2000

Dean of a-rabs takes a last ride

"Pistol," took his last ride in a horse-drawn a-rab's cart yesterday, his flag-draped coffin rolling west from stables near the Hollins Street Market, a cavalry of mourners behind it.

After holding hands in prayer at the corner of the alleys called South Carlton and Lemmon streets, friends and family moved to a dirge of clip-clops and jingling bells as the horses hit West Lombard Street for a four-mile journey to the March Funeral Home on Wabash Avenue.

No one stopped to hawk strawberries or string beans. No one bellowed the urban field holler that heralds the arrival of fresh produce at a rowhouse door.

More important business was at hand.

They were laying a stable master to rest: Willie "Pistol" Brown.

The son of an a-rab, Mr. Brown worked with horses and wagons nearly all of his 80 years.

"When we were young, he'd put us on horses and we'd ride bareback in parades," said Patricia Smith, one of his 10 children.

"Daddy said a horse could be your best friend. I've never known him to be without one."

Born in rural Anne Arundel County and a longtime resident of the 1000 block of Vine St., Mr. Brown died of pneumonia Wednesday at the Veterans Administration Hospital on North Greene Street.

He was preceded in death by his favorite horse, Bum, which he'd raised from a colt.

"He sang like Nat King Cole and Billy Eckstine, and he was a great dancer," said William Brown Jr., a retired autoworker who sat in the first carriage behind the canopied red wagon that carried his father's body.

"A while back, we tried to get him to stop coming down to the stables. We thought he was getting too old," he said.

"If we'd have made him stay home, he would've died a long time ago."

A World War II Army veteran, Mr. Brown worked his father Wesley's trade since the days when nearly everything was carted through Baltimore on horse-drawn wagons — ice, rags, wood, coal, fish, stone wheels to sharpen knives, and of course, fruit and vegetables.

When a-rabbing was slow, Mr. Brown did labor on such construction projects as the Baltimore Civic Center and hustled extra cash on the waterfront moving fruit and other cargo.

Although the source of Mr. Brown's nickname wasn't exactly in dispute yesterday, some folks did try to put a gentle spin on it.

Soft-spoken in his old age, it seems that Mr. Brown was a bit wild in his youth, took grief from no one and wasn't averse to backing himself up with something that packed a bigger punch than his fists.

Hence the moniker, "Shoot A Pistol," shortened to "Pistol," according to his daughter Charlotte Dumas, with whom he had lived in the 5900 block of Key Ave. for the past three years.

Added his son William Brown: "He had that kind of fun-loving personality. Everybody knows what it means when you talk about somebody and say, 'He's a pistol.'"

Although he had given up a-rabbing in the streets about five years ago, Mr. Brown continued to pick up produce at the Jessup Farmers Market for his buddies and truck it to the Carlton Street stables, where he often napped beneath a portrait of Jesus.

In the old days, the men kept goats and chickens under the huge tree that shades the yard there.

"I'm going to miss seeing him every morning," said an a-rab who said his name was Blue. "Gonna miss drinking coffee with him."

Next to Blue sat an a-rab who'd identify himself only as Big Daddy, a man who remembered the days when there were more wagons on the streets than cars; who said that when a horse died, a guy known as the "Killer Man," would come and take the corpse away.

When Shannon Stokes of the March Funeral Home showed up on South Carlton Street to oversee the transfer of Mr. Brown's coffin from the back of a Cadillac hearse to the back of a wooden wagon, she acknowledged a wide experience in funerals, but nothing like this.

"Never," said Stokes, as Donald "China" Waugh drove the coffin-laden wagon west on Lombard Street toward South Fulton Avenue and a 5 p.m. service at the March home.

Mr. Brown, who is also survived by his former wife, Alverta Wright, will be buried this morning at the Garrison Forest Veterans Cemetery in Owings Mills.

Baltimore is believed to be the only city in the country where hucksters still work on horse-drawn wagons and share the streets with cars and trucks.

The last stables survive on South Carlton Street, Retreat Street and Bruce Street, all on the west side.

Adele Stolte and Frances Mason — a pair of elegant, elderly women about as different from a-rabs as peaches are from parsnips — were on hand yesterday to pay respects to Pistol Brown and make sure a way of life does not die with him.

Stolte and Mason are members of the A-rabbers Preservation Society. Two years ago this week, the society filed a federal class-action suit against Baltimore City to protect a-rabs from what they claim is a campaign to shut them down.

The suit followed efforts by the city animal control agency — at the prompting of animal rights activists — to close the stables on allegations of poor living conditions for the horses.

"These are independent businessmen who don't have to depend on anyone," said Mason, who lives on a horse farm in Howard County where retired a-rabs' ponies are put to pasture. "The city should be smart about this and have them down at Harborplace every weekend."

In 1998, about two dozen a-rabs took part in the still-undecided lawsuit.

Today, there is one less.

July 11, 2000

Gilbert Lukowski, 75, led ILA local

GILBERT LUKOWSKI HAD A SPECIAL WAY OF MAKING HIMSELF UNDERSTOOD TO fellow longshoremen and company officials sitting across the negotiating table during labor disputes.

He would scream in their faces until they got the point.

"You'd ask Gilbert a question, and he would explain why you should have known the answer already," said Albert "Sin" Kowalewski, a childhood friend who served under him when Mr. Lukowski was president of Local No. 1355 of the International Longshoremen's Association from the 1950s through the 1960s. The local represented ship's carpenters.

"When he'd talk to the men at a union meeting he'd bang the metal table with his fist until you couldn't hear anything else," said Mr. Kowalewski. "You had to know the guy real well or you might have thought he was crazy."

Mr. Lukowski, a Thames Street scrapper who went from working waterfront labor gangs after World War II to heading the ILA pension fund in Maryland, died of lung cancer Monday at Stella Maris Hospice. He was 75.

"His bark was worse than his bite," said a nephew, Gregory Lukowski, a Baltimore tugboat captain. "He was one of them in-your-face guys, but every holiday, he was at your house, dropping off loaves of Polish raisin bread with the crumbs on top. When my father [Jerome] was dying, Gilbert came over every morning and they'd talk and cry together."

He said one pungent memory from his childhood summed up his uncle's no-nonsense approach to life.

On Saturdays, all of the Lukowskis would gather at the home of family matriarch Veronica — Gilbert's mother — in the 1700 block of Thames St. One weekend, they were grinding fresh horseradish.

"I was 8 years old and was bugging them to let me taste it. They didn't cut this stuff, it wasn't the kind of horseradish you get at the supermarket," said Gregory Lukowski. "My parents kept telling me I wouldn't like it, but Gilbert said, 'Come here, kid,' and let me take a whiff. I almost passed out. It was my first reality check."

On the waterfront, Mr. Lukowski worked for years to get as much money and benefits for the men he represented as possible.

In his later career with the pension fund, he spent hours explaining complicated benefits to men who sometimes could neither read nor write.

As a union president, he often urged the ship's carpenters — whose active ranks are down to fewer than two dozen men in the age of container cargo — to go on strike and stay out as long as necessary to win concessions.

"We had plenty of rough times because of that," said his wife, the former Katherine Mazzie. "The union was his life."

The son of a bootlegging longshoreman, Mr. Lukowski was the middle child of three brothers born in the Thames Street house that did business as the Seamen's Cafe. His older brother Frank died in 1971, and Jerome, the youngest, passed away in 1997.

A graduate of St. Patrick's parochial school on Broadway, Mr. Lukowski dropped out of high school to join the Navy during World War II.

After the war's end, he worked at Bethlehem Steel in Sparrows Point for a short time before going to work as a stevedore.

He married Katherine in 1950, the year he became president of Local No. 1355, and the couple settled in the Belair-Edison neighborhood near Catholic High School. Mrs. Lukowski still resides there.

When he wasn't doing union business, Mr. Lukowski read local newspapers and history books. His knowledge of Fells Point, known simply as Broadway in his youth, was encyclopedic.

"When I was growing up, the foot of Broadway was the greatest place in the world," he said a few years back. "They say nobody remembers the old days, but I think about it every day."

Until his cancer was diagnosed more than a decade ago, he enjoyed stopping in Kissling's Tavern at Fleet and Chester streets for a sandwich and a beer. Before his mother's death in 1990, he visited her every morning.

He will be buried tomorrow after a 10 a.m. funeral Mass at the Shrine of the Little Flower at Brendan Avenue and Belair Road.

In addition to his wife, he is survived by a son, John Thomas Lukowski of Baltimore; two daughters, Beverly Atkins of Ashbury, Va. and Janet Ewing of Abingdon; and two grandchildren.

September 7, 2000

From chutzpah to chic

A CHIC NEW BROOM IS SWEEPING THE CRUSTY LEGACY OF BERNIE FINK OFF FALLS
Road in Mount Washington.

The flamboyant owner of Fink's Liquors — a man who regularly amazed
his staff by selling people cases of booze they didn't know they needed —
Bernie Fink died at age 76 in late April after doing business for 30 years at Falls
Road and Fairfield Avenue.

His widow, Doris Fink, sold the store to an enterprise headed by local wine
expert T. Nelson Carey III. The Baltimore County Board of Liquor License
Commissioners approved the license transfer this week, and tomorrow will be
the last day the one-time clapboard grocery does business as Fink's.

"The sale came suddenly," said Mrs. Fink. "We started getting calls the minute
the obituary hit the papers."

No longer will a picture of Bernie — wearing a white cabbie's cap, aviator
glasses and an unlighted, extra-long cigarette while staring down the world —
look over his customers from the wall.

No longer will the eight guys who worked for Fink and stayed
on after his death tell "Bernie stories" while punching up lottery tickets.

How he decided to get an earring near the end of his life, only to endure the
ridicule of his staff for putting it in his right ear. He promptly switched it to the
other ear.

The time he accused a Roman Catholic liquor salesman of being a "religious
nut" because the man refused to come into Fink's on a Sunday to do business. Yet,
Bernie was likable enough that the salesman, Alphonso A. Ventrice, never held it
against him.

"Nobody told Bernie what to do," said Ventrice, laughing. "God bless his soul."

Or the time when the store was robbed at gunpoint and Bernie reimbursed
a customer named Tom Minton the $140 the man was forced to turn over during
the holdup.

"He was a little bit Edward G. Robinson and a little James Cagney on the hard
side and a little Spencer Tracy on the soft side," said Bill Chambers, the "senior

stock man and driver," for the past 16 years. "If you worked for Bernie Fink, you had to be tough."

Next week, Chambers and the other tough guys who survived Bernie and his bluster will be out of work. On Monday, Fink's Liquors opens for business as The Old Vine.

"I plan a complete transformation, inside and out," said Carey, a 36-year-old chef who manages the wine department at North Charles Liquors in Rodgers Forge. "I would like the store to mirror my personality instead of Bernie's."

Although Carey has said that Fink's employees may apply for any jobs still open after the new staff takes over, the men who took orders from Bernie don't buy it.

Pointing to Bernie's collection of faithful wisenheimers, Fink's general manager Mark N. Goldstein, 59, says: "The new man may want his staff to wear coats and ties. These guys don't fit the profile."

While the big sign that says "COLD BEER / WINE / MUNCHIES / CIGARS" on the building's north side is sure to come down during renovations, Carey promises that cut-rate diehards will still be able to pick up a six-pack of National Bohemian in a "dressed-up" beer section.

Beyond that, The Old Vine will offer fine wines, a smaller selection of hard liquor and some gourmet foods. "We're going to offer a sophisticated store where people can come and learn about wine," said Carey.

Carey intends to continue the Fink tradition of selling live lobsters on weekends, but it's doubtful he will tell customers — as Bernie reportedly did — that the truck broke down every time the delivery was late.

Fink sold 1-pound lobsters at or near cost, anywhere from $4.99 to $7.99, just to get people in the store. Last Christmas, according to Goldstein, they moved 500 lobsters.

If the crustaceans weren't selling briskly enough, Bernie would telephone regular customers and tell them to "come get your lobster before it's dead," said Ben Paskus, an assistant manager.

Whether it was a bag of lobsters or a case of liquor, Paskus says, Bernie made payment easy by telling customers he'd already charged the sale to their credit cards.

"And then they'd thank him," marveled Paskus.

Such acumen and chutzpah, says Paskus, 28, is the stuff he never learned in business classes at the University of Maryland, Baltimore County.

While Paskus plans to return to school and some of the other help will gravitate to bar or restaurant work, Bill Chambers isn't sure what he'll do.

Asked if he thought the new owner would keep the old boss's picture on the wall, Chambers said: "If he didn't want none of us, he sure don't want Bernie."

October 6, 2000

JIM BURGER 1981

"We come into this life alone and we go out the same way..."

ESSAY AND FAREWELL

Essay: Down at the end of a lonely street

HUMAN BEINGS ARE INDIVIDUALS AND THAT MEANS EACH OF US IS ALONE IN THIS world. We enter life alone. We go out the same way.

And, doctors and insurance companies have documented, if we spend too much time alone between our entrance and exit the odds are greater that we will leave this world sooner than necessary.

It is hard to imagine that a soul was ever born who didn't feel lonely at one time or another in his life. It blows over us all, nipping at some, nagging after others and knocking more than a few to the ground.

Unlike joy or anger, you usually cannot see loneliness in a person's face.

When severe enough, it will be pronounced in sadness or depression, sometimes bitterness, but more often it is a dull ache mixed in with half a bag of other emotions, at once the cause and result of all kinds of problems.

Joe has been haunted by loneliness for some time now, a good part of his otherwise successful 29 years.

A mid-level executive in the medical field, he fears the void may be beginning to define his life instead of simply disrupting it.

"It's frightening," he said. "Outside of my parents there's very little that is familiar for me to hang onto."

There seems to be no obvious reason for Joe's loneliness.

Fresh-faced and youthful, he is not a bad-looking man. Although a bit short with a slight paunch, Joe is thoughtful and articulate with interests ranging from literature to photography to wind surfing.

Exceedingly polite, he is always the gentleman, yet a bit timid, and often cautious — perhaps from a lack of confidence — to the point of inaction.

Well-groomed and clean, Joe is what every mother could hope for in a son-in-law, the quintessential "nice boy." So nice, in fact, that the mothers of his dates often like him more than his dates do.

"I've always sort of felt like an outsider," he said, describing a feeling that extends back to grade school. "Even though I'm almost never alone."

The week isn't so bad, says Joe. Monday through Friday there is always some type of time-consuming or mindless chore to do around the house, like washing his clothes or paying his bills.

And, while his job keeps him busy, a recent pattern of his staying later and later at the office for lack of some thing better to do has begun to worry him.

What is bad, Joe says, are the weekends. In this he is not alone. For many of the other lonely people mentioned here — all of whom asked that their identities be disguised — the weekend is a vacant cellar where loneliness holds a full-length mirror up to their empty lives.

"There's a time I call 'magic time' — on Friday, after work from about 5:30 to 9 p.m.," he says. "A time when you don't feel guilty about hanging out or relaxing [at home], because it's been a long week ... you look forward to interaction.

"So on a Friday I come home feeling good, I change into jeans and a T-shirt, pop a beer ... [and wait] for something to come up." The "something" could be almost anything — Joe says he'll usually accept almost any social offer.

During this time, Joe, who dates but has no steady girlfriend, will not pick up the phone and call friends to initiate some activity because, he says, it would only be "admitting defeat."

When two hours have passed and fun has not presented itself, he heads to the neighborhood supermarket to get a salad for dinner.

"There are times you don't want to shop at the Giant because it's a drag to see mirror images of yourself," he says. "At 7:30 on a Friday night [it seems] the only people there are social outcasts and I don't need that reinforced. At the same time you don't want to get there at 6 p.m. on a Friday because [couples and partners] are there, happy, getting their dinners before going home..." to what he imagines will be a romantic night.

Because such evenings have been absent from his life — and because he believes everyone else is enjoying romance and intimacy — it makes him jealous, angry and bitter.

So Joe buys his salad and goes home. He doesn't get dessert for later in the night, he says, because he doesn't yet want to commit — or admit — to the fact that his time won't be occupied.

If an empty Friday evening still yawns before him after he eats, Joe begins to pace.

"I walk around, go downstairs, maybe stand on the front porch awhile," he says, and watch the traffic roll by. "Then it's time for another beer."

Careful not to drink too much in case opportunity should knock, Joe will listen to music or wander around the house or the neighborhood for another hour or so — until about 11 p.m., when he'll either watch the news or a video movie.

By 11, the promise of "magic time" has evaporated for another week, and although depressed and times intoxicated, Joe has survived the anxiety it brings.

"I gotta kill those two hours between 9 and 11 p.m.; somehow that's the lowest time," he says.

"But the longer [loneliness] hangs around, the more a part of my life it seems to be," says Joe. "I try to stay busy. When I start to think about it is when I really feel down."

If there is one constant in the life of lonely people it is that they are unhappy, whether they are alone or not.

Yet being alone does not breed loneliness, the emotional state in which a person feels a strong yearning for the company of others. Different from this is solitude, where one is alone but content.

A person involved in a positive emotional relationship, one involving love and security, might be able to enjoy the magic time — the solitude — Joe has created for what it is: a chance to get away from the rat race and unwind from a hectic week.

But for Joe, this time has become a frustrating, regular reminder of what he doesn't have.

Dr. Laura Primakoff, an assistant professor of psychology at the University of Maryland at Baltimore, has dedicated her career to the study of loneliness and living alone.

"Loneliness is part of the human condition that has existed since humans have existed," she says. "What's different in America in the last 10 or 20 years is that the psychiatric and media professions are talking about it. And there are now more single people — one out of three adult Americans are single — and that has encouraged more frank discussion of loneliness."

While loneliness exists within marriages and large families — some folks are more lonely in a bad relationship than on their own, while psychiatrists know many patients who prefer imperfect companionship to none at all — loneliness appears to be most evident in the lives of people like Joe.

People who have failed to find, or hold onto, a special someone to share their life with.

"We all need someone to tell us we're great," says Leo, a 24-year-old unemployed truck driver who lives with his mother and is always looking for that certain someone.

"I come from a large family and to be the only one solo at large family functions is a very empty feeling, very lonely. Like being the third wheel all the time when your friends go out. That stinks, but it's better than being home alone," he admits.

Leo is one of the youngest in a family of nine. All of his older brothers have found a serious companion, and since he isn't any better- or worse-looking than any of them — and no smarter or less intelligent — he wonders what might be wrong with him.

Leo blames his predicament, his sense of being not only emotionally awkward but out of touch with intimacy, on the four years he spent in the Navy after leaving high school.

"While I was sailing around the world having sex with prostitutes my friends were home meeting girls, learning how to talk to them," he says. "I see myself as being behind in the game of life."

More than anything, Leo wants to find a "nice girl" — not a centerfold knockout, a party girl or a high-salaried professional — just a nice girl with a good mind whom he can fall in love with.

And, more importantly, who will fall in love with him.

"When I finally do go out with a woman," he says, "I figure she must not be that good if she wants to go out with me."

Dr. John R. Lion estimates that at least half of his dozen or so weekly patients, who see him for problems as mild as wanting someone to talk to and far more serious mental ills, suffer from significant degrees of loneliness.

"It's a great quest of people to find sustaining, intimate companionship — a very complicated challenge," he says. "It involves trust, an ability to be intimate ... to share without the fear of being abandoned or neglected. It's a tough job — surprisingly tough for many people. People are shy, anxious, frightened. We see these patients daily."

For most people, Dr. Lion says, being alone at times is "refreshing, compatible with a full life."

There seem to be a million causes for loneliness and the sense of being disconnected that it breeds in personalities both gregarious and shy.

To talk to the friends of lonely people who try to help their buddies, you would think there are also a million possible solutions. And yet, in the density of Manhattan and the open spaces of Arizona, loneliness not only persists, it thrives.

Some causes: The death of a spouse; children moving from home; old age; a job transfer; a divorce; being an only child; being single; sickness; a new school, a new neighborhood or the culture of a foreign country; being either a workaholic or unemployed.

Add to these time-worn situations the cold age of technology and the impersonal, man-interacting-with-machines mentality it has spawned, with television, video recorders and automatic bank machines.

Even air-conditioning has played a big role. Before homes were centrally cooled, families and neighbors sat on the front porch or steps on hot summer nights to catch a breeze and shoot the breeze. But sitting in an air-conditioned house watching TV, as inviting as that may be on a humid evening, cuts us off from each other.

"There's something very autistic about sitting at home and watching a movie on the VCR," says Dr. Lion. "The question we have to ask is, 'As we evolve into a more dehumanized society are we fostering more problems with isolation and loneliness?' "

"These technologies isolate people from each other," says Dr. Primakoff. "For single people or families, they keep people from interacting. Often in bad relationships one or the other person simply turns on the TV, and we [Americans] find that acceptable. Single people use the chatter of the TV in the background for the illusion of company."

The result, says Dr. Lion, is "a depressive state; a certain hopelessness ... despair, a lack of enthusiasm in life."

A few easy solutions to loneliness which can take the edge off a vacant life but in no way guarantee an introduction to that special someone: Take a college course; learn a craft; volunteer at a hospital; hang out in a library; talk to the person in the next seat; join a club; visit the elderly; develop a hobby; take walks; go to church; force yourself to strike up conversations in unlikely places; learn a language; or write to a prisoner.

John D. Conway, an inmate at the Maryland House of Correction in Jessup with four years left on a five-year burglary sentence, would certainly write back.

"People in prison get lonely for all types of reasons, no different from those that make people lonely on the outside," wrote Conway in a recent letter. "Separation from loved ones, from friends, from pets, lack of meaningful work — or no work — dull and unimaginative recreation ...

"But I do believe that we prisoners seem to have better defenses and are more adept at denying loneliness. Yet the denial comes out in our behavior and often in strange ways.

"One guy who shares my dormitory with me can be seen and heard every night carrying on a most lively and animated conversation with Sally Thorner on the 11 o'clock news. I have actually seen him sit in front of the TV and comb his hair in preparation.

"The kind of loneliness I see in here is of a type that is the most brooding and distressing. It is the loneliness of men trapped within themselves ... of men crowded together with nowhere to go and no one to talk to.

"True, I miss my physical freedom," he writes, "but even more than it, I miss some of those little things that you don't realize you miss right away after you're locked up.

"Such as children, I miss children, seeing them and hearing them, I miss house plants and pets, and I miss working on the annual vegetable garden in my sister's back yard. Little things. I miss taking walks in Herring Run Park with my nieces and nephews and pointing out to them the names of trees and how you can tell their names by the shapes of their leaves.

"I miss talking to the longshoremen and tugboat crews over coffee in Jimmy the Greek's Restaurant down in Fells Point at the foot of Broadway; I miss eating with a knife and fork and plate ... just little things."

"When people see something beautiful," says Dr. Lion. "The general response is, 'I wish so-and-so could see this.'"

And when there isn't a so-and-so around to share the beauty, the beauty itself — something as simple as a flower in bloom — becomes a negative reminder to the lonely of just how empty their life is.

But it doesn't have to be that way, if you are willing to work at it, says Dr. Primakoff, who earned her doctorate with a thesis entitled "Patterns of Living Alone and Loneliness."

The human desire to group together is very basic, she says, affirming Dr. Lion's observation that all social functions "from the Moose Lodge to the singles bar" are attempts to combat loneliness.

"But I'm saying that people who think that the only way to be happy is from another person are going to be in trouble," she says.

While Dr. Primakoff does not encourage her patients and students to abandon the search for meaningful companionship, she counsels that a well-adjusted, productive life need not be lost to that search.

"The traditional idea is you would rather be with someone else, but that's the assumption we're questioning, the assumption we challenge," she says. "The single people who feel quite lonely often have a basic assumption that a [love] partner will be their source of happiness, meaning, self-esteem and excitement, and without that they are lost."

Instead of living in a place where one merely eats and sleeps, Dr. Primakoff urges people to create homes where they can be comfortable, a place they not only want to come home to but one they can invite others to.

Those who live alone should take pleasure in shopping for their food, trying out new recipes, and learn to do tasks traditionally performed by the opposite sex, such as sewing or fixing the car.

Outside the home, Dr. Primakoff says, "People can choose their own company, and not by default. I encourage them to go out alone; there are no compromises [to make with someone else's restaurant or movie choices] in taking yourself out, and that's a powerful motivator. It's more adventurous; you're more likely to meet people."

Dr. Primakoff, who has taught her program at the University of Texas and the University of Pennsylvania but not in Baltimore, believes you are more likely to meet someone while pursuing an interest rather than spending all your time chasing after that special someone.

"We all know the stereotype of people who move into an apartment and literally don't take things out of boxes, don't decorate, and are out every night of the week looking for Mr. or Miss Right and wonder why their lives are so empty.

"These people are not developing friendships, they're looking for this elusive partner and that gets old. If one spends all of one's energy in that pursuit, it doesn't leave time for friendships that may be more stable than love relationships."

The absence of sexual relations can reinforce a lonely person's self-image as someone not worthy of intimacy, she says.

"Like companionship, it's a basic part of human life to want to be physically affectionate and sexually intimate with another person and, to varying degrees, if a person is deprived of physical affection and/or sexual contact, it will result in a type of loneliness," says Dr. Primakoff. "Over a protracted period of time [this lack of sexual contact] contributes very strongly to a basic sense of being cut off from other humans."

And it just doesn't afflict single people, she says. "Unfortunately, there are more sexless marriages or relationships with [poor] sex than we would like to contemplate."

Sincere affection can be obtained, she says, from friendships where there is "mutual physical affection, where people can touch each other, hug each other, engage in contact sports and dancing, or spend time with children — opportunities to touch and be touched. It's comforting."

What Dr. Primakoff is saying is that if you cannot find all you want from life in one person, get as much of it as you can from yourself and a combination of other relationships. But to the lonely, this advice just sounds too easy or not worth the bother.

What good is it to spend time making an interesting meal for yourself, argues Henry, a 33-year-old transportation worker, if, without a companion, "nothing is right — food doesn't taste right, music doesn't sound right, sleep doesn't feel right?"

Lucy, a mental health worker in her late 30s, says she's familiar with Dr. Primakoff's program. But, nonetheless, she's been prone — often in the past, but not so much lately — to lonely periods of such intensity that she becomes lost in them like a woman trapped in amber.

"I feel cut off," she says. "I walk around and I see a couple talking, clearly being intimate, and I feel that is not possible for me. . . . Sometimes I don't even answer the phone when it rings. I slip into this state, a withdrawn state, and it's hard to get out of, almost like you have trouble feeling."

While loneliness might be thought of as a more natural part of life for the expanding population of senior citizens who have watched friends and spouses pass away over the years, it makes it no easier to bear.

With people living longer, there are more senior citizens around today than ever before.

Around this group has grown support organizations such as the Golden Age Club, the Eating Together program, the American Association of Retired People, retirement communities, and agencies like Baltimore's Waxter Senior Center.

The possible solutions to loneliness for these people are no different from those offered to the young and lonely — using almost any constructive reason to get together with other people with similar interests. If it's possible, older people might consider buying a pet such as a dog: besides the sure companionship that a pet itself offers, neighbors and strangers are more apt to strike up a conversation with someone walking a dog, than someone just walking down the street by himself.

But the loneliness of the elderly is often complicated by illness and disease, a lack of mobility, and the feeling that they are unwanted in a world in which they have lived all their lives. A world — in America at least — geared to and dominated by youth.

Albert V. Contarini, the real name of an 87-year-old retired stonemason living in Glen Burnie, hates living alone, and blames society for turning its back on old people.

A bachelor who never married, his life became empty after his mother died 16 years ago. Although he was instrumental in beginning an Anne Arundel County program several years ago in which volunteers drop in on the elderly, the "Friendly Visitor" program has been unable to find a regular visitor for him.

"At the age I am now it's not right to leave a person alone ... all these years, to eat alone in that room and not have contact with people . . . every day I'm fighting, fighting loneliness. To study it is one thing, to live it is another.

"To live like this is to drop into a spider's web; you go down. It's like you have no purpose, you walk around and wonder, 'What's the use?' You wake up, you say, 'Oh well, what the hell am I gonna do today?' After a while you don't know if it's day or night. It's not normal, it's inhuman. It makes me angry."

Those feelings are no better for a teen-ager like Daisy, nearly 70 years Mr. Contarini's junior and able to go and do just about anything she wants.

"Whenever I feel lonely and like I don't have friends, I want to go out on the street and yell at people: 'I'm here!!!'"

May 3, 1987

Fare Thee Well

I COME FROM PEOPLE WHO ARE TIGHT WITH A BUCK.

When they go, they go first-class — Tio Pepe's for special celebrations, good schools for the kids and solid furniture. But they don't splurge often and rarely risk money earned with the kind of sweat that good schools have spared me.

My father's father could have scooped up a nice parcel or two of beachfront property in Ocean City after World War II. Mr. Sanchez, his good buddy from Rappolla Street via the Canary Islands, was buying and exhorted my grandfather to get a piece of the action.

But the prospect was too risky for a Sparrows Point shipyard worker who'd grown up milking cows in Pontevedra — the West Virginia of Spain — and the old man passed.

In the 1960s, a federal highway was scheduled to destroy Fells Point. My father was a veteran tugboat engineer for Baker-Whiteley at the time and Polish tavern owners around Thames Street were offering him their gin mills for half a song. But my folks had two boys in Catholic school and a mortgage on a brick rancher in the suburbs and Dad played it safe.

Mom — who still thinks the Depression is on and used to say, "You've never been hungry, mister!" when we'd turn up our noses at leftovers — wrestles bank statements to the mat until dawn looking for 17 cents she is sure has been stolen from her checking account. So you can imagine the flock of fears that flew around my parents' Linthicum kitchen the day I announced I was quitting *The Sun* — my employer since I was a teen-ager — after 23 years.

A good paying job!

With seniority and benefits !

And union security!

As my Polish grandmother often lamented from her Dillon Street lawn chair: "Yezus, ka-hah-nie . . ."

(That's "Lord have mercy" to you and me.)

Like singing convicts breaking big rocks into little rocks, Mom and Dad took turns saying: "I guess you know what you're doing."

This is what I'm doing: I'm buying that ocean-view property whether I live to see it developed or not; I'm grabbing a million dollars worth of Fells Point real estate before outside money comes in to give the bars stupid names and insipid motifs; I'm trusting that the God which brought me this far will not drop me on my head because I have embraced the idea that art is worth more than news.

I have no doubt that this is right — right for me, right now — in the way I imagine that married people leave their spouses in their hearts long before sharing the decision.

As the not-yet-famous John Lennon often asked the other unknown Beatles as the band paid its dues in Liverpool dives: "Where are we going, boys?"

"To the top, Johnny!"

"Where's that, boys?"

"To the toppermost of the poppermost!"

I'm going for it, Johnny.

Faithful to the frugality of my forebears, however, my leap from the roof of 501 North Calvert St. is calculated.

America doesn't give its rank-and-file parachutes lined with gold, but I am leaving with a reasonable check and subsidized health coverage in a buy-out offered to longtime Sunpapers' workers by its new owners.

And, having paid my dues on the city desk — from chasing cops to obits to the callous surgery of rewrite and the free verse of a thousand weather stories — I am leaving with pencils sharpened to the fine edge that knife-grinding legend Pio Vidi used to lay on local meatcleavers.

What will I do with this bag of tricks?

For nearly two-and-a-half decades — all in the service of the paper you are now reading — I've sliced the rough cloth of life in Baltimore into ribbons just long enough for a single bow.

My first byline, at age 20, was an interview with Studs Terkel in Chicago during a break in the Rolling Stones "Some Girls" tour at Soldier Field. It ran on the front of the features section.

My last as a staff writer came about a week ago, a deadline rewrite of a dispatch on a College Park provost taking the president's job at Iowa State University. It ran deep inside the local section, beyond the lost and founds.

In between, I have chronicled men who wanted to read their obituaries before they died; women who owned corner bars that sold more egg sandwiches than beer; sewing machine mechanics who dreamed of being composers and way too many teen-agers who found their way to coffins.

Now, in the vestibule of middle age — not a mid-life crisis, but a mid-life epiphany that arrived with a get-out-while-the-gettings-good check — I want something different.

Ribbons are pretty, but they don't cover very much. I want to try my hand at ball gowns and tailored suits: novels and screenplays and memoirs set in the city which this newspaper paid me to study for 20 years.

As a journeyman reporter, I will pick up what factory hands used to call "piece work" to keep my kids in good schools and the mortgage paid on Macon Street. But I will only take as much as necessary.

That challenge — not to take jobs out of fear — is greater than the decision to quit *The Sun*. While I do not share my family's aversion to risk, I did inherit the belief that work is the true Alvarez religion and fight the temptation to take every assignment that comes along.

For now, I am worshipping at a new altar: I will only do what I want to do for as long as it lasts.

I have plans to go back to sea — the last job I held before taking a job in *The Sun*'s circulation department in 1977. As a long-haired graduate of Mount Saint Joseph, a kid convinced that adventure was the only way to a life in letters, I worked as an ordinary seamen the summer after graduation and sailed again the following summer as a wiper in the engine room. Both tasks were too close to real work and this time around I hope to go out as a galley hand.

On board, I will be writing a memoir of my family's maritime history. Between ships, I'll be filing long-playing record albums at the Musical Exchange on Charles Street, washing dishes at the Viva House Catholic Worker house on South Mount Street, walking from Greektown to Curtis Bay with a notebook in my pocket ...

And turning all of it into art which I pray will survive me.

February 4, 2001

627 South Macon Street

About the Author

Rafael Alvarez was born in Baltimore in 1958 and educated in Catholic schools.

The father of three children — Amelia, Jake and Sofia — he lives in the Greektown neighborhood of East Baltimore. He works at a record store on Charles Street.

Alvarez is the author of two books of short stories, *The Fountain of Highlandtown* and *Orlo and Leini*, as well as *Hometown Boy*, a previous collection of his articles for *The Sun*.

A fan of the rock band Cheap Trick, he admires the writers Richard Ford and Tim O'Brien. Alvarez can be reached at rafael@alvarezfiction.com.

"I am deeply grateful to my friend Ron for writing this book. He reinforces Gospel hope that has been lost in too many circles, either abandoned for false teaching or set aside as wishful thinking. With selfless honesty and humility, Ron extends the healing Jesus died to make possible."

—Adam T. Barr, author, *Compassion without Compromise*; lead pastor, Peace Church

"Insightful and intriguing. Ron Citlau offers a compelling voice not often heard in today's conversation surrounding this topic. Throughout God's Kingdom *Hope for the Same-Sex Attracted* will prove to be helpful and inspiring."

—Bob Bouwer, senior pastor, Faith Church

"Glorious. Without demonizing his opponents, Ron burns off the debris and reveals Jesus to persons impacted by same-sex attraction. That's everyone. Read and bask in the Hope that redeems the struggle and invites us into a new way of being and loving. Best evangelical book on the subject today. Maybe ever."

—Andrew Comiskey, founder/director, Desert Stream/Living Waters Ministries

"When it comes to navigating the complex topics addressed in the pages of this book, Ron Citlau is on the top of my list of people I trust to handle the conversation biblically, compassionately, and pastorally. As you read, you might find yourself agreeing strongly, disagreeing profusely, or somewhere in between. But, wherever you come from on this important and contemporary topic, you will appreciate Ron's wisdom, grace, and honesty."

—Rev. Dr. Kevin G. Harney, pastor, author, and founder, Organic Outreach International, KevinGHarney.com

"Ron Citlau exhibits warmth, insight, and courage in *Hope for the Same-Sex Attracted*. I am grateful for this book!"

—Peter Hubbard, teaching pastor,
North Hills Community Church

"Pastor Citlau has written a helpful book for Christians struggling with homosexuality. He thoughtfully addresses some of the theological errors of our day—including the embrace of a 'gay Christian' identity and 'same-sex marriage.' He vulnerably shares his own struggle and gives realistic, biblical hope for those who forsake homosexuality and pursue Christ."

—Jeff Johnston, Issues Analyst—Marriage,
Homosexuality and Gender, Focus on the Family

"A must-read for pastors, counselors, lay leaders, and same-sex strugglers! Citlau addresses current popular roadblocks in Christian circles and suggests solid ways toward transformation. He highlights practical ways the body of Christ can aid the struggler in 'straining forward to what lies ahead . . . the prize of the upward call of God in Christ Jesus' (Philippians 3:13–14)."

—Anne Paulk, executive director,
Restored Hope Network

"Ron Citlau bravely supplies compassionate, biblical counsel on perhaps the most divisive issue of our day. He challenges same-sex-attracted Christians not to identify with their temptation, and he calls the church to be their community of love, healing, and family. This is an important book for all same-sex-attracted Christians, and for the people who love them."

—Michael Wittmer, professor of systematic theology,
Grand Rapids Theological Seminary, Cornerstone University

HOPE

for the

SAME-SEX
ATTRACTED

Books by Ron Citlau

Compassion without Compromise
(coauthored by Adam T. Barr)

Hope for the Same-Sex Attracted

HOPE

for the

SAME-SEX ATTRACTED

BIBLICAL DIRECTION FOR FRIENDS, FAMILY MEMBERS,
AND THOSE STRUGGLING WITH HOMOSEXUALITY

RON CITLAU

BETHANYHOUSE
a division of Baker Publishing Group
Minneapolis, Minnesota

© 2017 by Ron Citlau

Published by Bethany House Publishers
11400 Hampshire Avenue South
Bloomington, Minnesota 55438
www.bethanyhouse.com

Bethany House Publishers is a division of
Baker Publishing Group, Grand Rapids, Michigan

Printed in the United States of America

Library of Congress Cataloging-in-Publication Data
Names: Citlau, Ron, author.
Title: Hope for the same-sex attracted : biblical direction for friends, family members, and those struggling with homosexuality / Ron Citlau.
Description: Minneapolis, Minnesota : Bethany House, 2017. | Includes bibliographical references.
Identifiers: LCCN 2016036487 | ISBN 9780764218682 (trade paper : alk. paper)
Subjects: LCSH: Homosexuality—Religious aspects—Christianity. | Gays— Religious life. | Church work with gays.
Classification: LCC BR115.H6 C565 2017 | DDC 261.8/35766—dc23
LC record available at https://lccn.loc.gov/2016036487

In keeping with biblical principles of creation stewardship, Baker Publishing Group advocates the responsible use of our natural resources. As a member of the Green Press Initiative, our company uses recycled paper when possible. The text paper of this book is composed in part of post-consumer waste.

17 18 19 20 21 22 23   7 6 5 4 3 2 1

green press INITIATIVE

Cover design by LOOK Design Studio

To my wife, Amy.
There is no one else
that I would rather live this life with.
God has been good to me
by giving me you.

There are many people I want to thank on this project. First, Andy McGuire for his and Bethany House's support of this book. Your team is amazing. Second, I am so thankful to Ellen Chalifoux, who was the primary editor. Her suggestions, questions, and feedback made this a better book. Finally, I want to thank Dr. Todd Billings, Dr. Brian Dennert, Andrew Comiskey, Dorothy Greco, Nate Pyle, and Troy Westercamp, who provided feedback on various chapters. Any mistakes in this book are mine, but the good was refined by these good men and women.

CONTENTS

INTRODUCTION

Bob Dylan's song got it right: "The Times They Are a-Changin'."
We are now witnessing the emergence of the most gay-affirming
culture in human history. Our country's view of homosexuality has changed seemingly overnight. A majority of Americans
now see absolutely nothing wrong with same-sex relationships,
and gay marriage is now a constitutionally protected right.
Secular culture has spoken: Gay marriage provides the best
relational framework for gay persons to flourish and find happiness. Sadly, even some Christians agree. Meanwhile, the rest
of us struggle to explain why following Jesus is better for a
same-sex-attracted person than a lifelong, love-filled, committed same-sex relationship.

Seizing on the cultural upheaval, some in the church are
now asserting that the church's current stance against homosexual activity is not just wrong, but actually detrimental to
same-sex-attracted Christians. For them, such a prohibition
stands in the way of gay Christians flourishing in their relational and sexual lives. They believe that for the good of
same-sex strugglers, Christians need to embrace same-sex
marriage. Why would the church deny gay men and women
something that will make them so happy?

For them, it all seems so obvious if one is willing to consider the evidence. There are many men and women who have accepted their gay identity, are in committed same-sex relationships, and are Christians. They happily proclaim that gay marriage is a gift from God. They seem to be flourishing. And then there are stories of men and women who tried to live faithfully from a traditional perspective but only experienced pain, loneliness, and failure. If we take such stories seriously, what conclusions are we to draw? What are we to think?

All of this creates a challenge for evangelical Christianity. We must be able to give adequate and hope-filled answers to the questions of those who disagree with us and show why following Jesus can lead to a life of flourishing for the same-sex struggler. We need to be able to show same-sex-attracted Christians how they can live out their sexual and relational lives in ways that honor Jesus and fulfill the deep aches of the heart. If we believe that same-sex strugglers must refuse to act on their same-sex desires for the sake of following Jesus, then I think it is up to the church to show the ways they can find relational fulfillment in Jesus and his church. Until we do this, the good news will not be very good to the same-sex struggler.

Obstacles and Gifts

This book is an earnest attempt to biblically reflect upon the remarkable relational gifts available to a Christian who struggles with same-sex attraction and who desires to faithfully follow Jesus in his or her sexuality. It also seeks to answer the most pertinent challenges facing the evangelical church today as it relates to homosexuality and relationships. To do that, this book is divided into two parts. First, it seeks to remove the obstacles that stand in the way of God's gifts to the same-sex struggler.

From my perspective, those obstacles are gay Christian identity, gay marriage, and the spiritual friendship movement. I hope to show that these obstacles really limit the relational and sexual good that God wants to offer the same-sex struggler. Once the obstacles are cleared, this book gives five real and substantive biblical gifts that are available to the same-sex struggler: the gift of the church, the gift of therapy, the gift of singleness, the gift of marriage, and the gift of lament.

My hope in this book is to give these various gifts a fresh hearing. Please do not assume that you know everything that could be said about these various gifts, and please do not dismiss any of them without being willing to engage honestly with each one. Our goal is the same, I am sure: We want same-sex-attracted Christians to flourish in their relational lives. Let's journey together and see if these gifts might be the means of such flourishing. I believe they are.

Compassion without Compromise

If you are looking for a book that seeks to show how the Scriptures stand against homosexual behavior, the book in your hand is the wrong book. This book assumes that the Scriptures firmly and clearly stand against same-sex activity and seeks to reveal the ways a same-sex struggler can find relational and sexual fulfillment as they live out a traditional view of Scriptures even as they refuse to act on their same-sex feelings.

For a more in-depth discussion on what the Scriptures say about homosexuality and biblical ethics, you might want to read *Compassion without Compromise: How the Gospel Frees Us to Love Our Gay Friends Without Losing the Truth*. Co-written by my good friend Adam Barr and me, the book seeks to clearly show what Scripture teaches about homosexuality and how to live that out winsomely in a doubting world. *Compassion without Compromise* looks at what Scripture teaches about homosexuality and provides practical tips for Christians who want to love same-sex strugglers well.

Who Is This Book For?

This book is for pastors, church leaders, parents of a same-sex struggler, and Christians who want to work very hard to make their churches a place where same-sex strugglers can relationally flourish. With God's help, I hope to stir your imagination and give you some tools to better serve the same-sex struggler. I want to help you see just how much is relationally available to these brothers and sisters in Christ. This way, you can help make the church the place it should be—the place God wants it to be.

This book will also be helpful to the same-sex struggler who is seeking answers to how he or she can faithfully follow Jesus and fulfill the deep relational and sexual longings of the heart. For these readers, it is my desire that you find, in a more meaningful way, the deep relational riches that are in Christ for you. I will be praying for that!

A Word to Skeptics

Maybe you are reading this book and see homosexuality as a gift from God. Or at the very least, you think God doesn't really care as much about someone's bedroom behavior as some in the evangelical church seem to care. The way you see it, same-sex committed relationships are God's answer to the same-sex struggler. Period. End of story. Why stand in the way of something so good? To you, I want to say two things. First, I hear you. I have very close friends who believe as you do. I love them dearly. This book takes seriously the possibility that gay marriage might be God's concession in a broken world. While you may not agree with my conclusions, this is my honest and sincere attempt to add meaningfully to the conversation. Maybe we will all learn something together.

The second thing I want to say is this: I might be wrong (according to my wife, it would not be the first time!). I am a faithful follower of Jesus, a student of the Scriptures, and convinced of my position, but still I accept that I might be wrong. I try to engage this topic with that in mind. I want to learn and find out what is actually true. I humbly ask the same of you. You might be wrong, too. Perhaps you have gotten caught up in the cultural whirlwind and are really lost—maybe much more than you would like to admit. Read this book with an open mind. I hope that you, like me, will decide to follow the Truth wherever it leads. I am sure you will be glad you did.

Hope

It is such an honor to be going on this journey with you. I am hopeful that, together, we are going to find remarkable gifts for the Christian same-sex struggler. My hope, in part, lies in my own experience. I am a same-sex struggler. I am committed to Jesus and a traditional view of Scriptures. I have found relational and sexual fulfillment even as I refuse to act on my same-sex inclinations. I am flourishing! Christ has been good to me. But that is not the only reason I have hope that we can find remarkable gifts for the same-sex-attracted Christian.

Right now, as you read this book, there are countless men and women around the world who struggle with same-sex desire, love Jesus, have submitted their sexuality to him, and are flourishing. Their lives give us reason to hope.

I know unmarried men and women who struggle with same-sex attraction and who live glorious lives in their singleness. They flourish in the church without a spouse. They are bright lights of God's love in a broken world. They aren't lonely people; instead, they are full of life. Sure, they have struggles and issues, but they have decided to use their energies, relationships, and resources for the Kingdom of God. They simply are spectacular people. Their singleness doesn't seem to be a burden; it seems to be a beautiful gift.

I know men and women who are same-sex attracted and living in beautiful heterosexual marriages. They have children, love one another, have good sex lives, and are gifts to the church and the world. These marriages aren't convoluted messes filled with lies and deception. Instead, these marriages give us reason to hope that there are gifts available to the same-sex struggler who wants to follow Jesus.

I also have known men and women who deeply struggle with homosexuality. They live in between wholeness and brokenness. They know more of pain than joy. They want the joy of marriage or even singleness, but it eludes them. At times, their struggle overwhelms them. But even among these good men and women, I have found deep reason to hope. Even in the valley of homosexual brokenness, there are gifts available to same-sex strugglers who want to follow Jesus.

I believe that what Jesus has done for me, what he has done for countless others, he wants to do for everyone who will give their life to him. I have every confidence in the goodness and kindness of Jesus. Our God provides amazing gifts! So let's trust him together and see what he has for us.

PART ONE: **OBSTACLES**

I love to hike. I live in a suburb of Chicago. And all around Chicago are amazing nature preserves with hundreds of miles of walking paths used by runners, hikers, and horseback riders. One of the most beautiful paths, I think, is right by my house. It is about eight miles long, goes through forest and grasslands, and is utterly spectacular. One summer day I was walking the path and was about halfway done when I came to a sign that said "Path Closed." Not willing to let a large orange caution sign stop me, I went on. As I turned the corner there were trucks, workers, and tree debris everywhere. The path was nearly impassable. They were clearing brush, fixing the trail, and making sure it would be usable for years to come. Though I broke the rules and passed, large groups of people and folks on horseback would never be able to use the path until the workers were finished. There were just too many obstacles in the way.

This book has one aim: to show the rich biblical possibilities for flourishing that are available to the person who loves

Jesus and also has same-sex attraction. There is an ancient path that untold thousands through millennia have walked, but very recently the path has been closed. Not because it does not work but because there are many who say there is a better way. Unfortunately, this "better" way puts debris and wreckage on the older path. For this book to really show what is available to the Christian same-sex struggler, we must clear the obstacles that stand in the way.

The first part of this book seeks to clear the paths that are available. This will mean looking at three central ideas that permeate the church and the culture and seeking to show why they aren't actually helpful for the flourishing of the same-sex struggler.

1

The Obstacle of
Gay Christian Identity

I was working on my undergraduate degree in English literature from a great public university in Southern California. I
was five years into my relationship with Jesus and seeking to
deal with my same-sex attraction in ways that honored him
and stayed faithful to a traditional view of Scriptures. For me,
that meant sexual purity, a lot of accountability, and seeking the good Jesus might offer me through the opposite sex.
Unlike some other same-sex strugglers, my same-sex reality
was filled with shame, shadows, and a lot of pain. It was
never something I wanted to publicly embrace. Then I met an
amazing, generous gay professor in the English department.

This professor was kind, he was in a committed relationship, and he seemed totally at ease with his embrace of a
gay identity. This was the first time I had met a gay man who

was not in deep conflict and seemed genuinely at ease in his own skin. It was also the first time I felt a yearning to have the same freedom he did—a seeming integration of desire, personality, and life. What I learned from the professor and from other gays and lesbians who are my friends is that for some, the embrace of a gay identity has been a significant step into a life of integration and psychological wholeness. The caricature of gay men and women all hanging out in dark alleys just didn't fit the experience of many gay and lesbian people I was meeting both in real life and through the writings of many gay people.

Some Christians seeing the seeming good of embracing one's gay identity have asserted that it is utterly essential for a Christian to do so if he or she is to live a healthy and full life. Justin Lee, author of *Torn*, sees it as simply naming what is true:

> When I called myself "gay," I wasn't referring to any kind of behavior in my life. I had never had any kind of sexual or romantic relationship with a guy, and I didn't ever plan to. But even if I never acted on my feelings and never allowed my mind to turn to lust, there was no denying that I was different from other guys in one major way: Where they were attracted to and tempted by girls, I was attracted to and tempted by guys. I was *gay*.[1]

Lee has started an organization seeking to provide a space for those Christians who identify as gay.[2] The very name of the network, Gay Christian Network, embraces a gay Christian identity.

Wesley Hill, a celibate Anglican priest, sees his identity the same way Lee does, but as something even deeper and more interwoven into personality and life:

22

Being gay is, for me, as much a sensibility as anything else: a heightened sensitivity to and passion for same-sex beauty that helps determine the kind of conversations I have, which people I'm drawn to spend time with, what novels and poems and films I enjoy, the particular visual art I appreciate, and also, I think, the kind of friendships I pursue and try to strengthen.[3]

Both of these men are gay *and* Christian. Hill holds to a historic, orthodox sexual ethic while Lee is "open and affirming."[4] They are devout Christians, leaders in the church. They are well respected and sought out to speak on issues of sexuality and Christianity. They affirm the Apostles' Creed and salvation through Christ alone and see the utter necessity of integrating one's Christianity with one's gay identity. To do otherwise is, from their perspective, to do untold damage to the gay self.

The idea of happily joining a gay identity with your Christian identity is a new perspective. At no time in Christian history has it even been considered. Is this because of oppressive cultural realities or because to do so undercuts the good available in the gospel? The goal of this book is to show the rich provisions available for the same-sex struggler who wants to follow Jesus. To receive the rich provisions that God has available means removing the obstacles of those ideas that will actually do more harm than good. I believe that a gay Christian identity is one of those things that stands directly in the path of the same-sex struggler's flourishing.

In this chapter I want to share three reasons why embracing a gay identity will actually stand in the way of true Christian flourishing. Then I want to explore the biblical category of sexuality to embrace for those who struggle with same-sex attraction and want to follow Jesus. By the end of this chapter, I hope to show you that God provides something better than a gay identity.

Setting Up to Fail

I am going to be running a full marathon in the next few months to raise money for World Vision. When they came to my church to invite the congregation to commit to running a marathon, they told us that anyone can run a marathon if they are willing to do these three things: (1) commit to the process; (2) follow a fairly rigorous schedule of training; (3) use the right equipment, specifically great running shoes. If you do these three things, and you have a reasonably healthy body, they guarantee that you can run a full marathon. But let's say for the sake of argument that I decide I will not follow all three things they are recommending. What if I only run in my dress shoes, train occasionally, and gain fifty pounds? You, of course, would call me crazy and say that I have little chance of running a marathon and a better chance of ending up in the hospital (or maybe even getting to meet Jesus face-to-face!). I think something similar is happening when a Christian embraces a gay identity.

The writer of Hebrews tells us this:

> Therefore, since we are surrounded by so great a cloud of witnesses, let us also lay aside every weight, and sin which clings so closely, and let us run with endurance the race that is set before us, looking to Jesus, the founder and perfecter of our faith, who for the joy that was set before him endured the cross, despising the shame, and is seated at the right hand of the throne of God.[5]

Here is the question we have to ask: Does embracing a gay identity enable you, or those you lead, to "run with endurance the race that is set before us"? I want to suggest that a gay identity is a weight that hinders good running. Just think about what a gay identity is: It is seeing your same-sex desire, inclinations, and feelings as a good to embrace. How does this enable one to run a life of holiness? Doesn't one's embrace of a gay identity lead one, quite naturally actually, into situations and relationships that are sinful or at least morally dangerous? If, as Paul states in Colossians 3, all sexual sin, including same-sex activity, needs to be completely gotten rid of, how does embracing a gay identity help you do that? I think whether intentionally or unintentionally, the embrace of gay identity leaves the door open for sexual sin and temptation. And since we are commanded in Ephesians 4 not to give the devil a foothold, it would be best not to embrace a gay identity.

The Possibility of Transformation[6]

I have to insert a bit of my story right here and I think it will help show how embracing a gay Christian identity actually hinders us from what God might have for us. As I was coming alive in Jesus, he was the only hope I had. My life was a mess. My same-sex desire and sin had only caused chaos and pain. I was ready for God to do amazing things. For some reason, I just assumed that God would transform me. Change me. Meet me. From the church I was a part of to the people who discipled me, my overall experience was one in which transformation was something to be expected. Something to be on the lookout for.

Now here is the question: Does embracing a gay Christian identity, which at its core says this part of my identity is something that is unchangeable and integral to who I am, create a barrier to what God might have for the same-sex follower?

25

This reminds me of a great story in the gospel of John.

> Now there is in Jerusalem by the Sheep Gate a pool, in Aramaic called Bethesda, which has five roofed colonnades. In these lay a multitude of invalids—blind, lame, and paralyzed. One man was there who had been an invalid for thirty-eight years. When Jesus saw him lying there and knew that he had already been there a long time, he said to him, "Do you want to be healed?" The sick man answered him, "Sir, I have no one to put me into the pool when the water is stirred up, and while I am going another steps down before me." Jesus said to him, "Get up, take up your bed, and walk." And at once the man was healed, and he took up his bed and walked.[7]

Jesus walks by the healing pool of Bethesda and encounters a man who has been an invalid for thirty-eight years. And Jesus asks him this staggering question: "Do you want to be healed?" The man no doubt knows he is infirm, but could it be that he is more invested in being infirm than being well? Could it be that he has embraced an identity that stands in opposition to what Jesus is offering? Thankfully, Jesus moves beyond the man's limited view of what is available and fully and totally heals him.

These same questions are ones we need to answer. For the same-sex struggler, do you want to be healed? Are you willing to have Jesus touch your sexuality and make it whole? For the church, are you willing to stand for the hope of transformation? For healing and wholeness to be possible, like the invalid, we must see our condition as something in need of the mercy and healing of Jesus. We must see same-sex desire and gay identity as something broken that needs the touch of Jesus. Lee and Hill see their gay identity as an inherent good. They see it as something that God will work through but not change. In this way, they are in a worse position than the invalid. He knew he needed healing. He was confused by how this might happen. But he wanted it. He wanted the impossible. Jesus was the one person able to deliver.

One of the things I want for someone who deals with same-sex attraction is this: to keep the door open, to look out for the real possibility of God moving in their lives and bringing healing and transformation. I know there is a lot of controversy about whether such things still happen. But I know too many examples of people whose lives have been utterly changed by the gospel of Jesus to doubt the possibility.[8] If you deal with same-sex attraction, keep the door open to the possibility of God bringing about transformation; if you are a Christian leader, encourage strugglers to keep the door open. And whatever you do, do not name the fractures of same-sex attraction as good things to be embraced.

Not a Biblical Category

Probably the most important reason not to identify as a gay Christian is simply because it is not a biblical category. Nowhere does the Bible give us permission to identify ourselves in terms of our sinful desires, inclinations, or activities. This is basically the point I and Adam Barr make in *Compassion without Compromise*:

> There is not one biblical example of a person identifying with their sinful brokenness and then adding "Christian" to it. Could you imagine? I am an angry, unbelieving, porn-addicted Christian. Or I am a lying Christian.[9]

I believe, as has historic Christianity, that the Bible has the best information about the human condition and the nature of human identity. I don't think finding new ways to talk about what is happening inside of us is actually helpful. I want to encourage struggler and leader alike not to get caught up in cultural trends but instead to go back to the Bible. Study it, digest it, enter into it until you find what the Scriptures have to say. There are many areas where the Scriptures might be silent, but identity is not one of them. I think by using unbiblical categories to speak about sexuality, gender, and identity we begin to mix up categories, and it becomes unclear exactly what the good news has to say to us. We must name things as Scripture names them, call sin *sin*, and then embrace the cure that is found in Christ alone. Every other path is so filled with obstacles and problems that a full embrace of a biblical worldview seems like the only intelligible answer.

Remembering Who We Are

One of the most important conversations that we need to have as the Church is about how we intelligibly talk about sexual identity. If you agree that a gay identity is not helpful, then what is the best way to describe a person who struggles with same-sex attraction? And to be fair, a person struggling with same-sex desire aligning with a heterosexual identity does not seem to always be helpful either. Sure, heterosexuality is God's original intention,[10] but if a person feels totally different, what should he or she do? Lie? Pretend? Try harder? These are hard conversations that involve many dangerous cliffs. But I do think the Scriptures give us a way forward that actually puts us onto the path of human flourishing.

The best way to understand our sexual identity is to return to our original calling as sexual beings:

> So God created man in his own image,
> in the image of God he created him;
> male and female he created them.[11]

Male.

Female.

I want to suggest that these are the categories that the Scriptures give us to talk about sexual identity. We must understand what these words actually mean if we are to ever know how we should rightly express a biblical sexual identity. First, I think the categories male and female center sexual identity in our bodies. The great reformed theologian Herman Bavinck writes this:

> God is the Creator of the human being, and simultaneously also the Inaugurator of *sex* and of sexual difference. This difference did not result from sin; it existed from the very beginning, it has its basis in creation, it is a revelation of God's will and sovereignty, and is therefore wise and good. Therefore, no one may misconstrue or despise this sexual difference, either within one's own identity or in that of another person. It has been willed by God and grounded in nature.[12]

According to Bavinck, sexual difference (our biologically gendered bodies) is essential to our identity, and I think it is fair to say that it is the only way the Bible ever talks about sexual identity. If a person wants to live in accordance with God's will as it relates to his or her sexuality, the first thing he or she must do is embrace his or her gendered body because God has created it and willed it. And it is very good.

But there is more.

Biblical sexual identity is more than having a gendered body; there is a psychology of gender given by God that is developed through the traditional family model. Bavinck continues:

> The authority of the father, the love of the mother, and the obedience of the child form in their unity the threefold cord that binds together and sustains all relationships within human society. Within the psychological life of every integrated personality this triple cord forms the motif and melody.[13]

Through the discipline and love of a father and a mother a child matures into a healthy sexual identity. This healthy sexual identity enables a person to love well, either in singleness or marriage. The end result of such health will be someone who through his or her sexual identity can live out the ordinances and commands of God, including his ethical and relational commands.[14]

It is the psychology of the man or woman that has been largely ignored in Protestant circles when talking about biblical sexual identity. But if we are going to deconstruct modern notions of sexual identity, then the psychological reality of biblical sexual identity needs to be defined. Using the Bible as our guide, let me give some working definitions of what it means to be male and what it means to be female. I think the best way to understand a masculine sexual identity is sacrificial love. And the best way to think about a feminine sexual identity is creative and protective love. This is what makes up the psychological component of a sexual identity that has been formed well. Of course, this has been severely broken because of sin, but when we speak of healthy sexual identity, using the Bible as our framework, this is what we mean.

Now, if you are a Bible student at all this is what you should be thinking right now: *Prove it to me.* It might sound right, but in the end, the Scriptures are our guide for faith and life. It is quite possible to define the psychological component of sexual identity using the Scriptures, but one must be willing to study the text and the people who inhabit it. There are no proof texts on the psychological component of biblical sexual identity, but we see the proof of it everywhere.

A Caveat

When talking about biblical masculinity and femininity and the psychology in the midst of it, we are wading into deep waters. You might find what follows to be shocking definitions and assertions. But I am seeking to be faithful to the Scriptures and give biblical definitions. Your work is to decide whether I am right. Please don't disregard what I have to say just because the views proposed are radically counter-cultural. Perhaps this is a clue that we are going the right way. C. S. Lewis writes, "When the whole world is running towards a cliff, he who is running in the opposite direction appears to have lost his mind."[15] You will have to be the judge of which way I am running.

Biblical Masculinity

Paul writes in Ephesians 5:25, "Husbands, love your wives, as Christ loved the church and gave himself up for her." Christ loved the church by spending his life for her. It is sacrificial love that defines the life of Jesus from birth to the cross. And Paul makes the point that this should be the way a husband loves his wife. Paul's hope seems to be that through the love of a husband for his wife, she might know more fully the

31

love Christ has for her (and the world might get a glimpse of Christ's love for his bride). This is perhaps why Christian marriage should be held in such high regard.

Of course, Paul is speaking about marriage, but I think his definition of masculine love is for all men, married or not. I believe this is true because Jesus himself was single, and his life is the example of sacrificial love Paul gives in Ephesians.

Paul is another example of a man who lived out sacrificial love. Speaking to the church in Philippi, Paul writes, "Even if I am to be poured out as a drink offering upon the sacrificial offering of your faith, I am glad and rejoice with you all."[16] Paul saw his life as an offering poured out for others. I think he lived this way not only because he was an extraordinary apostle; he lived this way because he is an example of biblical masculinity.

This is not to say that women cannot live lives of sacrificial love. Of course they can and do. Look at any mother with her child and you will see such love on display. But it seems to be the biblical intent that men would through their lives have such love on display.

Missing in this definition is any mention of fulfilling one's desires as being tantamount to being true to one's sexual identity. Today, sexual identity seems to be tied up in sexual desire. If you have a desire for someone then that defines your sexual identity, and our work is to be true to one's self and pursue that desire. In the Bible, the opposite is the case. It is through sacrificial love and sacrifice that a man most fully lives out his sexual identity.

What I see bubble up from Paul, Jesus, and the biblical record is a calling to men to live sacrificially for others. Marriage is one place where this masculine love can be on display, and singleness is also a place where it can flourish. For the married man, God desires that such love be on display in how he loves his wife—physically, spiritually, and emotionally— his children, his church, and the world. For the single man, God desires that this be on display in devotion to Christ, his church, and the world.

Biblical Femininity

In Genesis 1 we are given the creation mandate: "Be fruitful and multiply."[17] This mandate was given by God to Adam and Eve. It was the command that through the male/female relationship children would be brought into the world for the plans and purposes that God has for humanity. Though both the man and woman have a role in the fulfilling of this command, it seems that women play a special role. It is in a woman's body that a child is conceived, protected, formed, grown, and birthed into the world. Afterward, the mother plays a special role in nourishing, protecting, and being with the new baby. This gift of biblical femininity is what I call *creative and protective love.*

But we must be careful here. Reducing femininity to a biological function and physical motherhood has many pitfalls and problems. And it could be offensive and hurtful to those women who have not had children or cannot have children. Though I believe that childbearing is the normative of creative and protective love, I do not believe it is the exclusive reality of feminine sexual identity. It is one window that shows us this unique love, but it is not the only one.

Creative and protective love finds its roots in God himself. He is the creator of everything. It is by him that a person can become born again.[18] When Jesus looks over Jerusalem, he compares his love to a mother hen who desires to gather in her chicks.[19] Isaiah compares God's love to the love a woman shows a nursing child and compares his comfort to the comfort that a mother gives her child.[20] And God's protective love is compared to a mother bear whose cubs have been stolen.[21] I want to suggest that God has ordained that this creative and protective love be uniquely expressed through feminine sexual identity.

As we have said, this can be shown through childbirth and child-rearing. It can also be shown in friendships and service. It is on display in kindness and protection of the least and the lost and the broken. It can be shown in leadership and sacrifice. It can be shown in the public square and in the church. It can be shown beautifully in marriage and brilliantly in singleness. We can see it in biblical examples like Mary, the mother of Jesus; Elizabeth; Ruth; Anna; Deborah; Esther; and Hannah. It is not just about having children, but about expressing and advocating for the love of God in all of his creation.

This is not to say that men can't love creatively and protectively. Of course they can. Jesus, the Son of Man, showed such love throughout his earthly ministry and life. But it seems to be the biblical intent that women will have such love on display in and through their lives.

Fallen Sexual Identity and Life in Christ

Biblical sexual identity can be hard to accept, especially if our core experiences have been far from what I have just described. The winds of personal experience, cultural change, and sin make it hard to see clearly. So what if we do not have a biblical sexual identity? What if our sexual desires flow from a fractured, sin-broken sexual identity? What if it is hard to embrace our God-given gender/sexual identity because of the pain it has provoked? I want to close this chapter with the hope of the gospel and why we can embrace our God-given sexual identity, even as we have to reckon with the distortion that sin has made of it.

In the book of Galatians Paul writes this:

> For as many of you as were baptized into Christ have put on Christ. There is neither Jew nor Greek, there is neither slave nor free, there is no male and female, for you are all one in Christ Jesus.[22]

Before I get to the good news of this Scripture, let me tell you what Galatians 3 is not saying. Paul is not advocating for the elimination of sexual identity. (He affirms sexual identity in Ephesians 5.) Paul is not equating sexual identity with the categories of slavery and nationality; the grammar construction is different, isolating sexual identity from the other two.[23] Instead, Paul is giving a new anchor for identity. It is no longer your position (slave or free), your nationality (Jew or Gentile), nor even your God-given sexual identity (male or female); instead it is the identity you received in your baptism. Jesus is your central identity! When Paul wrote this, people had authority, power, and influence based upon position, nationality, or gender. Now these things are consumed into the life of Christ. He is what is central.

And I think, at least for our discussion, this has two significant possibilities. First, if you, like me, struggle with same-sex attraction, disordered sexuality does not need to name us. Christ is our identity. He is the one who claims me and names me, not my urges. I need to hear this. When a same-sex feeling emerges, at times, it unsettles me. It causes me to fear what is true. But when I cling to Christ, I take on

35

his identity. This allows me to release my desires to him and choose to follow him.

Second, I think the life of Christ actually empowers us to live out our sexual calling as gendered beings. Is this not one of the major points of Ephesians 5? Christ uses sexuality and marriage and through them tells our purpose and the purpose of the cosmos (more on this later!). But this is the point I want to make: Whether we live out our sexual identity as Christians through marriage or through singleness, the life found in Christ empowers and enables us to be a good sexual gift—a man who can live an obedient life of sacrifice and service for the good of others; a woman who can live an obedient life of receptivity as a physical or spiritual mother bringing life into the world.

Conclusion

Gay identity is an obstacle that stands in the way of same-sex strugglers flourishing in the life of Christ. Such an identity sets us up for failure, closes us to the possibility of transformation, and simply is not a biblical category. For same-sex strugglers to flourish, we need to embrace the biblical category of sexual identity that is given to us: male or female. When this sexual identity is brought into the life of Christ, we find the ability to flourish as people under God.

2

The Obstacle of Gay Marriage

There is a married gay couple that is very close to me, my wife, and my boys. We have known them for years. We love them dearly. They are committed, smart, fun, morally conscientious, and devoted to their family and friends. They love life and are well adjusted. Both are professionals who are very successful in their jobs. They are deeply kind to me and Amy, respectful of our faith, and from every psychological measure that I know of, they are happy. The most fun we have with them is around food. Good drinks, good food, and lots of laughter. If psychological happiness, stability, and friendship are the measures of a good marriage, they have one.

In the Christian community, many have contended that gay marriage might be a way for gay men and women to stay faithful to Jesus and fulfill the deep desires of their hearts. No longer considered an outrageous proposition, gay marriage has gained traction in Christian circles. Jim Brownson, professor of New Testament at Western Seminary and probably the most thoughtful voice for progressive Christianity on the issue of homosexuality, writes,

Can we imagine a world in which the divine pronouncement at the beginning of creation, "It is not good for the man to be alone" (Gen. 2:18), might find a range of deeply satisfying resolutions, from heterosexual marriage, to celibate communities, to gay and lesbian committed unions?

For some Christians, this vision is imaginable as a form of "accommodation" in a broken world. . . .

Other Christians may be more ready to acknowledge that, throughout the natural order, same-sex attraction is a naturally recurring "minority" experience. These Christians may celebrate the way in which, by the providence of God, such "queer" folk can naturally deconstruct the pervasive tendencies of majority voices to become oppressive and exclusionary. In this vision, the inclusion of committed gay and lesbian unions represents . . . rather an offbeat redemptive purpose in the new creation.[1]

Even Wesley Hill, who stands with a traditional view of sexuality, seems to hope that within the institution of marriage, gays[2] will flourish. Hill quotes Alan Jacobs as he considered the Supreme Court decision to legalize gay marriage:

Perhaps I am soft on sin, or otherwise deficient in serious Christian formation—actually, it's certain that I am—but in any case I could not help being moved by many of the scenes yesterday of gay people getting married, even right here in Texas. I hope that many American gays and lesbians choose marriage over promiscuity, and I hope those who marry stay married, and flourish.[3]

Then Hill writes, "I know what he's saying. I felt that too."[4] For many Christians, there seems to be a hope that gay marriage will provide a way for the Christian LGBT community to flourish and be faithful to Jesus.

38

Of course, a majority of traditional Christians are quite skeptical of gay marriage and believe it brings great danger to the LGBT community and humanity at large. John Piper, theologian and pastor, writes concerning the legalization of gay marriage,

> [In the Supreme Court decision] there was massive institutionalization of sin. . . .
> In a 5-to-4 decision, the Supreme Court of the United States of America has ruled that states cannot ban same-sex marriage. . . .
> This is what the highest court in our land did today—knowing these deeds are wrong, "yet approving those who practice them."[5]

Many evangelicals, including me, see the legalization of gay marriage as the legitimation of behavior that the Bible strongly prohibits. And yet, at least in the Protestant world, we have not taken the time to show why gay marriage stands in the way of true human flourishing.

This chapter aims to show why gay marriage stands as an obstacle to true Christian flourishing for the same-sex-attracted Christian. I want to do this not by tackling gay marriage head on but by coming to it from the side door. To do this, I have to go back to the very roots of marriage and show you its importance and what it points to. Once I do that, we can draw some pretty clear, powerful conclusions about gay marriage.

A Theological Anthropology of Traditional Marriage

To understand why gay marriage cannot help a person struggling with same-sex attraction flourish, we have to understand why marriage exists. I have been married to my wife, Amy, for fourteen years. We have four boys, two dogs, lots of chaos, and even more love. My marriage and the family that flows out of it is one of the most special things that I am a part of. The special nature of my marriage, and all heterosexual marriages for that matter, is not just the relationships that make up those marriages, the happiness it creates, or the children they produce. According to the Bible, marriage points beyond itself. It is a sign that there is much more going on in the world than what we can taste, touch, hear, and feel. Marriage as the Bible sees it is not just another way for humans to pair and find happiness; marriage is a window into another world.

I suggest that if you want to get an idea of who God is, of what he is like, look to marriage, sexuality, and the family. It is within these relational realities that we get a window into who God is and why sexuality, heterosexual marriage, and family are so important.

Marriages are made up of distinct and different persons, and this points to God.

Marriages are made up of persons who are distinct but equal. In Genesis 2 God says, "It is not good that the man should be alone; I will make him a helper fit for him." Then the author of Genesis tells us what happens next:

> So the Lord God caused a deep sleep to fall upon the man, and while he slept took one of his ribs and closed up its place with flesh. And the rib that the Lord God had taken from the man he made into a woman and brought her to the man. Then the man said,

"This at last is bone of my bones
and flesh of my flesh;
she shall be called Woman,
because she was taken out of Man."

Therefore a man shall leave his father and his mother and
hold fast to his wife.[6]

God creates a helper for Adam; this helper is woman. Once
this difference is announced, God says, "Therefore a man
shall leave his father and mother and hold fast to his wife."
This "therefore" of God in Genesis 2 institutes marriage, and
it is presupposed upon gender difference. Marriage is about
two very different persons coming together. Two people living out of gender difference coming together to make up a
married life. Bavinck writes, "Within that unity, they are and
remain two. Each of the two has a unique nature, character,
and vocation."[7] Within marriage, each person has roles and
functions born out of gender difference. Such things are not
just cultural realities but are intrinsic to the very fabric of our
humanity and what marriage is as described in Genesis 2.

I want to suggest that this marital difference has a purpose;
it points to God. The Heidelberg Catechism declares this
about the uniqueness of each of the persons of the Trinity:
"The first is about God the Father and our creation; the
second about God the Son and our redemption; the third
about God the Holy Spirit and our sanctification."[8]

God is one substance and three distinct persons. The
theology of the Heidelberg Catechism teaches us that each
person of the Trinity performs a specific function. Mysteri-
ously, the differences between the persons of the Trinity come
together to make one God. I want to suggest that in biblical marriage the imprint of God's relational reality can be

seen. Two different persons, male and female, come together and make one marriage. The similarities between the Trinity and biblical marriage are clear and beautiful: The coming together of man and woman for life is a small echo of what God experiences within the Trinitarian community. For me, this is one of the reasons that gender difference in marriage is of such importance. We do not come together based on sameness, but difference. And this points, in some small way, to what is happening within the Trinity.[9]

At the core of family is union of persons that points to God.

When God speaks to Adam and Eve about the nature of their relationship, he says, "They shall become one flesh."[10] At the core of heterosexual marriage, as ordained by God in Genesis, is a unity of persons that is found in no other human relationship. This unity is physical, emotional, and spiritual. It is the mingling of persons.

At the foundation of the Trinity is unity of persons: "In the unity of the Godhead there be three Persons of one substance, power, and eternity: God the Father, God the Son, and God the Holy Ghost."[11] For sure each person of the Trinity is God, not part God. Yet somehow Father, Son, and Spirit in unity display the beauty and brilliance of God in a unique way.

It is the same with marriage. We bear the image of God on our own but somehow in the union of marriage the image of God is displayed in a unique and beautiful way. Marital unity points to the unity found in the Trinity.[12] Again, Bavinck seems to agree: "[Adam and Eve] Together in mutual fellowship they bear the divine image."[13] In their intimate fellowship we see a glimpse of the relational reality found in the Trinity.

It is in their unity of marriage that they point, in some small way, to the nature of the unity and fellowship experienced within the Trinity. God is a fellowship of such profound unity that the best language the church can use to explain it is to say that God is one. Do you want to see this unity on display in the natural world? Look at marriage between a man and a woman. It is when these two different persons come together—emotionally, spiritually, and physically—and become one that we get a taste of who God is.[14]

Marriage and family are about creating, and this points to God.

God is the one who creates. In the first chapter of Genesis, God creates everything. Planets, stars, water, and animals. He is in the midst of it all, creating and making the beautiful cosmos. He is so good at creating he can do it with his mere words. Quite a feat! Right before God creates humanity he says this: "Let us make man in our image, after our likeness."[15] Here, I think, we see two really important things. First, God is the God who creates. Second, being in his likeness means that there is something in our fundamental design that looks like him. We are creators too![16]

The most amazing experiences of my life were the births of each of my sons. So beautiful! And this is what blows me away: The love my wife and I expressed in our marriage bed would result in the creation of these beautiful human beings. Nothing in the human experience comes close to the creation of another eternal, unique person. Christopher West, a brilliant Catholic theologian, writes,

> God created us male and female so that we could image his love by becoming a sincere gift to each other. This sincere

giving establishes a "communion of persons" not only between the sexes but also—in the normal course of events—
with a "third" who proceeds from the both. In this way, sexual
love becomes an icon, or earthly image in some sense of the
inner life of the Trinity.[17]

And this is not only a Catholic idea. Bavinck agrees:

Father, mother, and child are one soul and one flesh, expanding and unfolding the one image of God, united within
threefold diversity and diverse within harmonic unity.
   This three-in-oneness of relationships and functions . . .
constitutes the foundation of all civilized society.[18]

Essential to marriage is the ability for the two to create
a third. Without getting into a significant debate about the
various things that must be considered when speaking about
procreation and marriage, I think this is fair to say: Procreation is essential to traditional marriage because it points
beyond itself to who God is and what he is about.[19] It is not
only the foundation of society but it also points to the very
nature of God. He is a God who creates, and in marriage
we get a small picture of what that means.

Marriage is about mission, and this points to God.

God is a community of love that wants his love to be known.
John writes, "God is love."[20] In his gospel he reminds us that
"God so loved the world, that he gave his only begotten Son,
that whosoever believeth in him should not perish, but have
everlasting life."[21] The persons of the Trinity relate to one
another by love, and since love is by its nature expansive, God
wanted to share this love with others. It is this love, rooted in
the Trinity, that sent Jesus, the Son. The Son came to bring

us into the love that God enjoys eternally without limits and is the source of all true human happiness. At the cost of his life, he did all that was necessary so that we could enjoy the love of God.

When a married couple—differentiated, equal, and united as one flesh—comes together for a lifetime, love is on display. Of course, this has been tarnished and nearly destroyed by sin, but when touched by the grace of God through Christ, something wonderful happens. The love they share in their marriage finds its source in God. And let me suggest that as they are immersed in his love, enjoying it within their union, it is only natural that they want others to know the love of Christ that is at the center of their marriage.

At the church I serve in Chicago, I have the honor of knowing some amazing couples whose lives are on mission. One couple that exemplifies living out of the overflow of love are my friends Derrick and Sandy. Derrick serves on the board of the church and has helped us over the last couple of years implement new ways of serving and reaching our community, especially the marginalized and broken. Sandy serves the kids almost weekly with great devotion and talent. They have three children who are great kids, who are growing and centering their lives in Jesus. What is so beautiful about this family is not all the things they do (though as a pastor I am grateful) but why they do them. They love Jesus. His love has shaped their lives. Now they overflow with the love that God has poured out to them. Their marriage is an outpost of his kingdom; it is a little church! Why does marriage matter? Because at its best, we see a small reflection of who God is and how he acts in the world. He is the God who loves, and his love propels him into the world. Christian marriages have this attribute as well.

Marriage is about intimacy and joy, and this points to God.

Do you know who is the happiest being in all of the cosmos? It is God. He finds this happiness in himself. God is a circle of sufficiency, finding all that he needs in the eternal, refreshing intimacy that God enjoys in himself. This is how John Piper puts it: "The chief end of God is to glorify God and enjoy Himself forever."[22] God's glory is his happiness with himself on display. It is the fruit of God's relationship within the Trinitarian community.

Humans flourish in relationships. Now, of course, there are many good places to be in relationship other than marriage (and we will explore some of these in the pages to come). There are many ways to be satisfied in relationship other than marriage, but there is no more intimate human relationship than marriage. In lifelong covenant, when a man and woman are whole enough (and even if they are quite broken), a unique and brilliant joy regularly bursts forth. Hang out with a newly married couple and you will sense a dignity (dare we say glory) that emanates from them. This is for a reason; marital joy and intimacy point to God.

Marriage shares a joy and intimacy that is unique to itself. Marital joy and intimacy are birthed out of difference and union. In some small way, marital joy and intimacy point beyond the marriage itself to the source and fountain of all: God. So I think it is fair to say that there is a decent argument to be made that God imprinted his image on marriage. Maybe this is why he said, "Let us make man in our image, after our likeness. And let them have dominion over the fish of the sea and over the birds of the heavens and over the livestock and over all the earth and over every creeping thing that creeps on the earth."[23]

Now, we are not quite ready to state why gay marriage and gay relationships will not cause true human flourishing because marriage doesn't just point us to God; marriage points to the purposes of everything.

Marriage Points to the Purposes of Everything.

Amy and I got married on a beautiful September day in Southern California. The weather was warm, we looked (really) good and we got married in an old church among lots of friends and family. When my soon-to-be wife walked down the aisle, I wept. I wept because she was beautiful. I wept because God had been good to me. I wept because my redemption, my longings, Amy's desires and dreams, and God's goodness were all coming together in one moment of celebration. It is one of the most wonderful moments of my life. But let me tell you something: The reason that marriage is amazing, special, unique, and holy isn't just because throughout it we can have perfect human moments; marriage is amazing, special, unique, and holy because it points to the purposes of absolutely everything.

Let me tell you a story, the story that tells us the purpose of everything.

Chapter 12 is one of my favorite chapters in the book of Genesis:

> Now the Lord said to Abram, "Go from your country and your kindred and your father's house to the land that I will show you. And I will make of you a great nation, and I will bless you and make your name great, so that you will be a blessing. I will bless those who bless you, and him who dishonors you I will curse, and in you all the families of the earth shall be blessed."

47

So Abram went, as the Lord had told him, and Lot went with him. Abram was seventy-five years old when he departed from Haran.[24]

God creates. Man rebels. God judges. God disperses. Then, right there in Genesis 12 something new, at least to us, emerges. God woos Abraham. He woos the father of Israel. He promises Abraham greatness, significance, and blessing. All that Abraham must do is leave the familiar and join God in this new relationship. I call this moment in history the wedding proposal. God has chosen for himself a bride. Now let's be clear, God is not proposing to Abraham individually but to the people of Israel collectively.

In Genesis 15, God and Abraham formalize their relationship with a covenant:

And Abram said, "Behold, you have given me no offspring, and a member of my household will be my heir." And behold, the word of the Lord came to him: "This man shall not be your heir; your very own son shall be your heir." And he brought him outside and said, "Look toward heaven, and number the stars, if you are able to number them." Then he said to him, "So shall your offspring be." And he believed the Lord, and he counted it to him as righteousness.[25]

God was making a covenant with Israel. Let me say something that you might never have thought of before. This is a wedding between God and his people. God was promising himself and all the good he provides to his bride, Israel. For Israel's fidelity (obedience), God promised to do amazing, miraculous things for his people. Israel would bear unbelievable offspring! Now, this is exactly how the prophets saw the relationship with God and Israel. Israel was the bride that God loved.[26] He was willing to do anything for her.

Now, Israel proved to be an unfaithful bride. She couldn't stay faithful; other "husbands" proved too alluring. This, of course, brought God's judgment and anger, but it also revealed something amazing: the beautiful husband heart of God.[27] God loved Israel, and even though she had failed miserably, he was faithful. This is exactly what we see in Isaiah; we see the Husband-God seeking to woo back the bride he loves (I call this marriage therapy God-style!):

> "Fear not, for you will not be ashamed;
>   be not confounded, for you will not be disgraced;
> for you will forget the shame of your youth,
>   and the reproach of your widowhood you will
>   remember no more.
> For your Maker is your husband,
>   the Lord of hosts is his name;
> and the Holy One of Israel is your Redeemer,
>   the God of the whole earth he is called.
> For the Lord has called you
>   like a wife deserted and grieved in spirit,
> like a wife of youth when she is cast off,
>   says your God.
> For a brief moment I deserted you,
>   but with great compassion I will gather you.
> In overflowing anger for a moment
>   I hid my face from you,
> but with everlasting love I will have compassion
>   on you,"
>   says the Lord, your Redeemer.[28]

Israel had committed adultery, had "played the harlot" and God had every right to judge her and cast her off. But he wanted a bride. He wanted his bride so much, the bridegroom came to do what was necessary to have that bride.

49

He became one of us. He lived for us. He died on our behalf and, through his resurrection, defeated the grave and won his bride once and for all.

We see it all come together in the book of Revelation:

> Then I heard what seemed to be the voice of a great multitude, like the roar of many waters and like the sound of mighty peals of thunder, crying out,
>
> > "Hallelujah!
> > For the Lord our God
> > the Almighty reigns.
> > Let us rejoice and exult
> > and give him the glory,
> > for the marriage of the Lamb has come,
> > and his Bride has made herself ready;
> > it was granted her to clothe herself
> > with fine linen, bright and pure"—
>
> for the fine linen is the righteous deeds of the saints.[29]

Finally, the bridegroom will have his bride, faithful and pure. You see all of history has been about this one wedding—between the Husband-God Christ and his bride, the church.

And he is a passionate husband. He pursues his bride like one lovesick. Alvin Plantinga writes this,

> The church is the *bride* of Christ, not his little sister. . . . These scriptural images imply that God isn't impassive, and that his love for us is not exclusively agapeic. They suggest that God's love for his people involves an erotic element of desire: he desires the right kind of response from us, and union with us, just as we desire union with him.[30]

Of course, God does not have sexual feelings for the church. Sexual intimacy points beyond itself to our union with Christ.

Though not physically erotic, Christ desires union with his bride, and the visible sign of that on the earth is marital physical intimacy. When a man and a woman have sex within the marital covenant, it reminds all of us that Christ desires his church and will pursue her for consummation, the marriage supper of the Lamb.

Now, let me tie it all together: Every marriage between a man and a woman points to the final purpose of the cosmos—the marriage feast of the Lamb. This is what Paul is getting at, at least in part, when he says this: "'Therefore a man shall leave his father and mother and hold fast to his wife, and the two shall become one flesh.' This mystery is profound, and I am saying that it refers to Christ and the church."[31] The mystery is that in every marriage there is a sign, a window into the actual meaning of the cosmos. If you want to know what life is all about, go check out a wedding.

Now we are ready to talk about gay marriage.

Why Gay Marriage Cannot Cause Human Flourishing

The following reasons are why gay marriage cannot help the same-sex-attracted Christian flourish:

1. Gay marriage cannot cause the same-sex attracted to flourish because there is no ability for oneness. As we have seen, marriage is about man and woman coming together as one. This oneness is seen in the very bodies that join together physically. And it points beyond itself to the very nature of relationship that God enjoys. In gay marriage there might be sexual activity and relating, but there is no union of persons.

51

And if human flourishing is about living into what God desires, gay marriage will not help you or me flourish.

2. Gay marriage cannot cause the same-sex attracted to flourish because there is no gender difference. Above, difference is essential for marriage because it points to a fundamental reality found in God.[32] This difference is male and female. Different in function, and equal in value and worth. In gay marriage two of the same come together. There is no difference. If human flourishing is about living in a covenantal relationship that points to the nature of who God is, gay marriage will not help you or me flourish.

3. Gay marriage cannot cause the same-sex attracted to flourish because there is no potential for procreation. Central to marriage is the potential for life to spring from the union. This, as we have seen, points to the nature of God, who is the God who creates. In marriage, we get to join with him in the creation of eternal persons. Gay marriage has no potential for procreation. As a matter of fact, as my hero, Dallas Willard, has remarked, "If all of society embraced gay marriage, there would be no society left."[33] If human flourishing is about living into our God-given mandate to be fruitful and multiply, gay marriage will not help you or me flourish.

4. Gay marriage cannot cause the same-sex attracted to flourish because a gay union can never be on the Jesus mission. The God we follow is the missionary God who sent his Son so that the world might know his love. This missional reality of God is central to who he is. Marriage

is meant to reflect this reality. Sadly, gay marriage is premised upon acting against the ethical demands of the Scriptures, and it is nearly impossible to be in rebellion to God's commands and also be or want to be on his mission.

5. Finally, and I think most important, gay marriage cannot cause the same-sex attracted to flourish because it tells fundamentally the wrong story. All of the Scriptures are about the one wedding.[34] From Genesis to Revelation, we are told a story of the Husband-God who desires a bride, the people of God. He has gone to great lengths, paying an unbelievable price, to have his bride. One day, he, the bridegroom, and his church, the bride, will come together in joy and celebration. This is the story of everything. Every marriage between a man and a woman points to this. This is why marriage exists. This is the story it tells. Gay marriage does not tell the same story. It changes the narrative, the characters, the purpose, and the reasons. Gay marriage tells a fundamentally different story. If human flourishing is about living in God's story, gay marriage will not help you or me flourish.

Conclusion

The only way to know whether gay marriage can be one of the means by which same-sex strugglers can flourish is to understand what marriage fundamentally is and what it points to. What we find is that heterosexual marriage points beyond itself; it is an icon, if you will, that helps reveal the very nature of God. Marriage also helps us understand the very purpose of the cosmos—the bridegroom and the bride. Gay marriage cannot be the means by which the same-sex struggler flourishes because it does not point to God and it does not tell the right story. Gay marriage, actually, is an obstacle to human flourishing.

3

The Obstacle of the Spiritual Friendship Movement

My second-born son, who is eight, loves baseball (specifically the White Sox!). This love affair with the game has been going on for the last couple of years. It started with my taking him to a game, where something happened to him. The smells, the people, the stadium, and the game cast a spell on him. He was hooked. Before long, we were watching games at home, learning about the players, and imagining what it would be like to be major-league players ourselves. But Sawyer didn't just want to watch the game and imagine playing the game; before long he became very passionate about *playing* the game. Soon we had balls, gloves, and a few bats, and every nice day we played baseball (and broke a window in the process). But still this wasn't enough. Sawyer wants to be on a baseball team; he wants to learn the game by practicing the game. He wants to find his place in baseball and have a swing at bat. Sawyer desires to be a baseball player.

Though the metaphor doesn't work completely, it does capture a very important desire that gay Christians want: They don't want to just watch other people being able to love; they don't want to just imagine what being in love would be like; they don't want to miss out on a part of life that their hearts desire. Christians who have same-sex attraction want to love. They want to *play the one game in life that seems to matter most*. I don't blame them, because I know the feeling of fearing that intimate love would never be mine to participate in as a Christian who experiences same-sex attraction.

As I began to walk with Jesus in the late 1990s, I was a brand-new Christian. I was in love with Jesus; I loved his church; I was feeling hope, but I also knew that the old ways that I had sought sexual intimacy in relationship to other men were no longer appropriate ways of connection. So here I was wanting to follow Jesus but having no idea how to relate as a Christian man. I was hungry for relationships, needed relationships, found myself attracted to people of the same sex, yet was not sure how to navigate it all. I remember feeling, at times, very alone and overwhelmed. I did not know how to deal with my feelings. I wanted to play the game but I did not know how.

A Seismic Shift

There is a profound, seismic shift happening in conversations around being gay and Christian over the last few years. Thought leaders like Wesley Hill, Eve Tushnet, and others are seeking to stay faithful to a conservative ethical understanding of the Scriptures and reconcile that understanding with their gay identity. These are men and women who understand that same-sex sexual behavior is not condoned but are suspicious of old evangelical ways of dealing with same-sex desire—reparative therapy, ex-gay support groups, etc. They want to play the game and wonder if there are different ways to play that enable same-sex connection and fidelity to the Scriptures. In their search for what might be available to them they have embraced a way of relating called spiritual friendship. In this chapter I want to explain spiritual friendship, its potential benefits and its dangers, and then conclude with my own story of friendship and how God used my friend Charlie to root me in the beauty and hope of the gospel.

Spiritual Friendship

The most important book on spiritual friendship was recently written by Wesley Hill. The book, titled *Spiritual Friendship*, is really concerned with one thing: In light of one's erotic and relational desires, how can these inner realities be channeled for holy living? In other words, in what kinds of relationships, and how, can a same-sex-attracted Christian love? *Spiritual Friendship* is Hill's answer. Though I do have some significant disagreements with Hill on a number of points, he is an engaging writer who is seeking to be faithful to the Scriptures and make a way for those who struggle with same-sex desires.

Keeping to the baseball metaphor, spiritual friendship is a specific way of "playing the game," a particular kind of relating. It has as its goal the desire to find faithful means to love people through one's same-sex attractions. The spiritual friendship movement proposes four particular ways of thinking about friendship, sexuality, and intimacy that make it a unique option for the same-sex struggler.

First, those who support spiritual friendship are holding to a traditional view of the Scriptures. Hill writes, "Paul is up in arms not about pedophilia or temple prostitution, it seems, but rather about how the original creation of male and female has been set aside."[1] This is important to state and it is no small thing. Hill, Tushnet, and others take Scripture at its word. For them, the question of whether same-sex activity is biblically permissible has been settled. Now, the question is, in light of the prohibition of Scripture, how can one love rightly? Whatever the (unintended) results of spiritual friendship might be, it is clear that it is being proposed as a way to be faithful to the Scriptures.

Second, spiritual friendships are friendships between two people of the same sex who are committed to each other. These are friendships filled with what Hill calls "fresh intentionality."[2] In his defense of spiritual friendship Hill shares his own experience of friendship that seemed satisfying but in the end was not grounded in commitment and community, and consequently, according to Hill, caused great pain. What Hill proposes are friendships that are bound like family or marriage so that there might be the security and commitment necessary for relational intimacy. For spiritual friendship to be a space where there might be intimacy that is satisfying for the same-sex-attracted Christian, there must be a stronger commitment in friendship. And not just private commitment but commitment that would be publicly acknowledged with liturgical rites. Hill wonders hopefully:

> We might choose, as a few friends have done with me, to
> seek a more formal acknowledgment of our friendship by
> making public promises to each other. Or we might, less

dramatically, choose to invite our friends to become more regular fixtures of our lives.[3]

For Hill such committed friendships provide the space for attachment, security, and love.[4]

Third, Hill hopes that such friendships will be the nucleus of the church. He writes,

> Priests and pastors have a vested interest in their congregations being filled with people who are friends with one another. They should look for ways to encourage the formation and nurture of those friendships. . . . Pastors and counselors could pray a blessing on pairs of friends, even in the privacy of their shared apartments or campus residence halls.[5]

Hill wants to reimagine, or he might say refocus, the way that the church relates within herself. He sees friendship as the means by which church finds community. This is not just for gay Christians but Christians in general. Committed friendships, for Hill, ought to make up the church and can be the doorway into real community.

Finally, spiritual friendship is a way, for Hill, to bless and embrace his gay identity as a "positive calling."[6] Hill writes, "My being gay and saying no to gay sex may lead me to be *more* of a friend to men, not less."[7] What Hill is exploring here is complicated and important. While not embracing homosexual activity, he is embracing what he would call his gay identity. As a matter of fact, he wonders if it might actually empower him to love well within the confines of friendship. Gay identity no longer becomes something to run away from, but by Christ, it becomes something to embrace.

The Good

There is good in Wesley Hill's defense of spiritual friend-ship. First, I have to say, right off the bat, I like Wesley Hill. I love his honesty, his intellectual curiosity, and his devotion to Jesus. This shines through the pages of his writings. He is asking important questions that I think the church needs to answer. His is an important voice in the conversation we need to have around Christianity, homosexuality, and the church. I am very thankful that he has decided to engage this topic with passion and carefulness.

Second, I am very thankful that Hill, and others within this movement, have defended a traditional stand on mar-riage. This is no small thing. Hill rightly finds revisionist arguments that the Scriptures mean something other than what they say to be totally unsatisfactory. In this way, he stands squarely within the historic Christian tradition. And it would be easy for him to embrace a more permissive path, especially in light of those like Professor Jim Brownson who are paving a way for committed gay relationships. Even as there is a cultural tsunami that is remaking everything inside and outside of the church as it relates to homosexuality, Hill is standing as a prophetic voice in the midst of his own desires and the Scriptures.

Third, Hill rightly points out that the church has bought into a cultural reality that puts an onus on individuality over commitment. Many churches are but one more destination in an ever-more-busy schedule that is passed through at about the same speed and importance as a McDonald's drive-through. Rootedness, commitment, vulnerability, and love are lost in many church relationships and seem to be only for those who have family. No spouse? Then tough luck. Hill points this out and asks us to consider a better way of doing church.

Finally, Hill gives an answer to how a Christian who has same-sex attractions could be faithful to Jesus and find love. I don't agree with his answer, but he has given one. This is the conversation that the church needs to have and the primary purpose I wrote this book. But we must give credit where credit is due. While many of us were fighting culture wars, Hill and others were seeking to make a way for those who see themselves as gay and Christian.

The Troubling

I think Wesley Hill gives us many gifts. But I think his proposal for committed same-sex friendships, if implemented, will actually have unintended consequences that will, I fear, do more harm than good. The biggest and most important problem I have with Hill's proposal for committed friendship is that it is birthed out of his gay identity. Hill is seeking ways to be faithfully gay. He is not in conflict with his gay identity but instead has, it seems, embraced it. Hill sees his gay identity as not just what one does in the bedroom but as a worldview, a worldview that does not need to be shied away from but embraced (in chapter 1, I shared some of his thoughts on gay identity). But how can this be? If, as Hill agrees, same-sex sexual activity is sinful, is not the inclination that pulls you toward such a union at the very least broken and in need of redemption? The embracing of gay identity but not same-sex sexual activity is an utterly new way historically to think about homosexuality within the Christian tradition, and I think it has fault lines that are dangerous. I am not sure how one embraces a gay identity that Hill admits decides for him whom he hangs out with, without it being a subtle form of erotic connecting, even if only in the mind. In other words, Hill enters into friendships in which he is attracted to someone; this is how he decides whom he will spend time with. Now, admittedly this might work for Hill, but for others might not using attraction be a very dangerous way to decide what friendships to invest in? Not to mention how the other person might feel about it if they knew. I think this is a subtle embrace of a queer worldview that I believe actually sets up men and women for moral failure.

I think the way of Christ is a total deconstruction of our attractions, worldviews, desires, and drives. As I understand the Scriptures, these are to be crucified. None of them can be trusted. They have all been tainted by sin. This is true for gay identity and true for heterosexual identity. Both must be crucified. There is the danger of objectifying those you desire; I think there are hidden motives that seem good but are driven by erotic desire outside of the heterosexual marital covenant. And there is danger of using the other for our own sexual needs even when there is no physical contact. Hill has come to the place, along with others, that one's gay identity is a good to be celebrated and engaged. I think this is a dangerous idea. At worse, I think unsuspecting same-sex-attracted men and women might deceive themselves into repetitive moral failure.

Second, I wonder if this is actually an interim step to a full embrace of committed same-sex sexual relationships. I want to repeat again that Hill has a conservative understanding of the Bible and there is *nothing* that indicates that this will change. But Hill has stepped into uncharted, dangerous waters. He has embraced gay identity as a qualitative good.

62

It is not very hard to imagine him embracing the logical next step . . . gay marriage. And if he does not, I can easily see this being a stepping-stone for others to embrace gay relationships.

As a matter of fact, this is exactly what has happened in the life of Julie Rodgers. Rodgers is a brilliant thinker and identifies as a gay Christian. She was until recently, like Hill, unabashedly celibate. She was hired as a chaplain at prestigious Christian college Wheaton and was a bright light of hope for many there. But then she began to change her mind on many fundamental things. First, she was part of the ex-gay movement that she saw as encouraging her to become "straight." Then she embraced celibacy; then a celebration of her gay identity and was a regular contributor to www.spiritualfriendship.org. Now she embraces full acceptance of gay marriage.[8]

Now, for sure, conservative evangelicals have many examples of men and women who have left orthodoxy, and this alone does not tell us whether a position is correct or not. But the very act of embracing gay identity and using it as a way to engage relationships seems like a tentative putting the toe in the water. Of course, you might put your toe in and decide that diving into the water just isn't for you. Or two other things might happen. One, you might like the water, wonder what all the fuss is about, and like Rodgers dive right in. Or two, while sticking your toe in the water you might accidently fall into a place you never expected to go. I am very concerned that the spiritual friendship movement in its attempt to stay faithful actually is preparing a lot of people to get wet.

Third, I wonder if the pathway of spiritual friendship that Hill is embracing actually is the embracing of same-sex relational idolatry and sin. In chapter 5 of Hill's book, he talks about an intense same-sex friendship he had and how that relationship fell apart when his friend decided to marry a woman he really liked. Over the next couple of days, Hill was undone. He wept. He was depressed. He was lost. He was deeply troubled to his core. Speaking of what he had, Hill wrote, "The intimacy of which our friendship partook wasn't different in kind from what married partners enjoy; it was more like a different species of the same genus. We were almost married, I thought, so deep was the affection we felt for each other."[9] A good pastor friend of his helped Hill see the truth: Hill had fallen romantically in love with this man. In light of this Hill passingly wonders, "Then didn't that mean I was also admitting that the friendship was all wrong? That it had to end?"[10] But Hill doesn't seem to answer the question straightforwardly. Instead, after sharing Henri Nouwen's own journey with relationship and same-sex attraction, he speaks of disappointment, failure, pain, and grief, but there is no language of sin, idolatry, or mortification.

This is not to say that any person who deals with same-sex attractions and wants to follow Jesus won't struggle with what Hill is speaking about, but the issue of language and framework does matter. Hill wants to move the whole conversation into the realm of relationships, interpersonal satisfaction, and trying to find how we can, to some extent, feed the hungers within. This is a very different way of speaking of sin than the Bible speaks about it. Paul speaks of putting it to death, making sure it is gone for good, and has the profound wisdom of calling sin . . . sin. Language matters. I want to suggest that we stick as close to the biblical language as possible when talking about homosexuality. The goal of our life is not relational satisfaction but holiness. I think Hill misses the mark. I think that the Bible simply has the best view of the human condition and its cure. And this is why I think language matters. Hill doesn't see homosexuality as something to be transformed. He thinks he is better for it. In such a conversation there is no room for God to change us. Isn't a large part of the gospel about transformation? I think spiritual friendship loses the biblical language and sets folks up to accept and embrace sin while losing the opportunity for profound change.

One Example

Now, one could think that I was not a big fan of friendship based upon what you have read so far in this chapter. Nothing could be further from the truth! I am a person who is blessed with deep friendships, and I think they have been integral to my growth as a follower of Jesus. We will speak in much more detail in the chapters to come about how community in the framework of the church can help the same-sex struggler, but I wanted to give an example of what I would propose is a framework for a godly friendship. I want to do that by sharing a bit about one of my closest and dearest friends, Charlie Contreras.

I met Charlie in the summer of 1995. I was nineteen years old, he was thirteen years older than I, and I was a complete and utter mess. Actually, a group of mutual friends who had been experiencing spiritual renewal at the Vineyard Anaheim brought me to Charlie in hopes that something could be done. From the very beginning Charlie embodied for me gospel hope. I was in real darkness and sin, and I had never let anyone into the mess before. Charlie knew my story from afar (it traveled before me), and he was genuinely kind. He opened his house to me, spent time with me, shared life with me, and never made me feel like a project. I felt genuinely loved by him.

Importantly, this was not an only Ron/Charlie relationship. That would not have served me and it would not have been life-giving to Charlie. What made this friendship beautiful was not its exclusivity but its inclusivity. It became part of a small group that organically began meeting in 1997. Every Friday night a group of thirty to forty young adults gathered for worship, teaching, and prayer. Some of my deepest friendships were formed there. The beauty of it was that there was an ability for shared vulnerability and shared authenticity. It was one of the most special communities that I have ever been a part of. It was in this framework that my friendship with Charlie and others stayed healthy for me. It allowed me to engage, disengage, and learn appropriate boundaries with other men. I do not think this would have been possible if I had found only special friends, no matter how committed, where I could seek to feed my hungers. No, it was friendships in community that created the space for me to grow.

Next, our friendship was based on a common need. Now, I mean this in a specific way. We were brought together not out of common interests or desires but out of a deep need to find Jesus. Charlie was broken. I was broken. The community that gathered weekly was filled with broken young adults. There was brokenness everywhere. We were sin-sick men and women and we all knew it. It was our focus on Jesus and our need of him that made our friendships beautiful. Again, I think all worthwhile friendships will have Jesus at the center. And not in some blithe way. No, a common pursuit birthed out of a common need. This is what I experienced with Charlie, and I have been radically transformed by the Jesus I (we) have encountered.

Our friendship has been long-term. We have been friends for over twenty years. We have been friends during the high points and low points of our lives together. This longevity of friendship allows for something really important: trust. Charlie is one of those people whom I trust deeply. I can talk about absolutely anything and hear a gospel answer in return.

I think one of the reasons there is such shallowness in the church culture is that we lack long-term gospel friends, friends who can be honest with one another and stay connected beyond geography and common interests. I probably have five friends like this. I am so thankful for them. My Christian life is richer for them. I would be much sadder without them. They provide profound good in my life. If we are to get very far in our Christian journeys, we need friends who will walk with us long-term. Of course, my wife is one of those friends, but she is not the only one.

Finally, our friendship has borne amazing gospel fruit. When we met, both of us were single and broken, and there did not seem to be a real way forward into hope. But then Jesus moved. Then Jesus had his way. Then, God began to transform the men and women in this little community. Now, twenty years later, there is profound gospel fruit. I have been married fourteen years, Charlie for twelve. I have four beautiful boys; he has a son and a daughter. I am the senior pastor of a 1,400-member church in Chicago. He is the pastor of spiritual formation at a 5,000-member church an hour from me. I have deep holiness and purity in my sexual life; Charlie has been totally set free from the sins that used to easily beset him. More than that, Charlie has had significant friendships

67

with dozens of other men from around the country; many of them have had their lives totally transformed. This is the final and most essential litmus test of friendship in the way of Christ. What kind of fruit does your friendship produce? More hunger? Blurry boundaries? Or does your friendship propel you into the way of Christ, and as a result there is fruit everywhere?

Charlie Contreras is one of my closest and dearest friends. I am the man I am today in part because of his friendship. He also modeled for me what Christian friendship looks like. My hope for those who struggle with same-sex attraction and want to pursue Christ is that they would have the great gift of friends like Charlie. I think Jesus is right. Seek to save your life and you will lose it. Seek to feed your sexual hungers and satisfy them through same-sex relationships and you will find yourself more lost than ever. But lose your life, starve the hungers, and pursue Christ with fellow sojourners, and you will find yourself satisfied, transformed, and I believe filled with a life of fruit.

Conclusion

The spiritual friendship movement raises many good questions. I think it has the best intentions and a real desire to follow Jesus even in the hard ways; it also stands as a prophetic accusation against a church and culture that does not know how to form friendships that can actually be life-giving to all involved. But there are troubling things within the spiritual friendship movement as well: the embracing of gay identity, a real danger of entering into a train of thought that will end up with the full embrace of gay relationships, and a loss of biblical language that speaks of sin, idolatry, mortification, and transformation. I think friendship is important, but only in its proper place. When it is rooted in community, centered around Christ, and long-term, I think such friendship will bear amazing gospel fruit. This is what we want for our friends who have same-sex attraction and who desire to follow Jesus.

PART TWO: GIFTS

Recently, I spent a couple of weeks in Germany with my wife and family. It was such a great time. Germany is a beautiful place. It has hundreds of miles of walking paths, and if you haven't figured it out yet, I love to hike! In Germany, trails are everywhere. So we walked a lot during our vacation. We walked along the Rhine, we walked through old cities, and we walked through the countryside. One morning I decided to go on a long hike/walk on my own. So out I went. The total distance was well over ten miles. It was long but it was worth it.

On my journey I saw a castle, beautiful valleys, and amazing landscapes. But there was one part of the journey that was especially wonderful. At one point I came to a beautiful wooded valley; it was like something out of a Grimm fairy tale. It was breathtaking. And right off the path in between me and the valley was a life-size crucifix. There he was, Jesus crucified. There was something about all that beauty juxtaposed with the mutilated body of Jesus. Somehow the two scenes came together. I was going on a hike to explore Germany and found Jesus. I have found this to be a common occurrence in my life: Wherever I am, the point is always Jesus.

We have been going on a journey, you and I, clearing the obstacles that stand in the way of the same-sex attracted, keeping them from flourishing in the kingdom of God. But now, let's get to where we want to go. The second part of this book is about what Jesus offers relationally to the same-sex-attracted Christian. This part is about what we can embrace. What will give us life? What are the relational possibilities available to a person like me—a same-sex struggler—so that I can experience the abundant life Jesus said was available?

It is my hope that the second part of this book is intensely practical. I want leaders and strugglers alike to be equipped. So there will be some theology (answering the *why* question), but also practical tips and benefits to the options explored. There will also be testimonies of people and churches that are pursuing Christ well. It is my hope that these chapters will encourage those who struggle, equip churches to serve same-sex strugglers better, and serve as a contribution to the wider conversation of homosexuality and the church. The goal is to provide pathways of hope for the same-sex attracted to flourish in Christ. Simply nothing less will do.

One last note: The second part of the book is best read in order. The chapters are written in the order I believe they must happen in a person's life for the sake of human flourishing.

4

The Gift of the Church

Right now, around the world, a cultural phenomenon is happening through an organization called CrossFit.[1] Boiled down to its essence, CrossFit is about working out with other people without shame and making sure that no one is ever left behind. With four million participants worldwide,[2] people are joining for the sake of personal and physical transformation; and key to this workout phenomenon is the community it engenders:

> The members exhibit a close-knit community of people trying to better themselves and those around them through physical fitness. Members have organized fundraisers and other drives to aid friends and other CrossFitters who are going through sickness and other extraordinary circumstances.[3]

Two researchers from Harvard Divinity School see the rise of organizations like CrossFit as driven by the human need

GIFTS

for community. All of us need places where we can experience
"deep community building."⁴ This longing for community
and relationship runs deep in us. We need it to survive. And
for those of us who are Christians and desire to faithfully
follow Jesus, we need the community called the church. And
what is true for all disciples of Jesus is very true for the same-
sex-attracted Christian. One of the fundamental needs of
a same-sex struggler who desires to follow Jesus is to have
a place to belong and grow. Without deep, holy relational
connections, the life of Christ will be nearly impossible for
us. The church will be foundational to the same-sex struggler who wants to follow Jesus. It is in the community of the
church where humans flourish.

The goal of this chapter is threefold. First, I want to show
you just how amazing the church is; second, I want to show
you the kind of disciplines you need to practice at your church
so that you will flourish; finally, I want to share an amazing
example of a church that is brightly shining the light to the
same-sex struggler.

The Church Is Amazing

I *love* the church. I have been blessed, loved, challenged, and
trained through the local church. The best and most important decision the same-sex-attracted Christian will make will
be joining a local church. If a same-sex-attracted Christian
gets involved in a great church, he or she will flourish no
matter what is going on in his or her life.

When I say that a local church is foundational for the
same-sex struggler's flourishing, I mean a specific kind of
church. Let me be bold: The church you and I need is a
church that looks as close to the church found in the book of

74

Acts as possible. Maybe you think that such churches don't exist. But let me tell you something: There are churches in your city where God is moving in amazing ways; there are also churches that are as dead as a doornail. What we need is a way to discern the difference between the right kind of church and the wrong kind of church. Acts chapter 2 helps us:

> And they devoted themselves to the apostles' teaching and the fellowship, to the breaking of bread and the prayers. And awe came upon every soul, and many wonders and signs were being done through the apostles. And all who believed were together and had all things in common. And they were selling their possessions and belongings and distributing the proceeds to all, as any had need. And day by day, attending the temple together and breaking bread in their homes, they received their food with glad and generous hearts, praising God and having favor with all the people. And the Lord added to their number day by day those who were being saved.[5]

Acts 2 is about "the birth of the church."[6] In the book of Acts we see the church as it ought to be, the church in its best form. I think we can pull from these verses what Christ's church should look like and what you should look for in the church you attend (or if you lead a church, what kind of church you should partner with the Spirit to become). We, of course, are not looking for perfection, but we are looking for communities that actually want the life of Christ in their midst. So, keeping our friends who are struggling with same-sex attraction in mind, we can see the kind of church that they need to flourish in the Kingdom of God.

A Biblical Church

If the church is going to be a place where the same-sex struggler can flourish, it must be biblical. The first church "devoted themselves to the apostles' teaching." These were the teachings of the apostles about Jesus, both what he had done and how the Old Testament pointed to Jesus. They gathered for one main purpose: to learn about the living Christ. This focus was the source of all the power and life of the first church. The first church was profoundly biblical. It centered its existence on Jesus through the teachings of the apostles and the writings of the Old Testament.

If we desire the same-sex-attracted Christian to flourish, then they must be in churches that love the Scriptures and point everyone to the living Christ. Sadly, not everyone sees the centrality of Scripture this way. Rachel Held Evans wrote a blog about why millennials are leaving the church, and she had this to say:

> What millennials really want from the church is not a change in style but a change in substance.
>
> We want an end to the culture wars. We want a truce between science and faith. We want to be known for what we stand for, not what we are against.
>
> We want to ask questions that don't have predetermined answers.
>
> We want churches that emphasize an allegiance to the kingdom of God over an allegiance to a single political party or a single nation.
>
> We want our LGBT friends to feel truly welcome in our faith communities.[7]

Now there is much to commend in what Rachel Held Evans says in general and some to commend specifically in the blog post I just quoted. She's correct about the attitude of many millennials, and I also want my LGBT friends to be welcome in my church. But we disagree about what that means. Like many in our culture, Rachel Held Evans wants the church to leave its biblical moorings behind for a cultural tolerance that embraces a new moral framework around sexuality.[8] Instead of being guided by the Scriptures, she is embracing a totally new worldview. To be fair, she will say she is seeking to follow Jesus in this new moral framework. Unfortunately, I am not sure if the Jesus of the Bible is the one she is following.

What I want for myself, and for every person who struggles with same-sex attraction, is to encounter the living Christ. What I want is an Acts 2 reality—God breaking in—to happen for me, for you, for all of us. And I can tell you the worst thing you can do is throw out the Bible for something more palatable. Both traditional sexual ethics and the promise for profound transformation are found within the Bible.

When you choose a church, or if you are considering the kind of church you will be, make sure those there love Scripture, teach the full council of God from it, and devote themselves to it. This includes the ethical demands of Scripture and the cure to the things that ail us. Make sure they call sin *sin*, love people where they are at, and seek Jesus in all that they do. This is what it means to be a Bible-believing church. Don't join a church that is not clear on their love of Scripture and the Jesus it points to. Your flourishing depends upon it.

A Church With Power

If the church is going to be a place where the same-sex struggler can flourish, it must believe in and experience the power of the Spirit. When the first church devoted itself to the Scriptures, something powerful happened: "Awe came upon every soul, and many wonders and signs were being done through the apostles."[9] This is what happens when Christ is preached and the Scriptures are persistently followed—power is unleashed. And we need power! Power for holiness to break the reign of sin in our bodies. We need power to stand rightly. And we need power if we are going to find transformation in our lives. If you are struggling with same-sex attraction and want to follow Jesus, or you want to serve the LGBT community, make sure you go to a church that believes that God can move in power.

The two fundamental ways you can know that a potential church moves in power:

1. Christ and the power that comes from him should regularly be preached from the pulpit.
2. There should be examples of life change throughout the church.

Does your church preach Christ resurrected? Do they believe that God can transform your whole life, including the broken areas of your sexuality, or have they theologically given up? Does the pastor share from his own life how Christ has transformed, and is transforming, him or her? Or is the preaching of God's word devoid of power? If a church believes in the power of Christ, you will hear it from the pulpit. If you don't hear it from the pulpit, it is not a place where you will flourish as a Christian dealing with same-sex attraction.

If Christ's power is in a local church, you will see the effects of it everywhere, specifically in the people who go there. They will have a quality of life quite different from non-believers. They will have an eternal kind of life. They will be living out Colossians 3 and 1 Corinthians 6 right before your eyes.

You should be able to see people who were once in the mire of sexual sin and brokenness and have found life; you should be able to see among the leaders a transparency—I was once this, but God has done this. Don't dare go to a church that has no testimonies. And if you are a church leader, testimonies of gospel transformation matter; they give hope to weary souls. No one gets tired of hearing how God can change lives.

If you are struggling with same-sex attraction and sin, you need a church that believes in and is experiencing the power of Christ through his Spirit.

Church as Cruciform Community

If the church is going to be a place where the same-sex struggler can flourish, it needs to be relational. Your church needs to be your family. The apostle Luke, sharing what the first church experienced, describes it this way: "They devoted themselves to . . . fellowship, to the breaking of bread . . . And day by day, attending the temple together . . . they received their food with glad and generous hearts, praising God and having favor with all the people."[10] At the core of a church that can serve someone struggling with same-sex attraction will be a church that focuses on relationships. I call the kind of community portrayed in the book of Acts cruciform community—community centered in the life, death, and resurrection of Jesus. Notice in the text that Luke goes out of his way to show that they broke bread together. Some commentators think this is an allusion to the reality that their very meals were communion services. Their meals together were centered in Jesus and were in the midst of their relational lives. The men and women in the book of Acts were living in close proximity with one another, immersed in the life of Christ. This nearness, centered in Christ, can best be described as family. Paul calls it "the household of faith."[11] It is here where you will experience healthy love, acceptance, nonjudgmental friendship, and most of all the life of Christ mediated through other men and women who want Jesus as much as you do.

One of the profound needs of all people, and especially the same-sex struggler, is to have places to be loved well. We all need places where we are cared for, accepted, and drawn into the life of the kingdom. This is one of the fundamental gifts of the church through cruciform community. This is lived out for the same-sex struggler perhaps most profoundly in smaller healing communities within the church. We are going to talk about these healing communities in the next chapter. But when you find yourself in one, expect your life to change.

It is this kind of community that is so life-giving to the same-sex struggler. It is a community where the Scriptures inform, the power of God sustains, and the people of God are the means of each member knowing that he or she is loved. It is a family. I want to suggest that one of the reasons people in general, and same-sex-attracted strugglers in particular, don't thrive in Christ is a lack of cruciform community. We are all so busy, with no time for relationships, and the result is that church is reduced to a sixty-minute service on the weekend. Reduce church to that and you will get very little out of it. The opposite is true as well. Give your life to the cruciform community and you will experience life.

The Benefits of Being in Such a Church

There are four real benefits of being in a Bible-believing, Spirit-filled, cruciform church community. First, there is acceptance.

There is no *us* and *them*. It is *we*. Church centered in Jesus is open to anyone. He is the hope and he is the answer for the sin of every person, and that includes the same-sex struggler. In this kind of church you will know real acceptance and very little judgment because those who make up the community understand that each one of us has our own sin and struggle to deal with. What a great gift it is to be accepted just as we are.

Second, such a church allows you to be yourself—struggles and all. There is no need to be fake. There is no need to hide. If Jesus is our sufficiency then he is enough. We don't need to pretend we are something we are not. We can be ourselves. What a beautiful thing it is to be yourself and to have people authentically love you. This is what happens in the body of Christ.

Third, you will experience transformation. I am flourishing today because I experienced more than a few amazing encounters with Jesus. I know that each person's journey with Jesus is different, and what transformation looks like can be different for each one of us, but I also know that Jesus loves to break into our lives. And when you are in a church that believes this and expects it, it happens! We need Jesus to show up, and he shows up in this kind of church!

Fourth, such a church is a safe place to learn godly relating. Same-sex strugglers have to navigate tumultuous waters of attraction, connection, and need; the church is a place where this can be worked out well. We are all growing in love, and those who deal with same-sex fracturing need a training ground to learn to love well. The church is such a place. It is with healthy enough men and women who are themselves seeking to follow Jesus that strugglers can learn to love and relate in healthy ways.

Finally, such a community is the place where we learn that we are loved. This is the need of every person, including those of us dealing with same-sex attraction. The deep ache of every human heart is to know love. There are many places to receive love—family, friends, marriage—but I believe that the church is to be one of the primary places where we learn how much God loves us. I am heartbroken by the stories of those who are same-sex attracted and deal with deep loneliness and ache for love. This should not be! This is one of the reasons that the church exists: so you would know your value and belovedness before God. When you find the right church, these benefits can be yours.

What Is Expected From You?

The church is foundational to human flourishing, and when you find the right church, you will flourish. But it is not a one-sided relationship. If you want life out of your church, if you want to flourish, then you need to engage the local church. You are not called to be a spectator or a consumer. Instead, you are called as a member of the body to take your place. Only when you do your part in a Christ-centered church will you experience a life full of kingdom flourishing.

This is what is required of you:

You must decide to follow Jesus.

No one can do this for you. It can be hard to have same-sex attraction and know that to live into your attraction means acting against God's Word. This one decision to be part of a local church and follow Jesus no matter the cost is the single most important decision you will make. It is this decision to align with the cross of Christ that will determine the kind of life you will have. But let me say this, a settled decision to follow Jesus in the context of a local church following Jesus will be the grounds of personal (and corporate) revival.

You need to be real.

You have a choice: hide or be known. Sexual brokenness and sin can be shameful, and it can be scary to share so intimately. But remember the words of James 5:16: "Confess your sins one to another and pray for one another, that you may be healed." Do you want gospel healing? Then live a confessional life. Find one or two people to begin to share with. If you don't know who to do it with, meet with your pastor and ask whom you can speak with. They will help you. Honesty in a church that is alive creates the space for God to move.

You need to worship regularly.

I have seen recent studies that show most committed Christians only go to church at most twice a month. If you want to flourish, you need to be at church every week, hearing the Word, singing songs about God and redemption, and growing. Some of the most profound moments of transformation in my journey have happened in the gathering of the people of God. What if I would have slept in that day or gone to see a movie? I might have missed out. I don't want you to miss out on the life available in Jesus. *Go to church often!*

You need to serve.

No matter what is going on in your life, you need to find a place in the church to give of your time, talent, and resources. Your same-sex attraction does not make you a second-class citizen. You are a person in need of Jesus just like everyone else. Roll up your sleeves and help your church live into the gospel mission. It can be easy to focus on ourselves and what is broken inside of us. Service gets our eyes onto the larger world and God's mission on the earth. When this happens in the local church, you will flourish.

The Result

When you find the right church, alive in Jesus, and you commit to it, you will flourish. You will find yourself knowing love—love from God and love from fellow brothers and sisters. You will see that your sin and fractures are just like everyone else's: brokenness in need of a Savior. You will know that people love you just as you are. And most of all, it will be in the body of Christ that you experience the life of Christ. You will flourish. Your life will never be the same again. I am not sure of all that God will do in your life as it relates to your same-sex attraction, but you will know his love. And his love is enough.

An Example of a Church Doing It Well

Peter Hubbard is a colleague in the gospel, a fellow pastoral member of the Restored Hope Network, and the author of a wonderful book, *Love Into Light: The Gospel, the Homosexual and the Church*. He is also somebody who is part of a church providing a beautiful community for the same-sex attracted. I sent him some questions about the church he is a part of, and he was gracious enough to answer. Below is our conversation.

What is the name of your church and position?
I am the teaching pastor at North Hills Community Church.

Why do you have a heart for the LGBT community?

Every person is a divine image-bearer, no matter what "community" they live in. They resemble and represent their Creator. They are loved by Jesus. In the past, we failed to intentionally communicate that love, but we are changing that.

In what ways are you reaching out to the LGBT community?

Our people reach out in love in many different ways, usually relationally rather than formally. For example, one family loved their neighbors (who were living a gay lifestyle) through simple acts of kindness for sixteen years before their neighbors trusted Christ.

Could you share a story of a gay person coming to Christ (or returning back to Christ) and what that looked like?

Recently a young man testified at his baptism, "When I look back four months ago, I don't even recognize the person." He is a new man. He gave his life to God and has peace. He had been living in a relationship with an older man, yet he was friends with some men in our church and began attending with them. When he trusted Christ, he soon after ended his relationship with the older man. He continues to meet weekly with his new Christian brothers to receive help and encouragement.

Does your church provide healing spaces for those dealing with same-sex attraction (SSA), and what are they?

Our church does not have any special "healing spaces" for those who struggle with SSA. Our desire is that our entire church would be a healing space. We try to downplay cultural identity markers that tend to separate us from one another. For example, we have about seventy life groups that meet throughout the week. Some groups have SSA strugglers, some do not. When, for example, men who experience SSA share their experience with men who experience OSA (opposite-sex attraction), they are united in their need of grace. They challenge one another toward biblical manhood in surprising ways. We do provide individual and group counseling as well as periodic special fellowships to share stories and seek healing. I suppose these could be viewed as healing spaces. But our primary goal is to unite people with all kinds of battles (SSA, addiction, depression, anxiety, anger, fear, eating disorders, etc.) so that the body can edify itself in love.

What is your hope for a same-sex-attracted person who comes to your church and wants to follow Jesus as it relates to his or her sexual identity?

Our prayer is that each one of us would see ourselves first and foremost in Jesus. We self-identify as Christ-followers. Every other identity (whether a true identity or a lie) must be viewed through the lens of our gospel identity. This unites us at the cross and empowers us through Jesus' resurrection!

What are one or two guiding biblical principles churches should have as they seek to reach out to the LGBT community?

I have been surprised by how many pastors view "God gave them up" (in Romans 1:24–25) as a permanent condition. This view shapes the way they speak about homosexuality, and this view is a rejection of the gospel. The words "gave them up" (*paradidomi*) are used more of Jesus than of any other person in the New Testament. He was given up to death and the cross. If that were a permanent condition, then we are all hopeless.

When I, as a pastor, speak about SSA with words full of gospel hope and help, people feel safe to share their struggle.

If I fail to talk about SSA or speak about it as an incurable disease that is ruining our country, then I should not be surprised when SSA strugglers do not feel safe coming to our church. I would encourage pastors to spend a lot of time face-to-face with SSA strugglers, hearing their stories and praying with them, and then speak words from the pulpit that are full of hope.

Conclusion

In order for Christians who wrestle with same-sex attraction to flourish, they will need a healthy and beautiful church home. This church home needs to be Bible-centered, Spirit-filled, and encouraging all to follow Jesus. The church is foundational for a life that flourishes in the gospel. When the same-sex-attracted Christian does the work of finding the right church, engaging that church, and serving there, he or she will grow and find profound gospel transformation.

5

The Gifts of Healing Communities and Christian Therapy

It was the summer of 1997. I had just begun to follow Jesus. I was earnest. I was also deeply in conflict about my sexual identity and needed to do something with the same-sex desires I was experiencing. And I was in bondage to gay pornography. I was living in Southern California, and a friend invited me to a group that was biblically based for those, like me, who dealt with sexual brokenness. So I went. This is how I was introduced to Andrew Comiskey and Desert Stream Ministries.[1] Living Waters, the main program that Desert Stream trains local churches to run, saved my fledgling Christian life. It was there I was able to be honest about my sexual sin and conflict. It was there that I experienced the grace of God through intensive prayer. It was there that I found radical transformation that enabled me to embrace my God-given sexual identity and be a good gift to others, especially my wife.

During this time, I also found much good through competent Christian therapists. I needed places to talk about what was going on as it related to my sexual identity, process my journey, and think through the possibility of dating women. Most of the care I received was rooted in the church, and rightly so; but the amount of care I needed necessitated that I find other avenues for care. These good therapists provided it.

For some, such groups and the idea of therapy don't sound appealing or necessary. And this might be true for some who struggle with same-sex attraction. But others of us will need healing communities and/or competent Christian therapists who can journey with us as we seek to follow Christ. In this chapter I want to first try to give a psychology of sexual identity; second, discuss the goal of healing communities and Christian therapy from a biblical perspective; third, give an overview of what a healing community and Christian therapist look like; and finally, give two practical on-ramps that you can provide as a leader or that you can take as a Christian same-sex struggler.

A Psychology of Sexual Identity

In chapter 1, we discussed how sexual identity from the biblical perspective is rooted in our gender.[2] This biblical sexual identity is expressed through our gender in two ways: (1) our bodies; (2) our psychological makeup. In other words, it means something psychologically to be male; it means something psychologically to be female. It seems fair to say that one of the signs that we are operating healthily through our God-given sexual identity is that we have sexual desires for the opposite sex. If heterosexual desire is a sign that one has a whole-enough sexual identity, same-sex attraction and activity reveals a fracture in our sexual identity as male or female. If this is true, it follows then that when we have fractured sexual identities that manifest themselves through same-sex desire, we are in need of help.

I want to suggest that the journey of following Jesus for the same-sex attracted is, at least in part, the redeeming of this fracturing. This is the work of Christian psychology. Because we are using terms that can be defined in a number of ways, I want to take the time to define *Christian psychology*. I like Dr. Ervene Bragg's definition of Christian or biblical psychology:

> Biblical Psychology is the description and explanation of man's spiritual, psychical, and physical constitution, by creation, the fall and redemption from the Holy Scriptures. That is what he was in the original creation, what he is by reason of the fall, or the presence of sin in his members, and what God makes of him in regeneration.[3]

Dr. Eric J. Johnson says it even more succinctly: Christian psychology studies the "nature of human beings and their psychopathology and recovery."[4] Let's apply Bragg's and Johnson's definitions of biblical psychology to our conversation on sexual identity and same-sex attraction: Christian psychology seeks to define our sexual identity and its purpose as described in the Scriptures; then in light of sin, it seeks to understand the cause and roots of same-sex attraction as a result of a sexual identity in crisis; and finally and most important, as a person lives in union with Christ, Christian psychology seeks to help one experience regeneration in his or her sexual identity so that he or she can live a holy life through his or her gender for the glory of God.

So to bring it all together, same-sex attraction is caused by sin and finds its roots in a fractured sexual identity. Christian psychology seeks to give biblical answers of hope that actually help the same-sex attracted move into a more healthy sexual identity. Christian healing communities and Christian counselors are some of the means by which this happens.

I need to say two important things so that we do not lose our way. First, the help we are looking for through Christian psychology is not first and foremost for the emergence of heterosexual feelings. Our aim is to become whole in our sexual identity as male or female. For some, heterosexual feelings will come, and for others this will not happen, but there will be an ability to be a relational gift through one's singleness. Healing communities and good counselors can help us find healing in our sexual identity.

Second, we must be careful about how we describe the causation of homosexuality in persons dealing with same-sex attraction. For some, same-sex attraction will be an expression of relational deprivations. Others will find their same-sex attraction a result of abuse. Some will find homosexuality a welcome choice based on a relational opportunity at some point in life. While others will have same-sex attraction from no apparent relational source or abuse at all; in fact, their relationships might be quite warm and healthy throughout life. *What is true about everyone's same-sex attraction is that the root of it is the fall of man. And all homosexual activity is sinful idolatry.* And while I do believe that the fracturing of a sexual identity that has expressed itself through homosexuality can be caused by a myriad of factors, the cure is one—Jesus Christ. We need places within the church and outside the church where men and women can experience this cure. Christian psychology, I think, can help in that journey.

A Caution and a Rant Before We Move On

Sadly, I think one of the ways that people have set themselves up for failure in the past is that they have made one's sexual feelings changing to be the litmus test of wholeness. I don't want to minimize the possibility of this happening (because it did happen for me), but nowhere in the Bible is this given as the only marker for a holy sexual identity. Instead, as we talked about in chapter 1, a male is living into his biblical sexual identity when he lives obediently unto sacrificial love; and a female is living into her biblical sexual identity when she lives obediently receptive to being a life giver, a mother spiritually and/or physically. Thus, whole sexual identity is not just about certain sexual desires and activities but being a good gender gift in every area of life. This is possible to do in heterosexual marriage and this is possible to do in and through singleness.

Secondly, a rant. I think one of the great misfortunes in our conversations around same-sex attraction is that we are afraid to talk about how this particular "imprint of the fall" fractures one's sexual identity and the possible Christian psychological models that might help the restoration and transformation of the human person. It is my hope that godly Christian theologians and psychologists will not bow to the cultural demands inside and outside the church, but seek the Scriptures for what a biblical sexuality looks like, how sin fractures our sexual identity, and how it can be healed. What we need are not platitudes or sentimental hopes, but concrete pathways that the same-sex struggler and church can use for the sake of fidelity to Jesus.

But we need not wait on this critical work; there are church communities and counselors right now providing healing communities and spaces for the same-sex attracted.

What Does a Healing Community Look Like?

Maybe you are like me and you deal with same-sex attraction and want to find healing spaces to encounter Christ and move from fractured to wholeness. Or maybe you are a leader and you want to provide healing places within your community for same-sex strugglers to encounter Christ, embrace their God-given sexual identity as male or female, and move into being a gendered gift. Below are attributes you should look for in a healing community:

It will be centered on the Scriptures.

It might use therapeutic models and techniques but its understanding of the problem and the cure will be biblically saturated. If the aim of the community is anything other than discipleship to Jesus, it probably won't be all that helpful for you.

It will believe that you can become (more) whole in your sexual identity.

A healing community wants to help you, whether male or female, enter into your God-given identity. Whether this is through marriage or singleness, this community should help you grow as a gendered being.

It will have prayer as a major focus.

There might be talking, even advice giving, but this will not be central. What will be central is a focus on bringing

God into your life and asking him to give what only he can give.

It will be a small-group model divided by gender.

It is my experience that small groups are the healthiest ways to work through the shameful, painful, tender areas of sexuality. These small groups should be gender defined (men with men and women with women). Churches and strugglers need to be wary of one-on-one care. It can do more harm than good.

It will be a confidential group.

Disclosure of one's past and sin is hard work. Same-sex strugglers deserve to know that what they are sharing will be held in confidence. It is up to each person what he or she will share publicly. To share someone else's story without their permission is to do great harm to them.

The leaders will have experienced significant transformation themselves.

First of all this means that most of the leaders are men and women who know from their own lives what it means to have dealt with sexual sin and brokenness and the gospel that saves them. This also means freedom from habitual sexual sin and also the integration of their sexual identity. Whether through singleness or marriage, they will be becoming good gender gifts.

There will be testimonies.

You will look around this healing community and people will be getting radically transformed. If there are no testimonies, run!

It will be under the authority of a local church.

This means that local churches will have the courage to
have such communities. Second, it means that these healing communities will be under pastoral authority. This
matters. God cares about it. Be very wary of going into
a healing community not under the authority of a local
church.

What Will Christian Counseling Look Like?

Maybe you want to go to a Christian therapist and work
through issues relating to your same-sex attraction. Maybe it
seems safer to you or maybe you feel like you need the extra
care. Or maybe you are a leader and you wonder what kind
of therapist you should send someone to who is under your
care and deals with same-sex attraction. Below is what you
should look for in a Christian counselor:

The Christian therapist believes in the Bible.

They might have been trained at a secular school, but what
you want to know is, do they believe that Jesus is central? You
want the cure, not just some pain management. You want
the therapeutic model to be gospel-saturated.

They believe in transformation.

They will be an ally as you seek gender wholeness. Ask
up front; make sure they know what you are expecting.
You are not putting your healing journey on the therapist,
but make sure they agree, at the very least, that healing is
possible.

They have walked with others who have dealt with same-sex attraction and have been helpful.

You would want your heart doctor to know what he is doing; expect no less from your Christian therapist. You want a counselor who is comfortable in the deep waters of sexual identity. Ask.

They are trained.

Licensed therapists have had at least hundreds of hours of experience, years of education, and oversight from a more mature and competent therapist. Be careful who you go to.

They follow a counseling code of ethics.

They have appropriate client-counselor boundaries; they aren't overly emotionally invested. It is a safe place.

On-Ramps for Healing Communities and Christian Therapy

Below are four ways you can enter into a healing community or find a trained therapist.

Living Waters

This is a 20-week group that meets in a local church and is designed specifically for men and women who deal with same-sex attraction (and other sexual sin and brokenness). It is Christ-centered, believes in transformation, and is centered in prayer. I cannot recommend it enough. For more information, go to www.desertstream.org.

Restored Hope Network

RHN is an interdenominational network of ministries that provide hope, care, and encouragement to the same-sex struggler. I serve on their board and am so thankful for their witness and stand for the gospel of Jesus. For more information, go to www.restoredhopenetwork.com.

Celebrate Recovery

CR is for anyone who has "hurts, habits, or hangups." It is a Christian small-group program run by the local church and centered on the twelve steps. This can be especially helpful for a same-sex struggler who is also dealing with sexual addiction. It fosters beautiful, authentic Christian community. I have benefited greatly from Celebrate Recovery. For more information, go to www.celebraterecovery.com.

American Association of Christian Counselors

This is an association of Christian therapists who believe in the Bible, love Jesus, and also believe in transformation. If you are looking for a trained therapist who is Christ-centered, check out their website: www.aacc.net.

Humble Yourself and Remember It Takes Time

To my friends who are same-sex attracted and love Jesus, don't let pride and fear stand in the way of entering into communities and spaces of healing. It is very easy these days to dismiss such options. Many folks are doing it. But when you have biblical expectations and are part of a Christ-centered church, these healing communities and therapists can greatly help you.

And remember, wholeness in one's sexual identity takes time. It does not happen for most overnight or even in a few years. It is a long journey toward having a sexual identity that honors Christ and that flourishes in relationship. This is true about anything in life that matters. So don't get discouraged. Stay faithful, believe in the goodness of God, and God will do extraordinary things!

A Bright Healing Community

One of my dearest friends in the world is Tracey Bickle. She has been one of the key leaders in the healing community of the International House of Prayer (IHOP) in Kansas City, Missouri, over the last fifteen years. Tracey is a godly leader, gifted, and committed to make sure that as many people as possible encounter the healing mercy of Jesus.

IHOP itself is a prayer movement that has as its unique offering a 24-hour prayer room lifting high the name of Jesus. Thousands of people are connected to IHOP in some way either locally or globally. Every year, 400 to 500 men and women go through one of their pastoral support programs in Kansas City. And a significant number of the men and women who go through their program deal with same-sex attraction.

IHOP's pastoral program for the same-sex attracted has one goal: to remove everything that hinders love—love of God and love of others. The unique prayer-room environment creates an atmosphere where people's "stuff" rises to the surface and can be more easily dealt with. So at IHOP, healing and transformation begin with interaction with the Spirit of God. Then these pastoral group options provide spaces for prayer and accountability. IHOP is unique in that it provides a diversity of programs because of their belief that Jesus healed in different ways in his earthly ministry and that probably means he continues to heal us in a variety of ways as well. They offer programs like Living Waters, twelve-step groups, counseling, and theophostic prayer opportunities. And all of their programs are filled with leaders who have been through the process themselves and have experienced a significant amount of transformation and healing. It is this unique environment of intensive prayer, softened hearts, and healing opportunities that makes IHOP such a great example of a healing community.

And IHOP has amazing fruit. Many of the men and women who come in bondage to sexual sin and same-sex desire find significant freedom. For Tracey and her team, getting folks married off is not the sign of a job well done (though many same-sex-attracted men and women have found the transformation necessary to be good gifts for marriage). Instead, when men and women fractured by homosexuality find peace and hope in their sexual identity as male and female and can begin to connect in healthy ways to other people, they know that God is at work.

IHOP, through Tracey Bickle's leadership, is a bright healing community. I share them as an example because God is doing amazing things throughout this country. IHOP is but one example. Maybe you are a church leader and you wonder what you can do at your church to serve the same-sex attracted. My encouragement to you is to start small but do something. It is fairly simple to start a Living Waters or Celebrate Recovery course. It just takes a committed core who love Jesus, have experienced some transformation, and want to offer it to others. Your church can be a safe place of healing for the sexually broken, including the same-sex attracted.

Maybe you are a same-sex-attracted Christian and wonder if there is a place for you to experience the mercy of Jesus in community. I want to tell you, in your city or nearby are ample opportunities for healing and transformation. I pray you do the work to find one.

Conclusion

The same-sex-attracted Christian has a sexual identity that is in some way fractured. Christian psychology provides answers and spiritual medicine to make whole what has been broken. Healing communities like Celebrate Recovery and Living Waters can serve the same-sex attracted well. These groups are safe, confidential, filled with leaders who have been through the process of healing, and radically centered in the hope of Jesus. A good Christian counselor can do much good as well. Centered in the Bible, believing that God transforms lives, Christian counselors can help individuals enter into the healing mercy of Jesus.

6

The Gift of Singleness

I love *The Lord of the Rings* trilogy. They are some of my favorite books. Central to them is the story of Frodo, Sam, and the fellowship of the ring. Their goal: destroy the ring of power and end the oppression of Sauron. The journey takes Frodo from comfort, ease, and normalcy to hardship, danger, and pain. Eventually Frodo and Sam separate from the rest of the fellowship and take the long journey to destroy the ring. Facing orcs, spiders, and all kinds of evil, their friendship is central to their ability to keep going. They accomplish the audacious goal they set out to meet. They do what is nearly impossible. These two little hobbits save Middle-earth.

Something that I have not really thought about but I think is quite beautiful is that Frodo was single. His character has no love interests; he forgoes many normal relationships of home and country for a greater calling. His calling to destroy the ring requires his full attention and life. Though his singleness is really secondary to his calling of destroying the ring, I do think Tolkien paints a wonderfully biblical picture of what biblical singleness looks like. Singleness is not just the absence of something; it is the embrace of a special calling and life.

In the last few years there has been a beautiful resurgence of men and women publicly embracing celibacy and singleness as they follow Jesus. This has important implications for those who struggle with same-sex attraction and desire to follow Jesus. Before this time, unfortunately, when someone came into the church and dealt with same-sex attraction, the goal for that person was the kind of transformation that would end in heterosexual marriage. But for many people marriage just did not seem like a reasonable option, and they were not sure where that left them relationally. For much of the good of the ex-gay movement, in which I flourished, I wonder if the seeming total fixation on heterosexual marriage as the mark of wholeness did harm.[1] Thankfully, singleness is regaining a hearing and helping many same-sex strugglers find a viable path into fidelity to Jesus and faithfulness to the demands and ethics of Scripture.

The goal of this chapter is to show the beauty, the viability, and the ability of singleness to be the means of a same-sex struggler who follows Jesus to flourish. Also in this chapter I want to explore, practically, how the same-sex attracted, and the leaders who are seeking to care for them, can know if a person is called to singleness; next, I want to give some practical tips on how the same-sex-attracted Christian can embrace singleness and live out one's sexual identity as male or female; finally, we will end with a few testimonies of lives flourishing in the midst of celibacy and singleness. By the end it is my hope that this chapter helps to put singleness in its proper place: a gift to the same-sex struggler.

What Is Biblical Singleness?

If you remember, in chapter 2 of this book, I sought to give a biblical meaning of marriage and show how heterosexual marriage points to the purpose of everything. Christ is the Husband-God who is pursuing his bride, the church. And one day—may it come soon—there will be the Wedding Supper of the Lamb. The bridegroom and the bride will come together never to be separated again. Heterosexual marriage points to this reality.

Let me suggest that singleness can also point to the purpose of everything.

In Matthew 19, Jesus gives his teaching on divorce. For the disciples, what Jesus teaches is very hard to hear. So they tell Jesus as much and he responds. Here is the exchange:

> The disciples said to him, "If such is the case of a man with his wife, it is better not to marry." But he said to them, "Not everyone can receive this saying, but only those to whom it is given. For there are eunuchs who have been so from birth, and there are eunuchs who have been made eunuchs by men, and there are eunuchs who have made themselves eunuchs for the sake of the kingdom of heaven. Let the one who is able to receive this receive it."[2]

Eunuchs are those who do not have the physical ability for procreation and usually have a very weak sexual drive if they have one at all. And Jesus tells his disciples that some people will choose to make themselves eunuchs for the Kingdom of God. This of course is not speaking of self-mutilation but a choice.³ Some men and women who follow Jesus choose the Kingdom of heaven over a marital relationship.

John Paul II has written one of the most important books on theological anthropology in the last hundred years, *Theology of the Body*. This is what he writes about choosing singleness and celibacy for the sake of the Kingdom of heaven:

> [A celibate and single man or woman] indicates the eschatological virginity of the risen man. In him there will be revealed, I would say, the absolute and eternal meaning of the glorified body in union with God himself. . . .
>
> Earthly continence for the kingdom of heaven is undoubtedly a sign that indicated this truth and this reality. It is a sign that the body, whose end is not the grave, is directed to glorification.⁴

Sexual intimacy is temporal; Jesus said as much: "For in the resurrection they neither marry nor are given in marriage, but are like angels in heaven."⁵ When a man or a woman gives up sexual intimacy and marriage for the sake of Jesus, he or she is pointing to the reality that sex is only a temporary reality. There is something more important than sex, the Kingdom of heaven. And the full revelation of the Kingdom of heaven will be the union of the Bridegroom Christ with his bride—the glory of God on full display. In the body and actions of a single person who follows Christ is the sign that there is an intimacy, a union, a reality of love that is more important and more real than sexual intimacy, and by abstaining from sexual intimacy they are giving their whole selves to that. A married person is obligated to serve and love her spouse. This is her calling and this is how she lives out her faith. For the single person, his calling is to use the energies of his life for service to the Kingdom of heaven. He has the time and the energies to live fully for God. In this way he shows humanity's deepest calling. In this way he shows what the purposes of the cosmos are all about.

The Marks of Singleness (How You Know You Have the Gift)

There are two texts in the Bible that speak explicitly about singleness and celibacy and give the marks of this gift. The first I quoted previously (Matthew 19:10–12); the second is found in Paul's letter to the Corinthians:

> Now as a concession, not a command, I say this. I wish that all were as I myself am. But each has his own gift from God, one of one kind and one of another.
>
> To the unmarried and the widows I say that it is good for them to remain single, as I am. But if they cannot exercise self-control, they should marry. For it is better to marry than to burn with passion. . . .
>
> I want you to be free from anxieties. The unmarried man is anxious about the things of the Lord, how to please the Lord. But the married man is anxious about worldly things, how to please his wife, and his interests are divided. And the unmarried or betrothed woman is anxious about the things of the Lord, how to be holy in body and spirit. But the married woman is anxious about worldly things, how to please her husband. I say this for your own benefit, not to lay any restraint upon you, but to promote good order and to secure your undivided devotion to the Lord.[6]

From the Matthew text and the Corinthians text we get a very clear idea of the marks of singleness and whether it is the gift that you have.

First, singleness is a voluntary vocation.

After Jesus shares about the gift of celibacy and singleness, he says, "Let the one who is able to receive this receive it." Paul echoes the same idea: "Each has his own gift from God, one of one kind and one of another." It is a gift that one must decide to receive. It is not forced; it is not mandatory. If the vocation of singleness is too much, consider the possibility of marriage.

It is a gift that is both situational and vocational.

Jesus tells his disciples that some are eunuchs by choice and for others it is a forced reality. This is the nature of Christian celibacy. You might have the gift because there simply is no other option—heterosexual marriage is not available or desirable, or what you desire (same-sex relationship) is something the Bible condemns. Or singleness might just be a season for you. You are not married but you are open to it if the right spouse comes along. Until then, you are embracing the gift of singleness.

Singleness can be both a delight and a source of great pain.

Jesus' using the imagery of being a eunuch for the sake of the Kingdom seemingly evokes imagery of both suffering and joy. Becoming a eunuch is painful. Tom Wright, commenting on Jesus' words on celibacy writes, "For some, the decision to postpone or renounce marriage seems every bit as hard as physical mutilation."[7] When one thinks of the ache and pain that can remain when one forgoes sexual (same-sex) intimacy, I think this is the type of pain that Jesus is alluding to. But the Kingdom is the source of all true delight: "For the kingdom of God is not a matter of eating and drinking but of righteousness and peace and joy in the Holy Spirit."[8] When Jesus is your one delight, you get to enjoy that relationship in a very special way. Not bound by other relationships, you can put Jesus at the center. Such a life is a life of joy. Celibacy carries the tension of joy and sorrow at the core of its calling.

Singleness can be either lifelong or for a season.

Paul seems to intimate that one should pursue celibacy and singleness until desire for someone of the opposite sex gets in the way: "To the unmarried and the widows I say that it is good for them to remain single, as I am. But if they cannot exercise self-control, they should marry. For it is better to marry than to burn with passion." As a person dealing with same-sex attraction, you might never find a person of the opposite sex who causes you to "burn with passion." In that case, celibacy is a gift given by God to you. But it might be the case that in one's journey with Jesus a person comes along that ignites the heart's ache for physical, emotional, and spiritual union.

The gift of singleness is a calling to something greater.

A single person can fill his or her life with the "things of the Lord." The time and energy usually spent on family and marriage can be spent in devotion to Jesus and his cause. I think this means that singleness always comes with a mission. Maybe not quite as extraordinary as saving Middle-earth, but nonetheless a mission that requires one's full devotion and energy. Both Jesus and Paul are great examples of singles living lives in gospel mission.

How Do You Embrace Biblical Singleness?

Though much could be said about how to practically live out biblical singleness, I want to give you five really important things that the same-sex-attracted Christian must do, and what leaders must be mindful of, so that singleness can be a gift by which the same-sex-attracted Christian can flourish in the Lord.

1. Singleness is a gift insomuch as you take the time and energy that you would use to invest in a marital relationship and invest that energy and time into your relationship with Jesus and his church. To do singleness well, you need to make your life with Jesus your one aim. You must find concrete ways to stir your affections and serve his Kingdom. Singleness allows you to focus on Jesus. Do not miss out on the opportunity that singleness affords you.

2. For singleness to be a gift for you, you must be part of a church community where singleness is valued. If church is only about a Sunday-morning church service, biblical singleness will be nearly impossible. Does your church value singleness as a gift of God? Is it held in esteem? Are the single men and women in your community thriving? Do they serve in leadership positions? Biblical singleness is rooted in a healthy church community.

3. For singleness to be a gift for you, you need friends. Friends to eat with, live life with, go to movies with, and even vacation with. Singleness is a gift when church is family and family is church. Isolation will destroy any Christian, but especially the person who is seeking to live out biblical singleness. This means that you need

to take responsibility to find places where you are fed relationally. In a healthy church, your proactive work will be met with other men and women looking for the same kind of healthy community.

4. For singleness to be a gift for you, you need healthy same-sex mentors who can be guides for you on your journey in Christ. There are things you will navigate: attractions, longings, crossed boundaries, and growth. A faithful mentor can be a safe place to work through all the things that come up in the journey of life. He or she can help you make sense of what is happening in you and around you. This kind of community is essential if one is to thrive as a single Christian.

5. For singleness to be a gift for you, you need to serve. The secret of serving for the sake of Christ's kingdom is that we get more than what we give away. You want deep satisfaction? Serve. Do you ache for relational connectedness? Serve. Are you afraid of loneliness? Serve. Singleness gives you the special ability to serve others. And it is when this service happens that you will thrive in your singleness.

Opposite-Sex Relating and Singleness

One of the dangers of the spiritual friendship movement that we considered in chapter 3 is that it is very fixated on same-sex relating in friendship. There is hardly any mention of the good of opposite-sex relating among those who are single. But I think that such relating is absolutely essential in our singleness if we are to live out of our God-given sexual identity. If you are a single man, the women in your life need the gift of your masculinity to thrive. If you are a single woman, the men

111

in your life need the gift of your femininity to thrive. This relating and being good relational gifts to one another can be deeply satisfying and a profound way of living out your sexual identity. Healthy biblical singleness will mean having friendships with both men and women. Without such relating, you can miss out on a wonderful way of being a gift to others.

Fiery Singleness and the Hope of the Gospel

Jim is in his fifties and has been a follower of Jesus for decades. His life has been hard. I connected with Jim through a mutual friend in Oklahoma City. Jim grew up Catholic, was molested multiple times, was exposed to pornography at an early age, and early in adulthood embraced a gay lifestyle. He found physical connection and relief in the club scene of the early eighties. Jim had multiple gay encounters but was never satisfied.

Then Jim met Jesus and it seemed like his life was turning around. In 1984, Jim got married to a young woman and had two children. He thought this marriage would take care of everything wrong with him, but instead his marriage became a pit and a mess. Jim was still involved sexually with other men, and his faith and his marriage were torn into shambles. Jim's Christian life seemed to be over. He got a divorce and entered right back into his gay life. He went from relationship to relationship, just trying to fulfill the deep hungers in his soul. He sinned, and he sinned boldly.

At this time in his life, Jim worked as a waiter and was totally lost as a man. But then God intervened, and he has not been the same since.

One evening while he was working, a woman came into the restaurant. While he was serving her she told him that

God had a word for Jim: "God wants to speak to you like a father speaks to his child." This one prophetic word broke through Jim's hard heart, and things began to change. He began to experience God's great love for him. Jim responded to God's love by pursuing Jesus. In 2003, Jim got connected to a ministry in Oklahoma City that serves those struggling with sexual brokenness and began to do the work of faithfully following Jesus. Through this, along with a healthy church life, Jim began to experience profound freedom. He set up friendships of accountability, installed Internet filters for both his phone and his computer, and is serving others. He still has same-sex attractions but sees his attractions as a manifestation of something lacking or broken in his sexual identity. His boundaries keep him holy, and his journey with Jesus is slowly transforming him.

Jim is single. He wants to get married but doesn't know when this might happen. In the meantime, he is happy. His embracing of a gay identity was miserable and distorted. All he knew in that life was pain. Now Jim describes his life as happy and grateful. There are some days he hardly deals with same-sex attraction at all. He is getting to the place in life where he is sensing the call to full-time ministry. He wants to serve other men and women broken in their sexuality with the same good news that he has received in his life. He knows that he is being called into something greater than what he has right now. God has more for him. His life is one of fiery singleness filled with the hope of the gospel.

Singleness and Hope

Tanja lives in England and goes to St. Mary's Anglican Church. She was born in South Africa and was always attracted to men.

Then, in university, Tanja met and grew in friendship with another young woman named Toni. Their friendship grew and Toni shared with Tanja that she was sexually attracted to her. Tanja liked Toni and the relationship and so they entered into a gay relationship that would last for over four years.

The relationship at its core was not very healthy, and after a lot of turmoil, Tanja and Toni broke up. Tanja thought her same-sex relationship was all just a phase and dated a man, but her attraction to women continued. Though she was a Christian and felt bad about her sexual sin, she tried to push aside her Christian ethics and worldview. She tried to run away from God, but God would not stop pursuing her. And in a Pentecostal church in South Africa she encountered the risen Lord.

There she met Jesus and was never the same again. Tanja was honest with the community that made up that church. And they prayed for her. Life seemed to be changing right before her eyes. Then she emigrated to England and met a man and they got married. Could life get any better? It seemed that God was answering all of her prayers.

But this was yet another painful relationship for Tanja. Her husband abandoned her when she could not have any children. Now she was forced into singleness and still wrestling with same-sex attraction. Still a Christian and knowing that same-sex relationships were sinful, Tanja decided to cling to Christ.

This is when Tanja began going to St. Mary's. There she met Sam Allberry, a pastor who also happens to struggle with same-sex attraction and has committed himself to Christian singleness. This beautiful church supports same-sex-attracted Christians by fully embracing the gospel in all that it does. This church also provides a support group for those in its midst who have same-sex attraction. This support group meets quarterly, is filled with men and women—some married and others single—and is led by the senior pastor and his wife. This group is an expression of what Tanja experiences at St. Mary's: community. It is a church that supports her, equips her, and stands with her as she follows Jesus.

Though Tanja's singleness was forced upon her and she would gladly remarry if the right man were to come along, singleness has been a gift. As a single woman she has much more time to serve the Lord. She teaches Sunday school and can provide personal care for those in need in her church community. She also has been able to pursue in-depth Bible training from a local school that required a significant time commitment. This school has taught her how to exposit Scripture, how to teach the Bible to others, and how to disciple others. She was able to do this training because she was single and did not have a family. Perhaps most beautifully, her singleness enables her to spend a considerable amount of time with the Lord.

Her same-sex attraction, though by no means a good in itself, has drawn her near to the Lord. Tanja has been through a lot. Her life has had difficult moments, but she has joy. In her singleness she has found hope.

Conclusion

Biblical singleness is a gift of grace that enables the same-sex struggler who is not married to live in spiritual health. More than that, it is a calling into the special purposes and mission of God. It is only possible when a person has a healthy church community and has received enough healing to be a good-enough gift through his or her sexual identity. And though the hunger for same-sex intimacy might always remain, it will no longer be central.

Biblical singleness can be a profound good gift to the same-sex struggler. It can provide a path for deep connection, gift giving, and healing. Singleness can be a season of life or a lifelong vocation. It is filled with both joy and pain. And most of all, it can be a profound way to live out your faith in Jesus.

7

The Gift of Marriage

I have been married for fourteen years. My wife, Amy, is smart, beautiful, funny, wise, and my best friend. When not totally stressed out by life, we have so much fun together; no one can make me laugh like my wife. I am also very attracted to her; no one turns my head like Amy does. She is an amazing mother who loves our four boys with passion and faithfulness. She is my equal partner in every way. She has taught me so much about life and Jesus that there is no way that I would be the man I am today except that God has given her to me. She has also been one of the key ways that God has grown me as a man.

When I got married, I had sexual purity and had grown considerably as a man but I was self-centered, self-concerned, and far from being a sacrificial servant. I also had whispers of same-sex desire still in my soul. All in all, I was immature but earnest. In marriage, every area of immaturity has been brought into the fire of our covenantal relationship. The same is true for her. She has been beautifully transformed by Jesus through our marriage. And though my journey of maturity is far from complete, God has used my marriage to bring profound good into my life.

One of the most precious spaces of our relationship is the good love I have received from my wife even as I still occasionally struggle with same-sex temptation. I have throughout my married life kept the moral boundaries in both my mind and actions as it relates to my sexuality, but there are moments of attraction or uncertainty that still bubble up. I do have good male friends whom I can bring these to, but I can also bring them to my wife. Because I have never crossed any moral lines in our marriage, she is able to give mercy to my weakness. She is able to partner with me as I pursue vigorous holiness. Over fourteen years of marriage, she has listened, prayed, and stood with me in my true identity as a man called by God. God has used her faithfulness to encourage and empower me to stand faithful.

What I am experiencing in my traditional marriage is what countless others have experienced as well—marriage is a place to be loved and encouraged to run the race of faith well. This is the good of marriage and why it can be a profound gift even to those who struggle with same-sex desire. I know this is a controversial subject and it has challenging edges to it, but I do believe that traditional marriage can be an option for many who deal with same-sex attraction.

In this chapter I want to first share how traditional marriage can be dangerous for a same-sex-attracted Christian, then share the good of marriage for the same-sex attracted. I want to give some of the criteria that can help a person know if marriage might be an option for them, and I hope to bring together all that we have learned about marriage and redemption; and finally, I want to end with two amazing stories of the good of biblical marriage in the midst of same-sex attraction.

The Pitfalls of Marriage for the Same-Sex Attracted

For all the good that biblical marriage can provide the same-sex attracted, it can also be dangerous. The same union that is a beautiful good can also be a very painful one. For the same-sex-attracted Christian, marriage must be entered into carefully and wisely; otherwise the damage and calamity might be great. There are three realities that must be faced by the same-sex-attracted Christian if marriage is to be a gift.

The first reality is that marriage will not fix a person's same-sex attraction. Marriage can be a support, a great help, and even bring healing, but if you think that your marriage can "fix" what is broken in you, I am afraid that you are setting yourself up for failure. If a person has deep, unresolved same-sex conflict, he or she should not bring that into a marriage. Marriage is not a place to live out of brokenness. Marriage will not fix what is broken in a person, but entered into lightly it can break more than just someone who has same-sex attraction.

The second reality that must be faced is the necessity of the same-sex struggler to be open about his or her past same-sex sin and current sin struggles. Long before anyone says, "I do," each deserves to know what they are getting themselves into. The spouse deserves to know where his or her partner's body and mind have been. Before marriage can even be considered, there needs to be complete disclosure of past sexual relationships, problems with pornography, and any historic strongholds of lust. There is also a need to make sure your potential spouse knows current sin issues. Do you struggle with same-sex lust? Emotionally dependent relationships? All of this needs to be brought out into the open. It breaks my heart when I meet a same-sex struggler who is married to someone of the opposite sex and his or her spouse does not know of past or current sin. Without such disclosure, marriage becomes a prison of deception and darkness.

The third reality that must be faced is finding a spouse who is willing to journey and partner with you in the uniqueness of your same-sex struggle. I was talking to someone recently who told me that when she told her soon-to-be husband about her same-sex attraction, he did not know what to do with it and was not pleased about it. For a person dealing with same-sex attraction, desiring to be married is not enough. He or she needs to find a spouse who is not afraid of navigating these challenging waters. It is more than possible to do so, but it makes marriage a more challenging relationship.

This all being said, for those who are in the darkness of same-sex lust and activity and are married, there is still profound, beautiful hope. I know of countless stories of redemption of those who have fallen and the Lord has lifted them up. It is no easy thing, but the grace of God is extraordinary. If you find yourself lost in sin, go to a pastor or counselor and begin the good, hard journey of redemption. You will be glad that you did.

There is a final consideration. There is a real possibility that the same-sex-attracted person is called to singleness. If this is the calling, entering into marriage will be a painful and costly covenant. Here we need to state what I hope is obvious: Marriage is not the best option but one of the options available to the same-sex attracted. Whether a person is called to singleness or marriage, both are gifts from God.

How Can Marriage Be a Gift to the Same-Sex-Attracted Christian?

Marriage is a gift from God that serves those in it and all of society. It is one of the great gifts that God has given humanity. As someone who has dealt with same-sex attraction, I have experienced great good in marriage. This good has sustained me, satisfied me, encouraged me, given me joy, and been one of the primary means of my journey into holiness. For those same-sex strugglers who have the gift of marriage, it is a beautiful gift.

Christian marriage is a beautiful gift because it is covenantal.

Marriage is a lifelong commitment between a man and a woman that God blesses. When two people with eyes wide open commit to one another for life, it creates a space in which we can fully disclose our whole selves. This has been a beautiful gift to me. I do not need to hide my same-sex temptations or weakness (or all the other ways in which I need Jesus) from my wife. This is no one-sided thing. Amy can bring her weakness and fears into the security and safety of our marriage; she can be fully known. Together, we pursue Jesus. We speak his truth into each other's lives. We hold out for the best for each other. And, we have promised to never leave until death rips us apart. Such intimate community is a beautiful gift.

Christian marriage is a gift because it is a place to live into your calling as a gendered person.

My wife is not like me. She is different in her body, in the way she sees the world, and even in the ways she engages those around her. She is a woman! Her difference is such a gift to me. In Christian marriage we are intimate with someone totally other. This, of course, is rooted in God's purposes and it is also rooted in the reality that what we need is not someone like us but someone totally different. Andrew Comiskey says, "Marriage displaces the shadows of same-sex brokenness and constantly reminds me that I am called to be a man for this woman."[1] It is a great gift to be called into one's true identity and to serve out of that identity.

Christian marriage is a gift because it is the place to express sexual intimacy.

Biblical sexuality, according to Paul, is about serving the other. In marriage this is fully possible, even for those with the residue of same-sex attraction. Though care must be taken, and many conversations must be had, marriage can satisfy the sexual yearnings for both involved. Again, I know countless stories where one of the spouses comes with same-sex attraction and they are able to find amazing sexual good in their Christian marriage.

Christian marriage is a gift because God has ordained it as the best place to have children.

We all long to instill the best of who we are, and our faith in Jesus, into the next generation. This is best done with a father and a mother raising a child together. Though there are good gospel reasons that a single person might raise a child by themselves, what is best and normative is for a mom and dad to raise their children. The best thing in my marriage to Amy are our four beautiful boys. They are an amazing mosaic of God's love and our marriage. I choose marriage because I choose them. There is simply no reason that a man or a woman with same-sex attraction who loves Jesus and wants children cannot have the opportunity of marriage with someone of the opposite sex. The gift of children is a great gift.

Christian marriage is a gift because of the deep friendship it can produce.

Marriage is unique from any other relationship. There are nearness of proximity, common goals, physical intimacy, and it lasts for life. Such relationship can produce amazing friendship. It is a great gift to do life with someone else. Marriage enables this in a special way.[2] In marriage, life is done together for common purposes and goals. There is simply no other kind of human relationship like it on earth. For those who are same-sex attracted and long for such friendship, marriage very well might be for them.

Christian marriage is a gift because it is the ground of holiness.

In Ephesians 5, Paul gives a beautiful teaching on Christian marriage. It should be a place of submission, service, and love. In marriage, these fundamentals of the faith are the means by which marriage is successful. But let me tell you a little secret: Most of us are not all that great at submission, service, and love. We want others to do these things for us, but we do not really want to do them. Marriage is the ground in which these vital fruits of the Christian life are cultivated in a beautiful and wonderful way. I believe this very well might be a valid reason for a same-sex-attracted Christian to pursue Christian marriage—he or she desires to become like Jesus.

Finally, Christian marriage is a gift because of the ability to live out Jesus' mission together.

In a marriage where both spouses are believers, there is the great joy of together serving the world in Christ's name. In some ways, this can make service easier. Of course, in singleness being a person of the gospel is quite possible. And it is also quite possible in marriage. My wife and I are running after Jesus together, and our very marriage is a missional outpost of his kingdom.

Marriage is a great gift. If you are a Christian with same-sex attraction, do not reject marriage out of hand. Though we need to enter into marriage with caution, honesty, and a potential spouse who understands what he or she is getting into, marriage can be as much a gift for you as it can be for anyone else.

How Can Someone Know They Have the Gift of Marriage?

Marriage is not for everyone. Paul in his letter to the Corinthians declares, "Each has his own gift from God, one of one kind and one of another."[3] For the same-sex-attracted Christian, the first step is to view marriage as a potential gift. The next step is to decide if, at this stage of life, you have the gift of marriage. Based upon my own experience and what I have learned by watching other Christians who have same-sex attraction, I think the following criteria can help you, or those you serve, learn whether marriage might be an option:

The same-sex-attracted Christian needs to be in a church community of hope and discernment.

By hope I mean a place that actually believes that the gospel could take two broken people and make something whole and beautiful. When you are part of a church community that loves the Lord and believes he can do great things, then the possibility of marriage for a same-sex-attracted Christian is seen as one of the many things the Lord can do. You also need a church community for discernment. A safe and wise community can help you answer questions like:

- Are you healthy enough and ready for marriage?
- Is there a sense in the community that this potential marriage is a good thing?
- Are there blind spots that need to be pointed out?
- How can the church support this potential marriage so it can thrive?

The same-sex-attracted Christian needs to have sexual purity.

For such a marriage to thrive it is necessary that those within it are not bringing darkness into the marriage. By no means does a person need to be perfect, but he or she does need freedom from sexual bondage. If that has not happened yet, marriage is probably not a good idea.

A mutual attraction between two persons of the opposite sex is needed.

You cannot marry someone to whom you are not attracted. By attraction I mean a pull toward another person of the opposite sex. This pull, to varying degrees, will exist emotionally, spiritually, and physically.[4] There will be a desire to spend time and energy with this person. And this person of the opposite sex will experience the same thing.

The same-sex-attracted person needs a willing spouse.

Well, duh! By this I mean a spouse who sees with eyes wide open what he or she is committing to. This is necessary in all marriages, but is especially important when one of the spouses has same-sex attraction. There will be unique things to navigate: your spouse being attracted to a same-sex friend; unmet needs; and the potential shame that might come from having to navigate these waters.

The same-sex-attracted person and his or her spouse need to be willing to fight.

Marriage is not easy, but for those willing to fight for each other and to stand into what God has for them, marriage can be a beautiful, amazing gift. You must be willing to fight for it.

The same-sex-attracted person can use these criteria to see whether he or she has the gift of marriage at this season of life. To be honest, you might need to come back to these again and again through a life of singleness. What is true in one season might change in the next. What God has not gifted yet, he might gift later.

A Final Word on Marriage

In conversations around same-sex attraction and marriage, it used to be that biblical marriage was the sign and goal that someone was really healthy and following Jesus. In the last decade the pendulum has swung. Now marriage is hardly seen as an option at all for Christians who have same-sex attraction. I do believe that in the past singleness has not been honored enough in the church; I hope that the many voices in our midst honoring singleness will rectify that. I have a final word about marriage to leaders and same-sex-attracted Christians: Do not throw out this viable, biblical option because it is not a popular option at this moment in cultural history. Marriage is a great good and has the potential to serve the same-sex-attracted Christian in many profound ways.

PCA Pastor, Same-Sex Attraction, and Marriage

Allan Edwards is a PCA (Presbyterian Church in America) pastor, is married, has one son, and has had same-sex feelings since adolescence. By age six, Allan's family was in a good church, hearing the good news of the gospel. He struggled with his relationship with his dad, and throughout childhood most of Allan's friends were girls. Allan is gifted artistically and remembers at the age of thirteen or fourteen being called a "faggot" by peers. Though he doesn't see any single thread in his life as deterministic, by high school Allan had exclusively same-sex desires, and by early adulthood was acting out sexually in anonymous gay encounters.

In college Allan would swing between being a Pharisee and embracing licentiousness. Though never outwardly rebellious, he had a secret life of sin. As a senior in college he tried to reconcile his same-sex reality with the Scriptures. He even tried to leave Christianity, but he just could not escape Jesus. The Jesus of the Bible would not leave him alone. Jesus had captured Allan's attention.

After college Allan returned home and began to come to grips with the gospel. He told his pastor about his same-sex attraction and experienced love, discipleship, and the truth that same-sex activity is idolatry. Then Tim Geiger, executive director of Harvest USA, discipled Allan in a profoundly important way. Allan was having a hard time and needed to tell his mentor something important. Allan told Tim that he was never going to change.

Tim replied with grace and truth, "You are not changing because you do not want to. You get something by identifying with your same-sex feelings." This was the beginning of a profound season of repentance. From this season of repentance, Allan aligned his identity with Christ and not his feelings.

Allan found support and accountability with godly mentors and a biblical support group through Harvest USA, he started reading good books, and he implemented accountability before sin was conceived. He also had to face some lies. Allan had always struggled with his weight and believed that fat people were worthless and that beautiful people were to be worshiped. His same-sex attraction was and is a pursuit of a lie: pursuing something in another man that Allan thought he lacked. Through all of this, Allan began to grow.

In 2009, Allan entered seminary. And in 2010 Allan began to date his future wife. They had known each other since high school, but now something was different. Though Allan had never experienced strong heterosexual desires, he became quite interested in his future wife, Leeanne. He began to want to spend time with her, learn about her, and hear from her. It wasn't long until Allan wanted to serve and love Leeanne the rest of their lives. Soon, they got married.

Allan loves his wife. Though there are challenges, just as with every marriage, they choose God's best for one another over feelings. Both of them want to be part of a marriage that is fruitful, and with the birth of their first child, they see the good that their marriage can produce. Allan and Leeanne are experiencing the good gift of marriage.

A Beautiful Marriage

I have known Andy and Annette for close to twenty years. They are one of the most brilliant examples of what is possible in Christian marriage. They have been married for thirty-five years and have four adult children. Their years together reveal a beautiful marriage.

They met each other while both worked at a Christian bookstore in Westwood, California. Early on a friendship sparked. They enjoyed spending time with one another and could make each other laugh. As they spent more time together, Andy knew he wanted to share something with Annette. He told her that a few years earlier, he had left a gay life in pursuit of Jesus. Probably because Annette had a gay brother, she wasn't shocked or surprised. She thought maybe her friendship with Andy would help her understand and serve her brother better.

Though Andy and Annette were spending a lot of time together, Annette really liked another guy and she set up a Christmas party in the hopes that he would pursue her. Instead, he was dismissive. But Andy came to the Christmas party with a corsage and gave it to Annette. Her heart changed right there. She began to have feelings for Andy. They began dating soon after.

One of the defining decisions in Andy and Annette's life was their decision to go to the Vineyard church that was led by Ken Gulliksen. This church became crucial in their lives. They served and grew. In 1980, Andy shared his testimony with the whole church. Before long, men and women struggling with same-sex attraction were calling the church office for help like Andy had received, and a new ministry was born.

Andy and Annette decided to get married. They were part of a church that believed that God could do anything and surely he could take a man who had left homosexuality and a woman who loved Jesus and make a beautiful marriage. Right after they married, Andy enrolled at Fuller Seminary and was exposed to John Wimber, and Andy and Annette's ministry, Desert Stream, began to flourish. For close to four decades they have been ministering the hope of Jesus to the sexually and relationally broken around the world.

At the center of their lives is their marriage. They have decided that disordered desire does not disqualify either of them from being sexual gifts to one another. They are so thankful that their marriage has born amazing fruit—adult and spiritual children that are standing in the truth of the gospel. Marriage gives Andy the grace to be a man for his wife, Annette. It displaces the shadows and darkness of same-sex fracturing and calls him into his true sexual identity.

But their marriage, like all good marriages, has been hard. They each bring their own residual brokenness and immaturity into marriage. Andy on occasion struggles with pornography and the occasional friendship that becomes a little too close. Annette brings struggles with food and her own brokenness.

Such realities, they say, are shameful. But the humiliation is good because it forces both of them to Jesus and the cross.

Andy has good accountability with other men where he can work through the shadows that remain. Annette knows that Andy's struggles do not reflect on her so much as the sin that remains in him and the world. This enables them to serve well. And still, they work it out together, believing the best for each other, standing for what is true, and pursuing Jesus passionately.

Life is changing. Now they get to see the fruit of what they have labored hard for. Walking with their children, serving the local church, and still standing in the hope that God can transform lives. Theirs is a beautiful marriage.

Conclusion

Marriage can be an extraordinary gift to the same-sex-attracted Christian. Though definitely not for every person with same-sex attraction, it can provide life and goodness for many. What is needed is honesty, a good community, a willing partner, and a spirit of adventure. If God opens the door of marriage, it can do extraordinary good in one's life. Marriage is a gift.

8

The Gift of Prayerful Lament

I was just a few years into my journey of following Jesus. It was 1998 or 1999 and my life was being transformed from the inside out. I was embracing sexual purity, sober, living in community, and my life was totally turning around. As wholeness began to emerge I wanted to date a woman. I was still having same-sex feelings, but I also had heterosexual feelings. I wanted a relationship; I wanted marriage; I wanted kids someday; I wanted a full relational life. At this moment, I probably wasn't ready to date but I wanted it.

There was a wonderful young woman who went to the same church that I did. She was funny, nice, pursuing the Lord like I was, and I was attracted to her. We had fun together and I could see us getting along well. I wanted to pursue her but I was scared of what might happen. Just thinking about trying to pursue a healthy relationship with someone of the opposite sex filled me with excitement, anxiety, and fear all at the same time. So, I prayed. I mean I really prayed. Over several days I prayed and I got the distinct impression that God was encouraging me to ask this young woman on a date. I was scared but I felt God's favor and encouragement, so what did I have to lose? If God is for me who can be against me? So one day while we were hanging out, I asked her out on a date. Instead of the yes that I was expecting, it did not go well! She did not feel the same way that I did. I was crushed.

What followed was a hard season for me that lasted for several months. I was confused, angry, and sad. I didn't understand what the Lord was doing. I wanted to enter into the realm of opposite-sex dating but when I did, the door was closed. This wasn't just a one-time occurrence but seemingly a pattern of life. The realm of women and dating was completely foreign to me. I had no idea what I was doing or how to be successful. I did not understand what to do! I thought the Lord was encouraging me to pursue opposite-sex relationships, but every time I did, I fell on my face. It would have been easier to retreat into the world of homosexuality.

One night during this hard season, I was at the end of my rope. I just remember lying in my bed weeping. I was lost, confused, and didn't have anything else left to give. The weeping was from the gut. I was in the fetal position and I cried for what seemed like forever. I spoke to the Lord; I shared my deep pain with the Lord; I yelled at the Lord; I lay silently before the Lord. Then, I had these words pop into my head: "I am the potter; you are the clay."[1] I felt in that moment that the Lord was saying, "I called you, I saved you, and I encouraged you to ask that young woman on a date, but I never promised you that she would say yes. As a matter of fact, I don't promise anything to you except myself." I had encountered the living God. Over the next months I found great solace, strength, hope, and correction in the Psalms. They became my prayer language. It wasn't until years later that I realized that God was teaching me something profoundly important about him and about my same-sex brokenness.

My story of suffering is minor compared to what others experience. Loneliness, pain, sorrow, and doubt circle around many Christians who struggle with same-sex attraction. What happens when a person with same-sex attraction has a season (or a life) that is as much a valley as a mountain top? What are we to do for men and women dealing with same-sex attraction whose desires for the same sex are just as strong as ever even after doing all the right things? What about the same-sex struggler who can't imagine marrying someone of the opposite sex, yet singleness seems like a prison sentence? Or what about the earnest Christian who hates his or her sexual sin and repents after every fall, but can't get free? Today, the most common answer to these questions is to advocate gay relationships and gay identity. Such advocates say, "We would not want to stand in the way of a person's flourishing, especially when there seems to be no other choice." But even here, in the midst of pain, loneliness, and suffering, God provides a way. It is the way of biblical lament.

In this chapter I want to show you the gift of the Bible in general and lament specifically for the same-sex struggler. I want to show you what biblical lament is, I want to share the benefits of lament for those of us in the valley of sexual and gender brokenness, and finally, I want to explore how to lament.

What Is Lament?

Biblical lament is one of the types of writing found throughout the Bible and specifically in the Psalms. Todd Billings[2]
writes, "Writers of laments and complaints in the Psalms
often seek to make their 'case' against God, frequently citing God's promises in order to complain that God seems to
be forgetting his promises. They throw the promises of God
back at him."[3] He goes on to describe the way of lament: "For
psalms of lament, the pattern looks like this: coming before
the almighty Lord, laying open our emotions and complaints
before him, and then openly declaring trust in his promises."[4]
It is a primary way of coming before the Lord and saying,
"Lord, this is not the way this is supposed to be."[5]

The Benefits of Biblical Lament for the Same-Sex Struggler

Before I show you how to apply lament to same-sex brokenness, I want to share what I think are the numerous benefits
of using lament in the midst of the pain and struggle that
inevitably come with same-sex attraction and following Jesus.
My goal is to convince you that lament is the best language
to talk about the unhealed, unfulfilled, and unsatisfied places
of the heart. It is the language given to us so that we might
journey well with Jesus and flourish even in the dark places.

The first benefit of biblical lament for the same-sex struggler is that it gives us biblical language for our struggle and
pain. One of the most important things we need to do as
Christians who walk with same-sex strugglers or struggle
with same-sex attraction is to give a framework for struggle,
failure, pain, and sorrow. I want to submit that using secular

language—no matter how insightful—is not as helpful or life-giving as using the language found in Scripture to describe who we are, who God is, and our hope. I love the language of Psalm 69:

> The waters have come up to my neck.
> I sink in deep mire,
> Where there is no standing. . . .
> I am weary with my crying;
> My throat is dry. . . .
> You know my reproach, my shame, and my
>   dishonor. . . .
> Hear me, O Lord, for Your lovingkindness is good;
> Turn to me.[6]

This describes how I have felt many times in my same-sex affliction. It describes not just sin and judgment but emotional turmoil and pain. The Psalms give us rich language to describe our failures, weaknesses, and pain. Of course, the psalmist is speaking about something different than same-sex affliction, but I believe his language can help describe what is happening in sexual sin, longing, brokenness, and pain. I want to encourage you that if there is biblical language to be used to describe what is going on in you, use it. If the Bible is the inspired Word of God, then it must be the best language available.

The second benefit of biblical lament for the same-sex struggler is that it shows us that pain, struggle, and even failure are not the end. The Psalms are filled with guilt, contrition, sorrow, anger, and pain. When these things happen to us, especially if they are not transient but more permanent fixtures in our lives, they seem final and authoritative. Lament shows us that we are not alone in our pain and grief. Listen to this: "Wait on the Lord: be of good courage, and he shall strengthen thine heart: wait, I say, on the Lord."[7] Lament is a transitory place. It is a place of waiting. It is grounded in the sure hope that in this life and the next God will be found faithful. Same-sex strugglers need to know this. What we are experiencing in our longings and in our pain is not the final word. Even if it lasts a lifetime! God will move. He will be faithful. He will have his way!

The third benefit of biblical lament for the same-sex struggler is that it shows that God and his kingdom have resources for us. Psalm 26 begins with this plea: "Vindicate me, O Lord." Underneath this plea is a belief that God is someone who has the resources to change things. He is powerful, competent, and near. Lament reminds us that we might be weak sexually, broken, and sinful, but this is not fatal. God has resources for us. He loves us. Billings reminds us that at the core of every lament is the lovingkindness of God. This is why we lament. This is what we need. This is the key difference between the same-sex struggler floundering and flourishing.

The fourth benefit of lament for the same-sex struggler is that it gives us a story to live in. We live in an age when sexuality is used to label identity, and one's desires are to be followed no matter the cost. The sex culture of our age is sadly one of the most lived-in stories of our time. Lament places us in an utterly different story—the story of the saving God who confronts our enemies and delivers his people. Lament places the Christian in Christ, where every pain, sorrow, and regret has been swallowed up in his resurrected life, and one day this will be our experience. This is the better story. This is our story. It is only within this story that words like *victory*, *transformation*, and *hope* make sense.

The final benefit of lament for the same-sex struggler is that it gives us a structure for our prayer lives. When I am in despair or struggling with attractions I don't want or wondering why I am stuck in old patterns when all I want is freedom, the Psalms help me. Not just as a place of hopeful assurance or as a reminder of God's goodness, but as an actual pathway, through prayer, to the God that the Psalms portray. And this is where I think we can make our point: Prayer is the foundation of all the good that can be offered to the same-sex struggler, prayer that gives us a language, narrative, and access to resources that can actually help us.

Learning to Lament

In a beautiful essay called "My Messy House," Kathleen Norris writes,

> I have found that when I have asked children to write their own psalms, their poems often have an emotional directness that is similar to that of the biblical psalter. . . .
> Once a little boy wrote a poem called "The Monster Who Was Sorry." He began by admitting that he hates it when his father yells at him: his response in the poem is to throw his sister down the stairs, and then to wreck his room and finally to wreck the whole town. The poem concludes: "Then I sit in my messy house and say to myself, 'I shouldn't have done all that.'"[8]

This little boy knows how to lament. For him, the Psalms are not a distant poetry but an outlet for pain and anger, and most of all, a place for encounter. We need to learn how to lament if we are to flourish even in the hard places in our lives.

We lament by living in the Psalms. I love all the Scriptures, but I find myself drawn to the Psalms again and again. And I find myself drawn to certain psalms where I find just the right furniture to live and to flourish. If your same-sex struggle is painful, overwhelming, or hard, you will find great comfort in the Psalms, but you must live in them. Skimming a few paragraphs just will not do. You and I need to memorize, repeat, dwell on, and live in the text. I have done this repeatedly with Psalm 27. The psalm begins in confidence. David trusts the Lord even as his enemies surround him, but by verse 7, there is a tone change, a sense of urgency:

Hear, O Lord, when I cry aloud;
    be gracious to me and answer me!
You have said, "Seek my face."
My heart says to you,
    "Your face, Lord, do I seek."
Hide not your face from me.
Turn not your servant away in anger,
    O you who have been my help.
Cast me not off; forsake me not,
    O God of my salvation!
For my father and my mother have forsaken me,
    but the Lord will take me in.[9]

I think I know exactly how David feels. I trust the Lord, but then "my enemies" stir fear and angst in me. This psalm helps me pursue the Lord when I am feeling troubled. By living in the texts, you will find sustenance for flourishing in the hard places.

We lament in our prayers. Some of us are afraid to be sad, angry, confused, or lost in our prayers. Yet the Psalms are filled with these very emotions. If you are angry or sad about something relating to your sexuality, let God into it by prayer. Prayers need to be the place of honesty. Don't hide. Through lament we will find intimacy with God and even joy. If we hide these more unappealing emotions, we unintentionally hide ourselves from God.

We lament through fasting. Though much could be said about fasting, I think it is a discipline that can help to reorient us and focus on what actually matters. When I feel overwhelmed, or when boundaries begin to blur, if I feel lost and confused, I will fast so that I can refocus my life on what actually matters even as I experience loss, lust, or pain in my sexuality. Fasting has been one of the great gifts that has taught me that what I feel is not the same as what is real. Fasting dislodges me from temporal longings and helps me put my eyes on God. It teaches me to hunger for the world to come.

We lament through community. At the center of lament is the admission that life is not perfect. It is rigorously authentic. Our communities need to enable such authenticity. We do not need to be victoriously happy all the time. Sometimes life is hard. For some of us, life is hard much more than we like to admit. Lament in community allows such sorrow in our midst. It does not hide it. How helpful this can be for the same-sex struggler. Sometimes life does not make sense and God seems distant. Lament enables us to live in the tension of faith and pain.

A Beautiful Lament

Jen is forty-three. Her life is good, but it is hard. She grew up sheltered in a Christian home. In first or second grade she just felt like she wanted to be a boy. So from early on

she was a tomboy. As she grew, her gender confusion grew
into same-sex desire. By college Jen had strong sexual feelings for girls. She began to enter into gay relationships. She
was deeply emotionally immature and many of the women
she dated were too, but she was hungry for relationship so
she didn't care. She also knew that what she was doing was
wrong but had no idea how to stop. Then, after her senior
year of college, a friend invited her to attend her church.

Jen was a musician and her friend's dad was a pastor
who was looking for musicians to play in the band. So Jen
came to church and joined the band. Jen's friend was a godly
young woman, and Jen trusted her enough to confide in
her. So over the next couple of years, Jen shared her same-
sex struggle, her pain, and her need with her Christian
friend. Jen had a live-in girlfriend that she would tell her
friend about. The relationship was tumultuous and full
of frustration. Finally, Jen had had enough of the chaos
of the relationship and told the girlfriend she needed to
leave. When Jen told her friend, she was glad to hear Jen
had finally made a good choice, but Jen became too needy
for her friend. She was overwhelmed and suggested that
Jen talk to her dad, the pastor. So Jen spoke to the pastor.
He became angry that Jen would bring her lifestyle into
his church. Jen wanted help, and what she received was
marginalization. Before long, Jen had to leave that little
church. But one good thing that this church gave Jen was
information about Portland Fellowship.

Portland Fellowship is a community of healing that provides intensive discipleship opportunities for those with unwanted same-sex desires. Jen went through their two-year
program, and God began to move in powerful ways. During
the journey, Jen was part of a singles group at church and

met a man she developed attraction toward. Before long they were engaged and married.

Life looked good and promising. Jen was married to someone she was attracted to in a marriage that honored God. But the marriage was doomed to failure. Her new husband was a binge drinker, which he hid before they got married. After marriage, there was no hiding. He drank, had trouble with the law, and then got caught up with crystal meth. She tried to work it out with him, but he did not want anything to do with working to save the marriage. Instead, he had an affair. Totally broken and devastated, Jen got a divorce.

She was mad at God and embittered. She had done all the right things and had ended up in a pit. In the pain of separation and divorce, for a brief moment, Jen found solace in a relationship with another woman. But then the Lord began to move in Jen's life and showed her that she had an addiction to relationships.

In a commitment to obedience, Jen joined Celebrate Recovery, worked the steps, and began to set healthy boundaries with other people, especially women with whom in the past she would have wanted to be in unhealthy relationships. She is seeing change. She has good boundaries, no longer is desperate for emotional connection, and has a fierce holiness. But life is still hard.

She does not see her singleness as a gift but as the means by which she keeps her sanity. She is frustrated by people and relationships. She knows that she needs them but cannot imagine being in a deeper more significant friendship or relationship. She is pure but the relational life that is available to others does not seem open to her.

When I interviewed Jen, I realized that her life is a prayer of lament. Her devotion and leadership in Celebrate Recovery, her standing for what is right even as she does not understand it, is a holy lament. She believes in the lovingkindness of God. She longs to see it, has even tasted it, but she yearns for more. Many enemies surround her. She is honest. Her healing is not complete. She stands in faith and trust. She waits for the Lord. Her life is a beautiful lament.

PART THREE:
FINAL THOUGHTS

9

A Note to Church Leaders

Two men have changed my life: Charlie Contreras and Andy Comiskey. In my sin, brokenness, and despair, God used these men to bring Jesus to me. Charlie has been there since the beginning. Before my sobriety from drugs or even my choice to follow Jesus, Charlie was a faithful witness to the hope found in Jesus. Andy stood in the gap and believed for me when there was not a lot of evidence for such belief. He encouraged me to believe and step into my masculine identity. His beautiful marriage and steadfastness stirred hope in me that such a life was possible. Without these good men I am not sure where I would be in my journey today. In my nearly twenty years of following Jesus, I have had amazing leaders shape my life. Many were pastors who have fathered me in the faith, and others were faithful lay leaders God brought alongside me at key moments to help form me. All of them God has used to grow me as a godly man. I would not be where I am in my Christian walk except that these leaders were faithful witnesses of the hope of the gospel in Jesus Christ. We live in a time when such leaders are essential.

On the topic of same-sex attraction, we are in desperate need of leaders who will be faithful and courageous. In this chapter I want to share what I think is essential for church leaders to remember and put into practice. I am a pastor, and it is my hope to encourage and equip church leaders to be bright lights in their communities for the same-sex attracted. So what follows are ten important reminders for leaders. I hope they serve you well.

Reminder #1: Remember the Goal

It is quite likely that in your church right now there are men and women wrestling with same-sex attraction. They are usually in one of two categories: (1) Men and women who are at peace with their same-sex attraction and have embraced a gay identity; (2) Men and women who are struggling with same-sex attraction, understand same-sex activity as sin, and want to know how to follow Jesus faithfully. The goals for each of these categories are slightly different though they flow from the same Jesus.

For those men and women in your church who identify as LGBT and are in a relationship, the goal is to introduce them to the living Jesus. This means pursuing them with friendship, kindness, a listening ear, and most of all, love. Sexual identity is not central; Jesus is central. Make much of Jesus and introduce them to the one man who holds eternity in his hands. The hope of every friendship is that all of our friends will proclaim Jesus as Lord.[1]

For those men and women who are struggling with same-sex attraction, understand that same-sex activity is a sin, and want to follow Jesus, the goal is to journey with them as they follow Jesus. From my perspective this goal entails that the same-sex-attracted Christian comes to make peace with his or her God-given sexual identity as male or female. Secondly, this means learning how to be a good gender gift whether in marriage or singleness. In this way, it is possible for the same-sex attracted to fully follow Jesus.

To be clear, the goal is not heterosexual desire. I really do believe that this is secondary to becoming good gender gifts. Our biblical sexual identities as male or female are essential to who we are as persons. Every follower of Jesus needs the power of Jesus to live a godly life as a man or woman. This is what we should encourage with those we pastor. This will help establish realistic and hopeful communities and put Jesus at the center.

Reminder #2: Do Not Be Silent

One of the number-one needs in our culture today is for faithful and thoughtful Christians to speak the scriptural truth about homosexuality and biblical sexuality. As a church leader, you need to know what you and your church believe. Take the time to do this. Also, if you are a preaching pastor, make time to preach the hope of the gospel for the same-sex-attracted Christian. I can promise you, there are many in your congregation who need to hear the truth and grace of the Scriptures.

It may seem that the safe thing to do is to be almost totally silent. I know many leaders who privately hold to a traditional view of sexuality and marriage but in a desire not to offend, stay pretty much silent. Unintentionally, this silence creates its own answer: Men and women must grapple with the issue on their own or with louder voices that encourage an embrace of same-sex attraction as a God-given identity. Silence on the biblical view of sexuality is affirmation of the cultural answer on homosexuality. If this is not what you intend, then in your realms of influence, speak up.

Reminder #3: Lead by Example

One of the most important things you can do is to create a church culture in which every member of your church is encouraged to authentically work through their own sin issues. Not privately but in community. This of course begins with the leader. One of the things I know is true is that my openness about my same-sex attraction, sin, and redemption provides hope for all kinds of people in my church. Their particular sins and weaknesses might be different, but when they see an example of what God can do, and my willingness to be open about it, this encourages them to seek Jesus for what they need.

As a leader, you need to lead by example. How has God pursued you? How has God transformed you? Where is he still working? Where do you still need him? There are men and women in your midst who want to know if Jesus is a real answer for what confronts them. You can show that he is by showing in your life what he has done. Living your life on display is one of the most powerful ways you can make your church safe for the same-sex-attracted Christian.

As a leader, encourage other leaders under your authority to live in the same vulnerable space. The goal here is to practice what you preach. When the leaders of the church are confessing sin, authentically sharing weaknesses, and praying for God's power, and God is redeeming and transforming these leaders, the rest of the church will follow. This all requires leadership. But in such a community, the same-sex-attracted Christian will flourish.

Reminder #4: Repent of Homophobia

I have heard the jokes and the demeaning comments and have seen the mean-spirited attitudes toward those who identify as LGBT a lot in my life. Here is the sad reality: Many times I have encountered this homophobia in the church. It is appropriate and right to stand for what is right and true even if it offends people. It is not right or Christian to couch one's disdain and disgust in religious terms. It is demonic and has no place in the body of Christ.

Please search your motives and the motives of your church. Make sure your stance against same-sex behavior is rooted in the Bible, not your bigotry. The salvation of many men and women in your midst might lie in the balance. And if you find homophobia in your heart and the hearts of your leaders, talk about it publicly and publicly repent. What a beautiful thing this would be. We need such leadership in our churches. I pray that our leaders would have the courage to put to death such evil in our midst.

Reminder #5: Build Friendships

One of the things that I have noticed among some of my conservative friends is a fidelity to truth without an embrace of love. What I mean is that truth is used as a weapon without ever knowing the enemy. Consequently, those on the other side feel attacked and wounded by the attitude in which truth is dispensed. I have noticed this attitude in my heart as well. To combat this, I have made the decision to build friendships with those with whom I disagree. I take Jesus' words seriously when he says love one another. Such friendships soften my rhetoric, sharpen my beliefs, keep my heart tender, and grow me as a witness of the gospel of Jesus.

Every Christian leader should work hard to build friendships with men and women who identify as LGBT in his or her community. You should hear their point of view and concerns and also share yours. You do not need to be afraid of those who are different from you.

Nothing but goodness can grow when you truly learn to love your "enemies." What a beautiful thing when foes become friends.

Reminder #6: Create Healing Spaces

It is your job as a leader to make sure that your church has places for men and women struggling with same-sex attraction to find and encounter the profound love and transformation of Jesus. There are multiple curriculums, ministries, and pathways that you can partner with to create a healing community in your church. But the most important thing is to make sure you offer *something*.

At Sam Allberry's church in England, the senior pastor and his wife lead a small group of those wrestling with same-sex attraction. This senior pastor has many responsibilities in his large church but wants to make sure his church offers a space for community and hope for the same-sex attracted. This is important for him, so he leads it himself. I pray that as a leader you will do what is necessary to create healing communities in your church. And if you do not have the resources to do so, partner with other like-minded churches in your area to provide a place of hope for same-sex-attracted Christians who deeply desire to follow Jesus faithfully.

Reminder #7: Do Not Minimize What God Can Do

When Jesus was on the earth, the lame walked, the blind received sight, the dead were raised, the sinful forgiven, and the hungry fed. The kingdom of God brought life, and that life can be defined by one word: *abundant*. I fear that in many of our Christian communities we have lost faith in the reality that God does extraordinary things all the time.

This is true of all of us and this is true for the same-sex attracted. I hope this book has made one thing abundantly clear: God has provided many profound pathways of relationship for the same-sex attracted. God, through his church, is faithful to the same-sex attracted. And he can, through the power of his blood, make each man and woman whole in his or her sexual identity. This he can do. Whether through singleness or marriage, God is faithful. There is no human need that God cannot provide a pathway for. As a church, your faith for others matters. If you lack faith, pray for it. If you have faith, boldly declare it. But whatever you do, do not minimize what God can do!

Reminder #8: Make Testimonies Into Leaders

One of the most beautiful things that happened to me on my journey was when a church made me a leader. I had been walking with Jesus for a few years, had grown significantly, and had grown in sexual purity immensely. Then I was invited to be a small-group leader. I cannot tell you how much I grew as a Christian because of this one decision by another leader. It was and is one of the most beautiful moments in my journey with Jesus.

If God is gracious to your church community, you will have men and women beautifully transformed by the power of the gospel, including men and women facing same-sex attraction. As these men and women encounter Jesus and grow, place them into roles of leadership. Your church will be better for it. When you have men and women who have seen Jesus be faithful even as they deny attractions and feelings that feel so innate, they understand the gospel in beautiful and brilliant ways. You need such people as leaders. Make a way for them; you will be glad you did.

Reminder # 9: God Is Sovereign

For the follower of Jesus it can seem right now in our cultural context that everything is being turned upside down. Sexual identity, appropriate sexual conduct, and marriage are all being redefined. The values and conduct that emanate from Scripture are being discarded for a reality that places personal autonomy at the center. For many of us this is scary and devastating. With the psalmist in Psalm 13 we cry out, "How long, O Lord?" It might feel for some of us that God is losing his grip and that events are tumbling out of his control. And even if we don't think that, we feel it deep within us. Fear can overwhelm us. But the Scriptures encourage us, "Our God is in the heavens; he does all that he pleases."[2]

God has ordained all that is going on. As a matter of fact, history must go this way so that the glory of his name and the good of his people might be known and realized. So we can relax. We can be at peace no matter what. Our God is in control.

Reminder #10: Have Joy

Around the world, Jesus is on the move. Sure, troubles and challenges are real for all of us. And on the topic of homosexuality, those who face same-sex attraction have many things to work through. But our God is in control and he is working redemption all over the world. Lives are being changed. Men and women are growing into their biblical sexual identity. The gospel is as glorious and strong as ever before. God is faithful!

So have joy. Choose joy. Turn your face to Jesus. As you lead men and women to Jesus who want to be faithful in the midst of same-sex attraction, show them with your joy just how beautiful and glorious Jesus really is. Gloomy and despairing Christian leaders give very little hope to anxious sinners. Cultivate joy.

Conclusion

Dear Christian leader, your leadership matters to the same-sex-attracted Christian. Don't just learn the issue; be part of a gospel solution. If you do not like the biblical possibilities I offer in this book, then it is your work to provide biblical pathways. It is not enough to know what you are against; the church needs to show what it is for and how it is possible to achieve it. It is my hope that the church provides the means for faithfulness.

One last word to Christian leaders: There is reason to hope. The title of this book begins with the word *hope*. The reason for this hope is that Jesus is the hope of the world. I pray that you would be filled with hope for the same-sex-attracted Christians that you are in relationship with. Just know there are countless leaders around the world who are doing what you are doing and seeing Jesus do what he does—change lives. Be filled with hope!

10

A Word of Hope to the Same-Sex-Attracted Christian

Recently, I was at a conference and had some downtime so I decided to go for a run. The conference was at a hotel near O'Hare Airport in Chicago, Illinois. The area around the airport is not really conducive to running outside—busy streets, lots of concrete, and not enough sidewalks! But I was determined and I set out on my run. Thanks to the people at the front desk of the hotel, I found a sidewalk to run on. So down I went. I wanted to go five miles, so that meant going out 2.5 miles. For the first 1.5 miles there was plenty of sidewalk, but then the sidewalk came to an end. If I was going to keep running and get the mileage I wanted, I would need more path to run on. Then I noticed that across the street from where the sidewalk ended there was a forest preserve and what looked like a dirt path. So I crossed the street and began to run on this dirt path into the forest preserve. For the first minutes everything was beautiful. The path was marked well, it was a nice scenery change (I even saw a deer), and I felt confident that I could get another couple of miles under my belt by running on this path. Then all of a sudden, the path ended in a large field. I wasn't sure where to go, and because I have gotten lost in forest preserves before, I had no wish to go further without a path.

Many of us who struggle with same-sex attraction know the discouragement that comes when it seems like there is no path for us to walk and follow Jesus. Others seem to have a clear path before them. But for us it seems like the path is nonexistent. This book has been my earnest attempt to show you that there is a path available for us. But as we end our time together, I want to make sure you enter into the journey with hope.

I am a pastor and I love the Bible. When I need hope that is where I go. I want to take this chapter and show you through Psalm 27, a psalm of lament, the hope that you can cling to as you follow Jesus as a same-sex-attracted Christian. I pray that God fills you with hope!

Psalm 27

The Lord is my light and my salvation;
  whom shall I fear?
The Lord is the stronghold of my life;
  of whom shall I be afraid?

When evildoers assail me
  to eat up my flesh,
my adversaries and foes,
  it is they who stumble and fall.

Though an army encamp against me,
  my heart shall not fear;

though war arise against me,
  yet I will be confident.

One thing have I asked of the Lord,
  that will I seek after:
that I may dwell in the house of the Lord
  all the days of my life,
to gaze upon the beauty of the Lord
  and to inquire in his temple.

For he will hide me in his shelter
  in the day of trouble;
he will conceal me under the cover of his tent;
  he will lift me high upon a rock.

And now my head shall be lifted up
  above my enemies all around me,
and I will offer in his tent
  sacrifices with shouts of joy;
I will sing and make melody to the Lord.

Hear, O Lord, when I cry aloud;
  be gracious to me and answer me!
You have said, "Seek my face."
My heart says to you,
  "Your face, Lord, do I seek."
  Hide not your face from me.
Turn not your servant away in anger,
  O you who have been my help.
Cast me not off; forsake me not,
  O God of my salvation!
For my father and my mother have forsaken me,
  but the Lord will take me in.

Teach me your way, O Lord,
  and lead me on a level path
  because of my enemies.

Give me not up to the will of my adversaries;
for false witnesses have risen against me,
and they breathe out violence.

I believe that I shall look upon the goodness of the Lord
in the land of the living!
Wait for the Lord;
be strong, and let your heart take courage;
wait for the Lord!

Hope in the Character of God for the Same-Sex Attracted

David, speaking of the Lord, uses the words *light*, *salvation*, and *stronghold*. God is light. He makes clear and seeable all that is real: The reality that sin breaks us. The reality that the enemy surrounds us. Above all else, this light imagery conveys the reality that God is real and present among us. God is a fiery light. God's light shows same-sex-attracted Christians what is real and most important, and this is not our sexual sin or proclivities. Instead, what is most real is who God is and what God has done for us. Namely, redeemed us and renamed us as new creations in Jesus Christ. This should give you hope.

God is our salvation. He is the one who saves us. Most important, God saves us from the Father's wrath because of the sin we have committed. He also saves us from the sin that is within us. This is where I want to speak a word of hope to the same-sex-attracted Christian. The same-sex sin you are perhaps currently struggling with is not the final word. Your salvation in Christ is the final word. He can equip you and empower you to mortify the same-sex sin that ensnares you right now. He can do this. He is the savior God. Does your same-sex attraction seem overwhelming? Are there relationships that are edging toward blurred moral boundaries? Have hope. God is our salvation.

God is our stronghold. Think fortress embedded in a mountain valley that cannot be attacked in any successful way. This is where God holds you. In the Lord you are perfectly safe. This does not mean life is easy or that horrible things don't happen to us. It does mean that we are cared for in such a way that our eternal security and joy are perfectly protected. Have hope; God is in control.

These three words—*light, salvation,* and *stronghold*—point to a God who loves you and has promised to be with you all the days of your life. This is what is most true about your life. This is where you need to find your identity. This is why you are utterly safe. This is why life is really a place of peace. Have hope.

Hope for the Same-Sex Attracted When Enemies Surround You

God is good but life is hard. Sometimes same-sex feelings or sin can feel like enemies that are seeking to overwhelm us. The language of David in Psalm 27 seems just about right. My enemies assail me. They are encamped around me. When this happens hope drains from us. But David has a different reaction. He remembers that the strength of his enemies is nothing in light of the strength of the God who is with him. David says, "My head shall be lifted up" (v. 6). In other words, even as his enemies surround him, David has hope because God is with him.

David's hope is in God. God will deliver him. He will cause David's enemies to "stumble and fall" (v. 2). David takes his eyes off of his circumstances and places them on God. This is the secret to hope when trouble surrounds us. Don't focus on the sin, fear, or fracturing; focus on the Lord. Like David, as you do this, you will feel hope rise up.

Hope in the Despair of Same-Sex Attraction and Sin

Something seems to happen in Psalm 27. David is filled with hope. His eyes are on the Lord. Then in verse 7, David begs the Lord to answer when he cries out. He reminds the Lord of his command to seek his face. All of this points to a situation where David is doing all the right things and God seems absent. God has not yet shown up. It seems that David is even worried that God might be angry at him and that is why he hasn't answered David's prayer.

I cannot tell you how many times I have felt like this in my same-sex attraction. Maybe you have too. Strong same-sex attraction. Difficult relationships. Ongoing sexual sin. A desire to have the same-sex feelings go away. Then, we earnestly pray and nothing seems to change. There is hope here too. David gives us a prayer to pray. He comforts us because we see that others, pillars of the faith, have been here too. We know that David is in the pantheon of the great heroes of the faith of Hebrews 11. He is commended for his faith. I think the anxious prayers of Psalm 27 are the fruit of amazing faith. Are things not as they should be? Pray. Do not give up. Do not be afraid of being angry. Ask God the hard questions. Remind him of his promises. Pursue him until he responds. Have hope.

Hope That God Is Not Done With You Yet

David asks the Lord to teach him his ways so that his enemies would not be victorious. David knows that there is more to grow into and more to learn. He is eager for the Lord to continue that journey with him. David had hope that God would continue in his training of him. David had not arrived at his final destination, and neither have we.

What you are experiencing right now is not all that there is for you. Maybe singleness or marriage is hard for you, or maybe it seems that you keep falling into a particular same-sex sin and you are just not sure how to get and stay free. Or maybe you cannot imagine being on this journey for the rest of your life. The word of hope is that God is not done with you yet. No matter where you are at in your journey with Jesus, you have just begun to experience God's goodness. It will take an eternity to see clearly what he has done in and for you. So cling to hope. God is not finished.

Hope in the Presence of God

Psalm 27 is one of my favorite psalms. The reason I love it is because one of the central themes of the psalm, in my opinion, is that the presence of God is the factor that can change everything. This is why he says his one aim is to gaze upon the beauty of the Lord. Enemies are all around. Things need to be learned. God might even be silent. But all of these things pale in comparison to the manifest presence of God in David's life. This is David's hope. The same-sex-attracted Christian needs to place his or her hope in the same place.

The thing to pursue in your life is not sexual desire change. Or heterosexual marriage. Or even singleness. While all of these things are important, they are not primary. They only have significance and can only be helpful categories insomuch as the Lord is near. You want hope to flourish in your life? Seek the face of the Lord! Seek his presence. Set everything else aside and make this your work. This can be counter-intuitive. When same-sex attraction or sin overwhelms us, we are tempted to focus on it. But this will sap hope. Instead, seek his beauty and do not relent until you see it. His presence brings hope.

Hope in Hope

My favorite verse of Psalm 27 is "I believe that I shall look upon the goodness of the Lord in the land of the living!" (v. 13). For David, this goodness hadn't necessarily arrived yet. For David, his enemies were near and dangerous. For David, real life looked really complicated. But in light of all that David was experiencing, he placed his hope in hope.

Hope is the settled sense of anticipated good. This is where David was placing his hope. He believed with his whole self that God—the essence of goodness—was going to be good to him. And so he clung to hope. Your life is complicated. Goodness has not fully arrived yet. You have enemies. But like David, let me encourage you to place your hope in God.

God will be found faithful. Your same-sex attraction and sin will not have the final word. The enemies of your soul will not be victorious. You will not be overwhelmed by same-sex hunger. The God you place your hope in will bring the goodness he has promised through his son. Do not give up. Place your hope in God. You too will see the goodness of the Lord in your life. Trust the Bible. Trust the Lord. Hope in hope.

Conclusion

I began this chapter with a story about running. I ended up in a field in a forest preserve and I wanted to run many more miles. I could have darted into the forest without a path and tried not to get lost. Instead, I turned back and found another path, a path that was clearly seen. What David offers us in Psalm 27 is the path of hope. You should keep this psalm and all the others close to you as you journey. It is easy to get lost in our same-sex attraction. It is easy to get lost in our sin. It is easy to lose hope. But Psalm 27 gives us a path into real hope. A hope that does not disappoint. This hope is for you even as you wrestle with same-sex attraction. Do not give up. There is real reason to hope.

NOTES

Chapter 1: The Obstacle of Gay Christian Identity

1. Justin Lee, *Torn* (New York: Jericho Books, 2012), 53.
2. www.gaychristian.net
3. Wesley Hill, *Spiritual Friendship* (Grand Rapids, MI: Brazos Press, 2015), 81.
4. The phrase usually used when one embraces gay relationships as God-honoring and biblically permissible.
5. Hebrews 12:1–2
6. Ed Shaw makes the point that transformation is possible beautifully in his book, *Same-Sex Attraction and the Church: The Surprising Plausibility of the Celibate Life.* He was the first person I've seen make a direct connection between the embracing of a gay identity and how this might shut us off from the transformation possible in the gospel.
7. John 5:2–9
8. In the second part of this book I will share many such stories.
9. Ron Citlau and Adam Barr, *Compassion without Compromise* (Minneapolis: Bethany House, 2014), 50.
10. If you wonder about this assertion, please read the book I co-wrote with Adam Barr, *Compassion without Compromise.*
11. Genesis 1:27
12. Herman Bavinck, *The Christian Family,* trans. Nelson D. Kloosterman (Grand Rapids, MI: Christian's Library Press, 2012), 5.
13. Ibid., 8.
14. By this I mean to do sexually what he commands in marriage and to not do sexually all that the Bible forbids.
15. This quote is attributed to Lewis, though I cannot find the direct source.
16. Philippians 2:17
17. Genesis 1:28
18. John 3:3
19. Matthew 23:37-39
20. Isaiah 66:13 and 49:15

21. Hosea 13:8
22. Galatians 3:27–28
23. I am thankful for the work of Timothy George in *The New American Commentary: Galatians*, which helped me interpret this text.

Chapter 2: The Obstacle of Gay Marriage

1. James V. Brownson, *Bible, Gender, Sexuality: Reframing the Church's Debate on Same-Sex Relationships* (Grand Rapids, MI: W.B. Eerdmans, 2013), 252–253.
2. I prefer the use of *same-sex attracted* but will use the term *gay* when arguing another person's point when they themselves prefer the term *gay* over *same-sex attracted*.
3. Alan Jacobs, "More Than 95 Theses," http://ayjay.tumblr.com/post/122589 515298/the-issue-of-gay-marriage-has-come-up-a-lot-since, June 27, 2015, quoted in Wesley Hill, "Hoping for Love," *Spiritual Friendship*, June 28, 2015, https://spiritualfriendship.org/2015/06/28/hoping-for-love/?utm_source=StandFirm.
4. Wesley Hill, "Hoping for Love."
5. John Piper, "So-Called Same-Sex Marriage," *Desiring God*, 2015, http://www.desiringgod.org/articles/so-called-same-sex-marriage.
6. Genesis 2:21–24
7. Herman Bavinck, *The Christian Family*, trans. Nelson D. Kloosterman (Grand Rapids, MI: Christian's Library Press, 2012), 5.
8. "Lord's Day 8." Heidelberg-Catechism.com,. www.heidelberg-catechism.com/en/lords-days/8.html.
9. It is important to clarify that this connection between heterosexual marriage, the Trinity, and difference does have limits. Man and woman are differentiated by gender, but God is not differentiated by gender. His difference is based on the difference of persons. It is similar in that the persons of the Trinity are differentiated based upon function, and this is also true of man and woman.
10. Genesis 2:24.
11. "Chapter 2." The Westminister Catechism of Faith, www.sites.online mac.com/trwmainst/west.html.
12. There is another place that God's unity is on display: in the church. Jesus in John 17:21 prays, "that they may all be one, just as you, Father, are in me, and I in you, that they also may be in us, so that the world may believe that you have sent me." My point is that in the created order, marriage alone points to the unity found within the Trinity.
13. Bavinck, *The Christian Family*, 5.
14. I want to thank Dr. Brian Dennert for helping me work through this section. Though any mistakes are mine, he helped make it better.
15. Genesis 1:26
16. We are not creators like God. He can create *ex nihilo* (out of nothing); we need substance and usually outside resources to make something. But still, the creation of human life and the beauty of human imagination does, I believe, point to the *Imago Dei* (image of God) within us.
17. Christopher West, *Theology of the Body for Beginners* (West Chester, PA: Ascension Press, 2004), 8–9.
18. Bavinck, *The Christian Family*, 8.

19. The conversation I am alluding to and that is beyond the scope of this book is this: Are all married couples biblically mandated to procreate? And if so, what does this mean for couples who cannot conceive?

20. 1 John 4:8

21. John 3:16 KJV

22. John Piper, *Desiring God: Meditations of a Christian Hedonist* (Colorado Springs: Multnomah, 2011), 31.

23. Genesis 1:26

24. Genesis 12:1–4

25. Genesis 15:3–6

26. A couple of examples: Isaiah 54:5; 61:10.

27. Read the book of Amos if you don't believe me!

28. Isaiah 54:4–8

29. Revelation 19:6–8

30. Alvin Plantinga, *Warranted Christian Belief* (Oxford University Press, 2000), 320.

31. Ephesians 5:31–32

32. This is also mandated because of the ethical demands of Scripture for marriage to be between one man and one woman for life.

33. Dallas Willard responding during a Q&A at the Valley Vineyard.

34. The Bible begins and ends with a wedding. I first heard this from a presentation given by Christopher West and then read it again in the work of Herman Bavinck. I am thankful to Christopher West, who helped this reformed guy see the essential tie between traditional marriage and the biblical covenant between God and his people.

Chapter 3: The Obstacle of the Spiritual Friendship Movement

1. Wesley Hill, *Spiritual Friendship: Finding Love in the Church as a Celibate Gay Christian* (Grand Rapids, MI: Brazos Press, 2015), 19.

2. Ibid., 108.

3. Ibid.

4. Hill takes considerable time in his book to explore covenantal friendships, especially liturgical rites that were practiced in the Christian East. For Hill, this seems to be a very important aspect of the kind of friendship that he is proposing.

5. Hill, *Spiritual Friendship*, 110–111.

6. Ibid., 76.

7. Ibid., 81.

8. Julie Rodgers, "How I Was Moved to Support Same-Sex Marriage in the Church," http://julie-rodgers.com/?p=16417.

9. Hill, *Spiritual Friendship*, 90.

10. Ibid., 93.

Chapter 4: The Gift of the Church

1. https://www.crossfit.com/

2. "CrossFit as Church? Examining How We Gather." Harvard Divinity School, http://hds.harvard.edu/news/2015/11/04/crossfit-church-examining-how-we-gather#.

3. Ibid.
4. Ibid.
5. Acts 2:42–47
6. John B. Polhill, *The New American Commentary: Book of Acts* (Nashville, TN: Broadman Holman, 1992), 96.
7. Rachel Held Evans, "Why Millennials Are Leaving the Church." CNN Belief Blog RSS. http://religion.blogs.cnn.com/2013/07/27/why-millennials-are-leaving-the-church/.
8. Evans has advocated for progressive thinkers like Jeff Chu and Matthew Vines. Both advocate for the celebration of committed same-sex relationships. See Rachel Held Evans, "Are we there yet?" Rachel Held Evans, April 4, 2013, http://rachelheldevans.com/blog/jeff-chu-are-we-there-yet?, and Rachel Held Evans, "Does the Bible really condemn committed gay relationships?" Rachel Held Evans, September 6, 2013, http://rachelheldevans.com/blog/matthew-vines-video.
9. Acts 2:43
10. Acts 2:42–47
11. Galatians 6:10

Chapter 5: The Gifts of Healing Communities and Christian Therapy

1. www.desertstream.org
2. This chapter is especially dependent on chapter 1 of this book; if you skipped ahead, please consider reading this chapter in conjunction with chapter 1.
3. E.C. Bragg, "Christian Psychology," http://docplayer.net/4245204-Christian-psychology-dr-e-c-bragg.html. I am a novice in Christian psychology and am sure that others can speak to these issues better than I can. I like Dr. Bragg's definition because it relies heavily upon the biblical narrative—creation, fall, redemption, and regeneration. For a reformed look at Christian psychology, please consider reading *Foundations for Soul Care: A Christian Psychology Proposal*, by Eric Johnson.
4. Phil Monroe, "A Christian Psychology Proposal 1," Musings of a Christian Psychologist. 2009, https://wisecounsel.wordpress.com/2009/06/10/a-christian-psychology-proposal-1.

Chapter 6: The Gift of Singleness

1. To be fair, singleness was a viable option for some. I think of Jonathan Hunter, a respected voice and former board member of Desert Stream Ministries. My point is that marriage seemed to be the high-water mark of healing.
2. Matthew 19:10–12
3. Origen took this text to mean that Jesus was calling some to a literal castration. Historically, the church has categorically rejected this idea.
4. Paul, John II, *The Theology of the Body: Human Love in the Divine Plan*. (Boston, MA: Pauline Books & Media, 1997), 267.
5. Matthew 22:30
6. 1 Corinthians 7:6–9, 32–35

7. N. T. Wright, *Matthew for Everyone, Part 2: Chapters 16–28* (London: SPCK, 2004), 47.

8. Romans 14:17

Chapter 7: The Gift of Marriage

1. Phone conversation, 4/14/16.

2. Of course, there are a variety of good ways to find friendship and enjoy it. My point here is to celebrate the good of friendship in marriage and the special way two people, in marriage, can know and enjoy one another.

3. Corinthians 7:7

4. There is a deep need to think critically about attraction and marriage. Today, most Christians think that attraction means solely physical/sexual longing for another person. Though this is an aspect of attraction, there are other important components: shared interests, emotional connection, and spiritual commonality. Defining attraction only as sexual longing, I think, has closed the door of marriage to many same-sex-attracted Christians.

Chapter 8: The Gift of Prayerful Lament

1. See Isaiah 64:8.

2. I am thankful to Todd Billings for his book, *Rejoicing in Lament*. I had Todd as a professor in seminary and always thought that being in his classes was worth the cost of seminary. A few years ago Todd was diagnosed with incurable cancer, and this book is his wrestling with this daunting diagnosis and the God he loves. It was within the pages of this book that I began to see how lament gives language to same-sex sin and brokenness.

3. J. Todd Billings, *Rejoicing in Lament: Wrestling with Incurable Cancer and Life in Christ* (Grand Rapids, MI: Brazos Press, 2015), 19.

4. Ibid., 43–44.

5. Conversations with Dr. Todd Billings.

6. Psalm 69:1–3, 19, 16 NKJV

7. Psalm 27:14 KJV

8. Kathleen Norris, *Bread and Wine: Readings for Lent and Easter,* "My Messy House" (Farmington, PA: Plough Pub., 2003), 4.

9. Psalm 27:7–10

Chapter 9: A Note to Church Leaders

1. In *Compassion without Compromise,* a book I co-wrote with Adam Barr, we take much more time talking about how to be a neighbor to the LGBT community.

2. Psalm 115:3

Ron Citlau graduated from the University of California, Riverside and Western Theological Seminary. He has served in ministry positions in Southern California and Kansas City. He is the pastor of Calvary Church in Orland Park, Illinois, part of the Reformed Church in America.

Ron has struggled with same-sex attraction his whole life and has worked with and walked alongside many others who have struggled with sexual brokenness, as well as equipped pastoral leaders to serve those dealing with sexual sin. He also worked with Andrew Comiskey, producing curriculum on sexual healing now used by Desert Stream Ministries in hundreds of churches throughout the country. When he isn't working, he loves to be with his wife, Amy, and their four boys: Jack, Sawyer, Eli, and Crosby.

More From Ron Citlau

In their role as pastors, Ron Citlau and Adam Barr have seen how homosexuality can tear apart families, friendships, and even churches. In this book, they offer compassionate, biblical answers about homosexuality and practical, real-world advice on how to think and talk about this controversial issue with loved ones.

Compassion Without Compromise
by Ron Citlau and Adam T. Barr

BETHANYHOUSE